THE
SLANGUAGE
OF SEX

THE
SLANGUAGE
OF SEX

Brigid McConville
and
John Shearlaw

Macdonald

A Macdonald Book

Copyright © Brigid McConville & John Shearlaw 1984

First published in Great Britain in 1984
by Macdonald & Co (Publishers) Ltd
London & Sydney

ISBN 0 356 10340 4

Photoset in North Wales by
Derek Doyle & Associates, Mold, Clwyd
Printed and bound in Great Britain by
Biddles Ltd, Guildford and King's Lynn

Macdonald & Co (Publishers) Ltd
Maxwell House
74 Worship Street
London EC2A 2EN

A BPCC Plc Company

CONTENTS

PREFACE

The authors would like to extend personal thanks and acknowledgements to everyone who contributed words and phrases for this dictionary; without them it wouldn't have been possible. But there's a special mention for Richard 'Alabaster' Evans for his patience (and for laughing in the right places), Mic 'Miracle Worker' Cheetham for getting everything together – and Liz Mellon, Jane Salvage, Nick Van Hear, Tom Jeffrey, Mark Cooper, Frank Dowling and Head The Ball, The Brutal Set, Pete Perfect, Jimmy The Blade, Tam The Bam, Fee Fee and the Fuckettes, "Moose" Caroll and Anne, Cocky, Stumpy and Harry from Dublin, Jon Frewin from New York, Big Al from Los Angeles, Mike Fry and his friends from Australia, Eddie Fitzgerald from the Chiswick Trades and various other shady places, the entire McConville family across the world, and everyone else from Tulse Hill Tavern to the Ramrod whose use of slang has been invaluable to us.

We'd like to dedicate this book to each other in the hope that if we can survive this we can survive anything.

BRIGID McCONVILLE
JOHN SHEARLAW
March 1984

Special Acknowledgements

The authors would like to acknowledge their debt of gratitude to the following sources, some of which inspired our work, some of which our work would have been impossible without. Several are mentioned in the text by name reference only, eg Partridge, Rodgers, Grose; the rest have proved invaluable in our search for a dictionary of contemporary sexual slang. Our principal published references were:

The Oxford English Dictionary (OUP)
A Dictionary Of Slang And Unconventional English Eric Partridge (Routledge and Kegan Paul)
The Queen's Vernacular – A Gay Lexicon Bruce Rodgers (Blond and Briggs)
The Dictionary Of The Teenage Revolution And Its Aftermath Kenneth Hudson (Macmillan)
A Dictionary Of Euphemisms Judith S. Neaman and Carole G. Silver (Hamish Hamilton)
A Dictionary Of The Vulgar Tongue Frances Grose (Follett)
Man-Made Language Dale Spender (Routledge)

INTRODUCTION

Sex, by its presence or absence, is a part of all our lives. But in the welter of publicity over the so called 'sexual revolution', the 'Pill generation' and 'Gay liberation' one vital factor is often overlooked.

We have little or no freedom of language for our sexual relationships, no respectable non-medical names which we can use freely in any company. Instead the language of sex is an underground language, a 'slanguage' in words and phrases, of simile, metaphor, euphemism and innuendo.

Perhaps it is the pressure of concealment on sex that has forged so much sexual language into its vivid and convoluted shape. But certainly it exists as hitherto uncharted territory, its images the signposts to the sexual taboos of our society.

The most striking pointer to emerge from the 'slanguage' we have gathered is that this sort of language is predominantly male. In researching this book – over several years and on three continents – it has been men who time and time again volunteered examples of slang which they used or had overheard other men using, in pubs and clubs, locker rooms and offices.

When women did have contributions to make – and theirs are much rarer – they were often personal words, coined for private use, or shared only with sisters, mothers and close friends.

No doubt this is partly a reflection of men's predominance in the public arena and of the greater ease with which men can and do gather socially, while women are more often isolated at home. But it is also a reflection of current attitudes about who has the right to 'consume' sex (a high proportion of slanguage is about the body as 'meat', 'crumpet' etc.). As such it parallels the way in which, visually, men have become the assessors of women's bodies, displayed universally in magazines, newspapers, on television, films and billboards. Men by their absence from advertisements and pin-ups retain the power of those who observe and make judgements, a power they retain in sexual slang. The comparative privacy of women's slang is also a way of dissociating themselves from male 'slanguage', so much of which is offensive to and offensive about women.

Our written sources, too, have been mostly male. Eric Partridge's brilliant *Dictionary Of Slang And Unconventional English*, to which we owe an enormous debt of gratitude, was gathered together over years as men corresponded with Partridge in his gentleman's club, passing on their items of slang. Many of these came from exclusively male groups in the armed forces.

Which brings us to the nature of slang itself. Most of those who use it will agree that slang is a system of identification – and of exclusion. The man who refers to his 'Hampton Wick' is identifying himself as (probably) a Cockney and, in speaking a language that only certain other English people will understand, is excluding all those who don't. In this way, slang connects the speaker with groups who hold certain attitudes – which makes the patterns which emerge for sexual slang most revealing. In heterosexual slang about homosexuality for instance, a recurrent theme is the 'masculinity' of lesbians, and the 'femininity' of gay men. (For the purposes of this book we used the terms 'straight' or heterosexual, 'gay' or homosexual, and lesbian, as the most widely understood terms in common usage which we hope are acceptable to these groups). Derogatory words to describe lesbians – like bull dyke, diesel dyke and bull dicker – imply that lesbians are really part male, even that they have pseudo-male organs. At the root of this is the old belief that only men and not 'real' women have sexual desires of their own, and so one in a lesbian couple must have male characteristics in order for sexual activity to take place. Conversely, heterosexuals commonly impute 'feminine' characteristics to gay men – hence 'queen', 'nance', 'limp wrist' and 'fairy'. (Note that 'feminine' characteristics are used to imply frailty.)

Again, the use of slanguage for sexual intercourse

overwhelmingly echoes assumptions that the male principle is 'potency', the female passivity. In the vast majority of the examples we have found, the male is the subject of the verb, actively 'mounting', 'tooling', 'riding' or 'screwing' the female object.

In the words for the male sexual organs, men do a great deal of what Dale Spender has dubbed 'willy waggling'. The organs are the 'family jewels' or the 'crown jewels'. In more aggressive tones, the penis is the 'sword', 'dagger', 'prong' or 'pistol', and its function is to 'spear', 'prick' or 'screw'. When it is erect the man can call himself 'proud below the navel', or refers affectionately to his EMBO. Contrast the mostly negative and frequently violent names for the female organs, in other dictionaries called the 'pudend' – from the Latin word for shame (as opposed to the male 'membrum virile').

Much of the time in slang, the vagina is not even there: it is a 'gash', 'gap', 'slit' or 'hole'. At worst the vagina is the 'cat with its throat cut', or simply 'cunt'. The clitoris (note that we have no native English word for the primary organ of female sexual pleasure, the name of which comes directly from the Greek root *kleitoris*) is rarely mentioned in slang except as the 'clit', or sometimes 'the little *man* in the boat'.

What can women call their own organs? If they say 'cunt' they can hardly escape the full force of hatred, fear and disgust which makes this the most serious term of abuse in slang, far more insulting than, for instance, 'prick'. The case known to the authors of a London woman who suffered severe abdominal pain without going to a doctor, shows how women are bereft of names for their bodies. Her friends realized she was embarrassed to seek medical care as she did not have 'respectable' words with which to tell the doctor about her gynaecological problem. Only when they showed her a text book with the official words written on a diagram would she go for help.

There are of course some pleasant terms for the female organs – like 'centre of bliss', and 'pleasure gardens' – but they are rare and archaic. There are also some humble, even self-deprecating, words for the penis – like 'button mushroom' – but the balance of proud and positive names work overwhelmingly in favour of men.

Women's breasts are subject to another kind of language – that of nursery-style comic rhymes. They are 'jalloppies', 'jigglies', 'baloobas', 'montezumas' – sounding wobbly, bouncy, round and funny. 'Bumpy jumpers' however, is an instance of another common trait in slang. It refers not only to breasts but generically to women. In the same way, many words which mean 'cunt', also mean 'woman'.

One of the most noticeable paterns to emerge from our published sources is that over the centuries the same words have had the concurrent (or consecutive) meanings – 'woman', 'harlot' and 'pudend'. A contemporary example is 'brass' (prostitute), rhyming slang with 'brass nail' for 'tail', which means also woman, *and* the female genitals.

Men, too, are equated in slang with their organs, but in quite a different way. One of the most popular ways of referring to the penis is to give it a male name – hence 'Dick', 'John Thomas', 'Peter', 'Percy'. Sometimes it is the 'man'. But this is giving the male organ the identity of an individual, and seldom is the male individual given the identity of his organ. It is true he might be called a 'prick', but if you really want to insult him, call him 'cunt'.

Again, the words referring to men and women as sexual beings are very different. In one linguistic study Julia Stanley (1973) discovered 220 words (from a sample) meaning sexually promiscuous woman, and only 20 for a sexually promiscuous man (which is why we have included the word 'promiscuous' itself in this book, as a word used in ways not accounted for by its dictionary definition). And in a study by Sue Lees from the Polytechnic of North London (reported in *New Society* 13 November, 1983), teenage girls complained about boys that 'if you don't like them, then they'll call you a tight bitch. If you go with them, they'll call you a slag afterwards.'

'The commonest insult, used by both sexes,' writes Sue Lees, 'is "slag". Girls and women are still often seen and judged primarily in terms of their sexual status (but) ... it is crucial to note that insults might bear no relation at all to a girl's actual sexual behaviour. One problem for girls – if the abuse came from boys – is that there aren't equivalent terms that they can use against boys. There are no words that amount to an attack on their whole personality or social identity. The only really derogatory word for a boy (a word such as "prick" is milder than "slag") is "queer" and "pouff". Because this refers to abnormal sexuality, there are limits to the occasions it can be used.'

Similarly, we have been unable to find a female equivalent for the term 'prick tease', while while words for male sexual prowess such as 'knob artist' and 'cocksman' have no female substitute. Slang shows clearly how the sexual double standard is alive and well.

But women are not the only ones to lose out because of the assumptions behind 'slanguage'. Many men we talked to said that they had no words which they were comfortable with to refer to sexual intercourse. 'Making Love' sounded too stuffy or pompous. But so many of the words available – like bang, knock and fuck – had such aggressive connotations that men preferred to avoid any explicit mention of 'doing it'.

Wayland Young (*Eros Denied*) illustrates the dilemma with this apochryphal tale: 'I was walking along on this fucking fine morning, fucking sun shining away, little country fucking lane, and I meets up with this fucking girl. Fucking lovely she was, so we gets into conver-fucking-sation and I takes her over a fucking gate and into a fucking field and we has sexual intercourse.'

Alternatively, there is the jocular tradition of referring to the penis as the 'tool' of the sexual 'trade', the 'equipment' or 'tackle' with which to 'do the business', or get 'on the job'. How can men express their own needs and emotions in this briskly businesslike usage?

Some women have attempted to 'reclaim' certain slang words – like 'cunt' and 'dyke' – to make them more positive. But as writer Michelle Roberts told a women's magazine recently: 'I don't think there is a word for what women do in heterosexual sex. The kind of words you want are "I embrace you", "I take you in", "I hold you" or "I absorb you".'

Terms about masturbation in their jokey jingles tend to reflect the embarrassment with which this subject is often treated. The 'five finger knuckle shuffle' with 'Mother Palm and her five daughters' are ways of saying that 'to gallop the maggot' is not an occupation that adults should take seriously (not unless they are 'wankers', that is). And for the most part, unless women adopt the male terminology (as many have done with 'wank'), it is an activity which they are absent from in slang.

There is no systematic or comprehensive way to research a book about such a volatile medium as slang. Our best sources were

13

personal contacts, mostly male. Many of their words and phrases are, to the best of our knowledge, original and elsewhere unrecorded. But a remarkably high proportion of slang which at first we thought was new, proved to have ancient roots and precursors.

In contrast, much of the slang told to us by women has no written source that we could trace, but sometimes draws on established slang. One woman for instance told us her private name for breast – 'tuds', an amalgam perhaps of 'tits' and 'buds'.

A questionnaire which we circulated to encourage contributors yielded disappointing results however. Perhaps writing down the kind of words rarely seen except in graffiti goes against the usual verbal habit of slang.

Anther important written source for us was Bruce Rodger's gay lexicon, *The Queen's English*, which is about a whole gay language, with sexuality as just one of its subjects. Apart from providing us with some of the best examples of outrageous and funny slang, Rodgers introduces a whole range of sexual practices, some hilarious, some mysterious, some stomach-churning, but most of which are beyond the wildest dreams (or nightmares) of the average heterosexual.

Rodgers' delineation of gay slang also made another point clear to us: that the same word can often have very different meanings in gay and heterosexual slang. Much of gay slang turns the table on heterosexual jibing, by making a virtue of referring to gays in the feminine. Male names are adapted to the female version, the term 'queen' is liberally sprinkled about. Rodgers expresses the defiance of much of gay slang like this: 'Slang is social protest, used to deflate the hypocrisy of nice-sounding labels that mean nothing to the people who use them. Slang is also the expression of the underdog – it is aimed against the establishment.'

But only a small proportion of slang is considered unprintable these days, and much of our material comes from contemporary newspapers and magazines, from the *News of the World*, the *Sun*, the *Guardian*, women's magazines, the Sunday 'pops' and 'heavies', and *New Society*.

We were surprised at how liberally the pages of the daily press are sprinkled with sexual slang. Much of this is euphemism and creaking innuendo – especially on the pages of pin-ups and in the pop papers where stories with a sexual theme are nearly as common as news.

But many are not innuendo at all: in contrast to a recent editorial in the *Sun* condemning the use of the 'foulest four letter word' on a radio show, the *Guardian* has recently printed 'fuck' and 'vag wash sex' on its women's page.

Even characters in such respectable TV shows as 'Jewel In The Crown' (ITV, 1984) have used the word 'fuck' or referred to 'losing one's cherry'.

And, after all, much of sexual slang is not obscene. Much of it is about love, affection and courtship, about 'dating people', having 'girlfriends' and 'boyfriends'. It crops up in conversations about ''er indoors' or simply 'my old China'.

It's there every time we call someone a 'berk', a 'prat' or a 'wally', or ask 'who are you leaning on these days?' It marks new departures in our style of relationships, whether we are 'on the market', 'in the closet', 'living together' or 'living in sin'.

Much of slang makes a needle-sharp point about sex — commercial or otherwise. It's not out of admiration for the Tory party that the women who come to London to seek work in the sex industry refer to themselves as 'Thatcher's girls', while a 'Have it Away Day' has come to mean a lot more than an idle shopping spree to the city.

All the fears and guilt and hilarity of human sexuality are reflected in slang too. Across the UK people have joked about their own sexual inadequacies and disappointments in local language — was it like 'chucking a worm up the Mersey Tunnel', or like 'pushing a sausage down Regent Street'? If withdrawal is your method of contraception and you live in Edinburgh, you might know what it means to 'jump off at Haymarket', or if your lover is in Sydney Australia, did you have to 'hop off at Redfern.'?

And who could do anything but smile at the ingenuity of terms like 'gorilla salad', 'pink oboe', 'tummy banana', 'where the monkey sleeps' and 'QUANTAS hostie'.

We suspected before we began this book that in recent years a rich vein of hitherto unexplored sexual language had come out of the closet along with a variety of sexual practices. Perhaps people in previous generations have indulged in 'bagpiping', 'bambi' and 'B&D', but these are the terms that are used today.

Some of the entries in this dictionary may seem shocking and upsetting. But perhaps by writing about them we can take some of the power out of the taboos that make them so, or some of the sting out of their function as abuse. Many more of the entries are imaginative, bizarre, affectionate and funny, and we believe *The Slanguage of Sex* is the first contemporary guide to the jungle of sexual slang in the US and UK. We will have left out some important items. Not only is slang ever-changing and ever-developing, but it means different things to different people in different places.

We hope that our readers will let us known about *their* use of sexual slang so that we can keep this dictionary up to date.

JOHN SHEARLAW
and
BRIGID MCCONVILLE

A

academy A brothel. Rarely heard in popular usage these days, and probably as outdated as the institution itself. Of the whole litany of synonyms unearthed by Victorian etymologists Farmer and Henley – academy, pushing school, nanny-house (q.v.), case, – all were well established by 1850, but only knocking shop remains popular. For today's equivalents *see also* RELIEF MASSAGE (for massage parlour) and KNOCK OFF (for knocking shop).

accoutrements The male genitals. Primarily camp gay and a comparatively dismissive word for what is normally regarded as precious and important to the male. *Contrast with* CROWN JEWELS, FAMILY JEWELS, and VITALS.

AC/DC Bisexual. In common usage from the late fifties onwards, spreading from the US to the UK. Obviously taken from the two modes of electricity – alternating current and direct current. Especially used by men of a man experimenting with homosexuality. The female equivalent is almost invariably *bi*. *See also* AMBIDEXTROUS. The rise to fame of Australian heavy metal band AC/DC in the seventies bore no relation to their sexuality – in Australia the combination merely meant high voltage long after its slang meaning was accepted everywhere else!

ace of spades The vagina. The phrase carries an appealing notion of play, unusual in words for the female sexual parts, but is also linked to the 19th century slang for female, widow or black-haired woman.

acorn The penis, or more specifically the exposed glans penis in a state of erection. Affectionate, colourful and direct from the Latin root (*glans*, acorn); one of the few words for the male organ not implying force, threat or power. UK and US usage from the 50s at least. *Compare with* BUTTON MUSHROOM.

acorn picker Anyone who enjoys fellatio, although mostly used by male gays.

action Also **piece of action** Either a willing participant in sexual activity (noun), or the method employed (verb). Thus to a pursuer a man or a woman can be 'action', but equally one's preferred type of sex will be one's own 'action'. Hence likely to be used in a question. 'Where's the action?' – where can one find sex? 'What's your action?' – which way do you want to have sex? Transported back from the US to the UK these terms are in widespread use by both gay and heterosexual men and women.

active partner Originally, the man who penetrates during anal intercourse; thus primarily male gay. Synonyms are legion and begin with arse bandit (q.v.). There is, however, a limited 'straight' usage, usually in the form of male complaint, as in 'I'm the active partner in our relationship,' which makes the assumption that women just 'lie back and enjoy it'.

ad, advert Indication of availability for sex, usually on a paying basis. This sexual use of the accepted American abbreviation for advertisement came into being from the seventies onwards. An ad can appear as a postcard in a shop window with a contact number displayed, as a few lines in the classified section of a sex magazine, or even as a few scribbled lines on a toilet wall. In all cases what is available is either obvious or insinuated (see, for instance, RELIEF MASSAGE). By the mid seventies whole magazines were published consisting entirely of ads, aimed either at straights, gays, wife swappers or those with more 'perverse' tastes, and this method of sexual communication continues to flourish. See CONTACT MAG.

Adam A male gay's first lover. US male gay slang (Rodgers).

Adamic Naked. Starting with the worthy OED definition (literally from the first man in the Garden Of Eden) there follows a whole slew of slang derivations. Principally, Partridge notes the grammatically incorrect but common adamical and adamatical – both meaning naked. However the root is now only found in compound form in phrases like Adam and Eve's togs (i.e. no clothes at all). A contemporary US phrase is Adam's PJ's (PJ's = pyjamas).

Adonis A male regarded as perfectly physically attractive; from the name of the Greek god. Just as likely to be used as a negative, jocular comparison – 'He's no Adonis'. Usage is particularly common in reference to 'holiday romances' – 'I went to Corfu this year and fell in love with a bronze Adonis'. Gay and straight usage.

advertise, to To behave in a sexually provocative manner. The sexual meaning has largely been adopted by the camp male gay faction (Rodgers), yet is still occasionally used by heterosexuals. Thus a woman wearing a low-cut dress at a party will be said to be 'advertising' herself.

affair A sexual liaison. Shortened form of love affair. An affair may simply be a relationship between two people but commonly carries the connotation of 'illicit sex'.
Also used as a noun, as in: 'She's my affair at the moment.'

African queen A black male homosexual. Mostly US. *See also* DINGE QUEEN.

afterbirth An 'ugly' face. From the term denoting the placenta after childbirth. Although in common usage since 1587 (OED) this is now a good example of a quasisexual word that has become a 'low' insult. Hence the pub joke: 'Is that a spot on your face? No it's the afterbirth.' Can also be used – invariably by males – to describe a person insultingly. A strong indication that male attitudes towards childbirth still tend towards disgust and loathing.

after his end, more commonly **after his hole** A man desirous of sexual intercourse. A common

catch phrase used by twentieth-century men usually in an open social situation. Can also be personally stated; thus, after my end, and after my hole. *See also* END and HOLE.

afternoon delight Sex in the afternoon. Conveys both the element of pleasure and of relative rarity. Affectionate euphemism amongst both sexes in the US and UK since the 60s at least. *Compare* MORNER, NOONER, QUICKIE.

agreeable ruts of life, the The vagina. Old-fashioned and almost whimsical, but nevertheless a comparatively positive term to describe the female sexual parts. (Early twentieth-century origins.) Male usage only. *Compare with* PLEASURE GARDENS.

A-hole Uncommon abbreviation for the US term ass-hole, most likely to be used as an expletive.

AIDS Acquired Immunity Deficiency Syndrome. This fatal illness became known as 'the gay plague' after gay men in America began dying at the end of the seventies. To date the disease has killed more than a thousand Americans – mostly gay men. Its cause is not yet known, but is thought to be a kind of a virus which prevents otherwise healthy people from resisting infections. Sufferers lose weight and may develop skin cancer or tumours. Nine out of ten die when they contract an infection. AIDS came to the UK in the early eighties and, by the end of 1983, 24 cases had occurred in Britain. The disease has changed the pattern of homosexual relations in the 'US' and the UK, especially in 'gay' cities like San Francisco. The former promiscuity amongst large groups of gays has been replaced by a fearful caution, with AIDS representing a death threat rather than a social inconvenience like herpes or VD.

air one's pores To be (or become) naked. Coy and fanciful English euphemism. Twentieth-century UK (mostly literary) usage, but now dated.

airtight (Of a male gay) penetrated in every orifice. Primarily US gay slang (Rodgers) and a strong indication that multiple sex is much more a part of the American gay scene than it is in Britain. Instigating 'airtightness' could involve upwards of three partners and, as such, the term is most likely to be used in pornography or other flights of fancy.

all arse, all bum The use of 'all' in its true sense, allied with one or several physical features, has been common descriptive sexual language since the 17th century (Partridge). As such the dominant physical (and thus sexual) feature

becomes the person. Usually dismissive rather than lustful and applied mostly to women.

Many of the compounds are still extant (as in the two above); also, all behind, all boobs, all cunt, all fanny, all tits and teeth. Some of these do still have positive sexual connotations, but several have become merely insulting – as with 'all fanny'. The venerable 'all mouth and trousers' itself a euphemism for 'all prick and breeches' was originally applied to a man whose words spoke louder than his sexual actions. Now it is merely an insulting (non-sexual) catch phrase. Others, like the convoluted 'all things to all men and nothing to one man', which meant prostitute in the 19th and early 20th century (Partridge), are now obsolete.

all dolled up *See* TART.

all forlorn An erection. Cockney rhyming slang for horn. *See* HORN, MARQUIS OF LORNE, COLLEEN BAWN.

all nighter Originally prostitutes' slang, meaning a customer who has paid for sexual services for the night, rather than for a shorter period of time. As such, dating back to early 20th century. (The opposite is part timer.) Now in more general currency (straight and gay) indicating a person whose desires are so great that they can spend all night in sexual pursuit and/or 'action'.

almond The penis, or more specifically the glans penis. Cockney rhyming slang from c.1890 (Partridge) from almond rock = cock. Now uncommon, but see next entry.

almond rock candy The penis head. As seen, and tasted, by a fellator. Gay slang, fifties onwards.

Alphonse A ponce. Rhyming slang (and also a pun on the unlikely name) and now rare.

alright, a bit of An attractive woman or man. *See* BIT. Also ALRIGHT, ALL RIGHT, and BIT OF ALL RIGHT. Contemporary UK slang.

Alsatian An 'unattractive' woman. For a fuller explanation *see* DOG. 'Straight' British slang only, attributing the 'unfeminine' qualities of the animal to the woman; in this case largeness and ferocity. Abusive, derogatory and lamentably common. Less commonly, 'she's a bear'.

altogether, in the Naked. The mildest of euphemisms, now almost invariably used jocularly. Suprisingly not yet recognized by the OED.

Amazon Big, 'aggressive' woman. Used by men in a derogatory sense of women whom they find threatening; the meaning from the original tribe of South American warrior women. But characteristically, feminists are reinterpreting the word in a positive sense, as in this piece from *Spare Rib* October 1983: 'Amazon (also aggressive woman, harridan, virago, lesbian) – all those women who don't comply with conventional ideas of feminity. Keep up the good work ...'

ambidextrous Bisexual. Probably the first recorded euphemism for a person recording an attraction to both sexes but now as old fashioned as 'double-gaited'. Almost invariably the common modern equivalents are AC/DC or 'bi'.

ammunition Sanitary towel or tampon. Hence the old-fashioned phrase from a woman delighted to discover she isn't pregnant – 'Praise the Lord and pass the ammunition!' World War II British usage, now obsolete.

anal virgin Gay man who has never had passive anal intercourse (Rodgers).

angel A male homosexual. Camp term, in this sense exclusive to the gay community. *Compare* QUEEN.

angry (Of the erect penis.) Related to the imagery of 'inflammation' and 'aggravation'. A good example of how male sex drive and aggression are linked in slang: here the organ (the weapon) is imbued with a mind of its own and reacts to provocation (i.e. sexual excitement). Contemporary UK male slang.

animal A person reputed to be without sexual restraint and/or discrimination. There are several shades of usage; notably a 'promiscuous' man to another man is an animal, but equally a sexually unattractive partner is an animal. A male may say (of a female) 'I'm not going to bed with that animal' (*see* DOG), while a female is as likely to say (of a man) 'Keep that animal away from me'.

anything in trousers, she'll have A British phrase directed at a female reckoned by others (male or female, but more often another female) to be sexually 'promiscuous' or indiscriminate. Semi-jocular and not as insulting as 'bike' or 'margarine' but while sexual double standards persist it is generally derogatory to women. It also implies a grudging admission of a degree of female freedom. *Contrast with* the expression applied to men – ANYTHING ON TWO LEGS.

anything on two legs, he'll fuck (or shag) One male's approbation of another's reputed sexual conquests or (sometimes) lack of discrimination. Originating in the services (WW2) and now widespread. For the full colourful litany of synonyms *see under* YOU'D ...

are you coming yet? A common

enough part of the (generally limited) verbal communication during coitus. Often uttered by the more considerate or 'liberated' male as he 'holds himself up', in order to ejaculate at the same time as his partner achieves orgasm. A modern phrase as a modern idea – only recently have men been urged to pay attention to the female orgasm. Variations include are you ready?, are you OK? or even, are you alright? A phrase like 'are you happy?' is more likely to be post-coital however.

are you keeping it for the worms? The anguished cry of the male denied the chance to 'deflower' a woman. 'It', of course, is the hymen. Becoming obsolete as virginity becomes less fashionable.

are you on the pill? Catch phrase which is currently a request prior to (or sometimes during) sexual intercourse between a man and a woman. Dating from the sixties when the Pill became a popular form of contraception among young people. The phrase took over from the clumsier – and more dated – are you fixed? or even, are you alright? For other pre-coital requests *see*, for instance, FLAGS OUT?, PAINTERS IN?, ARE YOU RED SAILS IN THE SUNSET? and HOW ABOUT A SWIM? *See also* NECESS-ARIES.

are you red sails in the sunset? Literally, are you menstruating?

For a fuller etymology *see* RED SAILS IN THE SUNSET.

armful of chairs, she wouldn't know if you'd been up there with an Bawdy catch phrase, probably Australian in origin; spoken by one man to another reporting a remarkably large vagina. There is also the inevitable accusation of the woman's 'promiscuity' – and an unconscious, but glaringly obvious double standard.

armswing An act of masturbation. As with most words for masturbation the force and power required to complete the act is colourfully exaggerated. This particular example is principally American.

Arschloch The anus. Direct from the German (= asshole) and briefly fashionable among US gays during the 60s.

arse The 'backside buttocks'. Standard English for over a century but still regarded in the UK as a highly sexual word. Compounds are multiple and while arsehole and shit arse are derogatory (and non-sexual) terms most terms have a sexual flavour; 'Look at the arse on that one!' and 'What a piece of arse!' are common terms of male approbation. Widespread straight and gay usage, male and female. Synonymous with the American 'ass', which is interchangeable in all phrases and compounds.

arse bandit A homosexual. British male usage only, implying disgust and 'theft'. Rarer and more archaic are arse brigand and arse king (occasionally, in the US, arse queen). *Compare* TURD BURGLAR.

artichoke The vagina. Connoisseurs take great delight in the use of this word and are wont to refer to the OED definition – 'a fruit ... with edible parts inside the bristly exterior.' Mostly affectionate male usage as women still tend to find themselves bereft of vocabulary for their own parts and inhibited by the implications of 'cunt'. Less common (and mostly US) is Jerusalem artichoke – the vagina of a Jewish woman.

article A woman, as described by a 'straight' man. Common in the Antipodes where the standard male question would be 'Did you feature with an article?' Undeniably dismissive, leaving the woman without identity. *See also* BAG.

artist *Also* **artiste** A virtuoso sexual performer. Heterosexual and gay male usage in the US and UK since the 60s at least. Often preceded by a word for the penis; *see under* KNOB. *Compare also* COCKSMAN.

ass The 'backside buttocks'. American – but also used in Britain – for arse (q.v.).

as the actress said to the bishop

23

A catch phrase from WW2 onwards, which has the function of pointing out a sexual innuendo in an otherwise innocent statement. It has since achieved everyday status by its widespread inclusion in plays, books and jokes. Partridge gives the worthy example: 'It's too stiff for me to manage it, as the actress said to the bishop.'

More recently it has served as an excuse for 'bad language': 'I'd give her one – as the actress said to the bishop'; the addition of the catch phrase is meant to render the real sexual intention innocuous. Thus almost entirely jocular. Older variations like 'as the soldier said' or 'as the monkey said' have been largely superseded by the above, which enjoyed a revival in the seventies and looks likely to last for ever.

Athenian Any active homosexual. Mostly camp gay usage and an extension of the 'ancient Greeks as pederasts' philosophy. *See* DORIAN.

Attila The Hen A woman considered by men to be aggressive and powerful, from an obvious pun on Attila the Hun combined with the common word for woman – hen. This has also become a back-benchers' nickname for Mrs Thatcher since her appearance as 'leaderene'.

aureolae The area directly surrounding the nipples. Although non-slang definitions include such notions as 'the radiant circle of light around the head in classic religious paintings' (OED), the word has become very much a part of the new pornography, especially in the realms of soft porn fiction in 'girlie' magazines like *Penthouse, Knave* and *Men Only*. In these pages the aureolae 'glisten', 'expand' and 'tantalise' – among other things. The arrival of the see-through dress in the sixties, the clinging T-shirt in the seventies and the boob tube and the wet T-shirt in the eighties saw a shift in attention from the cleavage to the nipples and their adjacent parts. Reference to the aureolae is no longer solely the province of the breast fetishist or the medical student, but part of the common sexual language.

auxiliary, auxiliaries The genitals. Like accoutrements (q.v.) an unusually dismissive word for the male organs. Mostly gay US usage from the 60s.

available Ready for sexual suggestion and/or consideration. Widely used, usually as a conversational enquiry in a social setting; for example, the middle-class enquiry, 'We're having a dinner party next week. Do you know any available men I could invite for Fiona?' The OED definition is 'within one's reach'. Add the sexual connotation and that is as precise as you can get.

away the trip Pregnant. Originally Scottish dialect only, but still extant.

awkward Pregnant. Male euphemism to describe a temporarily incomprehensible situation, e.g.

'She's awkward at the moment'. Like 'away the trip', this is old fashioned but used when even the coy 'preggers' is considered unacceptable.

B

baby Lover, and/or friend. Use among the fashionable elements of English society has been constant since the turn of the century. But it was the glamorous stars of Hollywood's heyday who gave the word its supercool American flavour — which still persists, especially in the common shortened form 'babe'. Straight and gay, male and female usage, invariably as a term of affection.

baby maker The penis. Coy, euphemistic UK usage, now virtually obsolete.

back cave The anus. Principally male homosexual usage but now uncommon. Sometimes also back garden (*see* PLEASURE GARDENS), and the more medical 'back passage'. There are however, far more popular and colourful terms — *see* BATCAVE, HERSHEY HIGHWAY.

back passage The anus. With the synonymous 'back door', used by UK males in relation to anal intercourse with a woman — 'She likes it up the back passage'. Some gay male usage also. *Compare with* FRONT BUM.

backs against the wall! Also 'backs to the wall chaps!' Hearty and jocular cry of the straight male to warn of the arrival of a male gay — perceived as a threat to his anal integrity. Especially used in drinking, sporting gatherings. *See also* SEPARATE SHOWERS, and DON'T DROP YOUR CAR KEYS.

bag A woman. Derogatory term widely used by both sexes in the UK (but rarely in America) — as in 'She's a silly old bag'. The word has a long history, traceable back to the 17th century, when 'baggage' was used to reflect discredit on men as well as women. Partridge gives the old meanings 'worthless man' and 'saucy young woman', but the word was soon narrowed down to apply to females only — and it came to mean prostitute or loose woman.

bag of coke Sexual intercourse. Cockney rhyming slang for poke. *See also* FRIAR TUCK.

bag off To form a sexual relationship with someone – i.e. to 'get off with'. Predominantly Scottish and northern English male expression. Popular and current usage, equivalent to the Liverpudlian 'cop off'.

'Bag off' features in Dave Robertson's *Edinburgh Poems* (1980) in 'I'm a gadgie':

'The fanny lap your patter up
They like it when you're rough
And if you dinnae fuck them
There's other bits of stuff.
We take them to the bar
And get them steaming first
And if you dinnae get a bag off
You can always steal their purse'

bag over the head job A woman with whom a man has sex, but whose face he considers too 'ugly' to look at. In the tradition of expressions which describe women as passive receptacles for male sexual activity, but whose disappointing unattractiveness just has to be ignored. A common catchphrase in the UK among men. *See also* 'YOU DON'T LOOK AT THE MANTELPIECE WHEN YOU'RE STOKING THE FIRE'.

bagpipe, to UK equivalent of 'huffle' (q.v.).

balaclava Sexual intercourse. Cockney rhyming slang with chaver. *See* CHARVER.

bald-headed hermit The penis. An old-fashioned English term, now virtually obsolete except maybe as a joke.

ball and chain Wife. American prison origin from the 20s. Adopted in the UK, it sounds like (but isn't) rhyming slang. Yet the term shares the common cockney image of the wife as a shackle. *See also* TROUBLE AND STRIFE.

ball breaker American term for a woman considered threatening or 'castrating' by men, usually because of her drive, aggression or success. The implication is that a woman in this role is attacking traditional male territory, and literally robbing men of their potency.

balls The testicles. The most common slang term with this meaning in the UK, and used by men and women of all social classes, often as an expletive – as in 'Oh balls!', or 'What a load of balls'. Also widespread US usage, but in America 'nuts' is probably more common. A popular UK and Irish variant is 'bollocks' or 'ballocks', which makes for a more emphatic expletive. Although dating back to the 17th century (and perhaps even farther) in the form of ballocks (now bollocks) the word was considered vulgar by the 19th century.

baloobas The breasts. Affectionate male UK usage. *Compare*

27

BAZOOMAS, BEJONKERS, JALOPIES.

bambi Straightforward homosexual and lesbian sex which does not involve sado-masochism, bondage or domination. A recently popular English gay and lesbian term. For instance, oral and anal sex, without embellishments, are 'bambi'. Taken from the name of the Walt Disney cartoon fawn, for its youth and innocence in the midst of the perilous forest. Equivalent also to 'vanilla' (q.v.).

bamboo stick The penis. Mostly West Indian and African male usage within the UK. *See also* BIG FOOT JOE.

B and D Bondage and domination, or bondage and discipline. Widely used contemporary term in the US and UK to describe the activities of tying up and/or forcing a partner into submission for sexual gratification. *Compare* S AND M.

bang, to Sexual intercourse. Common UK and mostly male usage, unrecorded before the 20th century. Comparable in its 'striking' imagery to 'knock' and 'fuck', and the male is assumed to be the active 'banging' partner.

The term occurs in the bawdy song 'Bang bang Lulu' (or 'Bang Away Lulu'), and in the originally Australian but now widespread catch phrase 'She bangs like a shithouse door in a gale'. *See also* GANG-BANG.

bang and biff Syphilis. Cockney rhyming slang with 'syph', with a pun on 'bang' (q.v.).

barge pole, I wouldn't touch it with a Catch phrase expressing straight male abhorrence of sexual activity with a woman, implying that she is 'ugly', diseased or simply unpleasant. Dismissive and aggressive UK male usage. Note the use of 'it' instead of 'her', common in abusive slang. *See also* I WOULDN'T DO IT WITH SOMEBODY ELSE'S.

Barrer Moke Sexual intercourse. Cockney rhyming slang for poke. *See also* BAG OF COKE.

basket, the The male genitalia seen in outline through clothing. US slang, originally male gay but now more common straight female usage. *See also* PACKAGE.

basketeer, basket-watcher Person who enjoys looking at dressed male crotches. US to the UK, mostly gay, but some straight female usage (especially in the US).

basket lunch, to have a To give a 'blow job' (fellatio) without undressing the partner. Some female usage, but mostly US male gay.

batcave The anus. With its suggestions of darkness, eeriness and fear, batcave has become one of the more popular male gay terms for the anus in the US and UK. At some time in the 80s,

London, New York and San Francisco have each boasted a Batcave Club, frequented by male gays. An alternative US and UK male gay usage is 'mineshaft' which also has a club named after it.

bathroom sex Sex in the bathroom, whether embellished by aquatic delights or not. Used by heterosexuals as much as by gays, in the US and UK. In British West Indian slang the phrase has been immortalized by General Echo in the song of the same name (taken from the album '12 Inches Of Pleasure'): 'Bathroom sex I have to sing/Is nicer than a double bed spring.'

bazooka The penis. Primarily American, straight male usage, occasionally extended to 'bazooka shooter'. The image of penis as weapon is a common one. *See* BULLETS.

bazoomas Breasts. Common English joke word, mostly straight male usage. Often heard in tandem with an alliterative adjective – thus 'big bazoomas'. *See also* BEJONKERS.

B.B. Bra. An abbreviation of 'bust bodice'. Female and mostly northern English usage.

bean juice Anal exudate. US male gay slang, derived from the Mexican slang 'bean queen' for a male gay. The reference is to beans as a cause of wind, and

hence the synonymous US 'fart slime'.

beard splitter The penis. Dating back to the 18th century, this is largely obsolete in the UK, but *compare* the contemporary phrase 'to spear the bearded clam'. In both senses the beard = the vagina or the vagina and pubic hair.

beast with two backs, making the Sexual intercourse. The first attributed usage is in Shakespeare's *Othello*, and although some lexicographers deem it obsolete, the phrase is enjoying a new run of popularity with young middle-class British people who make the most of its melodramatic and archaic flavour.

beat off, to Also 'beat the meat'. Male masturbation. The former is principally American, the latter more common in the UK where men have used it for decades. Both bear testimony to the self-flagellating imagery traditionally associated with male worship of Onan. *Compare* FLOG THE DONKEY.

Beattie and Babs The (usually) sexually transmitted infection of 'crabs' (q.v.). Cockney rhyming slang and so limited UK usage.

beaver The female genital area. Most often heard in reference to pornographic pictures as 'beaver shots'. One theory as to the origin of the term is that the dark and hairy shape of this part of the

29

body looks from above much like a beaver when swimming. Trendy UK and US usage. In the language of contemporary pornographic magazines for straight males (especially in the UK) the graphic term 'split beaver' means a vagina openly displayed, and magazines containing such pictures are often advertised as featuring 'split beaver shots'. There is also a current, but limited, usage of to split the beaver: to have sexual intercourse.

bed, to To have sexual intercourse with. One of the most popular euphemisms of the 'liberated' sixties and seventies, with a principally straight usage. Thus 'Did you bed her, then?' and hence the terms of approbation, 'bedworthy' and 'beddable', used by both males and females. Male gays eschew this polite usage and prefer to go for the jugular with 'fuckable' or 'shaggable'. *See also* SHARE ONE'S BED WITH.

bed mate, bed partner A sexual partner, male or female. Both euphemisms are now considered so polite that they may even occur in national newspaper interviews.

bee bites Small breasts or nipples. Originally male gay slang for men's nipples, now sometimes straight usage for small female breasts and/or nipples. Also 'dog ears', 'cherries'.

Beecham's Pills Testicles. From

30

cockney rhyming slang with pills. Often shortened to 'Beecham's'.

beefcake Male sex appeal and/or a sexually appealing male. Widespread UK and US, gay and straight usage. Hence this item on the *Sun*'s Page Three in the 'Me and My Man' series when women appeared topless with their men in briefs:
'Beefcake muscles appear on Page Three by popular demand. Today Karen Clarke, 20, displays her desirable property – estate agent husband Malcolm' (3 Sep. 1983).
Beefiness in women, however, is still widely considered repellent, despite the recent trend for female body-building. Hence the decision by Berni Inns to refuse employment to women who wear clothes larger than size 14. As the *Sunday Mirror* put it on 19 Feb 1984: 'Beefy barmaids at Britain's top steakhouses are in for a lean time ... (said a union official) ... "Berni just want dolly-birds to work for them".'
See also MEAT.

beef curtains The female labia. 'Beef' has the slang meanings 'penis' and 'man', and so this phrase, contemporary among UK males, refers to the female parts as drapery for the male. *See also* CHOPPED LIVER.

bejonkers The breasts. Another jokey, nursery type word: *compare*

BAZOOMAS, BALOOBAS. Sometimes also: majonkers.

bell The clitoris. Popular since WW2 among the American black community, now widespread in the US. Songs like 'Ring My Bell' by Anita Ward caused scarcely a raised eyebrow in the 70s. 'You can ring my bell any time you want to' would be regarded as a 'come-on' phrase in the US if used by a female.

bell end The penis. UK male usage. Contemporary and widespread. The reference to shape is comparable to the more popular 'knob', also 'helmet'.

belly fuck To rub against a partner's stomach until orgasm. Limited, mostly US usage, gay and heterosexual.

bender A male homosexual. One of the more common derogatory terms for 'gay' currently in use among heterosexual UK males. Also limited use to describe lesbians. Less common is the variant 'arse bender'. The modern usage derives entirely from the imagined activity: compare H, DOING THE and GENDER BENDER.

bent To be gay or lesbian. Very widespread UK male usage, despite the parallel slang meaning 'criminal'. Top-rated TV shows like 'Minder' and 'The Sweeney' have spread both senses.

bent as a nine bob note Gay. Sometimes in shorthand form, as in – 'he's a nine bob'. Sixties origin but the phrase shows no sign of dying out despite decimalization and the end of the 'bob'. The common US equivalent is 'queer as a three dollar bill'.

berk An irritating fool. Although this word is very common in the UK and applied (usually to men) without embarrassment and without much more force than 'twit' or 'wally', its origins are a surprise to many. Berk has the original meaning 'cunt' from cockney rhyming slang with Berkeley Hunt.

Bertie Woofter Male homosexual. See POOF.

between the sheets In bed, and often in reference to the delights of sexual intercourse. 'He/she was wonderful between the sheets.' Another example of a euphemism so polite that it has entered national newspaper speak.

BF The partner who supposedly takes the dominant role in a lesbian affair. BF stands for 'boyfriend' and it is a common idea that lesbians cannot be 'real' women, but must have male characteristics. US slang. See also BULL DYKE.

Bi A common abbreviation of 'bisexual' in both the UK and US. Hip and non-judgmental usage. Compare AC/DC, DOUBLE-GAITED, SWITCH-HITTER.

Big Foot Joe A male endowed

with a large penis. West Indian in origin, and in the seventies a part of British Creole. Immortalized in the chart hit 'Wet Dream' by Max Romeo in 1972 (banned by the BBC): 'Give the pussy to Big Foot Joe, give the fanny to me'.

Big J Anal intercourse accompanied by a simultaneous 'blow job' (fellatio), both performed by one gay male on his partner. Rare as a word, legendary as an activity – because of the contortions involved. US origin, but becoming notorious in London. Other US equivalents are 'shrimp job', 'High Russian' and 'High Texan'.

bint A girl or woman, as in 'I saw him with some bint last night'. Also a prostitute. The word is originally Arabic (from '*saida bint*', literally, a 'good day girl' (Partridge)) and was imported from Egypt by the Armed Forces after the first World War. Its history gives it strong 'colonial' and racist overtones, and it is commonly used both by ex-colonial types and working-class British men.

bird Woman, or girlfriend. The root is the Old English 'bryd' which meant woman. It evolved the related meaning 'bride' and developed into the modern 'bird', which meant 'girl' or 'maiden' in the 16th century and then took on the meaning 'sweetheart' and 'harlot' in the 19th century.

Today it is common UK male – and sometimes female – usage for woman, but it keeps the derogatory and sexual emphasis. As such it is similar to many other once 'respectable' words for woman which became devalued through taking on a sexual meaning – see MADAM, and DAME. 'Bird' also had the meaning penis in 60s US gay slang.

bird bandit A womanizer. Cockney, working-class slang, as in 'Minder' (11 Jan 1984) – Arthur, 'shocked' to find a woman in a dressing gown in Terry's flat calls the place a 'bird bandit's lair'.

bit Sexual intercourse. As in *Woman* magazine (Dec 83), about an old couple who tripped up together on a pavement and scrambled up quickly in case bystanders should think they were 'having a bit'.

bit Woman (and occasionally, man) as a sexual object. Very common and widely used by UK males. Comparable to 'piece' both in usage and implication that the woman is less than whole. Commonly often qualified as bit of fluff, bit of posh, bit of young, bit of rough, bit of crackling, bit of crumpet, bit of large, bit of stuff, bit of crumb, bit of black, bit of mutton, bit of skirt, bit of alright, bit of jam. Many of these have survived from the 1930s. Also 'bit of tripe' – rhyming slang for wife. *See also* BIT ON THE SIDE.

bitch Term of abuse for a woman, from its meaning of female dog. Widespread contemporary usage by both men and women across the English speaking world. The term has been applied to 'lewd' (OED) women since Middle English, while 'to bitch' had the 1675 meaning – 'to frequent lewd women'. For comparable usage of animal names for women, *see* SOW and ALSATIAN.

bite, the The vagina. 18th century UK originally, but now obsolete.

bite, to To contract the anus during anal intercourse. US male gay slang.

bit on the side Dismissive term for an occasional lover, usually extra-marital. Male and female UK usage. Hence this letter to the *Sunday Mirror* from a woman who had asked for a book by this title: 'In all innocence I asked the young man at our local library: "Can you get me *A Bit on the Side?*" He went scarlet!'

bits Genitals. Euphemism used by women, as in this comment: 'A picture of him naked was in *Playgirl*, but the bits were covered up'.

BJ *See* BLOW JOB.

blow job Fellatio. Widespread UK and US usage during the 20th century, heterosexual and gay. Sometimes abbreviated to BJ. In the US the more usual form is 'to blow'. For reasons lost in the mists of (albeit recent) history, 'blow' in this context is synonymous with 'suck'. *See also* SUCK.

blue Pornographic, obscene. A now widespread euphemism, and one in British usage since 1830. Often heard in reference to pornographic films (as 'blue movies') or to 'blue' language, as in the *Sunday Mirror* (18 March 1984) referring to the Terry Wogan/Jimmy Young morning chat: 'Her Majesty [the Queen] is not the only one to have her ears assailed by increasingly blue banter between Radio 2's morning hosts.' The word in question was 'knickers'. More generally used however as by the *News of the World* in their feature about stripping in pubs and clubs (4 March 1984) entitled 'Blue Blue Britain'.

blue balls The state supposedly experienced by males who are kept uncomfortably on the brink of orgasm. Straight and gay male usage since 1940 in the UK. Sometimes also LOVER'S BALLS.

blue veined steak The penis. Originally Armed Forces slang since before WW2. Also 'blue veined trumpet', more common among men in Scotland and the north of England.

boat and oar Prostitute. Cockney

rhyming slang with whore. *See also* BOLT THE DOOR, EARLY DOOR.

boggle, to To stare lecherously at women, usually from a secluded place. Current UK male usage. Hence one of the stars of Jackie Lynton's *Wanking Contest* (1980) is named 'Tom Boggle', in reference to his voyeuristic role. *Compare* PEEPING TOM.

boiler A woman. Widespread UK usage since the 60s, almost exclusively male. Its early 20th century origins are derogatory. Partridge records its earliest usage as 1925, and gives the definition 'a well-used woman of forty or over'. Given the use of 'hen' and 'chicken' to mean woman or girl, it seems likely that 'boiler' is a reference to the older and tougher variety of fowl. However, today's women are less accepting of names with such hostile undercurrents. Hence the 1980s pop song 'The Boiler' about a rape, which links the rape with the attitude behind the use of 'boiler'. *See also* RAKE OUT.

bolt the door Prostitute. Cockney rhyming slang with whore. Also boat and oar, six to four, early door, two by four.

bona omi A gay male, as described by another gay male. Traditional English theatrical usage, now widespread in the US and the UK. *Contrast* NAFF OMI. *See also* POLONE.

bone in the leg An erect penis, as noticed in a man wearing trousers. Hence 'She's given him a bone in the leg'. Common Dublin slang. A US gay equivalent is a 'boner'.

bonk Sexual intercourse. As in 'Did you have a good bonk last night?', and to describe the state of play in a relationship – 'They're not even bonking any more.'

This word is a favourite of the UK young, taking over from classics such as 'roger', or 'tup' from generations past. Entirely cross-sexual, with women being just as likely to say they bonk somebody as are men. Thus 'bonking', an acceptable part of everyday straight life.

bonk on An erection. As in 'I woke up with a bonk on', or more colourfully 'to nurse a giant bonk on'. The term has been in usage from the late 50s at least. *See also* STONK, and EMBO – both describing the early morning phenomenon.

boobs Breasts. Since the swinging 60s, by far the most common word used by UK women – and some men – for breasts. Hence the brief heyday of the 'boob tube', a tight sleeveless 'vest' of clinging material, invented at the end of the 70s.

bottle and glass Cockney rhyming slang for arse. *See also* KHYBER PASS, ELEPHANT AND CASTLE.

box The vagina. American slang, rarely used in the UK. A common US porn magazine term, and one immortalized in the joke by American comedienne Bette Midler:
    'Darling, you've got no tits and a tight box.'
    'Herbie, get off my back.'

boy The penis. Synonymous is lad; also, in Ireland, the 'boyo'. Affectionate straight male term, as in 'Wherever I go, I take the boyo with me.' For other examples of manly identity given to the organ, see DICK, PETER *et al.*

brand name One's sexual preference. 'What's your brand name?' Originally US gay, now straight also. *See also* WHAT NUMBER.

brass nail Prostitute. From cockney rhyming slang for tail. Commonly shortened to 'brass'.

brewer's droop Alcohol-induced impotence. The phrase has been around almost as long as the condition. Dating back to at least Shakespearean times, but showing no signs of waning popularity as a jocular catch phrase. *Compare* 'GET IT UP, HE CAN'T'.

bring off To stimulate to orgasm. Now in wholesale use for every combination of man and man, woman and man, and woman and woman, although Partridge notes that 'to bring off', i.e. for a woman to induce an orgasm in a man, has been colloquial English since the 16th century. Also to 'bring on' – to cause sexual excitement.

bring out To convince a person that they are homosexual, sometimes through physical seduction. Mostly US gay usage, though a US alternative is 'teach school'.

Bristols Breasts. From cockney rhyming slang with Bristol Cities = titties. Still in widespread usage. *See also* CAT and KITTIES.

brown hat, or brown hatter A male homosexual. Almost exclusively straight male UK term, emphasizing the supposed deviance and dirtiness of anal sex. *See* CHUTNEY FERRET, TURD BURGLAR, CHOCOLATE BANDIT.

brush *See* OFF THE BRUSH.

brush, the The penis. Almost entirely British West Indian usage. Thus Lloyd Chalmers on the 'Censored' LP (1972) 'I'm going to give you the brush, I'm going to give you the full length.'

bubbies The breasts. Affectionate UK usage, dating back to the 17th century at least.

bubble gum A condom. Teenage US slang from the fifties onwards, now a little outdated. 'Bubble gum machine' is an automatic condom vendor, usually found in public lavatories.

bull dicker A fantasy figure lesbian whose clitoris is supposedly so extended that she is

35

able to simulate 'straight' sex – i.e. penetrate – another female using her endowment as a penis substitute. The expression is US male homosexual camp in origin, again drawing on the ancient prejudice that lesbians are part male – because it's impossible to have sex without the male element!

bull dyke A 'butch' lesbian. Derives from the old myth that lesbians must be part male (hence bull), as 'normal' women do not have sexual urges. Its original use goes back several decades, but today it is used by men and women with a measure of fear and hostility.

The popular stereotype of a bull dyke is the cartoon lesbian with short cropped hair, boots and industrial clothes. Hence the straight joke: 'What's the difference between a bull dyke and a whale? Two tons of blubber and a hair shirt.' And the 'joke' definition of bull dyke: 'She rolls her own tampons and kick starts her vibrator.'
See also BF.

bullets Lumps of semen. Straight and gay male, taken from the image of the male who 'shoots' during orgasm. Hence 'to lose bullets' or 'to shoot bullets'. 'To run out of bullets', signifies an inability to ejaculate. *See also* BAZOOKA.

bum The backside. Currently the most popular word for this part of the body in British usage, and considered only slightly naughty. Dating back to Middle English as 'The posterior' (OED), it became a vulgarism in the 18th century.

bum cleavage The crease between the male buttock cheeks, as exposed when ill-fitting trousers are pulled downwards by the bending action. The sighting of a 'bum cleavage' often provokes comment between women in bars, but it is considered a comical rather than erotic sight. For a US gay equivalent, *see* HAPPY VALLEY.

bumper to bumper Rubbing vaginas together. US lesbian slang, virtually unheard of in the UK (Rodgers).

bumping pussies Two men unable to indulge in any other sexual activity than rubbing their bodies together, supposedly because of impotence or ineptitude. Contemptuous US male gay slang.

bumpy jumper Breasts, or occasionally, woman. English rural usage, intended to be amusing. First heard by the authors in darkest Somerset when a pub landlord was moved to comment after staging a Friday disco, 'Should be a good night tonight, there's plenty of bumpy jumpers coming in.'

bun in the oven, she's got a Pregnant. Common UK slang for many years – perhaps originating in the north of England.

bunk up To have intercourse. English working-class in origin: 'Did you get a bunk up last night?'. Forces' slang in the UK from World War II, from the sense to 'bunk' or 'bunk down' = to sleep. *Compare* SLEEPING WITH. Now limited male usage.

buns The backside, i.e. the buttocks. US male gay slang. Also 'bun-bun' and 'bunt'. Hence the title of the book of photographs of male posteriors, *A Woman Looks at Men's Buns* (Christie Jenkins, Perigee 1980).

butch *See* BULL DYKE. Also sometimes 'baby butch' – a US term for a young, boyish-looking lesbian.

butt The backside. An abbreviation of buttocks. Mostly US usage, and less popular in the UK than the venerable 'bum'. Hence the US 'butt fuck' for anal intercourse.

butter Semen. More common in the US than in Britain and liable to be used by both straight and gay males. Sometimes also 'love butter'.

button The clitoris. Well-established soft-porn usage for twenty years – as in 'I pushed her button till she came'. Mostly straight male usage, and sometimes more affectionately as 'love button'.

button mushroom A small penis. Contemporary and native English term used by men in an affectionate or self-deprecating way about their own organs.

C

cabbage The female genitals. UK male usage since the 19th century and still extant. Comparable with 'greens'. The 19th century synonym 'cauliflower' is, however, now obsolete.

cabman's rests Breasts. Cockney rhyming slang.

cadbury canal The anus. English gay usage, since the 60s. Comparable to the US equivalent 'Hershey highway', Hershey being a chocolate brand name in America. *See also* CHOCOLATE BANDIT.

camp A certain style associated with effeminate gays. Bruce Rodgers in his *Gay Lexicon* defines it like this: 'Camp is burlesque, fun, and ability to poke a jocular finger at one's own frustrations and guffaw at the struggles of other pathetics, homosexuals or famous influential people.'

Yet it is not confined to gays: any person can 'camp it up' by behaving in an outrageously effeminate or 'ducky' fashion.

Its root is from the 16th century theatrical term 'camping', describing young men wearing women's costumes on the stage. This in turn came from the French *campagne* – the countryside, where strolling players entertained. 'Camp' was in usage as an adjective for 'acting in an exaggerated manner' by 1906. Its 'homosexual' connotations followed in the 20s, and by the 30s it had the meaning 'effeminate' in theatre slang. By 1945 camp had developed its general contemporary sense – characteristic of homosexuals (Neaman and Silver) and still enjoys widespread popularity as a word, and as a style, in both America and the UK.

canoodle, to To fondle sexually. Still popular today in the UK as a slightly naughtier variant of 'cuddle', this affectionate term dates back to the mid 19th century, when it passed into English slang from the US. One suggestion as to its derivation is a combination of 'canny', i.e. gentle, and 'firkytoodle', a 17th century term for sexual petting (Partridge). A person given to much canoodling is known as a canoodler.

cap A common shortened form of 'Dutch cap', the contraceptive diaphragm. US and UK female usage, although 'phragmmie' is a popular middle-class equivalent.

captain has come, or **the captain is at home** Menstruation has started. A pun on catamenia from 1744 meaning menstrual discharge. From the 17th to the 19th century in the UK but now obsolete, as is its equivalent 'the cardinal has come'.

carry on A general term for sexual activity. UK and US usage, from the 1850s onwards. To be 'carrying on with someone' is to have an affair, and in the UK a whole string of mildly naughty films featuring women with big 'boobs' are known as the 'Carry on films', from their titles which incorporate the phrase, e.g. 'Carry on Camping'.

cash and carried Married. Cockney rhyming slang. Also cut and carried, and dot and carried.

cat and kitties Breasts. From cockney rhyming slang with kitties titties. *See also* BRISTOLS, MANCHESTER CITIES, TALE OF TWO CITIES, TOWNS AND CITIES.

cattle Women. A term of contempt from the 16th to the 18th century, but now obsolete, although 'cow' is still a common UK term of abuse. Cattle however most likely evolved from 'chattel' rather than from the animal, although this doesn't remove the sting.

cattle truck Sexual intercourse. From cockney rhyming slang with fuck. *See also* FRIAR TUCK, TROLLEY AND TRUCK.

cat with its throat cut The female genitals. Contemporary UK male usage, and possibly the most violent image in slang referring to the female body. Also as a 'cat's head cut open', since WW2 at least.

Cat has the old-fashioned meanings of prostitute, and of vagina, from its link with 'pussy'. Hence the US cat-house for brothel, and the old-fashioned English 'cat-party' for a group of women.

cave The vaginal and/or anal orifice. Usually gay slang, however, in reference to the anus, especially in the US. As in 'I've been exploring some interesting caves tonight'. *See also* BATCAVE.

centre of bliss The female genitals. UK slang from 1790, but now obsolete.

chalk mark, leave a A catch phrase used crudely by males, usually in the full version: 'Leave a chalk mark when you've finished.' The insinuation is that the vagina is so large that it becomes a 'competition' to fill it. UK only, always insulting.

Charlie Hunt Rhyming slang with cunt. Old-fashioned UK usage, now limited.

charlies Breasts. Current UK slang, mostly male and affectionate. This term dates back to the 17th century, and is still acceptable enough to appear on family TV programmes like 'Hi De Hi'.

In Australian slang, however, a charlie is a prostitute.

charver Also sometimes chaver. Sexual intercourse. UK slang since the mid-19th century – usually as the act of 'charvering'. The etymology is obscure, but possible connections are the French *chauffer* – to heat, the English 'chafe', and the Romany *charvo* – to touch or meddle with. Still popular as slang in the UK among men and women, and especially in London.

cheese and kisses Wife. Cockney rhyming slang with missus. Also cow and kisses, plates and dishes.

cherries The breasts, especially when small. Affectionate UK contemporary usage, mostly male, and comparable to 'poached eggs'.

cherry, to lose one's To lose one's virginity. Common UK usage since WW2, as in Paul Scott's *Jewel in the Crown* in which Sarah Layton's seducer

asks her 'Haven't you lost your cherry yet?' Still extant in Britain and the US, among men and women, gays and homosexuals alike.

cherry splitter A long thin penis, presumably useful for taking someone's cherry (q.v.). US gay slang from the 50s.

chew Cunnilingus. Mostly 20th century US male usage, comparable to 'eat'.

chick Woman. Common, if somewhat cool, UK and US usage – as in this phrase from Carol, a black woman, on a Channel 4 programme about women (23 Jan 1984): 'I speak to a lot of black chicks my age'. This sense first appeared in America during the 20s, and later spread to the UK, and has always suggested youth, defiance and independence (*contrast* HEN). However, it is now considered dated.

Note that its original slang usage in 1750 carried the meaning 'child'.

chicken in the basket A young man available for sexual favours, usually anal intercourse. US gay slang since the sixties.

china Wife. From rhyming slang of 'china plate' with 'mate'. Old fashioned but still some faithful UK usage.

chink The vagina. British slang from the 18th century, but now obsolete. For modern equivalents *see* CRACK, and CRANNY.

chocolate bandit Homosexual man. Modern UK male usage, generally as a term of ridicule from a heterosexual. *Compare* TURD BURGLAR, and CHUTNEY FERRET.

chopped liver The vagina. Modern UK male usage, in the 'body as meat' line. *See* CHOPPER, and also PORK, MEAT etc. Sometimes shortened to liver.

chopper The penis. Common contemporary UK male usage. In the same vein as 'pork sword', 'hammer' etc. A 20th century coining, now widely adopted by UK males.

chucking a worm up the Mersey Tunnel, like One of the more popular in the litany of catch phrases describing sexual intercourse in which the male feels his penis to be ridiculously small and dwarfed by the dimensions of the vagina. Invariably a male expression, and invariably one implying that he has derived no pleasure from the encounter. As such, insulting to women. The expressions have been around since the turn of the century and regional variations include: shoving a sausage up Regent Street; lobbing it through an open window (Dublin); chucking a sausage down the Old Kent Road; shoving it into the Lincoln Tunnel (New York); and the most explicit (and

colourful?) that the authors have come across, dangling a worm in a paste bucket (UK only). Further contributions to this limited list of similes will be welcomed, especially on the lines of 'stirring cold porridge with a punt pole' (Richard Evans, Oxford 1970).

chutney ferret Homosexual man. Contemporary UK heterosexual slang, and although humorous, distinctly derogatory. *Compare* CHOCOLATE BANDIT, and TURD BURGLAR.

clap Venereal disease, or more specifically, gonorrhoea. Widespread British and American usage – as in 'He's given her a dose of the clap'. The term goes back a long way, deriving from the French *clapoir* – a swelling in the groin – since 1587.

cleft The female genitalia. UK slang from the 19th century, and now virtually obsolete, but *compare* the modern CRACK.

click, to To hit it off with a member of the opposite sex. British slang since WW1, but now confined mainly to Scotland and the north of England where the question 'Did you click?' or 'Did you get your click?' is widely understood. And 'click' as a noun is also common – a person's 'click' being their girlfriend or boyfriend.

clinkers Defined by etymologists Farmer and Henley as 'Deposits of faecal or seminal matter in the

41

hair about the anus or the female pudendum' – and the meaning hasn't changed since 1830. Unfortunately the 1840s phrase 'to have clinkers in one's bum' – i.e. to be restless – is now obsolete, but 'clinkers' is still common UK slang. *See also* DINGLEBERRIES.

clit A common slang abbreviation of clitoris (from the Greek), in the UK and US. Note that the Greek is the only known source of this word. As immortalized in Jackie Lynton's tape 'The World's First Wanking Competition' (1978) which features a character called Honey 'Hammerhandle' Clit.

In the US a 'clit closet' is a gay term for a hotel which rents rooms to prostitutes and their clients (Rodgers).

See also BUTTON.

closet gay A person who does not admit to (usually) his or her homosexuality. Among gays this can be a matter of resentment: the 'closet case' or 'closet queen' is remaining in an Uncle Tom role – servile to the heterosexual community. 'To come out of the closet', or 'to come out', is to make one's homosexuality public knowledge. Predominantly American slang which since the 60s has been adopted in Britain. Its origin is presumably the American word closet, meaning cupboard – as in the UK phrase 'to have a skeleton in the cupboard'.

club, in the Pregnant. Widespread UK usage, old fashioned but still current. Short for 'in the pudden (or pudding) club', a rakish late 17th century organization. 'Pudden' is a double pun, referring both to semen and to the female *puden*dum (Neaman and Silver).

club The penis. 19th century UK slang, and now virtually obsolete, but *compare* the contemporary CHOPPER, and HAMMER.

coachman on the box Venereal disease. From cockney rhyming slang with pox.

cobblers Also cobbler's awls. Testicles. From cockney rhyming slang with balls. Hence the expletive 'Cobblers!' *See also* COFFEE STALLS, ORCHESTRA STALLS.

cock The penis. Along with prick, one of the most popular and venerable of slang words for the male organ in both the US and UK. It derives from the 1481 English meaning of cock as a tap or spout, and developed its present slang connotations in the early 18th century.

There are inevitably many compounds, such as cock tease (*see* PRICK TEASE), cock-stand – an erection, cock smitten – obsessed by men, cock sucker – a person deeply despised.

cock cheese Smegma of the penis. UK male slang, and modern.

cocksman or **coxsman** Also cock-artist. A man who is sexually successful with women. Note the approval implicit in the terms, especially 'artist'. Recently popular UK male slang.

coconuts The breasts. London slang from the 20s, but now rarely heard.

coffee stalls Testicles. Cockney rhyming slang with balls. *See also* COBBLER'S, ORCHESTRA STALLS.

collar and cuff Effeminate. From cockney rhyming slang with puff – *see* POOF.

Colleen Bawn The penis. From cockney rhyming slang with horn. *See also* MARQUIS OF LORNE, and ALL FORLORN.

come, to Also sometimes 'to come off'. To experience orgasm. This term originated in 19th century Britain as a euphemism, and is now the most common term of its kind in the US and UK.
   'Come' or 'cum', as a noun, is also a widespread term for semen.

come on To show strong sexual interest and encouragement. In the UK, if a person is 'coming on strong', or 'really giving you the come on', this is a more explicitly sexual form of flirting. Contemporary slang.
   Also with the contemporary UK sense among women – to begin menstruation.

come out *See* CLOSET GAY.

commodity The female genitals. British slang from the 16th century, but now obsolete. The 'property' theme lives on however: *see* PARLOUR.

confirmed batchelor A male gay. Current UK euphemism among straight males and females. The implication is that the man is 'odd', i.e. is never going to get married and have 'normal intercourse'. As such it may be used in speech or in newspapers to imply that a man – such as an MP – is gay, while to spell this out might invite legal action.

contact mag A magazine in which people advertise for sexual partners, explicitly stating their preferences and predilections. UK contemporary usage.

convenience Also 'a convenient'. A 17th century term for a mistress, now obsolete.

cop a feel To fondle sexually. Contemporary northern English male usage.

cop off with To 'get off with', or seduce a person. Northern English, especially Liverpool usage, among males and females. Contemporary – and acceptable – enough to appear on UK TV soap operas like 'Brookside'. Not to be confused with 'cop it' – Australian slang since the 40s for becoming pregnant.

copper stick The penis. 19th century UK slang, now obsolete.

43

From the slang for policeman's truncheon; *compare* the modern CHOPPER, also CLUB.

corker The penis. UK male usage, from the 1950s, but limited.

corn holer A homosexual man. US gay usage, from the practice in the days of the outhouse of using dried corn cobs for toilet paper (Rodgers). Hence the 'corn hole' is the anus – since the 30s – and 'cornholer' one actively interested in it.

cory The penis. 20th century male UK usage, often heard in speech, and usually among males as a joke.

cottage Gay slang for a public toilet where the practice of 'cottaging' – loitering in toilets to find gay sexual partners – takes place. Common UK slang since the 50s. The camp image is that of a cosy, comfortable place, whereas the reality is more sordid.

US equivalents are 'teahouse', 'clubhouse', 'cornhole palace' and 'penile colony'.

cow Derogatory term for a woman. UK slang since the 18th century, with the concurrent 19th century meaning – a prostitute. Still extremely common among men and women in Britain, as in the general insult – 'She's a silly cow'. Also sometimes as 'silly moo'.

cow and kisses Wife. From

44

cockney rhyming slang with missus. Sometimes shortened to 'the old cow'. *See also* CHEESE AND KISSES, PLATES AND DISHES. Roughly affectionate term, mostly confined to London usage.

coyote The female genitals. British slang from the 19th century, probably from the US, but now obsolete. *Compare* CAT (with it's throat cut), and PUSSY.

crabs Body lice which infest the pubic hair. UK slang since the 18th century.

crack The vagina. Current UK and US usage, dating back to the 16th century. Like so many words for the female genitalia, it also had the 18th century meaning prostitute, while in the 19th century the term 'crack hunter', for penis, enjoyed brief popularity.

crackling Women, as sexual objects. Still current UK male usage although dating back to the 1890s, as in 'I could fancy her, she's a nice piece of crackling'. Comparable to 'pork' and 'meat'.

cranny The vagina. 19th century UK slang, now obsolete, *but see* CRACK.

crawler *See* KERB CRAWLER.

cream Semen. Mostly US but also British contemporary usage. The 'creamstick' is the penis, while 'to cream one's jeans' is to become so sexually excited as to climax while clothed – although in the UK this

American term is usually spoken tongue in cheek, as in 'Don't talk about her any more or I'll cream my jeans'.

cream crackers The testicles. From cockney rhyming slang with knackers.

crown jewels The testicles, and/or genitals. UK and US contemporary male slang from the 50s onwards, homosexual and heterosexual. *Compare* FAMILY JEWELS, and NUGGET.

cruising On the look out for a sexual encounter. Originally from the fifties in the US where young males would literally 'cruise the streets' in cars looking for girls to 'pick up'. But by the late sixties the word had become almost exclusively male gay, both in the US and UK. To 'cruise' now means either walking in the street hoping to meet another man, or to circulate a bar or club with the same intention. 'What were you doing last night? Cruising?' or 'Look at that queen, she's cruising for a bruising'.

crumpet Woman. As in 'She's a nice bit of crumpet'. Common UK male slang, dating back to the 1880s. Now obsolete however is the 20s phrase 'to get a crumpet' – to have sexual intercourse. *Compare* TART, JAM TART (under 'bit of jam').

CT Initials for 'Cock Tease', a variant of 'prick tease' but one

which is more popular in the US. *See* PRICK TEASE.

cunni Abbreviation of cunnilingus. Affectionate UK middle-class usage among men and women. Contemporary. *See also* CUNNY.

cunny The vagina. UK usage from the 17th century, but although the root is from coney = rabbit, the term is still sometimes used in preference to 'cunt'.

cunt The female genitals. The term derives from the Middle English *cunte*, or *count(e)*, corresponding to the Old Icelandic *kunta*. It may be related to the Latin *cunneus*, wedge, or to the Old English ‾cwithe, the womb. A possible Old English root is *cu* (in OE *cwe*) which Partridge interprets as 'quintessential physical femininity ... (which) ... partly explains why in India the cow is a sacred animal'.(!) The OED lists this early usage: Gropecuntlane was a street name in the City of London in 1230. Since the 15th century the word was considered obscene and it was an offence to print it in full, except in the reprinting of old classics. So powerful are the taboos surrounding the word that it has been ignored by the OED until recently, although 'prick' has been included.

Cunt is also a term of abuse which reflects the deep fear and hatred of the female by the male in our culture. It is a far nastier and more violent insult than 'prick', which tends to mean foolish rather than evil. This violent usage is a constant and disturbing reminder to women of the hatred associated with female sexuality, and leaves women with few positive words to name their own organs. In reaction, since the late seventies, some feminists have attempted to 'reclaim' the word (*see* Introduction.)

cunt face Insulting term of address implying that someone is ugly. Contemporary usage in the UK and US and much more insulting than a term like 'shit face'.

cunt itch A derogatory term used only by males to describe physical desire in women. Contemporary.

cunt struck A man obsessed by women. As with the two last entries invariably used by men, and again contemporary. Derogatory in usage.

curse The menstrual period. Originally a euphemism during the 19th century, based on the idea that a woman's period was the 'curse of Eve'. Still widely used in the UK, despite recent efforts to banish the taboos associated with menstruation. There are still no slang words with positive connotations for the 'period'.

curtains The foreskin. *See also* LACE CURTAINS, BEEF CURTAINS. Male gay slang since the fifties.

cut out to be a man Circumcised. 20th century UK usage among men.

cylinder The vagina. Australian male slang since the 30s.

D

d.a. or **D.A.S.** Menstruation. A coy abbreviation of the even more coy euphemism 'domestic affliction'. This dates back to Victorian times and is now obsolete, but neither men nor women have yet found a way to talk about menstruation without embarrassment – and probably won't until prevailing love/hate attitudes towards women change.

daddy, or **daddy-o** Older man who showers his younger male lover with presents. US gay slang. *See also* SUGAR DADDY.

daffodil Young male gay. Also stereotypical effeminate homosexual. Post-war colloquial English records the meaning 'effeminate and precious young man' (Partridge).

dagger Penis. One of the many terms for the male organ which draws on the image of a violent weapon. *See also* DIRK, PORK DAGGER, BAZOOKA.

dagger 'Butch' lesbian. In the tradition of ascribing male characteristics – *see* dagger above – to lesbian women. As in the US gay phrase, 'You'd turn queer too, if your mother was a dagger'. *See also* BULL DYKE.

dainties Gay men. Derisive heterosexual term, especially in the US, from the 60s on.

dainties Women's underwear when worn by a male transvestite. Hence a generic gay term for underwear.

dairy, or **dairies** Breasts, or breast milk supply. Hence 'I had to bottle-feed the baby when my dairy dried up.' As such a polite euphemism, acceptable at any coffee morning.

But the lewd use of the term as breasts dates back to the 18th century. Partridge has 'sport the dairy' and 'air the dairy' as jocular expressions for revealing the breasts.

Dairy arrangements was a 1920s equivalent of 'boobs'. Milky

47

way, charlies, charms and (in rhyming slang) cabman's rests are in the same venerable tradition and still crop up in cockney usage.

daisy Man who sexually entertains more than one man at a time. *See DAISY CHAIN.*

daisy chain Group sex performed by a circle or chain of gay men, linked penis to anus. Widespread UK and US gay term since 1950s. Alternative forms are: chain gang, floral arrangement, ring around the rosey.

daisy duck Passive partner in male gay sex. US gay slang.

daisy picker Gooseberry. Old fashioned Anglo-Irish term for any third party accompanying a couple. The image suggests a bored chaperone left to idly gather flowers on a country walk.

damaged goods A person who is no longer a virgin. Common term used by men and women, principally in the US.

dame Woman or girl. Stars like Bogart in Hollywood movies familiarized the term and gave it a strong sexual emphasis, but it remains predominantly an Americanism. The word meant girl or sweetheart in Scotland throughout the 19th century and until the 30s. It also carries the venerable sense of titled woman, and Dale Spender gives its modern usage as another example of how 'respectable' words for women are systematically devalued.

dancer Stripper or prostitute. Common UK euphemism, often prefixed by 'exotic'.

dancer Male victim of constant rape and sexual oppression by other men. US homosexual slang.

dandy Gay man, usually as the stereotypical effeminate homosexual. As with 'daffodil' the term has come to refer to sexuality, while previously it described style. Originally it was an 18th and 19th century term for fop, or fashionably dressed man. Dandysette meant female dandy, and came to mean lesbian in the US in the 40s. Partridge suggests the root 'dandipratt' – insignificant person.

dang The penis. Not as common as dong.

dangle The penis. As in the well-known phrase: It's not the angle of the dangle, it's the little bit on the end that matters.

dangler, dangle queen Gay male exhibitionist, or man who wears tight trousers to show off his crotch. Occasionally also a gay man who wears long earrings – US 'camp' slang.

danglers Testicles. Partridge traces the usage back to the mid 19th century at least, yet it is still current amongst UK males.

Danish pastry A trans-sexual. US gay male term. The authors have been to many a bakery to investigate this image, but as yet its origins and implications remain a mystery.

dark meat A black man's penis. Also, less commonly, a black man. US, mostly gay, usage. *See* DICK for other instances of man and his organ sharing a name.

darling Affectionate form of address to a lover or a friend, not necessarily sexual. Widespread use by people of all sexual orientations. Also dahling, for a jocular, affected and/or camp variation.

dash Latent homosexual, or man willing to give homosexuality a try. US gay slang, possibly from the slang sense of 'dashing' (i.e. exciting), or 'dash' – a tiny bit, as in: 'He looks happily married, but he's dash around the edges' (Rodgers).

dash up the channel Sexual intercourse. Now considered an old-fashioned term. Originally English fishermen's slang.

date A meeting with romantic possibilities: 'Have you got a date with her on Saturday night?' Originally US, but now widespread in the UK.
  Also, the person invited to go out: 'He's my date for Friday'.
  The greater social importance for women of having a date, i.e. getting a man, is indicated by the post-war use of 'dateless' as a silly, foolish girl.

date The anus. Australian slang, presumably from the image of the wrinkled brown fruit.

date locker The anus. Primarily Australian term, but usually used by 'straight' males in a non-sexual context.

dead easy A woman whom a man expects will consent to have sex with him. This well-established, originally cockney phrase is the English equivalent of the US 'easy lay'.

dead end street The female genitals. This originally Canadian phrase is another variation on the widespread theme of the vagina as highway. *See also* pushing a sausage up Regent Street/The Old Kent Road, *under* CHUCKING A WORM UP THE MERSEY TUNNEL.

dead eye dick Active partner in male gay sex. Dead eye refers to the anus, dick to the penis and the whole phrase draws on the image of the male lover as gunfighter/marksman. US gay slang from the 60s.

dead meat Prostitute. Also frozen meat. As opposed to fresh meat, meaning a woman who is not a prostitute. This old-fashioned term (Partridge places it from 1900) is in the long, misogynist tradition of describing women as meat. For modern parallels *see* PORK, EASY (MEAT), SALAMI.

dead rabbit Penis that will not attain or sustain erection. This ruefully affectionate term draws its impact from the image of the limp, pathetic corpse. Also dead stick.

dear Affectionate form of address, which, like darling, has countless nuances. It can be camp, sarcastic, friendly or loving according to the context. A variation is dearie, the superlative is dearest.

Dear John A letter from a woman telling a man she wants to end their relationship. Originally US and Canadian Armed Forces slang from the 1940s, later adopted by the British Forces. Now so generally widespread that it has acquired the new meaning of a letter telling a man that he has given a woman VD. Also from one gay man to another. A more old-fashioned and less euphemistic version is VD letter.

debut A first homosexual experience. *See also* OUT.

decorations Semen stains lining the trouser leg. US gay slang.

decorative Pretty. Often used of women by men who *imagine* they are being complimentary. But as the use of this phrase in the recent Channel 4 TV documentary 'Sexuality' shows, the (male) boss who comments of a (female) secretary, 'Very decorative', may find himself accused of sexual harassment.

decoy Dildo worn beneath the trousers by a homosexual to give the impression that he has a big organ.

Also young male who entices gay men into having sex in a public place in order to shop them to the police.

deerstalking Chasing after women. Old-fashioned and largely obsolete phrase drawing on hunting imagery and punning on dear.

deflower, to To take someone's virginity. The word applies to males and females, although the original image is feminine and based on the old notion that a women's virginity before marriage is her most precious asset, ensuring purity of descent in the male line. Despite – or perhaps because of – its archaic flavour, the term is still in vogue amongst young people in the UK. *See also* CHERRY (to lose one's).

deft and dumb Old-fashioned post-World War II catch-phrase denoting the perfect female partner. A parody of the phrase deaf and dumb, it implies that man's ideal woman has the sexual skills of a geisha girl, but is as mute as a rubber dolly. The cockney songwriters Chas and Dave are modern proponents of this theory with their obnoxious song 'Rabbit'; 'You've got a beautiful face ... But with your incessant chatter, you're becomin' a pest.'

Note also the contemporary UK 'joke' that the perfect woman is 'a deaf and dumb nymphomaniac whose father owns a brewery.'

degenerate, or **DG**, or **deegy** Heterosexual slang word for homosexual. The assumption is that homosexuality is 'unnatural' as it precludes procreation, and is therefore a lower form of sexual practice.

It is also a contemptuous word for anyone who is aroused by 'perverted' sex also, and so carries different judgements, depending on the user's convictions about what is 'normal'.

degenerate bar Gay bar where nothing is off limits. Affectionate US gay term. Used for any bar or club which is renowned for 'cruising for trade' (looking for sexual encounters) or where encounters actually take place on the premises.

delicate-assen Trousers shop. US gay slang, using an obvious pun.

delicious Tantalizingly sexy. As in 'Look at that delicious smile' or 'Isn't she delicious'. Usually applied to women by men, but also gay usage between men. Sometimes abbreviated to delish in camp fashion.

As with so many sexual slang words, the image is of the body as food to be consumed. *See also* TASTY, CRUMPET, CRACKLING, MEAT.

deliver a baby Undressing to expose an erect penis. US male gay slang.

delo nammow Old woman. Backwards slang since the last century, now virtually obsolete, as is delo diam – old maid.

demure as an old whoreat a Christening *Extremely* demure. Colourful traditional English simile, probably of Armed Forces origin, polarizing the extreme images of piety and notoriety.

den Place such as a massage parlour, Turkish baths or brothel where people gather for clandestine sex. Found in phrases like vice-den, den of iniquity. Its usage is generally coy, as in the pop tabloid's: 'Plumber's wife ... turned on the clients at a massage parlour by offering sexy extras. She worked in a vice-den built at the back of the home of a car dealer' (*Sun* Oct 1983). Or camp usage: 'See you in the den of sin, dahling.'

derrick 'Butch' lesbian with 'mannish' features. US slang. Yet another term attributing male characteristics to lesbians. *See* BULL DYKE. In 19th century England the term meant penis, and was possibly compressed into 'dick'.

derriere Bottom. From the French word for behind. Usage is coyly euphemistic, 'She had an injection in the derriere', or camp.

desert disease In reference to a

man who habitually touches women in an unwelcome way – i.e. he is suffering from 'wandering palms'. Common UK female usage from schooldays onwards (J. Salvage 1984). *Compare* WHT, and WANDERING HAND.

design for living Group sex between three people. US slang.

destiny A woman's fiance, but note – rarely a man's fiancee. This semi-serious middle-class term, based on the old notion that finding a husband is a woman's be-all and end-all, dates back to 1910 and is now virtually obsolete.

dethroned Gay man forced to leave a public toilet (usually by police), which he has been frequenting in order to procure sex.

detrimental A male 'pervert'. This meaning has developed from the early 19th century sense of an ineligible suitor and/or younger brother of the heir to an estate. In mid 19th century it had come to mean a male flirt, and following the pattern of many modernized terms (*see* DANDY) it took on a much more explicit sexual meaning.

deviate, also **deviant** Homosexual man or woman. The implication is that anything other than heterosexuality is 'abnormal'. Hence the string of slang

words like queer and bent. *See also* DEGENERATE.

diamonds The testicles. An affectionate, if not boastful, term which denotes the enormous value a man ascribes to his parts. *See also* FAMILY JEWELS, VELVET ORBS.

diaphragm The contraceptive device. *See* CAP.

dibble The penis. Obscure but venerable term, from the pointed gardening implement used to make holes in the ground for planting. A welcome relief from the usual weapon imagery, but still the picture is of plunging into the passive soil. The more modern but less earthy equivalent is tool.

dick The penis. As an abbreviation of the man's name Richard, it is parallel to the usage of John Thomas, Peter and Mickey. There is often a striking and proud identification between man and his organ: hence many words – man, lad, chap, fellow – mean both.

Perhaps it was this perception that led a woman journalist to write that when a woman is with a man, she often feels that two is company but three (woman, man and his penis) is not.

Dick also carried the ancient meaning of man, as in Tom, Dick and Harry, from the 16th century.

Partridge traces the meaning of dick as penis to military, mid-19th century slang and suggests it could be a compression of derrick, which has the old meaning penis, or from rhyming slang with creamstick, also meaning penis.

In the First War the gallantry medal the DSO was facetiously known as Dick Shot Off.

Dicky diddle, like Jimmy Riddle, rhymes with widdle to mean urinate.

Dicky also has the old mid 19th century meaning of prostitute.

dick, to To 'fuck' somebody. Most often as 'Did you dick it?'. Contemporary, mostly UK male, usage.

dick-drinker, or **dick-licker,** or **dickey-taster** Man or woman who performs fellatio. Mostly US gay slang.

dickey dido The female genitals. Uncommon and mostly out of date except for the bawdy song which runs 'And the hairs on her dickey dido hang down to her knees'.

dickory dock The penis. Cockney rhyming slang with cock.

dick pedlar Male prostitute. US slang from the 60s.

dicky broad Lesbian who is reputed to have a clitoris the size of a penis. US slang from the 60s, mostly gay. Another in the catalogue of terms for lesbians, which impute male characteristics. *See also* BULL DYKE, and BULL DICKER.

diddies Breasts. This is a dated term, probably a corruption of titties, but rarely used today.

diddle To masturbate. Used by and of either sex. Now obsolete in the UK, but still widespread in the US – which can cause embarrassment for British travellers who use 'diddle' in the non-sexual sense of 'cheat'. In the 19th century 'diddle' also meant penis (among schoolboys) and to copulate with.

'Diddly pout' is an obsolete term for the female genitals, from rhyming slang with spout or possibly from pouter – an old term for the same. 'Diddle' is also a possible precursor for the modern 'dildo'.

did I buggery, or **did I fuck!** Expression of extreme protest or denial. Comparable to will I, fuck! and like fuck I will! Contemporary UK male usage, as in the boast: 'Did I give her one – did I buggery!'

diesel dyke 'Butch' lesbian. US slang. Another macho term applied to lesbians. *See also* BULL DYKE.

dig a ditch, to Also dig boy ass. Buggery. US gay slang. Ditch has the meaning anus.

dike *See* DYKE.

dildo Artificial penis-like implement, made of rubber, plastic etc. when sold in sex shops, or otherwise improvised.

In Australian girls' boarding schools, a dildo was a candle;

hence the catch phrase 'lights out at nine, candles out at ten.'

The root of the word could be diddle, or dillpickle – a phallic vegetable. The OED gives dildo glass as a cylindrical glass.

Possibly related is dillpot or dillypot, originally rhyming slang for twat, and then (in Australia) developing the meaning – a fool.

Dildo is also used in the sense of idiot or prick: 'Oh, he's a right dildo, that one!'

The European words for dildo, focusing on its entertainment function, are more positive: The French have *bientateur* (do-gooder), *consolateur* (relaxer) and *godemiche* (I enjoy myself). In Germany the word is *Phallus Phantom* (spectre penis) and in Italian *passatiempo* (pass the time).

dine in Entertain sexually at home. Hence dine out – going out to find sex: 'Are you dining in or out tonight?' US gay male slang.

ding The backside. From Australian and US surfers' slang. A ding is a hole in the bottom of a surfboard and has itself come to mean 'bottom'.

ding dong The penis. Ding and dong are each separate words for the penis, so it is not surprising to find them paired like this. Also ding dong bell. No doubt Chuck Berry fully intended the innuendo of his big hit 'My Ding-a-Ling'. *Compare with* BELL END.

ding dongs The testicles. An affectionate camp term, similar in tone to gongs and nuts.

dinge queen Gay black man. Dinge has been a slang word for black man in the US for the whole of the 20th century. *See especially* Damon Runyon *On Broadway*. The addition of queen (q.v.) has been common gay usage since the late 50s. An alternative is zulu princess.

dinger The anus. Australian in origin, and probably not used in a sexual context. As innocuous as bum. Partridge gives the example, 'Don't forget that he'll get more than a gentle tap up the dinger if something goes really wrong.'

dingle berries Dried remnants of faeces in the hairs around the anus. This becomes a serious sexual matter in some forms of gay sex. Rodgers gives this US example: 'Harvest your dingle beries Repunzel, and I'm sure someone will be along to irrigate your ditch.' Hence dingle-berry pie, the anus. *See also* WILNUTS. An old-fashioned and graphic English alternative is bum-tags.

dingle-dangle The penis. This usage dates back to the turn of the century and with its nursery rhyme ring appears in several bawdy songs.

dink, dinky A small penis. Either one not naturally large or, more commonly, shrunken with cold.

Hence the surfer's phrase 'What's up? Cold sea given you a dink?' The derivation is either from dinky – small, or possibly the Scottish dink, meaning neat.

dinner beneath the bridge Rodgers defines this as two partners having oral sex in the 69 position while keeping their knees bent throughout. He also implies that it is an activity necessitated by lack of space, but the authors remain mystified by the image and would welcome an explanation. US gay slang.

dinner music Humming to increase the pleasure of fellatio. US slang from the 60s. An alternative is choral sex.

dinners Men's nipples. US gay slang.

dip the wick To have sexual intercourse. A phrase as venerable (mid-19th century origin) as it is durable. Now almost acceptable, even boastful, male euphemism. Hence dipping the wick and burying the wick. The former has connotations of candle making in which the wick is stiffened and increased by dipping in hot wax, and the latter of snuffing out a candle.

dirk The penis. An old Scottish equivalent of the penis-as-weapon theme. *See also* BAZOOKA, BEARD-SPLITTER, PORK DAGGER *et al.*

dirt Pornography. *See also* DIRTY.

dirt road The anus. Principally a US variant, using the image of orifice as highway but at the same time one to be abhorred and/or shunned due to uncleanliness. Obviously in gay usage the term is affectionate. Also dirt run.

dirty Vulgar, pornographic or obscene. Also 'filth' and 'filthy'. This word is used to qualify many others with a lewd connotation (see below). Indeed this book in manuscript form was known amongst undiscriminating friends as the dirty dictionary! There are a multiplicity of terms such as 'you've got a dirty mind' and 'you've been thinking dirty thoughts again' that imply only the mildest of sexual innuendo. But contrast with standard newspaper usage, e.g. for 'kerb crawlers': 'Police girls posed as prostitutes to snare dirty drivers', (*Sun* Oct 1983). Here dirty is a term of disapproval; in other related terms that follow this isn't the case. The ambivalent usage is far from new – Partridge cites the 19th century punning catch phrase for intercourse as 'dirty work at the crossroads'.

dirty, do the To take sexual advantage of a person who is then abandoned. The traditional usage was 'to do the dirty on a girl', but since the Pill revolution 'doing the dirty' has become more egalitarian.

dirty barrel To have VD, in a

male. This dates back to turn of the century naval slang – another gun-for-penis usage – but has become widespread here and in the US. Also dirty dick.

dirty dog, you Affectionate term for a lecher and/or an ardent sexual performer. The phrase often betrays an element of grudging admiration and possibly envy, as in: 'You *didn't*, you dirty dog!' Mostly male UK usage.

dirty dowager A rich, ageing homosexual. Camp US, but very rarely a kindly epithet.

dirty old man Semi-jocular term for the most part, used to describe a male past his sexual prime and relying for kicks on the attractions of younger girls and boys – legally or illegally. As such the term is disdainful and disapproving and as likely to be used to describe a flasher or a paedophile as it is a resolute 40-year-old in love with a 16-year-old girl. [Often shortened to DOM.] *Compare with* the more affectionate RANDY OLD SOD, or RANDY OLD SO-AND-SO. A camp American equivalent is 'soiled senior citizen'.

dirty thing, you Often prefixed and affixed by you, and as such a joking chastisement of amorous and/or sexual feeling in a sexual opposite. With the addition of a laugh or a giggle it is a coy, almost schoolgirlish come-on. Without either it is a delighted camp admonishment. Also dirty girl!

56

Dirty boy! 'Keep your hands away from there, you dirty boy!'

dirty weekend, have a Principally to absent oneself for any length of time with one's lover for the purposes of sex. Original meaning was for a man and his mistress to pursue an affair away from their usual partners (and she was a 'week ender'), but now much more general, even having the possible connotation of two nights together without the children for a married couple. As above the equation of sex and 'dirt' is a telling point, and much more common in the UK than in the US.

dish A sexually attractive person. The word has male and female, straight and gay usage. Its US origin was put at around 1930 by Partridge, and until the 60s the word was applied by men to women.

It has also shared the meaning buttocks and homosexual during the 50s.

The image is again of the body as food as in crumpet, crackling etc. The adjective, applied to men and women, is dishy: 'Who's that dishy bird/bloke?'

dishonourable discharge Masturbation after failing to find a sexual partner for the night. Originally Forces, now gay and straight male catch phrase.

ditch The anus. Male gay slang. *See also* DIG A DITCH.

dive in the bushes Cunnilingus. US and UK slang from the 60s. Diver is a pejorative term for a person who performs the act. Also high diver, muff diver, 63, go South, sneeze into the cabbage etc.

diving suit Condom. This dated Australian term is an imaginative variant on the diver theme above.

divorced, be To lose one's sexual partner. The slang sense is a jocular parody of the OED usage. 'If you don't start treating her better, you'll soon be divorced.'

From the 70s on, divorced or get a divorce became a frequent usage for couples who, never having been married (or intending to), merely split up.

D.I.Y. *See* DO IT YOURSELF JOB.

do, do it, doing it A general and widespread euphemism for sexual activity, usually intercourse. Straight and gay usage by men and women in UK. 'I came home and found them doing it in the kitchen.' Also 'Does she do it?', and 'I haven't done it for months'. *Compare* 'I haven't had it for months', *under* HAVE, TO.

US usage has more gay applications, as in 'do a brown'. In Britain, the term lends itself to any number of colourful combinations – 'do a bit/of crumpet' etc.

Terms like do the business, do a ride, do a grind, do a mount and do a tread date back to the mid-19th century, but men use the same laborious imagery today. Do over, do a good turn to and do the trick are more dated and practically obsolete. Dobash, an old naval term for girlfriend, is a compression of – (she may) do a bash.

Do a perpendicular and do a knee-trembler – to have intercourse standing up – are also more than a century old but still in popular currency.

Do a job is a related Australian term for getting a woman pregnant.

Do a line with is a very common Irish term for going out with someone, like the Australian do a knock line with.

dockers ABC Ale, baccy, cunt. The three supposed requisites of a stereotypically happy, working-class male's life. British dockside, mostly Liverpool slang, from the turn of the century. Now outdated.

doe eyes Woman with large eyes and meek expression. The term is usually intended as flattery, submissiveness being traditionally considered a virtue in women. Also to make doe eyes, which has the sense of inviting sexual advances.

Doe was also an upper-class term for woman at the turn of the century, and is an old 18th century euphemism for prostitute.

does it wink? Jocular inquiry as to whether a penis is circumcised.

Much more common usage in the US where circumcision at birth for non-religious reasons is more widespread.

dog Unattractive or 'ugly' person, male or female. But more often applied to women, as beauty is considered a more important attribute in a woman than in a man. As in 'You should see the dog he's knobbing these days.'

In US slang, dog-lady or dog-woman is an 'ugly' prostitute, while dog's dinner is an unattractive person.

Dog's lady, dog's wife, doggess and puppy's mamma are old-fashioned ways of calling a woman a bitch. *See also* ALSATIAN.

Women as sex objects are commonly referred to in animal terms – *see also* COW, BITCH, SOW, PIG.

dog, to Also doggy fashion, dogways. To have sexual intercourse on all fours like an animal.

A variety of expressions draw on the dog image to convey a sense of distaste for sexual activity – like make a dog's match of it, an old English expression for having sex by the wayside. Similarly, dog's rig had the meaning of having sex to exhaustion and then turning back to back in indifference. Dog-drawn is an obsolete term for a woman from whom a man has been forcibly removed during sex.

Dog food is a contemporary male, gay expression for soldiers,

from the US Army slang dogface, a private.

do-hickies The male genitals. US slang. The root is probably Antipodean, where do-hickey replaced doings with its popular meaning of one's possessions or equipment. *See also* TACKLE.

do it The semi-comical usage of do it took on a new dimension with the rise in popularity of car stickers and T-shirt slogans, originally from the US in the early 70s, rapidly spreading to the UK. A complete litany would fill a separate volume, but among the most common are:

nurses do it with patience
windsurfers do it standing up
squash players do it against the wall
cricketers do it with bats (or balls)
surfers do it in the tube
farmers do it in furrows (or wellies)
men do it when they want to

do it yourself job Masturbation. Well-established UK term, more likely to be used by a male than a female.

dokus The anus. US slang from the Yiddish *tokhes* (Rodgers).

doll, dolly Traditionally an attractive person of either sex, but usually applied to women. But because of the stereotypical and synthetic image of 'fluffy' femininity it conveys and the modern emphasis on more 'natural' looks, it is now being increasingly used as a term of criticism: 'She was plastered with make-up like a little doll.'

Dollybird, once complimentary, is now sometimes derisive, although in England fine distinctions of social class make its usage more variable. To a working-class man dollybird might be a term of admiration, while in the mouth of a middle-class person it expresses a measure of contempt for a woman of a 'lower' social class.

And the word has a long history. In the 18th and 19th century dolly meant mistress. Doll-common and dolly-mop both referred to prostitutes, while a dolly-mopper was a womanizer.

Partridge records that the mid-19th century usage of doll was insulting and applied to older, usually well-dressed women. He quotes Mayhew, 'If it's a lady and a gentleman then we cries, "A toff and a doll".' But at the same time it meant girlfriend – a precursor of the modern American guys and dolls.

In the 60s Cliff Richard sang a love song to a 'Lovin, Livin Doll', but by the end of the 70s feminist Sheila Rowbotham had written about her rejection of this passive, 'pretty' image of femininity.

dollop the wiener Male masturbation. US slang. Wiener means sausage, and so is parallel to UK terms like wallop the sausage, and beat the meat.

doll spit Semen. Uncommon, but drawing on the image of penis as plaything. Thus more likely to be used about masturbation.

dolly The penis. This dates back to the 19th century at least, and although now virtually obsolete in UK it is current US gay male slang. One suggested source is the old saw about the little girl's daddy who answers her queries by telling her his penis is a doll. When he awakes to find her crying, she tells him she was playing with his dolly – until it squirted her in the eye. *See also* DOLL SPIT.

domestic afflictions Menstruation. *See* D.A.

dong The penis. Widespread male usage. Also donger. *See* DING DONG.

Don Juan The 16th century writer Gabriel Tellez (pseudonym Tirso de Molina) wrote a play about the adventures and amours of a legendary Spanish nobleman. The central character – and incurable playboy – was called Don Juan.

Mozart spread the reputation of the character further in his opera *Don Giovanni* and by the early 19th century when Byron wrote his epic *Don Juan*, the name was already synonymous with a womanizer. Still widespread slang.

donkey, also **donkey rigged** Very

59

large penis. Also hung like a donkey. Still current usage but dating back to the late 19th century.

Donkey serenade refers facetiously to the noises made by a person performing fellatio. *See also* DINNER MUSIC. US gay slang.

donning the beard Cunnilingus. Australian male usage, also spreading to the UK. *Compare with* YMCA, dining at the.

don't drop your car keys! Common jocular catch phrase among straight men when they are likely to encounter a gay male. The implication is that as soon as they bend down they will immediately be buggered. Underneath the jocularity there is fear on the part of the 'straight' male towards the homosexual. *See also* SEPARATE SHOWERS.

doodle, or **dood** Also doob. The penis. Old-fashioned children's slang, perhaps from the nursery doodle-doo – a cock, or from the Australian dood, a pipe.

Doodle sack is the vagina; a crude, passive image.

Dorian, or **dorian lover** Homosexual man. After the Doric region of Greece. In sexual slang, especially male gay, anything Greek is indicative of homosexuality. Hence the quip, 'A Greek is somebody who gets a little behind in his work'.

Academics might presume that this usage is in deference to the

classical Greek tradition in which every young Adonis was encouraged to loved his male comrade, rather than women – whom Aristotle classed with slaves as lower forms of life. (Note the modern, pretentious gay term for a large penis – doric column.)

But it is more likely the modern myth that prevails, one inspired by the forces in WW2. Greek men were lumbered with the image of thick sheep-farmers, who in reaction to the cloistered nature of their Catholic womenfolk would turn to any orifice – i.e. of sheep – in their extremes of frustration.

dork The penis. UK contemporary, mostly male, usage. Dork has the parallel slang meaning of idiot, hence its usage falls somewhere between prick and berk. Thus not always intentionally sexual and probably a carry over from schoolboy slang.

dose, a A case of VD, an abbreviation of 'a dose of the clap/pox etc.' Around since the 19th century and still very current.

do social work To have a relationship with someone of another race. The implication is that somebody is trying to be trendy by showing their 'broadmindedness'. US slang.

dot The clitoris in its most common usage, although it can also mean the anus in male gay slang. Thus dot the i = sexual intercourse (with the i standing for penis). *See also* BUTTON, BELL.

dot and carried Married. Rhyming slang.

do the bowling hold To arouse a woman by holding her crotch as if it were a bowling ball; forefinger in the anus, thumb stimulating the clitoris. Colourful US slang, virtually unheard in the UK.

double It is a long tradition in English slang to combine 'double' with other words for intensification or to make puns. Thus from the 18th century we have double act = getting married, double assed = large bottomed, double cunted = sexually large, double diddied = large breasted, double jug = the backside, double ribbed = pregnant, double hung = well endowed (of a male) and double sucker = large labia. The pattern of usage continues with the more contemporary terms below.

double date Two couples on a date together in 'straight' usage; 'cruising' in pairs for group sex in gay usage.

double event Simultaneous penetration of the vagina and the anus, usually with the penis and finger (or dildo). The alternative, old-fashioned use – to have syphilis and gonorrhoea at the same time (Partridge) – is now extinct.

double gaited Bisexual.

double header The 69 sexual position. Mostly US.

douche, to To wash the vagina, or, in gay male slang, to use an enema. The myth that douching after intercourse prevents pregnancy is mostly forgotten, but this old joke about bidets remains: 'Is that to wash the baby in? No, that's to wash the baby out.'

Douche bag is at once the equipment used for douching, and an extremely scornful insult applied to a man or woman. Mostly US, where the practice is more widespread.

dove Term of 'romantic' endearment from a man to a woman. Not just another 'bird' image, dove is the age-old symbol of purity and innocence and so is supposed to represent woman's 'sweetness and chastity'. Old-fashioned usage. A modern alternative is dove = ageing lesbian (US especially).

down Body hair of the softer variety, as in young men's beards or women's pubic hair. Hence, 'kiss somebody's down' is cunnilingus. Partridge cites downy bit as an old-fashioned term for 'half-fledged wench'.

down, to go To perform cunnilingus or fellatio. Perhaps the most widespread US and UK term for this practice, whether straight or gay. *See also* MUFF.

To down a woman is also to prepare her for sex, but the term is now obsolete.

61

down the rabbit hole Into the mouth and down the gullet (Rodgers). This US male gay term is a more comical image than the usual one of 'deep throat' for the same supposed pinnacle of pleasure in fellatio.

down there One of the oldest of all euphemisms for the sexual parts, male or female. Its very archaic nature lends it an affectionate, almost jocular quality. 'I let him kiss me down there' and 'What's he (or she) like down there' sound (and are) coy but very common.

doxy Girl or woman. Now virtually obsolete, but the word has an interesting history. From the 16th and 17th century it meant beggar's trull, or female begger and up until the 20th century carried the parallel meaning of mistress or prostitute.

By the 19th century the London working classes used the word for their wives, and it also meant a young woman, however virginal. And so before the term lost its currency in the later 19th century, its basic meaning of female had been coloured with all shades of meaning as regards a woman's age, sexual and marital status.

Partridge quotes Bishop Warburton in a play on its ambiguity: 'Orthodoxy, my Lord, is my doxy. Heterodoxy is another man's doxy'.

Its root is probably from the Dutch *docke*, a doll. *See* DOLL and DOLLY for similar changes.

DP The damp patch left on a bed or sheet after sexual intercourse. 'It isn't my turn to sleep in the DP again, surely?' is the modern query, whereas one contemporary catch phrase runs: 'True liberation is making him sleep in the damp patch!'

drab A prostitute. Virtually obsolete, but the adverb remains to describe a dreary, slatternly style in a woman. As such it is a male sexual insult.

Dracula's mother 'Ugly', old woman. An insult applied by men to women they find sexually unattractive, from the legend of the satanic blood sucker. The Australian equivalent is drack.

drag Women's clothing as worn by men. Hence a man in women's clothing is in drag, and Danny la Rue is a drag artist putting on a drag show. The usage dates back to the 1850s in Britain when drag referred to the petticoats worn by male actors in women's roles. Go on the drag, and flash the drag were slang terms as far back as the mid-19th century.

Male gay and especially camp usage in the US has the word in countless combinations such as drag face (a man in make-up), drag lips (man in lipstick), drag ball (an occasion for men to dress up), drag butch (a woman dressed as a man), drag queen or DQ (a homosexual in drag), drag wig (a woman's wig on a man) and the use of drag to mean any clothing: 'I'm changing into different drag tonight'.

Probably unrelated is the Australian teenage usage of drag for girl.

dragon A fierce woman, usually an 'old dragon'. The slang usage is decidedly hostile. It had the 17th to 19th century usage 'a wanton' and came to mean an old prostitute. In the US it means any woman with masculine characteristics.

That the usage of the word reveals a lot about stereotype 'femininity' and male fears of women is shown by this definition of dragon given in the feminist magazine *Spare Rib*, November 1983: 'A mythical monster, usually represented with wings and breathing out fire. It has come to describe a fierce older woman. Something to be proud about, sisters!'

drain The vagina. Also 'drain pipe'. As in the drooling and overconfident Australian and UK male expression – 'I'd be up her like a rat up a drainpipe'. Another crude receptacle image of the vagina as an empty space. Now dated and rare. *See also* DOODLE SACK.

draped Having a large penis. *See also* WELL HUNG, probably the root of the analogy here, and DRAPES.

drape queen Gay man who pads his crotch with socks, hankies and other items to give the illusion of a large 'package'.

drapes The foreskin. Draped takes the meaning uncircumcised. Also any number of variations like dusty drapes (an unclean foreskin), drawing the drapes (pulling back the foreskin). Also synonymous in US slang with blinds, curtains, opera capes. Hence to draw the blinds etc.

dream Ideally attractive woman or man. Also as dreamboat, dream-lover, dream-boy. The aura of romance is rather over the top and has been hacked to death in soap operas, advertising and soft porn, as in the *Sun*'s description of their topless model on 21 November 1983: 'Dreamboat Beoley – Water baby Beoley Ashley likes to plunge beneath the waves for a spot of skin-diving when she's not making a splash on dry land. But ... we've got the saucy Liverpool lass to surface on Page Three.'

dream whip Nocturnal emission of semen. Drawing on the American brand name of an artificial cream, this US phrase puns at several levels. *See* the English and more prosaic WET DREAM.

dress, how do you? Sometimes,

63

which side do you dress? What originated as a tailor's enquiry when measuring for a pair of trousers – to ascertain which way the genitals hung, to the left or right – has now become common parlance with women in particular enjoying the usage in phrases like 'It's easy to see which side he dresses' when observing a man's genitalia through trousers and/or underpants.

drinking from the furry cup Cunnilingus. Contemporary working-class male usage in Dublin (F. Dowling 1984).

drip dry lover A man with a small penis. Affectionate US camp slang.

dripping for it (Of a woman) Ready for sexual penetration. This term dates back to the turn of the century and is invariably used in a derogatory context as a sign of 'unnatural' lust in a woman. *See also* READY FOR IT.

drive, to To have sexual intercourse. A common image of power and control in the male dating back to the 19th century, but still common UK and US male usage, as in, 'I drove it into her'. *See also* DRIVING POST.

drive it to home base A macho American extension of the image described under 'driving post' (q.v.).

driving post Euphemism for penis. Often used in 'sex for sale'

adverts; 'Young lady seeks driving post' (followed by a phone number). As noted above, 'to drive' is well-established slang for sexual intercourse of any nature, in the same line of aggressive, penetrative imagery as 'screw' (q.v.) and the obvious drilling. Drill, of course, means penis.

droopers Sagging breasts in a woman. Now fairly dated.

Duchess of Fife Wife. Cockney rhyming slang. *See also* FORK AND KNIFE, TROUBLE AND STRIFE. (Origin of 'my ol' Dutch'?)

dyke The stereotypical 'mannish' lesbian. Generally intended as a term of abuse, originating in the US, now widespread in Britain.

But in this country the term has been 'reclaimed' by more politically conscious lesbians who will call themselves and each other dykes. Carol Uszkurat in her song for a benefit concert in aid of Lesbian Line and London Gay Switchboard (December 1982) has the satirical lyrics

'What's it like to be a dyke
Are you butch or femme
Do you really hate men?'
And the feminist magazine *Spare Rib* defines it like this: 'Probably expected to wear (dungarees) ... reclaimed by lesbians as in, for example, dynamite dykes.'

One unlikely suggestion for its source is -dite, from hermaphrodite. But at least this is consistent with the entrenched idea that any woman whose sexuality is not dependent on stimulation by the male must be part male herself (*see* BULL DYKE).

Rodgers perpetuates the stereotype with his definition 'swaggering, cigar-puffing lesbian'. It is enshrined in popular British mythology in this 'joke':

'What's the difference between a whale and a dyke?

Two tons of blubber and a flannel shirt.'

But the aggressive and insulting usage is now being countered by the proud usage by lesbians.

E

early door Whore. Cockney rhyming slang. Not to be confused with early doors = drawers.

early spurt Premature ejaculation. An attempt through assonance to make light of a problem that has made life a misery for many men and women.

earth mother An all-providing female, usually one with a baby, an Arran sweater and left-wing leanings – according to the derogatory stereotype. Mostly a jocular term.

ease oneself, to To ejaculate. Old-fashioned euphemism dating back to the 18th century. The image is a pleasant one of relief from tension – *see also* RELIEF MASSAGE.

East and West Breast. Cockney rhyming slang. Limited male usage.

Easter bunny queen Gay man who 'comes' as quick as a rabbit. US slang (Rodgers). *See* EARLY SPURT for the less colourful UK equivalent.

easy Sexually compliant. The word is generally applied by men to women and implies criticism of lax morals. The judgement is a reflection of the old double standard of sexuality, i.e. a decent woman should be 'difficult' for a man to bed. There is no equivalent concept applied to men.

'Easy' is mostly commonly found in compounds like easy lay – widespread in the US and growing in popularity in the UK. An old-fashioned English equivalent is easy virtue, usually (women of …). Easy meat carries on the tradition of referring to flesh as meat, and is a widespread heterosexual and gay term, in British usage since the 1920s. Easy make and easy mark are less common US equivalents.

Easy on the eye and easy to look at mean attractive and again are generally applied to women.

eat, to Oral sex; either cunnilingus or fellatio. Widespread gay and heterosexual usage, originally US but now more common in the UK.

Variations are eat fish (cunnilingus, *see* FISH), eat pussy (*see* PUSSY), eat somebody out, and eat dick (fellatio). In America these terms are also commonly used as angry expletives; if someone on the streets tells you to 'Eat dick, man!', he or she means 'fuck off', or more literally 'suck cock'.

eat with your hands To grope someone. Jocular and witty US camp expression as in 'Didn't your mother tell you it isn't polite to eat with your hands?'.

eccles cake as in 'like stuffing an eccles cake into a slot machine.' Unsatisfactory sexual intercourse. A Northern English expression, comic and dismissive, alluding to lack of firmness in the male organ – in contrast to the imagined steely and voracious nature of the female orifice. Contemporary and mostly female usage.

eclair queen Rich homosexual man. A multiple pun in the camp tradition, playing on the meaning of rich, the phallic imagery of the pastry and the cream it contains.

Edie A prostitute. Obscure and virtually obsolete London police slang for prostitutes literally 'walking the streets' in areas outside of Soho. The term was used to distinguish lower paid operators from the 'escorts' operating at the richer end of the circuit.

eff A stand-in for fuck, as an expletive. Effing and blinding is a well-established English euphemism for swearing.

effie Stereotypical effeminate homosexual. Just as lesbians are labelled part male in the popular imagination (*see* DYKE), so gay men are commonly ascribed what are thought to be 'feminine' attributes – like weakness, fickleness and cowardice. That the effie is lumbered with this image reveals as much about stereotyped views of women as it does about attitudes to gay men. *See also* FRUIT, FAIRY.

egg A boy too young to be considered in a sexual light. This innocuous US gay term combines the idea of something smooth and unformed with an image of fragility. Hence egg-sucker, meaning a gay 'cradle snatcher', is abusive.

eggs in the basket The testicles. Clearly a universal image: in Spain the equivalent is *huevos* (eggs) and in Hebrew, *betsim*.

Egyptian queen Black gay man, especially if tall and stately. US camp slang. Also ebony queen, dinge queen.

elephant, see the To be seduced. Now obscure, this colourful term originally meant 'to see the world'.

It took on its sexual connotation by association with the idea of gaining experience, becoming worldly. There is an equivalent in French: *avoir vu le loup* (Partridge).

Elephant and Castle Anus, arse or bum. From cockney rhyming slang with arsehole. *See also* KHYBER PASS, BOTTLE AND GLASS.

elephant's bollocks Large breasts. *See* 'tits like elephants' bollocks', *under* TITS.

elrig Girl. Back slang. Dated UK usage. *See also* DELOW NAMMOW, TENUC.

EMBO Early Morning Bonk On, or to put it clinically, a matutinal erection. With this colourful abbreviation − pronounced as a word, not as initials − there is an element of jocularity; the everyday occurrence has happened again for reasons man knows not. *Contrast with* PISS HARD ON, and PISS PROUD.

encirclement Sexual intercourse − from the female point of view. First heard by the authors in early 1984, this is clearly an attempt to counter the great bulk of slang words which describe sexual acts with the male as the active party. Hence this paragraph in a letter to the feminist magazine *Spare Rib*, April 1984: 'We feel that (the rhythm method) is the best that scientific research has produced to ensure that encirclement (or do we mean penetration?) does not lead to an unwanted pregnancy.' Limited usage in the UK so far.

encore, to get an To get a second erection during one session of love-making. A double pun on the sense of 'doing it again' and the standing ovation. 20th century UK male usage. *See also* SECOND INNINGS.

end The glans penis, mostly used in compounds like bell end, red end, blunt end. To have an end on, means to have an erection.

Perhaps the most common usage is in the English compound expression for sexual intercourse 'to get one's end away'.

endless belt prostitute. Australian slang; belt = sexual intercourse.

end of the Sentimental Journey The vagina. Virtually obsolete English term which Partridge connects with Sterne's novel. *See also* DEAD END STREET.

endowed *See* WELL ENDOWED.

English muffins Buttocks, especially when pert and rounded. In gay usage the term refers to boys' buttocks. US slang. Another equivalent is buns.

English style/method 'Fucking' the thighs. Camp gay expression. This US terms sheds an interesting light on American views of British sexual practice. The assumption is that this is what boys in British public schools do. The only US parallel is Princeton style, meaning the same.

entertain, to To have sexual intercourse with. Originally a coy Victorian euphemism; 'Have you been entertaining your lady friend?' then and now means 'Have you been to bed with your girlfriend?' The meaning has also attracted widescale camp interest and is used by many gays. One example is 'entertaining royalty' – i.e. having sex with a 'queen'.

envelope, or **love envelope** Condom. Late 19th century UK usage. Now virtually obsolete, but perhaps a relative of the more common 'French letter'.

equipment The male genitals. Widespread US and UK usage. A workmanlike phrase in keeping with the sense of 'doing the business' and 'on the job'. *See also* MARRIAGE GEAR, and WEDDING TACKLE.

'er indoors Sometimes **her indoors** A wife. A common, originally cockney and working-class expression. Thanks to TV exposure in series like 'Minder' it is now widely aped all over the UK. Hence this recent advertisement in *The Standard*: 'This Saturday, Arsenal play Aston Villa at Highbury. What better way to escape those little chores her indoors has lined up for you?'; and this quote from a *Sun* bingo winner (27 February 1983): 'It'll be up to 'er indoors what we do with the rest of the money.'

etchings, would you like to see my? One of the most venerable catch phrases of sexual innuendo. The origins lie in the clichéd image of the bohemian 'artistic' way of life as sexually permissive; hence an invitation to see one's 'art' was an invitation to the bedroom and thence to sex. So old and worn that it is now only used as a joke or in self-parody.

ettie Girl or woman. Cockney and working-class slang. From the girl's name.

eunuch Medically, a man who has been castrated, but in slang the term is applied to a man who lacks 'balls', i.e. verve, courage, power and the other characteristics popularly associated with virility/masculinity. As a political correspondent writes in the *Guardian* (14 Nov 1983), 'The last thing that Whitehall needs is political eunuchs who do not hold strong views about the political issues of the day ...'

Eve *See* CURSE (of Eve).

even with somebody else's *See* I WOULDN'T DO IT EVEN WITH SOMEBODY ELSE'S.

ever-loving Wife. Cheerful working-class and lower middle-class expression, likely to be used as a term of stoical endearment.

69

every night about this time ... Sexual intercourse. Coy euphemism dating back to WWI, now rarely heard.

Eve's custom house The vagina, i.e. where Adam made his first entry. This colourful phrase, dating back to late 18th century Britain, is now obsolete.

evil A wife, or marriage. 18th-19th century English slang. Now obsolete. *Contrast with* EVER-LOVING.

ewe dressed lamb fashion, an old *See* MUTTON (dressed as lamb).

ex Previous spouse or lover, whether male or female. Originally High Society slang for ex-wife or ex-husband during the 20s, the expression has gained in popularity in all social classes and is now the widely accepted term for ex-partner, regardless of marital status or sexual orientation. In a society where serial relationships and remarriage have become the norm, it is generally used without rancour or embarrassment.

exchanging loads The practice whereby a fellator deposits a mouthful of semen into the mouth of a partner. Initially popularized by American 'groupies' serving rock musicians but also common among gays. *See also* SNOWDROPPING, SNOWBALLING and WHITE RUSSIAN.

exchanging spits French kissing, also more rarely sexual intercourse. Initially working class, now used as a joke euphemism (especially for the latter meaning).

exercise the ferret Sexual intercourse. Originally Australian, popularized by Barry Humphries, this is another somewhat cute image of the penis as a jumpy little rodent forever popping into holes. *See* DRAIN and EASTER BUNNY QUEEN.

exhaust pipe The anal opening. One in the legion of terms denoting dirt, odour and pollution – plus in this case expellation – to the anus. Originally US.

exotic Beyond a person's usual sexual experience, if spoken euphemistically. Hence 'exotic dancer' becomes a euphemism for prostitute. 'Exotic delights' are sexual experiences, usually gained in exchange for cash.

expressive button The clitoris. Hackneyed and coy term usually used by the 'liberated' male. The liberated female finds such terms embarrassing. *Contrast with* the simpler, and more widely used, BELL.

extra-curricular activities Illicit sexual activities, whether unfaithful behaviour to a regular partner, adultery or just plain sexual intercourse. The phrase relies upon its schoolteacherly mock-formality to make the point that something 'naughty' is going on.

Hence it is a rather, pompous euphemism, largely middle class. It first became current in the 1940s amongst the 'cultured' classes (Partridge) and at the time meant solely adultery.

eye The anus. Hence a whole string of compound expressions, many of them male gay and predominantly US, like eye doctor – the active partner in anal sex. However, to wink the brown eye is to expose the bum by 'mooning': the expression, like the practice, is common among rugby players.

The use of eye for orifice is a venerable one, and at times it has also meant vagina. Hence eye opener, meaning penis, a term which dates back to the 19th century. Eye hole has also meant the urinary opening.

In another more direct sense, eye is important in sexual slang, because of the visual stimulation by an attractive person, and because of eye contact, which is a major element in flirtation. Hence an eyeful is at once an attractive person (usually applied to women), and a glimpse of naked flesh. To make eyes at someone is to flirt, and to have eyes for a person is to fancy them sexually. As usual the US slang unceremoniously cuts through the foreplay with eye-fuck, meaning to undress somebody visually. Contrast with the sizzling style of British romantic fiction, 'He undressed me with his eyes'.

eyeful, an A glimpse of something sexually provocative. Either 'I got a real eyeful when she took her dress off' or, with the word used slightly differently, 'Look at Jane, she's a right eyeful!' Mostly working-class usage, more by men than women (although not exclusively).

Eyes out like organ stops Catch phrase applied to an ogling male. Current UK usage, jocular.

F

faggot Male homosexual. In the US – where it is most popular – commonly shortened to fag, so that the British habit of referring to cigarettes as fags causes frequent amusement to Americans. (Indeed, Partridge cites a 1946 Canadian sense of fag as a girl who smokes.)

Slang etymologists have widely different theories about the origins of the word. Rodgers suggests four possibilities, beginning with the somewhat fanciful idea that homosexuals were dubbed fags because of the notions of macho, cigar-smoking men that cigarettes were an effeminate habit. He also suggests the source of fag as the British schoolboy name for the servant to older boys, or as an abbreviation of Fagin – as the character who taught little boys dishonesty, or as the middle-English name for the heretic condemned to be burnt alive.

Partridge however notes that faggot was a pejorative term for a woman, equivalent to the modern baggage, and as so many words intended to insult men have developed from words meaning 'woman', this seems like the most likely source. In this country however, faggot has never been as popular as the ubiquitous 'queer'.

fag hag A woman who consorts with homosexual men. This US term is contemptuous.

fag mag A magazine for homosexuals. UK journalists' slang for magazines like *Gay News* (Hudson).

fairy Homosexual man. UK and US heterosexual usage, but also used by some homosexuals to describe someone they consider to be an effeminate gay. The image is based on the stereotype of homosexual man as 'feminine', dainty and fey. *Compare* NANCE, and 'FLUFF' (under 'FLUFFIE').

fall off the roof, to For a woman to menstruate. Apart from the association with blood, this catchphrase (mostly US gay usage) is based on the notion that a menstruating woman is 'irritable, cranky and unavailable for sex' (Rodgers). Which all goes to show just how deep the antipathy to a woman's 'curse' still runs.

falsies False breasts on a transvestite or drag act, or a heavily padded bra.

family jewels The testicles. Mostly jocular male usage. Not only attributing inestimable worth to these 'nuggets', but implying that herein lies the family's wealth, to be passed down from father to son.

fancy, to To be sexually attracted to a person. One of the most widespread, classless and ageless of slang terms. Until recently however it was primarily working class and as such shunned by the middle classes (Hudson).

fancy a swim? Query from a man to a woman to ascertain if she is a likely candidate for sex. The 'joke' is that women supposedly avoid going swimming when they have their periods, and so if the answer is 'no' the man asumes it's 'the wrong time of the month'. Of course, he doesn't assume that she simply doesn't want to have sex with him – but then he hasn't asked her this ...
Australian in origin, after Barry Humphries, but by now a cult phrase among UK connoisseurs of bad taste.

fancy bit or **fancy piece** Girlfriend – usually in an illicit relationship. *See* BIT ON THE SIDE, and FANCY MAN. *Contrast* use of 'bit' or 'piece' for females, and 'man' for males.

fancy man Boyfriend – but generally in an illicit relationship. As such, equivalent to 'bit on the side'. The term dates back to the beginning of the 18th century, when a fancy man was a 'harlot's protector or lover, a sweetheart or kept man' (Partridge).

fancy work The male genitals. 20th century UK slang, but this delicate euphemism is not widespread.

fanny The female genitals. In the UK this contemporary sense has become distinct from the earlier sense of 'backside'. It was not long ago that to 'have a big fanny' was to have a big bum, or 'or to park one's fanny' was to sit down. The sense of 'bum' still persists in the US, however.
Yet according to Partridge, fanny has had the simultaneous sense of 'female pudenda' since the mid-19th century, and even, he suggests, from the publication of the 1794 classic about life in a brothel, *The Memoirs of Fanny Hill*.
Today, it exists as one of the less objectionable words for 'cunt', and is used as an equivalent for 'rubbish' or 'nonsense' (hardly flattering to women) in phrases

73

like 'Don't talk such a load of old fanny.'

fart catcher A male homosexual. The term dates back to the 30s and is rarely heard today (Partridge).

fartleberries *See* DINGLE BERRIES.

fast Sexually 'promiscuous'. Almost invariably applied to women and a reflection of the sexual double standard. 'Fast woman' or 'fast lady' invariably springs to mind. Also 'fast and loose' as a catch phrase for a person (again, usually female) who is considered sexually available – except in the sense 'to play fast and loose' with someone's feelings, which can apply equally to both sexes.

The latter phrase dates back to the 16th century, while the 18th century meaning of fast was 'dissipated' (Partridge).

favour sexual intercourse – as performed by the male. There could hardly be a more self-congratulatory term, as in the catch phrase said about any attractive woman – 'I could do that a real favour'. Amazingly, it is used without a sense of irony by many men. Even Partridge uses it to define slang about intercourse as 'the sexual favour'. And so mild is the euphemism that even Fred Gee, *Coronation Street*'s barman, has been heard to crack jokes about the dividends to a workman

of 'doing a favour' for some old ladies (13 Feb 1984).

feature, to To succeed in having sex with a woman (of a man). Australian in origin and popularized by the notorious Barry Mackenzie, this is now becoming widespread UK usage. It is equivalent in usage to 'coming across with' a woman: as in 'Did you feature with her last night then?'

federating Having sexual intercourse. Australian slang of the 20th century (Partridge).

feed the monkey Sexual intercourse – of a man with a woman. US slang from the 60s, but rare. *See* WHERE THE MONKEY SLEEPS.

feel To touch with sexual intent. Comparable to the equally popular 'grope', both in regular usage by young people in describing – for instance – the activities at a party: 'Did you see him giving her a feel in the corner?' The word has had this form of slang usage since the 18th century (Partridge). Northern usage is commonly to 'cop a feel'; i.e. to touch somebody sexually.

In America the usage is more likely to be 'touchy feelie', which refers as much to emotional as to physical 'groping'. Hence the name given to a class in human relationships at a Californian college as the 'Touchy Feelie course' (*Guardian* 8 Feb 1984)

felch See VELCH.

female A woman. According to Partridge the slang practice of referring to women specifically by their gender 'has long been pejorative' – and it still is. The force of this is best felt in contrast with the use of 'male', which is not pejorative.

feminine The characteristics attributed to 'females' (q.v.). The stereotype generally includes softness, passivity and ladylike behaviour – and as such the definition is very much in dispute. The feminist magazine *Spare Rib* describes 'feminine' as 'what we are meant to be. No necessary connection with what we are'.

Also used as a euphemism for the sexual parts in advertising catch phrases like 'feminine freshness' – referring to products which are supposed to make the vagina smell not like itself, but like perfume/flowers etc. It has to be supposed that advertisers don't think the vagina is 'feminine'!

femme The stereotyped 'feminine' partner in a lesbian relationship. The assumption is that women duplicate heterosexual patterns of dominance and submission, and that the 'butch' partner will play the 'masculine' role.

Lesbians however tend to treat the stereotype as a poor – if not oppressive – joke. Hence these satirical lyrics about the kind of questions a lesbian is likely to encounter:

'Are you butch or femme?
Do you really hate men?'

Note especially that the 'femme' is supposedly the passive partner. Indeed, Rodgers defines femme as 'passive lesbian' and as 'passive homosexual' – transferring the 'womanly' quality even to male gays.

And of course at root of all this implied passivity is the original meaning of femme as the French word for woman, and the Standard English 'feminine' (q.v.).

femme fatale The fatally attractive woman of Hollywood tradition who lures the unfortunate male into her grasp – and then betrays him. This is probably the female equivalent of 'lady killer' and is a popular Page Three word – as in this piece from *The Sun*, describing 'Exciting Erica ... who loves both James Bond and dry martinis. Of course that's the lethal combination which gets him stirred and shaken. She's a femme fatale all right!'

ferret The penis. Also 'trouser ferret'. Australian in origin, this term has joined the list of UK terms which describe the male organ as a wriggly little animal. *See also* RABBIT, GALLOP THE MAGGOT, ONE EYED TROUSER SNAKE. Not to be confused however with 'two ferrets fighting in a sack' – the catch phrase that describes the sight of buttocks wobbling in a pair of tight trousers.

See also EXERCISE THE FERRET, which refers to this creature's supposed propensity for running up and down trouser legs.

ferry A prostitute. The implication is that she gives 'rides' to many men. This is Australian usage and little known in the UK, but *compare* the British 'TOWN BIKE'.

fetch Seminal fluid and/or sexual emissions (Partridge). UK slang from the 19th century but now obsolete.

fetishist A person who has a strong sexual feeling for particular parts of the body (the feet, the breasts etc.) or for particular objects or articles of clothing, e.g. boots, leather. Rodgers suggests the possible root as the French *fetiche* = artificial and descriptive of primitive charms, and the Latin *factitius* = factitious.

fife and drum Bum. From cockney rhyming slang.

fifty-nine Mutual cunnilingus. The joke in this gay male term is that oral sex between women scores less than a 'sixty-nine' – ten points off for the absence of a penis (Rodgers). Old ideas about penis envy are clearly not yet vanquished ... *See also* SIXTY-EIGHT, SIXTY-NINE.

fig The female genitalia. An old-fashioned term, unlikely to be used these days by any but D.H. Lawrence afficionados. Compare the Italian 'figa' for 'cunt'.

filly A young woman, generally considered attractive by men. Most men will use the term with the intention of showing affection: hence Partridge defines the term as 'since 1820 an unobjectionable name for young girls'.

But today's 'young girls' are likely to find the term not at all 'unobjectionable' with its overtones of the woman as an animal, valued for its breeding, youth and qualities as a 'ride'. The only comparable name for a male is 'stallion', which has quite different implications of power and virility. Extenuating circumstances however can be argued from the likely origin of filly in *fille*, the French word for daughter, and hence the paternalistic tone.

finger fuck To caress a woman's genitals manually. A modern term, generally confined to the bedroom or to erotic literature. The old-fashioned sense was to masturbate, from the 19th century (Partridge).

fire a shot, to To ejaculate. Largely obsolete, but an explicit part of the tradition of penis as weapon. *See also* HALF-COCKED.

firk Also ferk. Euphemism for fuck – and with less power to cause offence. Also firkin, for fucking.

fish Current US gay male term for women, also for female genitals. Usage is insulting, expressing contempt for the female parts as slimy and smelly. And as in so many slang words, no differentiation is made between a woman and a 'cunt'. This is still mostly US usage, where synonyms are fish tank and fish pond. To have a fish dinner is to have sex with a woman, and a fish queen is a homosexual man (Rodgers).

The fish, however, has been a symbol of sexuality and fertility down the ages, and featured as such in Greek art. But, ironically, the traditional means of depicting the fish was as a phallic symbol.

Partridge records an early UK usage of fish for 'female pudenda' from 1850, while a bit of fish meant sexual intercourse, a fishmarket was a brothel, and to go fishing was to 'hunt for a sexually obliging woman'.

This is evident in the 'joke' in circulation in New York City: 'Why don't they let women swim in New Jersey? They can't get the smell out of the fish.'

fish and shrimp Pimp. From cockney rhyming slang. Limited UK usage.

fist fuck The mostly gay male practice of inserting the clenched fist into a partner's anus. This is now a widely talked about practice in America where publications like *The Fist Fucker's Manual* give instructions on how to perform the act without causing too much damage. But there is no doubt that some gays are permanently harmed by this kind of insertion – rumoured these days to include feet and even head – and it is hard for any but afficionados to imagine how this is considered an erotic act at all.

Partridge records the 19th century usage as male masturbation: perhaps he wasn't willing to countenance anything 'worse' – or perhaps the very term gave people some ideas ...

five finger knuckle shuffle Male masturbation. Popular particularly with young men for the joke value of its rhymes and alliteration. *Compare* 'MOTHER PALM AND HER FIVE DAUGHTERS' for inventiveness.

flags out, to have Also to have flags flying. Said of menstruating women. This is another cartoon-like variation on the theme of sanitary pads seen grossly exaggerated into sheets, sails or in this case, flags. Almost always male usage and not without a trace of horrid fascination for the female functions. *See also* 'RED SAILS IN THE SUNSET', and (she's got the) 'PAINTERS IN'.

flange The female genitalia. Scottish slang, mostly young male usage. Also however, the corona of the penis in UK and US slang (Jimmy The Blade, Dingwall 1983).

77

flash, to To expose the penis, or other taboo parts of the body. Also to 'flash it', 'flash one's meat', or – in woman – 'to flash the upright grin' (Partridge). The activity is either confined to flashers – who generally cause offence to women – or is part of jokey flirtation on the part of both men and women. One of Beryl Cook's famous comic drawings is of a female flasher. The earlier (and still concurrent) sense of 'flash' dating back to the 17th century was to show off, be ostentatious.

fleece The pubic hair. Less popular than fur. UK slang from the 19th century.

flesh pots General term for sexual opportunities – as in the cliché about travelling abroad; e.g. 'visiting the flesh pots of Europe'. As a meaty image, flesh has a safe niche in slang: 'to go fleshing' is an old-fashioned UK term for sexual intercourse, as are 'to flesh it' and 'to flesh one's sword' (Partridge).

fletch The Irish equivalent of VELCH (q.v.).

flier, to take a To have sexual intercourse other than naked and other than in bed. The pun is presumably on the express train, but not to be confused with the US 'fly jockey', said of the male who copulates with his trousers on (Rodgers). *See also* MILE HIGH CLUB.

fling A brief affair. Also a flutter. This term assumes a degree of sympathy, even connivance in the user, based on the notion that a fling generally takes place away from home and if nobody is the wiser, no one will get hurt.

As in this *News of the World* feature (12 Feb 1984) about singles' skiing holidays: 'If you felt like it you could have an endless good time. I heard of one girl who managed a fling with 15 guys in two weeks.'

flog the donkey Male masturbation. Also flog the mutton, both seeing the penis in the animal/meat tradition. The sense of self-abuse is as apparent in the use of 'flog' as it is in 'beat the meat'. *See also* GALLOP THE MAGGOT, for a comparable use of the idea of 'riding'.

floosie A 'promiscuous' woman and/or girlfriend. A dismissive term, generally used by men. Partridge traces it to 40s naval slang, and notes that 'Flossie' is a South African word for prostitute.

flopper stopper Bra. Old fashioned, schoolboyish usage, using comic rhyme in the tradition of so many slang words for breasts. Note that this seems to be a particularly English predilection. The purpose of the flopper stopper is to support the 'flip flaps' or 'flip flops' (Partridge). The 'flip flap', however, can also be the penis. *See also* JIGGLIES, and BUMPY

JUMPER, for comparable treatment.

flower The female genitals. British slang from the 19th century. Now obsolete but notable for its pleasant and positive connotations. Other variations are flower pot, flower of chivalry. Not to be confused with 'monthly flowers' – periods. *Compare* CHERRY, and PLEASURE GARDEN.

flowers and frolics Testicles. One of the more fanciful examples of rhyming slang with 'bollocks'. Possibly Anglo-Irish origins; note that the preferred Irish pronunciation 'bollix' is a more accurate rhyme with 'frolics'.

fluffie According to the so-called 'masculist' movement a fluffie is a traditional woman, dependent on men, a doormat, a social and sexual coward, masochistic and self-effacing. The fluffie is functionally constipated, economically useless, and unable to cope with the world. Note the similarity of sound – and implication of women's prostitution – with 'floosie'.

This definition is from Hugh de Garis, of the 'masculists' in Europe, whose professed creed of sexual equality hides a deep misogyny and backlash against the feminist movement. Fluffies, say de Garis, are 'husband-killers, parasites on men's lives'. His solution is for women to become a bit more macha. (*See* MACHO)

The term 'fluff' has never showed kindness to women: *see* 'BIT (OF FLUFF)'. And like other words representing a stereotype of the 'feminine', men apply it to other men to convey distaste. Hence fluff is a gay term for an 'effeminate' gay (Rodgers).

food US gay term for 'men as sex objects' (Rodgers). Interesting to see spelled out what is otherwise implied in slang terms like crumpet, dish, meat etc.

fool around with To have sexual petting or intercourse with someone. Less common in the UK than in the US, where 'to fool around' is a quite presentable euphemism. 'Fool sticker' or 'fool maker' are old-fashioned UK terms for the penis, while 'fool trap' had the meaning female genitals, and 'harlot' (Partridge). Yet again, 'cunt' and 'prostitute' have been equated.

footsie footsie A form of gentle, and usually secretive, under-the-table flirtation, in which two people play at touching feet. However it is most often heard in joking banter between people who are slightly embarrassed about having accidentally touched, as in 'Playing footsie with me are you?'. A less common parallel is 'handsie handsie' – or hand touching.

foreplay Sexual activity leading up to intercourse, considered an essential part of the process of giving sexual pleasure – and one certainly expected by heterosexual women of the modern male. Hence the plethora of jokes about the notion of foreplay amongst 'foreigners'; e.g. the *Sunday Mirror* 12 Feb 1984: 'Shame on the Australian newspaper tycoon who, addressing a distinguished London dinner, said his countrymen's definition of foreplay went something like: "You awake, Sheila?".'

fork and knife Wife. Cockney rhyming slang. *See also* DUCHESS OF FIFE, TROUBLE AND STRIFE.

fornicator The penis. 19th and 20th century UK slang, now largely obsolete. Also 'fornicating member/engine/tool'. Note the active principle in these (by now largely obsolete) terms, in contrast to 'fornicator's hall' – the vagina (Partridge).

four letter words A blanket term for language considered obscene. And it is certainy a reflection on social attitudes that the 'obscene' in this sense means words about the sexual *and* excretory functions, (without much differentiation made between them) – as opposed to words about, say, violence.

Originally these were literally the words of four letters which Partridge lists as 'arse, balls, shit, fuck, quim, cunt, cock, twat, piss and fart.' He argues that the term entered the language with all the fuss about *Lady Chatterley's*

Lover, and became colloquial in the fifties.

fourth sex, the Lesbians. This US gay term (Rodgers) is presumably drawing on the notion of women as the second sex, gay men as the third, and lesbians as the fourth. The only winners it seems, are heterosexual men!

But the pecking order does come full circle: note that the gay term 'fifth wheel' means a heterosexual male (?) in a gay gathering.

Fred Sexual interest. This is a prime example of slang word developing in a small group of people. One regular habituée of the Windmill pub, south London, was heard to say in 1981 to a male friend – 'I'm sick of you going on about fancying that woman. Why don't you just call her ... Fred, or something.' The word subsequently developed so that all references to sexual interest or flirtation became instantly summed up as 'Fred'. (Thanks to F. Dowling.)

freeze, the The withholding of sexual intercourse on a woman's part. Interesting chiefly for its unselfconscious definition in Partridge: 'a wife's most potent weapon'! Australian, 1930s in origin.

french kiss A full sexual mouth-to-mouth kiss with lips parted. Sometimes known as frenching, although this has had further connotations of oral sex since the 19th century. Hence the US term for oral sex – 'to speak in a foreign tongue'.

For some reason the word French is widely used in slang to suggest sexual meanings (*see* FRENCH LETTER). Hence the classic euphemism 'French lesson', to advertise services offered by a prostitute. 'French prints' is a now old-fashioned term for pornographic pictures, while to be 'Frenchified' was to have syphilis (Partridge). In the US too, gays have adopted 'French revolution' to mean the advent of Gay Liberation.

french letter A condom. This has been a popular term in slang for at least a century. Note however that the French have retaliated in kind: *capote Anglais* is their equivalent. Also sometimes 'french safe' or 'frenchy' or, in a fancy style, a 'French tickler'. A possible origin is a lesser known term for a condom – 'frog skin', from which 'frog' might have developed into 'French'.

fresh Sexually forward. As in the reprimand to men by women – 'Don't get fresh with me'. Although very popular in the US and UK some years ago, it now has a dated ring, as do 'fresh bit' – for new girlfriend, and 'bit of fresh' – for sexual intercourse.

Friar Tuck Sexual intercourse. Cockney rhyming slang with fuck.

fried eggs Small breasts. This self-explanatory image has been popular in UK slang since the 30s at least.

friend Often a euphemism for lover, male or female, in these days of hard-to-define relationships. Not long ago, however, 'friend' was euphemistic for menstruation – as in 'My friend has come', or 'I have friends to stay' (Partridge).

frig, to To masturbate. Male and female usage, often as an expletive. The word has a long history: its root is from the Latin *fricare*, to rub, and it entered the English language at the end of the 16th century. And today it features in the lyrics of bawdy songs like 'Frigging in the Rigging'.

Note that it also, like 'wanking', has the sense of messing about and wasting time, a further reflection on popular attitudes to 'self-abuse'.

frisky Sexually eager, as in the term used by men and women – 'I'm feeling a bit frisky these days'. Not to be confused with 'frisking' – sexual touching or intercourse.

front bum The vagina. Male Irish usage. Intended as jokey and innocuous, but somewhat disturbing in its denial of the nature – and even the existence – of the female part. *Compare* 'TOP BOLLOCKS' – an Irish term for breasts.

Several doctors have also told the authors that the euphemism most women prefer to use for their own vaginas is 'front passage' – which sounds very much as if it also evolved from the word for bum, 'back passage'.

Partridge cites the (now old-fashioned) UK equivalents 'front attic/door/garden/parlour/room/window/gut', and 'front door mat' for women's pubic hair.

front suspension Bra. Australian slang, with the image of the woman as a hefty vehicle.

fruit Male homosexual. Widespread, mostly US, usage and acceptable enough to be used in banter on US TV shows like 'Soap', in which Carol says to an actor in a corn flakes advertisement 'Oh, just what the cereal needed – *fruit*' (12 Jan. 1983). Fruit salad is camp slang for a group of gays, while fruit machine is the male organ.

fuck, to To have sexual intercourse with. This classic 'four letter word' has a history as chequered as its modern usage.

Likely etymological roots are the Latin *futuere* and the German *ficken* (although, says the OED, this is unproven), meaning to strike. Other suggestions include the Sanskrit *ukshan* – bull, and the Cantonese *fook* – happiness (Rodgers).

Bruce Rodgers also hazards this suggestion: 'from naval commanders in the early 19th century who abbreviated For Unlawful Carnal Knowledge in their logbooks'.

However the image of sex as 'striking' remains a common theme in slang, with words like 'banging' and 'knocking' as synonyms for 'fucking'. And today the word is most commonly heard as an aggressive expletive, usually on the lips of men, although women do increasingly use it.

It has been a part of the English language since the 16th century at least. The OED notes first usage as a verb in 1503, and comments: 'until recently regarded as a taboo word and rarely recorded in print.' Indeed 'fuck' until only a few decades ago was considered one of the most obscene of all sexual words, and its absorption into daily speech has marked a revolution in slang. Particularly notable is the increase in the use of the word by women today, who before the last World War would risk losing all respectability should the word ever pass their lips. At the beginning of 1984 'fuck' appears as an expletive in an article about today's young on the *Guardian* women's page without arousing comment.

In America however, 'to fuck' has always been used more openly and US men and women today will apply the word without embarrassment to their sex lives. This freer usage has crossed the

Atlantic to make the word more generally acceptable in the UK today. Women's magazines like *Spare Rib* and feminist books like Cartledge and Ryan's *Sex and Love*, use the word to mean intercourse: 'the insistence that sex was good for you ... reinforced the pressure on women to fuck.' However, many women – and men – remain unhappy about applying the word to their own love making, because of its aggressive connotations, and it is still not acceptable as an expletive in many situations – hence this editorial in the *Sun* (23 September 1983): 'Keep It Clean. In a radio interview, 'Brideshead' actor Jeremy Irons outraged listeners by using the foulest four-letter word ... The radio is intended for family audiences. People who use it should observe standards of decency. After all, Mr Irons is supposed to be a serious actor. Not a Rolling Stone.'

fuck, a A sexual partner, male or female, as in the phrase: 'he/she's a good fuck'. Not to be confused with 'fucker' – a widely used insulting term for a man; as in: 'Look at that silly fucker'.

fuck me pumps A style in women's shoes with high wooden heels and a single sandal strap. The American equivalent is 'throw me down and fuck me shoes'. Both of these slang terms serve to illustrate how in the popular imagination at least the high, tottery style of women's shoes, emphasizing the swaying of buttocks and the wearer's vulnerability, are considered almost an 'invitation' to sexual assault.

fud The female genitals. Mostly male Scottish slang usage, also some UK and US variants – like 'futy' and 'fudy'. Usage dates back to the 18th century, when 'fud' meant pubic hair, from the word for a rabbit's or hare's scut.

fun and games Sexual intercourse. A fairly modern euphemism, as in 'Were you up to fun and games last night?'. Also 'funny business' or 'to have a bit of fun' – for any form of sexual activity, but usually clandestine. 'Funny bit' is a now obsolete term for the female genitals (Partridge).

fun bags Breasts. Modern UK male usage, with the sense that the breasts' function is entertainment of the male. *See* FUN AND GAMES.

funch Sex at lunchtime between gays. A collapse of 'fag' and 'lunch' (Rodgers). *See also* AFTERNOON DELIGHT, MATINEE, MORNER.

fur pie The female genitalia. Also 'hair pie'. 'Fur' has long had the sense pubic hair, while 'pie' is in the long tradition of referring to bits of the body as edible. Mostly UK, male and working-class usage. Hence the greeting of a cockney dustman to the authors at a London working men's club:

'Good morning, know what I had for breakfast this morning? Fur pie!' *See also* FURRY HOOP.

furry hoop The vagina. Mostly jocular usage between men, with the implication that the 'hoop' is something a man performs tricks in hopping through. Furry rug is another variant. *See also* HORSE COLLAR.

G

gal Generally as an affected pronunciation of girl. Like so many other names for women, at different times it has had the interchangeable meanings girl, sweetheart – and prostitute. *See also* GIRL.

gallop the maggot Also gallop the antelope. To masturbate. 20th century male usage, originally Cockney, comparable in comedy and rhyme to 'jerkin' the gherkin'. Gallop has the related meaning of erection. Hence to be 'unable to raise a gallop' is to be impotent. Note the connection with 'ride'.

game A person supposedly eager to have sex, as in 'Anyone can see she's game'. Also a generic term for prostitutes, carrying the noxious image of women as meat to be hunted for sport. Fair game – applied to women considered available for sex – carries the same overtones. And of course on the game is a venerable term for prostitution, from the mid-19th century. Now outdated are game woman and game pullet for prostitutes, or women considered sexually 'forward'.

On a more frolicsome note however are 'the national indoor game', an old-fashioned euphemism for sexual intercourse, and the synonymous 'first game ever played'.

gander A married man. This is very dated but is interesting historically. The 'gander month' was 'the month after childbirth in the 17th to 19th century when it was held excusable for men to err' (Partridge). A gander gang or gander party was the male equivalent of the modern 'hen party' – and a rather more equitable term than the current equivalent 'stag party'. *See also* GOOSE, for usage of 'gander month'.

gang bang Group sex. Also unfortunately used to refer to – and to trivialize – gang rape. Also the US usage gang-shag, and the UK pig-party.

gap The vagina. Dating back to 18th century Britain but still current in the UK. One of many slang terms which describe the female parts as an absence or lack, in the tradition of the belief in 'penis envy'. More common equivalents are 'hole' and 'gash'. Variants are gape, or gape over the garter – now very dated – and also gap stopper, the penis.

garden Also pleasure gardens. The female sexual parts. This charming piece of slang is still current – a nurse reported to the authors that an old cockney woman patient asked her to wash her pleasure gardens – although it has persisted from the 16th century. It is one of the most pleasant terms of its sort, with links to the image of the Garden of Eden, and other positive connotations of health and fertility. It has a string of associated, but now largely obsolete terms such as garden gate, the labia; garden hedge, the pubic hair; garden house, brothel; garden goddess, prostitute; gentleman's pleasure garden (and grotto), the vagina; pleasure garden padlock, sanitary towel; and –inevitably – gardener, the penis. It is quite likely that the common modern phrase 'leading someone up the garden path' is related, although today it is used quite innocently without awareness of its possible erotic connotations. *See also* GREENS.

gash The vagina. Although its sounds peculiarly modern in its crudity and violence, this term has been in use from the 18th century at least. It is another in the tradition of words that describe the vagina in terms of a bloody wound: *see also* CAT WITH ITS THROAT CUT, and SPLIT ARSE. And as with many other words meaning 'cunt', gash has also come to mean woman, or women – e.g. 'Is there any gash around?'

gasp and grunt The vagina. Cockney rhyming slang for cunt. *See also* GROWL AND GRUNT, GRUMBLE AND GRUNT, JOE HUNT, SHARP AND BLUNT.

gay Homosexual. Although the term is applied widely to both homosexual men and women, there is undoubtedly a sense that gay has been appropriated by men – gay bar, gay club, and gay disco refer to aspects of a male culture. As a result many women homosexuals, particularly in the UK, prefer to call themselves lesbians.

Historically the word has had a multiplicity of meanings. Since its medieval French origins gay has always carried connotations of 'immorality' – in addition to its standard sense of 'joyful'. According to one source (Michael Taylor), in medieval Provencal French 'gay' referred to 'female immorality'. This sense was soon carried into English: according to the OED it was often euphemistic 'of immoral life' (1637). By the

19th century gay was used to refer to 'women leading an immoral or a harlot's life' (OED).

To 'turn gay', or to 'lead a gay life' still had the meaning 'to become a prostitute' between the world wars. Partridge lists gay bit for harlot, gay house for brothel, gay in the groin for a 'loose' woman, to gay it for sexual intercourse, and gaying instrument for penis.

Only post World War II did the word take on the now almost exclusive sense of homosexual, which has quite usurped the sense of 'joyful'. The Gay Liberation movement and newspapers like *Gay News* can claim responsibility for this huge shift in meaning, marking a major change in social attitudes. By the end of the 70s singers like Tom Robinson were publicly celebrating a form of sexuality previously treated as criminal perversion in hits like 'Glad To Be Gay'.

gayola Bribes paid by gay men to police officers in order to evade arrest for sexual misdemeanours. A pun on payola. US usage.

gear The genitals. Nowadays the term refers almost exclusively to the male genitalia – as in 'wedding gear' – and is used jokingly and affectionately. The expression dates back as far as the 16th century, when it referred to both male and female parts.

There is also the alternative meaning of homosexual, from rhyming slang with queer, but this form is rare.

gee (or possibly **ghee**) The female sexual parts. A recently very popular form of slang among Irish males. Origins unknown – any association with the Indian word for clarified butter?

gender bender Men or women – usually belonging to pop culture – who adopt an androgenous or transsexual image. At the beginning of 1984 the term was coined to describe the new pop stars like Boy George and Marilyn (a sequinned male singer) who wear makeup and wear 'feminine' clothing, and Annie Lennox of The Eurythmics who appeared in both male and female roles in a video of the band's music.

The *Sunday Mirror* ran this special report on 22 January 1984:

'THE GENDER BENDERS – why girls like boys like George.

'They are shocking. They are outrageous. They call themselves the Gender Benders – the latest youth cult to follow in the high-heeled footsteps of bizarre pop idols Boy George and Marilyn.

'Gender Bender boys are mad about make-up and adore dressing up. And the girls love it. Amazingly, they find it tremendously sexy.

'Our research shows that most Gender Benders are anything but gay ... They make-up and dress

87

up out of a sense of fashion. And the girls find it a turn-on.'

Although the *Sunday Mirror* confined their investigation to males, a concurrent issue of *Woman* magazine depicted Annie Lennox as a part of the same trend away from traditional 'feminine' and 'macho' sexual delineations.

generating tool Also generation tool. The penis, from a pun on the electrical and procreative meaning of generating, combined with the well-worn sense of 'tool', dating back to 19th century Britain and now rarely heard. Not surprisingly the female counterpart is 'generating place' for vagina.

geography The female genitals. An allusion to the destination of 'exploring hands', now considered quaint and rarely used.

gert stonkers! A great pair of breasts. This is still current Somerset slang, 'gert' a dialect form of great, stonkers being a port- manteau word for anything considered tremendous. This is a true rustic term of admiration.

get off with To have a sexual encounter with. This is one of the most common expressions in use by the younger, courting generation in the UK, and it includes all forms of sexual activity from kissing to intercourse. It usually refers to a first experience – as in 'She got off with George at a party, and they've been going out ever since.'

But the phrase has a history far less liberated than most modern users appreciate. According to the OED it has the mid-19th century meaning 'to succeed in marrying one's daughters'. It evolved, meaning getting engaged or married, but was only jokingly used of males. The recent sense of mutual sexual attraction leading to action only evolved gradually between the world wars.

A variant, referring explicitly to sexual intercourse, is 'to get among it'.

get on my wick To get on a person's nerves. But the origins – wick/Hampton Wick – rhyming slang for prick are largely forgotten, and women often use the phrase with impunity. *See* HAMPTON WICK.

get it up, to To have an erection. Generally used (by men and women) in the negative form – 'He can't get it up' – and as such considered a deadly insult. Contemporary UK and US usage.

getting it Sexual intercourse. This bland euphemism generally occurs in question form – as in 'Have you been getting it lately?', or 'Have you been getting any?'. Yet so innocuous is the innuendo that even milk commercials on family television shows have used the slogan 'Are you getting enough?'. To 'get it' is almost completely interchangeable with 'to give it'. *See* GIVE HER ONE.

'To get' is also used in numerous compounds meaning sexual intercourse: *see* END, ROCKS OFF, HOLE, OATS, JOLLIES, KICKS.

giblets The genitals. Usually found in compound forms like to join giblets – to have sex, or to get married, and to have a bit of giblet pie, or do a bit of giblet – sexual intercourse. Old fashioned, but still used by some Londoners.

giggle stick Penis. Cockney rhyming slang for prick, this is an untypically allusive example of the genre. Also giggling pin, gut stick and joy stick. *See also* HAMPTON WICK, MAD MICK, PAT AND MICK.

gigolo Man who prostitutes himself to women or makes his sexual services readily available. More generally used however as a term of contempt for any man who fancies himself and his success with women. The modern sense has developed from the 1927 meaning, a professional male dancer, itself taken from the feminine 'gigolette' – a 'young woman of easy virtue' (OED). *See also* HUSTLER.

gimcrack The vagina. A combination of the image of a cheap toy – found elsewhere in slang, *see also* WHIM – and the long established 'crack'. UK slang dating back to the 19th century but now largely obsolete.

ginger beer Homosexual. From cockney rhyming slang with queer. Commonly shortened to ginger.

girl From its basic OED meaning of female child, girl has acquired a string of slang usages. The most common of these, dating back to the 16th century, are those of woman, girlfriend or female sexual partner. A man's 'best girl' is still in use after generations to denote the one he hopes to stay with or marry.

There are many slang compounds: girl show – a ballet or revue; girl-trap – a seducer; girlery, or girl-shop – a brothel; girlometer, or girl catcher – the penis. But, like the verb 'to girl', or 'to go girling' – i.e. consorting with or having sex with women – these terms are well out of date.

But the venerable 'old girl', an affectionate expression for a woman friend of any age, is still common. And the use of girl or more commonly 'girlie' to suggest sex is still the norm – hence 'girlie mag' for pornographic magazine, and 'girlie pictures' for porn photographs.

But there is a glaring anomaly in the modern usage of 'girl'. Mature and even elderly women are still referred to as 'girl' – whereas no male over the age of puberty is likely to be called 'boy'. This piece about Princess Diana (the *Sun* 28 Oct. 1983) is a prime example: 'The Princess watched a hair-care demonstration and told young mum Sherol Hansom: "Men don't know what we girls have to go through." '

And as such, the widespread application of 'girl' to women of all ages reinforces and reflects the assumptions of our culture that females are more vulnerable and childlike and less mature, responsible and logical than males. The origins of the word underline this point. In Middle English, 'girl' was used for a child or young person of *either* sex, until in the 16th century its usage was confined to female children.

The equating of girl with child is even more explicit in the traditional Irish question about the sex of a new baby – 'Is it a boy or a child?'

girlfriend Woman as a partner in a sexual and/or romantic relationship – with a man or sometimes woman. But often – especially in North America – when used by one woman about another, she simply means female friend without sexual connotation. *See also* GIRL.

With the continuing trend away from marriage, the meaning of girlfriend has been stretched to the limit, and women belonging to couples in committed relationships who have lived together for years are still given this label by uncomfortable friends and relatives – just as the woman in the earliest days of a relationship is 'the new girlfriend.'

Historically, the term is of US origin, arriving in London in the 20s, and once referred to 'illicit sexual' relationships!

gism or **gissom** Semen. Common UK male usage. Sometimes spelled jessom. A firm favourite with heterosexual porn magazines.

give head, to Fellatio. Widespread US term, gay and heterosexual.

give her one To have sexual intercourse with a woman. This is a very common phrase among Jack-the-lad types, who every time they set eyes on an attractive woman will say, 'Cor, I wouldn't mind giving her one ...'

The implication – as in so much sexual slang – is that the male is the only active partner in sex.

An old-fashioned equivalent, which incorporates the common theme of weaponry, is 'to give a shot'. Also 'give a thrill' and 'give her a bit of the other'.

glad eye A sexually inviting look, as in the phrase 'I saw him give you the glad eye, Beryl'. Outmoded, with a definite 30s flavour, but enjoying a new popularity with sections of today's youth. 'Glad rags', for party clothes, is however fading from slang usage.

glick, to To eat cottage cheese out of a woman's knickers. This is a term used by a limited group of people in Dublin, mostly for its shock value in conversation, but a certain amount of doubt remains as to whether the word was invented for this purpose alone, or whether 'glicking' is an established practice (E. Mellon, Dublin 1983).

globes Breasts. A universally understood image. In widespread usage for over a century at least.

glue pot In reference to the aromas of sexual intercourse. Principally found in the old-fashioned expression 'the glue pot is unstuck' which (according to Partridge) is a catch-phrase from 1890 meaning: 'He gives off the odour of a genital exudation or of a seminal emission.'

gnawing the 'nana Fellatio. One of the more engaging Barry Humphreyisms, and still largely Australian. *See also* TUMMY BANANA.

go Sexual intercourse, most commonly in the form 'go all the way'. This expression dates back to the 1920s, but is still widespread especially among young women – as in 'Have you ever been all the way?', or 'Did you go all the way with him?'

Among men, usage tends to take the form of crude enthusiasm about women's sexual appetites – as in 'She goes like the clappers', or 'I bet she goes like a train'.

goat A lecherous man. Generally used in disgust by a female of a male, as in 'Get your hands off me, you dirty old goat.'

It is a well-established meaning: the OED has the definition 'A licentious man' from 1675. Some old-fashioned compounds are goats gig, or goat's jig – sexual intercourse (from the 18th century); goat house – brothel: goat milker – prostitute, or vagina (early 19th century); and to look goats and monkeys at – to look lecherously at. *See* MONKEY, for comparable usage of an animal image.

gobble To perform fellatio or cunnilingus. Belonging to the widespread 'eating' imagery of oral sex common in the US and UK. Hence also 'gobbler', as one who performs the act.

The term had a related, but now outdated usage in Britain: A 'gobble-prick' was 'a rampant, lustful woman' from the 18th century (Grose).

go down Oral sex. One of the most widespread of US terms for fellatio and/or cunnilingus, its usage has spread to the UK but without losing the American flavour. *See also* GIVE HEAD.

goer A person considered sexually enthusiastic and/or athletic. More often applied by men to women than vice versa, as in 'I wouldn't mind giving her one, I bet she's a real goer'. *See also* GO.

go it alone Masturbation. Generally male, ironic usage only.

gold-digger Woman thought to be luring a rich man into marriage in order to get her hands on his money. The origin is American from the 1920s, but the term entered UK slang in the 30s and is now firmly established, especially in popular newspaper usage where stories of celebrities and 'fortune-hunting' females abound.

golden shower The practice of urine fetishism. It is becoming more common in US gay bars to 'take a golden shower' – i.e. be urinated upon, or 'give a golden shower'. Unwary visitors to the gents beware! This is not, however, an exclusively gay practice.

Champagne fountain, orangeade, warm beer are US synonyms. The term – like the practice – is as yet less common in the UK.

good Very commonly found in terms of admiration for a man or woman's sexual prowess – as in 'good at it', 'good in bed' (or 'GIB'), 'good at the game', and 'good lay'. To 'have a good time' has also had a sexual connotation since the 17th century, and today it means, explicitly, sexual intercourse. Less common these days is the synonymous 'have a bit of goods'.

And still very common as a throw-away phrase with strong sexual 'wink-wink nudge-nudge' innuendo is 'If you can't be good

be careful', uttered indiscriminately by men and women as a form of 'goodbye'.

good looker, good looking Attractive man or woman. Common both as a description and as a form of address – as in the famous US catch phrase – 'Hey, Good-looking!'

go off the boil To lose interest in sex, or a sexual relationship. Despite its reference to sexual 'heat', the cosy domestic image makes this phrase quite acceptable in 'polite' company. Affectionate but slightly dated, and used by novelist H.E. Bates in his books about the Larkin family, written in the 1950s.

goolies Testicles. One of the most widespread, non-erotic words for the male 'tackle', generally used in a hearty, sporting context – 'Poor old Johnny got a terrible blow in the goolies'. It has a venerable English history, dating back to the 19th century, but has yet to cross the Atlantic successfully. Partridge suggests its root could be 'gully', meaning a game of marbles – by association with the glass 'balls'.

goose To pinch the buttocks. Common UK heterosexual usage. Related is the US gay usage of inserting a finger in the anus, and also the Canadian meaning – a pederast.

In English, goose and its many compounds have long had a sexual connotation. Goose's neck or gooser had the 19th century meaning of penis, while goose was a prostitute, VD, a woman, and sexual intercourse. Goose grease had the meaning vaginal secretions, the goose month was the time of a woman's confinement in pregnancy (for the husband it was the gander month), and goose and duck was rhyming slang for fuck. Gooseberry puddin' was rhyming slang for old woman, while gooseberries meant testicles.

go out with To have a romantic and/or sexual relationship with. People who are 'going out together' are assumed to be unmarried, or at least, not *yet* married. The origin of the term is the old-fashioned 'dating' system in which 'boyfriends' took 'girlfriends' out for the evening, but by now it is so deeply entrenched that its origins are obscured. Hence the popular song by British singer Joe Jackson about a jealous would-be lover – 'Is She Really Going Out With Him?'

The Irish equivalent is to 'go with', a form which has survived from the 1890s when it meant both 'to go out with' and to have sexual intercourse with.

gopher tits Male breasts. Modern US gay male term, in affectionate reference to the comical rodent.

gorilla salad Pubic hair, especially when thick and coarse. This is a mostly US term originally gay

but increasingly popular amongst heterosexuals in America and Britain. Many long-established UK equivalents also use the vegetation imagery. *See* GREENS, and GARDEN.

go steady To have a regular, committed relationship with a 'boyfriend' or 'girlfriend'. The term was originally post-war North American, and probably came to the UK in the 50s through the host of Hollywood movies in which no greater bliss existed than the chance of 'going steady' with the hero. It is now definitely dated, but is enjoying a new semi-humorous vogue among some middle-class youngsters. Hence a young Oxford student recently, amidst gales of laughter from her friends: 'Guess what, Hughie has asked me if we can go steady ...'

gowhunk A Limerick man who indulges in the practice of sniffing women's bicycle seats (J. Jackson). For UK regional variations *see* SCHNARF, SNURGE. These describe the activity, but we know of no British word for the participant. Contributions very welcome.

grappling Heavy petting. Mostly Anglo-Irish female usage. The comic image is more intense and suggestive of struggle than the similar sounding 'groping'.

gravy Sexual transudate, male or female. Hence to give gravy – sexual intercourse, gravy giver –

the penis, gravy maker – the vagina.

greens Sexual intercourse. Also 'after one's greens', and 'go for one's greens'. Although rarely heard today, this image is in the same tradition as the still extant 'pleasure gardens' and 'gorilla salad'. Related terms are green-grocery and green meadow, for the female parts; fresh greens, for a new sexual partner or prostitute, the price of greens – the cost of a prostitute and green grove – pubic hair (Partridge).
'Groceries' is still in use as a US gay term for genitalia.

grind Sexual intercourse. Another in the aggressive, penetrative line of slang – *see also* SCREW. Considered crude and so more widely used by men than women, although the phrase 'bump and grind' for sexual intercourse is less likely to offend.
First usage goes back to the 16th century, since when 'to do a grind' has become a common term for sexual intercourse. On the grind referred to prostitutes, as on the game does today. A grinding house was a brothel, grinding tools or the grindstone were the female sexual parts.

grope To fondle sexually. Very widespread among younger people and often used without condem-nation – as in 'I haven't had a good grope for ages', or 'Did you see any groping going on at the party?' But at times women use the term with disgust at unwanted sexual advances – 'My boss won't stop groping me', and, as a nickname, 'Groper' for men with 'wandering hands'.

growl and grunt Cockney rhyming slang for cunt, often shortened to growl. Hence the old-fashioned 'growl-biter', for cunnilingist. *See also* GASP AND GRUNT, GRUMBLE AND GRUNT – all suggesting the animal noises of sexual intercourse.

grumble and grunt Cockney rhyming slang for cunt, often shortened to grumble. It also has the meaning sexual intercourse. *See* GROWL AND GRUNT.

gut entrance Also front gut. The vagina. Based on the same deliberate mistake as 'top bollocks' and 'front bum', but the effect is repellent rather than amusing. Related and equally unflattering are gut fucker or gut sticker for male gay, and gutter – the vagina. The predominant associations of these words are filth and disgust – from their sound as much as anything else.

gutter crawler *See* KERB CRAWLER.

H

H, doing the The act of buggery. The shape of the letter is supposed to represent the figure of one man behind another person. Currently a popular slang term among London male media folk.

had *See* HAVE.

hair A woman. To 'be after hair' or a 'hairy bit' is to pursue a woman for sex (Partridge). These uses are now virtually obsolete, but *see* HAIR-PIE etc. for current variants.

hair-pie The female genitals. Also hairy-hole, sometimes addressed abusively to women. Widespread male working-class UK and US usage. *See also* FUR-PIE. Less common synonyms are hairy oracle and hairy ring, and the now sadly lost 'Hairyfordshire' (Partridge).

hair splitter The penis. Apart from punning on the sense 'to split hairs', this term depends upon the use of 'hair' for the female genitals – *see* HAIR, and HAIR-PIE.

half-cocked, to go off For a man to break off a sexual encounter midway to orgasm and so be semi-satisfied – or, to ejaculate prematurely. The euphemism puns on the image of the penis as a gun, and has been used in James Bond films when the hero is interrupted by a call from HQ in the middle of a love-making session. *See also* FIRE A SHOT.

half-mast With trouser flies open, and also, having a semi-erect penis. To tell a man that he is 'flying at half-mast' is the social equivalent of saying 'you've got egg on your chin', and passes as an acceptable way of dropping a hint to do up his trousers.

hammer The penis. Canadian slang since World War II. This is an obvious phallic image, which also conveys the action of violent striking common in sexual slang – *see also* BANG, and FUCK. At the same time the hammer is a 'tool', another recurrent image in slang. Surprising then that this rather unpleasant term isn't more popular.

Hampton Wick Penis. Cockney rhyming slang for 'prick', often shortened to Hampton. The name comes from the London suburb, and this is one of the more widely known rhyming slang terms.

handbag Male homosexual. UK male heterosexual slang, drawing on the stereotypical effeminate image of the gay male as a pseudo-woman who minces about with a handbag on his arm – that this is what women do is taken for granted. *See also* NANCE, MOLLY, EFFIE etc.

hand job Masturbation, generally male. Widespread UK usage among men. Also to 'go off by hand', and 'to bring down by hand', while 'to bring up by hand' is to raise an erection. Related American terms are 'hand reared' – to describe a man's large penis, and 'hand made' said of a large penis supposedly developed by frequent exercise (Rodgers). And an old-fashioned UK term for the penis is 'handstaff' – not to be confused with 'handwarmers' – the breasts.

hangers The testicles. (Also sometimes the breasts.) Perhaps used most graphically to mean the former by the jockey Willy Carson: When asked by *Woman* magazine (June 1983) whether he thought the new fashion for women's bodybuilding was attractive, he replied with an emphatic 'NO', arguing that if women were meant to have muscles, they'd also have 'two hangers and a night fighter'. *Woman* didn't print this reply.

96

hanky panky Sexual activity, usually illicit, from casual kissing at a party to full scale intercourse. Originally in mid-19th century Britain the term meant conjuring, from which it quickly developed the sense of trickery, underhand or naughty activities. The term has retained its popularity for generations and today's youngsters still use it frequently for its Benny Hill quality of naughtiness. Hence a *News of the World* feature (12 Feb 1984), about a singles' skiing holiday, quotes one 'brunette Jan Dubois' as saying, 'If you're looking for hanky-panky, you'll find it everywhere.' However it is not a classless term: according to *The Complete Naff Guide* to call sex 'hanky panky' is about as 'naff' as talking about a 'leg over situation'.

Hansom cabs Crabs. Cockney rhyming slang, now virtually obsolete, but *see also* BEATTIE AND BABS.

happy hunting ground The vagina. Male slang. The notion of heaven here rolled up with the age-old language of sexual pursuit. The male is hunter, the female the hunted. *Compare* HAPPY VALLEY.

happy valley The cleavage between the buttock cheeks. US male gay slang. This is primarily the name of a US ski resort, and the term puns on the notion of a pleasurable place in which to slide the phallus.

hard-on An erection. Widespread UK and US usage. Contrast 'hardly' – a very small erection. In Britain the term dates back at least a century, with variations like 'to give soft for hard' – sexual intercourse (Partridge).

haricot A homosexual. From rhyming slang with haricot bean = queen. *See also* IRON.

hatter *See* BROWN HAT.

have, to Sexual intercourse. Extremely common form of expression in the US and UK, among men and women. Generally found in phrases like 'to have it off', 'to have it away', 'I haven't had it for months'.

have it away day In jocular reference to the day-return ('Away Day') train tickets on which an increasing number of women are travelling to London in order to earn money as prostitutes or by working in the sex industry. Contemporary slang among women in Soho.

have the painters in, to *See* PAINTERS IN.

Haymarket *See* JUMP OFF AT HAYMARKET.

head The bulb at the end of the penis. Hence the mostly US term for fellatio – 'to give head'. Slang since the 1960s at least. *See also* HELMET.

headache, to have a The classic excuse from a woman to a man, given as a reason to avoid having sex. Now widely used in the jesting catch phrase – 'Not tonight darling, I've got a headache.'

heart throb A person who is the object of sexual desire and fantasy. Hence many pop stars who appeal to youngsters are known as 'teenage heart throbs', and a February issue of *Woman* magazine ran the headline 'Heart throbbing' on its cover to commemorate Valentine's day.

heavy petting Intimate sexual fondling, but excluding penetration. A widespread term predominantly in the US but also used in the UK. Associated largely with youthful explorations of sex, when boys and girls are either reluctant to lose their virginity and/or afraid of pregnancy.

heeler *See* LITTLE HEELER.

heirs The unisex form of the pronouns his/hers, rolled into one – as suggested by the so-called masculist Hugh de Garis.

hello sailor The camp greeting intended as a joke about homosexuality, from the popular notion that sailors spend their long ocean voyages perpetrating acts of buggery. Hence also the gay disco song 'In the Navy', and the song 'Frigging in the Rigging'. 'Hello Sailor' has been in circulation since the 1940s when it became a popular radio catchphrase in the UK.

helmet The 'head' of the penis. Sometimes as 'German helmet'.

he-man 'All confidence and coition' – Partridge's definition shows that the meaning of he-man hasn't changed for generations, and he traces it back to 1906. *See also* MACHO.

hen Woman or girl. Affectionate name, used by men and women. Mostly north of England slang. However the affection is less evident in derivatives like 'henpecked' – of a man supposedly bullied by a domineering woman, and 'hen house' – a household where the woman rules the roost. Nor is the all-female 'hen party' ascribed much glamour or dignity – in contrast to the male equivalent, the 'stag party'. *See also* BIRD.

her indoors *See* 'ER INDOORS.

hermes A carrier of the infectious venereal disease herpes. The joke stems from the name of the aircraft carrier, and is increasingly widely told in the UK:
Q. Have you got herpes?
A. No, Hermes – I'm a carrier.

hershey bar Male homosexual. This is originally US slang, from the name of the famous American chocolate bar (*see also* CHOCOLATE BANDIT), but is becoming increasingly common in the UK. Also growing in popularity is the term for the sexual route chosen by many gays – 'up the hershey highway'.

hickey A 'love bite', generally on the neck. This is a widespread term – and preoccupation – among Canadian and US youth.

hide the sausage Sexual intercourse. Mostly male UK slang with strongly childish overtones of hide and seek. Sausage is a common image for the penis – *see also* 'chucking a sausage down the Old Kent Road', *under* CHUCKING A WORM UP THE MERSEY TUNNEL.

high Russian *See* BIG J. Also sometimes 'high Texan'.

hit or miss Kiss. From cockney rhyming slang.

hole The vagina. Dating back at least to Shakespearian times, very common UK male slang, as in 'Did you get your hole last night?', or 'How's your hairy hole?' Women however generally find the usage offensive – not surprising in view of the fact that it describes the sexual organs in terms of a nothing, or an absence.

Drawing on this sense is the phrase 'a hole in one' – a pun on the rare golfing achievement – referring to the unusual accident of getting pregnant as a result of having intercourse for the first time.

homework Girlfriend (Partridge). A part of the old-fashioned tradition of describing the female

98

partner as – literally – one to be worked on at home, and so the passive recipient of the male's propensity for 'tooling' and 'doing the business'. *See also KNITTING*.

homo Widespread abbreviation of 'homosexual', and when used by heterosexuals – as it has been for 50 years – not intended kindly. A popular taunt among English schoolboys is to abbreviate this even further and shout 'Mo' at a boy they wish to brand as 'queer'.

hooker, a A prostitute. Still a mainly US term, but widely understood in the UK and found in the recent Sunday supplement headline like 'Havens for Hookers' – about prostitution in Soho.

hop on Sexual intercourse. A popular phrase with men and women in the UK and – especially – Ireland, where the standard question after a night out is often 'Did he hop on you then?' or 'Did you hop on her?' Note the male does the 'hopping' – as in 'hop into the horse collar' (*see* HORSE COLLAR).

horizontal exercise Sexual intercourse. Also 'horizontalize'. Not often heard in slang, but more often in epithets like 'dancing is the vertical expression of a horizontal desire'. 'A horizontal' was a 19th century term for a 'courtesan' (Partridge).

horn An erection. Also the penis. 'To feel horny' is to feel sexually excited, and 'to cure the horn' is for a man to have sexual intercourse. This is still very common UK slang among men, from its phallic imagery and implications of hardness. However women – especially in America – do at times refer to themselves as 'horny'.

horse collar The female genitals. Hence 'to hop into the horse collar' is a male term for sexual intercourse.

Horseshoe is also an old-fashioned UK term for the 'pudenda' (Partridge), while 'to horse' is shorthand for intercourse. The latter dates back to the 17th century.

horse's hoof Homosexual. From rhyming slang with poof. Less common than iron hoof or iron.

hortus The female genitals. From the Latin, meaning garden. This is by now obsolete, but remains of interest for its connection with still-contemporary terms like 'pleasure garden'. *See also* GREENS.

hospitals, playing Sexual intercourse. Mock-childish slang, based on the sexual play of children who undress and inspect each other's bodies in the game of 'hospitals'. Equivalent to 'playing doctors and nurses', from the same source.

hot To be sexually excited or to fancy someone. Used by and of both men and women, as in – 'He (or she) has the hot's for you', or 'he's got hot pants for her'. 'Hot stuff' is anything or any person who is sexy.

An article on male impotence in the March issue of the young women's magazine *Cosmopolitan* quotes the case of Angela: 'Both my recent boyfriends have been hot and randy on the way back to my place – but as soon as we get into bed – Pssssst ...'

Partridge notes 'hot session' and 'hot roll with cream' for sexual intercourse, and 'hot milk' for semen, while 'hot meat', 'hot mutton/beef' had the old-fashioned UK meaning of woman *and* the female genitals. Yet another equation of woman and 'cunt'.

housewife The female genitals. Several old-fashioned UK expressions have depicted the female parts as a warm and cosy sanctuary as in 'home sweet home' and 'house under the hill' (Partridge). However, given the negative force of the synonymous 'cunt', this hardly reflects well on the 'housewife': note also that the term 'hussy' for woman, is also a decendant of the term.

huffle, to The mostly gay male practice of having sex by inserting the penis into a partner's armpit. *Also* 'to bagpipe'.

hump, to To have sexual intercourse. A venerable (from the 18th century) and still widespread term in the US and UK, among men and women. Equivalent to 'bonk'. Not so offensive as to prevent quick sales in Australia of T-shirts bearing the single motto 'hump'. Compare the image with 'beast with two backs'.

hung like a donkey Referring to the (large) size of a man's penis. Also often as 'well hung' – a term popular in pornography, and as the genial Irish inquiry between men about the state of the world – 'How's it hanging?'

hunk A sexually attractive man. Also sometimes as 'hunky'. The origin is probably Australian from 'a hunk of beef', and 'hunk' still conveys the sense of a man who is big and muscular. Generally used by women as a term of high praise for a man's physique. Widespread in the US and UK.

husband's supper, warming the A jokey catch phrase referring to the practice (in women) of standing in front of the fire and raising one's skirts to warm the behind. UK slang from c 1860, but now obsolete.

hustler A prostitute, male or female. This is related to the old-fashioned term 'to hustle' – to have sexual intercourse. The term is more common in the US than in the UK: the actor Jon Voigt in the film 'Midnight Cowboy' aspired to being a hustler. *See also* HOOKER.

I

IBM Small penis. Initials stand for 'itty bitty meat' and also as a pun on the computer firm. US origin and usage, mostly camp slang.

iceberg Sexually cold person. Usually applied by rejected men to women who, they rationalize, must be 'frigid'. Derogatory but also jocular, as in 'You haven't a chance with her, she's a real iceberg.'

ice cream machine The penis. Somewhat dated US usage from the 60s. Enough to put anyone off Mr Whippy. Note the exaggerated, cartoon quality of the image, implying impossible bulk and creaminess of semen. *Compare* LOVE BUTTER.

ice job Fellatio performed with ice cubes or ice cream in the mouth. Hence the fellator becomes the 'icing expert'.

icky A US term of distaste for some of the less pleasant, more tangible manifestations of sex.

Hence the joke about the WASP couple who go to the doctor to find out why they are failing to procreate. The husband eventually confesses that his wife won't let him 'come' – 'Buffy says it's icky!'

I couldn't eat that Male expression of distaste for a woman. As in so many such phrases the female's identity is reduced to an object as 'that' or 'it'.

ID The penis. From the abbreviation for identification. Mostly US male gay/camp usage, as in 'let's see your I.D.'

I didn't ask what keepsyour ears apart! Sparring riposte in answer to the exclamation 'Bollocks!' Sounds like it has parade-ground Sergeant Major origins, which indeed it has.

if you can't be good, be careful! Common as a parting comment from one woman to another – especially as one goes out for the evening – implying that if she

101

can't say no to a man's sexual advances, at least she can protect herself from pregnancy. The tone is generally arch and conspiratorial, a bit of 'wink, wink, nudge, nudge' disguised as advice.

if you drop a fiver in Bandon, kick it all the way to Cork An Irish catch phrase referring to the supposedly numerous male homosexuals in Bandon, Co. Cork. The fear of 'straight' men that it is dangerous to bend over in the company of gays lest they be immediately buggered is a recurrent theme in slang. *See also* DON'T DROP YOUR CAR KEYS.

impale To penetrate sexually. Yet another in the aggressive weaponry line of images.

in-and-out Sexual intercourse. This old-fashioned English term has become established in the US. Often embellished as a compound phrase, as 'a quick in-and-out job' – hurried sexual intercourse – indicates. *See also* 'WHAM, BANG, THANK YOU MA'AM (or man)'.

inch (or sometimes **incher**) The penis; thus to inch is to have sexual intercourse. Often the inch element is quantified, indicating the male obsession with the length of his organ. Hence the boastful 'I gave her my full nine inches'.

in circulation Socially available, but with the implication of being also sexually available.

in flagrante In the act of sexual intercourse. A comon middle-class and slightly risqué expression abbreviated from the Latin *in flagrante delicto* – which is the formal legal euphemism. It is now trendy, dinner party set usage, more classy than 'in the act'.

ingle-nook The vagina. From the word for chimney corner. Rather twee image, with warm and cosy connotations but also not the only one to represent the female part as a hot and gaping hole. Note that 'ingle' has the old 1631 meaning 'to fondle', and also the mid-19th century sense 'catamite' (OED).

inhale the oyster Fellatio and/or cunnilingus. By association with inhale as a US slang word for 'eat', and the traditional sexual connotations of the oyster meaning the penis, the vagina or semen.

in honour of someone In reference to masturbatory fantasies as discussed in male-only conversations: 'I had a wank in honour of so-and-so ...'

in-laws In slang, the parents of one's girlfriend or boyfriend. Originally the term referred only to the relations of married people – Queen Victoria is recorded as using the term in 1894 (Blackwoods) – but today with the decline in the popularity of marriage it is used in rueful reference to the mother or father of any sexual partner. As in 'I'm stuck with the in-laws this Christmas. Might as well get married!'

102

inner sanctum The vagina among heterosexuals, the anus among male gays. In the same line of mock-pious imagery as 'temple of love'. US and UK usage.

in season Desiring sex or available for sex. From the animal imagery of the breeding season.

intentions, are they honourable? Like other expressions which once referred formally to marriage or betrothal (*see* IN-LAWS), the old fashioned form has been maintained in semi-parody of the traditional idea. At one time the assumption was that if a gentleman's intentions towards a lady were honourable he would ask her to marry him. Today the same question means 'Are you trying to get him or her into bed?'

Similarly, a person's 'intended', previously their fiance(e), is now used ironically as simply a girl-friend or boyfriend.

interested in only one thing Catch phrase traditionally uttered by indignant women about men whose prime objective is to have sex. Now considered primly old fashioned and more likely to be used in flirtatious reproof than in condemnation.

interested in the opposite sex(or **not interested**) A euphemism still very common among the older generation to indicate what shape a person's sexuality – usually a son's or daughter's – is taking. *Not* interested can be a polite way

of saying 'gay', while interested is usually relieved confirmation of 'normal' heterosexuality.

Interflora Sexual intercourse between 'hippies'. Now dated, this was a 60s pun on intercourse, flower power and the florists' service.

in the closet *See* CLOSET.

in the family way Pregnant. A very common and polite euphemism, more likely to be used by older people. Now almost Standard English.

in the game Being a male gay. Mostly US usage. *Contrast with* the UK term for prostitution – ON THE GAME.

in the hay Sexual intercourse. From the fanciful idea of sex as a 'roll in the hay'. Less common than 'in the sack', mostly male usage.

in the nip Naked. Widespread innocuous usage by men and women – as in 'I always sleep in the nip'. Also in the nub, in the nud, in the nuddy – from nude.

in the pudding club, also**in the club** and **in for it** Pregnant. Widespread, mostly lower middle-class and working-class usage, late 19th century origin and still common. *See also* BUN IN THE OVEN.

into a woman, be or get Sexual intercourse. A common male expression, as in 'I'd really like to

103

get into that one' or 'into her knickers'. Interestingly, the same form when used of a man by a man in the UK – 'he laid into him' – means to fight. The recurring theme of weaponry and attack in sexual slang suggests these usages are not far apart in meaning.

introduce Charlie Sexual intercourse. Charlie represents the penis, in the pattern of male names given to the organ – *see* DICK, JOHN THOMAS, MICKEY etc.

in trousers, anything *See* ANYTHING IN TROUSERS.

invert A homosexual. More dismissive than the normal 'gay' but less offensive than 'queer'. 20th century usage but dated in the UK.

invitation to the waltz Sexual intercourse. *See* WALTZ.

Irish fortune The vagina. Presumably the idea is that to have a vagina is a woman's bad luck. Hence derogatory male usage only.

Irish root The penis. Dating back to WW1, it's hard to fathom this image, but in English slang anything 'Irish' is traditionally a joke.

Irish toothache An erection (or sometimes a pregnancy – *see* ITA). The 'joke' is lost in the mists of time – this phrase dates back to the turn of the century – but if current Irish jokes are anything to

go by, it was probably something to do with the supposed ignorance of the Irish. The expression has survived, at least in working-class London.

iron Male homosexual. From rhyming slang with iron hoof = poof (or even iron hoove = poove). In the UK it has also had the meaning male prostitute, now obsolete. One of the most enduring and popular working-class expressions for gay.

irrigate, to To have sexual intercourse. A coarse working-class expression with obvious imagery. *Compare with* LUBRICATE.

it Perhaps the most widespread and variable of all euphemisms for sexual activity, 'it' stands for the penis – as in 'shove it', 'stick it up', or in the song 'Lie down girl let me push it up, push it up' ('Wet Dream', Max Romeo) – and also for the vagina – 'You're not allowed to touch it'.

But more often than not 'it' stands for sexual intercourse – *see* DO IT. so pervasive is the euphemism that catch phrases like 'It's naughty but it's nice', originally a line from a popular song at the turn of the century, swiftly developed a sexual innuendo, and today advertisers use the same phrase to advertise cream cakes – with more than a hint of subliminal imagery.

'It' also has the long-established meaning of sex appeal. During the 20s, Clara Bow – one of Hollywood's first screen goddesses – was known as 'the It girl'.

ITA (Irish toothache) Pregnant. It also has the meaning erection – *see* IRISH TOOTHACHE. Long-standing UK usage.

itch, the Sexual urge. Generally occurs in expressions like 'she's a bitch with an itch', or 'the seven-year itch', widely known as the time when after several years of marriage a husband or wife gets restless and starts to look for extra-marital liasons. This use of 'itch' dates back to the 17th century.

Related expressions are 'to play at itch buttocks' – to have sexual intercourse – and 'itcher' or 'itching Jenny' – the vagina.

To 'have an itchy back' is an old Australian euphemism for sexual desire – purportedly from the requests of women to their husbands to scratch their backs, in the hope that one form of contact will lead to another.

it takes two to tango Euphemistic expression implying that in any sexual indiscretion both partners take a share of the blame. Originally this was a line from a popular song. Australian, from 1933, but now dated.

ivory gate The vagina. An old-fashioned literary euphemism (Partridge).

ivory pearl Girl. Rhyming slang. Less common than ocean pearl.

I wouldn't do it even with somebody else's UK male expression of disgust towards a woman. But the phrase betrays extraordinary arrogance: in effect the man is saying he would not do the woman the favour of having sex with her even if he (somehow) didn't have to use his own penis!

Comparable is the phrase in which a man shows his distaste for what he considers another man's lack of sexual discrimination: 'I wouldn't stick my walking stick where you put your prick.'

J

Jack Today principally found in the form 'to jack off' meaning to masturbate. This is almost exclusively male terminology – women being generally far more reluctant to refer to masturbation. Also the US 'jack journal', for pornographic magazine.

But Jack, like other words that stand for 'man' (*see* DICK), has a long and varied history of usage in sexual slang. As far back as the 15th century Jack meant a male lover: the children's nursery rhyme 'Jack and Jill' has preserved this usage and it has been argued that the whole verse is about a sexual encounter.

Jack has also had the meaning penis, and erection, while 'to jack' meant sexual intercourse and 'to jack it' was to have an orgasm. Note that jack comes from the same linguistic root as jerk and compare jerk off, jerk the gherkin, jerk job etc. – all meaning masturbation. Note also, however, that 'Jack Nasty Face' was an old word for the *female* sexual parts.

Other usages of jack – now obsolete – are as follows: Jack in the box – penis, or foetus, or syphilis (rhyming slang with pox); Jack in the orchard – sexual intercourse; Jack Nasty Face – the female parts; Jack Robinson – the penis; Jack Straw's castle – the female parts. In slang Jack Straw was a 'nobody' (Partridge); Jack whore – a 'masculine' woman.

jacksie Also jaxy. Backside or bum. Widespread term, originally from the Armed Forces. It also has the meaning 'fanny' or vagina in the north of England. Possibly related to the mid-16th century term for privy – a 'Jakes' – which still survives as 'jacks'.

jacob The penis. Old-fashioned, largely obsolete usage. Jacob's ladder was the vagina. Biblical names for the sexual parts are not uncommon; *see* for instance NEBUCHADNEZZAR.

jail bait Female under the legally permitted age for sexual intercourse. The implication is that the girl tempts the male to break the

106

law. Widespread, from the US to the UK by the sixties.

jaisy Homosexual. According to US sources this is from the combination of Daisy and Jane. But 'jessie' is an old-fashioned English and Scottish word for 'effeminate man', comparable to the modern 'pansy', and Partridge gives the root of jessie as jassamine, or more correctly jasmine.

jalopies Breasts. Mostly north of England usage, from the slang word for an old car or cart bouncing along the road. This is an affectionate and comical word, like many others meaning breasts – *see also* JIGGLIES, BOOBS.

jam 'Just A Man' from the initial letters. This is a US gay term for a heterosexual man.

jam, bit of Woman or girlfriend. UK slang from the turn of the century. To have a bit of jam is to have sex, and 'lawful jam' is a wife. In the tradition of talking about women as 'tasty' morsels, *see also* CRUMPET, PORK etc.

By association with woman, jam and jam pot also had the meaning vagina.

Jamtart was rhyming slang for sweetheart, and from the mid-19th century also meant wife, mistress and prostitute.

jane Girl or girlfriend. Janey also had the meaning vagina. Both very dated.

jars Breasts. Widespread usage, especially in Ireland. *See also* JUGS. Not to be confused with 'to have a jar' – to have a drink.

J. Arthur J. Arthur Rank. Masturbate. Cockney rhyming slang for wank.

jaw queen Fellator. US gay and camp usage.

jelly Semen. Rarely used on its own, but common in compounds. *See* JELLY BOX.

jelly box The vagina. Also jelly bag, which dates back to the 17th century. Jelly has the old-fashioned meaning semen, hence jellybag was the scrotum.

The vagina is often referred to as the 'home' of the male apparatus – *see also* JACOB.

See also BOX – modern usage for orifices in both sexes.

jerk off To masturbate. Mostly US, but now increasingly widespread in the UK. *See* JACK for some old-fashioned English equivalents.

The word jerk is usually found in rhyming or alliterative combinations, such as jerk the gherkin, jerk the jelly, jerk the juice, jerk the turkey, jerk the mutton.

Also JO for jerk off, and jerking iron for penis.

See also GALLOP THE MAGGOT.

Jerusalem artichoke *See* ARTICHOKE.

jessom, or **gizzum** or **jizzum**

107

Semen. Widespread modern English usage.

jet stream Semen as ejaculated. US term.

jet the juice, to To ejaculate. Mostly American.

jewellery, or **jewels** The male genitalia. A high value is set on these indeed! *See also* CROWN JEWELS, FAMILY JEWELS. There is no equivalent meaning for the female genitals.

Jewish compliment A circumcised penis. US slang, mostly gay. An English parallel is Jewish nightcap – the foreskin. In both cases the reference is to circumcision in Jewish men. A Jew's compliment is an old-fashioned term for having a large penis but no money (Partridge), by association with the expression 'Yorkshire compliment' – 'a gift useless to the giver and not wanted by the receiver' (Farmer and Henley).

JGF Conversational shortening of 'just good friends', largely adopted by middle-class youth. Thus it becomes a euphemism and a joke. 'Are you in love with her? No we're JGF' means that a man is sleeping with a woman. A 'JGF scenario' is a sexual mating. Mostly male usage, and thus slightly derogatory – often used in reference to 'affairs' or 'bits on the side'.

108

jig, also **jig-a-jig, jig-jig, jiggy-jig** Sexual intercourse. From the image of the jerky dance and also for the fun of the rhyme which appeared in English street ballads as far back as the 1840s. *See also* ZIG-ZIG.

jigger The penis. Also the vagina. *See also* JIG.

jiggle Sexual intercourse. Hence jiggling bone – the penis. *See also* JIG.

jigglies Breasts (*see* JARS).

JO An act of masturbation. *See* JERK OFF, and JACK.

job, on the Sexual intercourse. One of the more widespread and socially acceptable phrases in modern slang, comparable to 'doing it' and 'doing the business'. Few other current favourites can be said to date back to the 16th century as this term does.

But note that to 'do a woman's job for her' had the meaning of having sex with a woman, while to 'do a man's job for him' meant to kill him (Partridge). The same shift of meaning exactly occurs with the use of 'into'.

Jo bag Condom. UK Forces slang. *See* JOHNNY BAG.

jock A hunky, athletic male. This is a very widespread term in the US, but surprisingly not many English people are aware of its meaning, perhaps because of the different English usages. *See below*.

jock Referring to the male genitalia, usually in compound forms like jock strap – an athletic support for the genitals, jock itch – 'athletes' foot' of the pubic area in men, jockey shorts – men's underpants.
These are derived from the older meanings of jock. At the end of the 18th century jock referred to the genitals of men or women, but came later to refer only to men. 'To jock' was a 19th century term for sexual intercourse, from the mid-16th century and 17th century words jockum – penis, and jockum cloy – sexual intercourse. A 'jockum gagger' was a man living on his wife's earnings as a prostitute.
Note that Jock, like Jack, also means 'man' – *see also* DICK.

Jodrell Bank Masturbate. Cockney rhyming slang for wank. *See also* LEVY AND FRANK.

Joe Buck Rhyming slang for fuck. Australian.

Joe Hunt Insult applied to a man, taking its venom from cockney rhyming slang with 'stupid cunt'. Now virtually unknown outside the East End of London.

Joey Menstruation. An upper-class English euphemism. 20th century but already obsolete.

jog, to To have sexual intercourse. Rare and dated, *but see* JIG.

John A prostitute's client. The name John is often used in slang to refer – sometimes contemptuously – to outsiders or people without identity.

Johnny bag Condom. Widespread slang in the UK, used by men and women. *See also* JO BAG.

John Thomas The penis. Made famous by D.H. Lawrence's *Lady Chatterley's Lover* which went to an obscenity trial in the 1960s for using terms like this – which today seem ludicrously mild. But the term dates back to the 1840s at least. Sometimes abbreviated to J.T. Another variant is John Willy (*see* WILLY). Related – but dated-words for penis are Johnnie and Johnson. *See also* JOHNNY BAG.

joint The penis. This is principally US usage. A camp variant is 'jointess' for clitoris.
In English slang, joint had the old meaning – a wife, because 'joined' i.e. married or having sex ('joining giblets') with a man.

jollies Sexual excitement. A common and humorous euphemism in the US and UK, used by male and female alike, and favoured by the younger generation. The word applies to any form of sexual activity – 'she gets her jollies from B and D'. Note that the old-fashioned sense of 'jolly stick' =

penis is now obsolete. *See also* ROCKS OFF, GET YOUR.

jolt, to Sexual intercourse. Also to jottle, and jottling. Presumably because of the comic suggestiveness of the words. *See also* JIG, and JOG.

joybag Condom. *See also* JOHNNY BAG.

joy boy Homosexual. UK, midsixties heterosexual usage. Also limited US usage for male prostitute.

joy of my life Rhyming slang for wife.

joy prong The penis. Again the weapon image: *see also* PORK DAGGER, MUTTON SWORD *et al*.

Joy stick The penis. Also jolly stick.

JT The penis. *See* JOHN THOMAS.

jugs Breasts. Crude, mostly male usage from the image of jugs of milk, comparable to jars. 'Jug' in days gone by was also a contemptuous name for a mistress.

juice Sexual transudate in women or semen in men. 'The juicy feeling' is slang for the state of sexual arousal in women. 'Give juice for jelly' is a phrase for orgasm in women that dates back to the 19th century. *See also* JELLY.

juicy 'Sexy'. A very widely used expression considered less explicit and more socially acceptable than 'juice' above. Almost anyone – but more usually young people – will talk about 'a good, juicy novel', or a 'bit of juicy gossip'. Yet its roots are sexual – it meant 'piquant, bawdy ... amorous' over a hundred years ago (Partridge).

jump To make sexual advances, or sexual intercourse. 'He invited me back to his office and then he jumped on me' – is an embarrassed woman's way of saying someone made a pass at her, or even assaulted her.

Jump has had the meaning to copulate from the 17th century, and to 'go for a jump' has the old-fashioned meaning sexual intercourse.

jump off at Haymarket, to To practice the withdrawal method of contraception. A Scottish catch phrase, in reference to Haymarket as the last stop before Edinburgh Waverley (Central) station.

Compare 'get off at Redfern' – i.e. the last station before Sydney Central, in Australia.

Both are contemporary slang among young local people.

jungle up To sleep more than one in a bed. US slang.

jupper Sexually 'up her'. Partridge gives the source as loose Australian rhyming slang from the 1930s. A parallel term, also Australian is 'skinner' – rhyming with 'in her'.

K

Kama Sutra In reference to any sexual practice considered exotic or adventurous. As in 'the sex was unbelievable – real Kama Sutra stuff.' From the famous Indian classic describing a huge variety of sexual positions. Now virtually synonymous in slang with X-rated – and as dated.

kanakas Testicles. Mispronunciation – often deliberate – of knackers. Australian, 20th century usage.

KD'ed Made pregnant. An abbreviation for knocked up.

keen on To be sexually attracted (to). This usage is widespread and utterly innocuous, conveying the pure romantic enthusiasm of one person for another. Hence a middle-class mother is likely to say to her young daughter, 'He's very keen on you, isn't he dear?'

In Canada and the US, the word keen is commonly used on its own as an expression of great admiration – as in 'Have you seen Chuck's date? Man, is she ever keen!'

keep down the census! To masturbate. This imaginative way of dealing with the guilt of Onanism in the male deserves to survive, but sadly has become increasingly uncommon since the 19th century.

keep it clean! A catch phrase likely to be used admonishingly when sexual slang or innuendo creeps into conversation. The idea that sex and any topic connected with it are 'dirty' is a deep-seated one. *See also* DIRTY.

keep one's end up Although this term is common in everyday slang to mean 'do one's bit', it has the underlying sexual implication of keeping the male organ up. The two meanings subtly mingle when one man sees another going out with yet another woman and says, 'He keeps his end up, doesn't he!'

111

Less directly sexual in connotation is 'keep one's pecker up', i.e. stay cheerful. *See* PECKER.

keep the horse's ears warm! Referring to the large and pendulous nature of a woman's breasts. The authors heard this imaginative phrase from the mouth of a young and hilarious woman at the bar of a pub in the heart of Somerset. She was describing another woman to her friends: 'You'd need arms from here to Dunster to get hold of her,' she said. 'Bend down and she keeps the horse's ears warm.' Who says women don't ever use sexual slang?

kennel The vagina. Hardly a pleasant image, associated as it is with a dark and smelly animal's lair, but in keeping with the use of 'dog' and 'alsatian' for woman.

kept woman, or **kept man** A woman, or a man, who depends financially on a sexual partner. The enormous shift in the meaning of this phrase mirrors the change in our thinking about sex and marital status. Originally the Victorians and their successors referred to a rich man's mistress as a kept woman, and so among 'respectable' people it was a polite way of calling a woman a prostitute – albeit a high class one.

But today, with fewer women choosing to get married than ever before in recent history, the term is more likely to be a parody of the original, suggesting that one partner is giving financial support to the other. Hence if a woman today is earning more than her boyfriend, or if he lives in a house or flat which she owns, he may refer to himself ruefully as a kept man. The term has also come to refer to a married partner – as in 'I'm not getting married, *I* don't want to be a kept woman.'

Gay usage is just as common, with the punning sense of 'keptive' for the supported partner, at the same time suggesting dependency and obligation.

kerb crawler Man who drives a car at walking pace through an area frequented by prostitutes. The term has recently become widespread in the UK since police campaigns and public pressure to stop the practice have been headline news – hence this recent *Sun* story: 'New Blitz on kerb-crawlers. Another police force is set to join the blitz on kerb-crawlers. In Nottingham, where police girls posed as prostitutes to snare dirty drivers, 15 men have already appeared in court and 25 more cases are due in the next fortnight.'

kettle The vagina. A rather obscure image but perhaps associated with spout, also meaning vagina. It has been suggested that kettle, which dates back to the 18th century, was a precursor of BOILER (q.v.). Related is the rather flowery, and now very dated, kettledrums = breasts.

key The penis. Naturally enough the adjunct is keyhole – for vagina. And apart from the obvious imagery, these words carry the old ideas that a woman's chastity is to be protected until 'unlocked' by one, unique man. The Victorian lexicographers Farmer and Henley comment that the key 'Lets a man in and the maid out'.

Khyber Pass Arse. From cockney rhyming slang. One of the more enduring and better known examples of this esoteric form of slang.

kicks Excitement, thrills. A direct steal from non-sexual slang, it was inevitable that this word would take on sexual connotations. And today the question 'What do you do for kicks?' spans the whole gamut of modern excitements, from drugs through sport to sexual tastes; just like the phrase 'whatever turns you on'. The meaning was immortalized in the pop song 'Route 66' by Chuck Berry – 'You get your kicks on Route 66'. The song was taken up by the Rolling Stones in the sixties and the meaning still survives. *Compare with* the more recent ROCKS OFF and JOLLIES.

kid A term of affection addressed to women, generally northern English and working class. Women use the term to their women friends – it is always on the lips of Vera Duckworth and Elsie Tanner in 'Coronation Street' – and men use it to women in the sense of 'babe'. But the term has some startling implications. Apart from the fact that it also means child, historically kid meant a pretty young prostitute. Kid-leather was generic for young prostitutes, and a kid-stretcher was a man who used young prostitutes. Kid as a verb also meant to get pregnant: nap the kid was to become pregnant. Kidded, or with kid still means pregnant.

kidney wiper The penis. Obscure, from an old ribald song.

killer *See* LADY KILLER.

kindness Sexual intercourse. Although entirely one-sided – it was the man who did the kindness to the woman – this old-fashioned, originally Scottish expression has an element of generosity sadly lacking from many more modern terms for sex.

King Lear Homosexual. Rhyming slang with queer. Obscure.

kinky Any form of sexual activity or inclination which is other than conventionally 'straight'. As such the adjective is used to describe a huge range of practices, from slight variations on the missionary position to the most esoteric of fetishes – depending on one's idea of what is 'straight'. And up until the mid-70s slang dictionaries still defined kinky as exclusively homo-sexual, an indication of how ideas have changed. But few people today believe that sex *should* be confined to heterosexuals in the missionary position, and so kinky can now refer to anything sexual or even sensual, and to any person who displays an interest in sex.

kip, in the Sexual intercourse. Although kip historically meant brothel it now means merely a bed as a noun or to sleep as a verb. As a compound it is synonomous with euphemistic terms such as 'in the sack' and 'between the sheets'.

Kippersville The vagina. Dismissive male usage, implying that the female sexual organ has a fishy odour. From the US, now as common in the UK. *Compare* FISH.

kiss The 'straight' sense of the word kiss has been extended in slang to include fellatio and cunilingus. In America, where if US jokes are anything to go by, people are obsessed by oral sex, the current phrase is 'to kiss someone off' (fellatio) or 'to kiss someone down' (cunnilingus). But dabblers in slang should be sensitive to its application – if someone tells you to 'kiss off!' or to 'kiss it' in other than a seductive setting, they mean 'fuck off!'

Kissing fish – from a novel with that title – has the US meaning lesbians. *See* FISH.

kiss and tell To reveal the secrets of one's sex life with a partner, usually in a newspaper. The phrase came into currency from the sixties when popular newspapers would pay the former lovers of film stars or pop stars to 'tell all' about what went on in the bedroom, no matter how brief the affair.

Now generally applied to any person who isn't shy about describing their sexual encounters – and causing embarrassment to previous partners.

kit The male organs. Now rare, but many other phrases in the same line of imagery continue. *See* EQUIPMENT, WEDDING TACKLE *et al.*

Kit has come Menstruation has begun. Now quite outdated, but in the same tradition of euphemisms for periods as 'the captain is at home', and 'the cardinal has come'.

kitty The vagina. Old fashioned and derived from 'pussy'.

knackers The testicles. Possibly from the old slang word for castanets or other 'strikers'. Mostly schoolboy or male sportsmen's slang – as in post-football match analysis, 'He got me right in the knackers'. But most commonly occurring in the form of knackered, meaning exhausted, without strength – which has evolved from the same slang root, to knacker, i.e. to emasculate.

kneel at the altar Cunnilingus. Mock-reverent phrase for a practice usually described more bluntly – and a parody of the ceremonial aspect of marriage.

knee trembler Sexual intercourse while standing. The term is as widespread as the practice, and so is most often heard among young people who don't have the luxury of privacy at home, and among men who are having a 'bit on the side' and go to alleyways etc. for illicit liaisons. The term dates back to at least 1850 (Partridge).

knick knack The vagina. Suggestive of a not very valuable trinket. Male, dismissive usage.

knitting Girlfriend, or women generally. As in 'the sailor's knitting' – BBC 'Start the Week', 5 Dec 1983. This had been mainly Forces slang from about 1930 (Partridge). *Compare* HOMEWORK.

knob The penis, or the end of the penis. Also, as a verb, sexual intercourse. Knob is one of the most common of all slang terms – in both its forms. Both men and women refer to the penis as the knob, and it is a word less likely to cause public offence than synonyms like prick. It is never for instance, used as an insult – unlike 'stupid prick!' or 'dickhead!'

Knob as a verb has a similarly innocuous status, although note that the use of knobbing implies that the male and his penis are the essential and active elements in sexual intercourse. One will often hear 'He's been trying to knob her for years', but rarely 'She's been knobbing him ...'

Also 'knob artist' – a man admired for his 'pulling power'. Note that a parallel term for women would be almost inconceivable!

knockers Breasts. One of the most widespread terms for breasts in slang and found on the lips of everyone from schoolboys to TV comedians. It belongs to the genre which sees sex and the human body as comical rather than erotic – *see also* BOOBS, BAZOOMAS, NORMA SNOCKERS.

knock off (or **up**) To have sexual intercourse with. Originally working-class slang, this is now a widespread phrase – but still considered 'crude' in polite circles. It is certainly not a very loving term, and is often used with more than a hint of disapproval – e.g. 'He's been knocking off his old friend's wife for years now'. As with knobbing, it is usually the male who is doing the knocking.

Other related phrases, still very common, are knocking shop – brothel, and knocked up – pregnant.

Knock also has the old meaning of penis, dating back to the 18th century.

knock out Devastatingly attractive. As in 'That bird's a real knock out'. The metaphor is from boxing, but both men and women use the term about each other.

knot, the The end of the penis. Rare, but for similar visual imagery *see* ALMOND, and ACORN.

knot, tie the To get married. Clichéd and widespread middle-class term, hardly encouraging to would-be spouses – as in 'Don't you think it's time you two tied the knot?'

know, to Sexual intercourse. Venerable – even Biblical – this euphemistic term is now outdated, but the original idea from the Garden of Eden that sex = knowledge = sin, is still very much with us.

knuckle shuffle Male masturbation. A more flowery version is 'five finger knuckle shuffle'.

kumquat A lump or drop of semen. A camp American peculiarism, punning on the name of the fruit.

KY KY Jelly. Brand name of a common lubricant jelly used by gays *and* heterosexuals to aid sexual penetration. It has become so much a part of everyday sexual experience – and in the popular imagination, of gay experience – that the letters KY are now combined jokingly with other phrases to suggest homosexuality. JY Kelly means a gay, as Fred Bloggs means a man. K.Y.M.C.A. is an extension of the joke about the Y.M.C.A. being a gay haunt, and K.Y. queen or K.Y. cowboy are US terms for any homosexual.

Another, American, form of lubricant is the cooking fat Crisco – hence the expression for a homosexual 'Crisco kid'.

116

L

labia The lips of the vagina. The word has meant lips since the 16th century (OED) but its now commonly accepted usage is to describe parts of the female body which have only recently escaped from the medical textbooks (in which a clinical distinction is made between the inner and outer labia) and sex manuals. Still a strong favourite in soft porn magazines, where 'to labiate', meaning to perform sexual intercourse, also survives.

lace curtains The foreskin. Semi-jocular camp gay usage, US and UK. See also DRAPES.

ladder The vagina. Now largely obscure, but the imagery is of woman as object and man as the one who climbs up (or on) 'it'. Dating back to the 19th century but now obsolete.

lady killer A male who is sexually 'successful' with women. Current UK usage by men and women, although with an old fashioned ring, as in – 'Just watch out for him dear, I've heard he's a real lady killer!' The term, although with the milder connotations of a flirtatious male, dates back to 1810.

laid See LAY.

lamp of love, the The vagina. A flowery literary euphemism, outdated and now rarely heard, but for the female more pleasant than most other words describing her sexual organs. Also there is the coy female expression 'light the lamp' = to have sexual intercourse.

lance The penis. Predictable male organ = weapon imagery, but more dated than most. Also 'lancing', to have sexual intercourse. See also PORK DAGGER.

lap land The vagina. Originally from the pun on Lappland, now rare, as is 'lap clap' meaning sexual intercourse (Partridge).

lardsack A fat, unsightly (to the beholder) body. Insulting and usually applied by men to women (although gays also use the word to describe a man with a fat stomach). The lard imagery is also popular in descriptions of women – like lump of lard and tub of lard. Hence the contemptuous – and contemptible – putdown 'It was like fucking a lump of lard', by a man who considers the woman to be fat and sexually unresponsive.

larking Any form of sexual activity. More common is 'larking about' which can be applied to anything from a stray kiss at a party to full sexual relations. As such an enduring, and very British, euphemism (it's perhaps no coincidence that H.E. Bates' series of novels about a lusty, liberated family enjoying life to the full in rural England in the fifties featured the Larkins. See, for instance, *The Darling Buds Of May*).

lather Sexual transudate. The word dates back to at least the 19th century and remains neat and inoffensive imagery. The same can't be said, however, for compounds in soft porn parlance such as lathered up – prepared for sexual intercourse; or lather maker – the vagina.

launch pad(occasionally **launching pad**) The bed. Literally the place where things 'take off'. Mainly US male gay usage.

lawnmower A man's mouth when performing cunnilingus. An amusing update of the venerable meaning of grass = vagina/pubic area (since 17th century) and the 20th century implement. *See also* GREENS, GARDEN.

lay A sexual partner, or an act of sex. Accepted young usage from the sixties onwards and very widespread in both the US and the UK. Thus someone can be 'one's lay', or somebody can 'lay' somebody else. Interesting because one of the few words used by both sexes – a woman can talk about laying a man, and vice versa.

layer cake The male buttocks. Camp usage. The image is one of a delectable item in 'at least two parts'.

LBJ Fellatio of the highest quality – i.e. a 'presidential' blow job. A throwback to the sixties and the days of Lyndon B. Johnson's reign at the White House. Dated US camp usage, now surviving on humour content alone.

leading article The vagina. 19th century and some 20th century usage, but now obsolete. *Contrast with* LEAK.

lead in your pencil, put some Old fashioned but still contemporary expression used by UK males of the hearty variety. As in 'Have a pint. That'll put lead in your pencil' – suggesting a need for increased potency.

leak The vagina. Unusually graphic, and, as is so often the case, conjuring up images of 'a hole' that needs 'plugging' or 'filling'. *See also* GASH, GAP, CAT WITH ITS THROAT CUT.

leap, or **do a leap** (Of a man) to partake in sexual intercourse. Recorded as far back as 1530 (OED). The usage is almost exclusively male, representing the male as the active partner. Thus to leap is simply to possess (a female), while a leap in the dark (= sexual intercourse) carries the same implication. Archaic to the younger generation, and thus used only humorously.

leather The vagina. Popular a century ago (Partridge), but now, with all the compounds and related phrases, largely superseded by the contemporary usage of leather as a sexual fetish (*see* LEATHER BOY). Equally outdated are to bash leather, to pound leather, to rub leather and to stretch leather, all meaning sexual intercourse. Yet, as an anachronism, leather stretcher, meaning penis, survives.

leather boy Also leather man, leather queer and leather queen. One who obtains sexual gratification either by dressing up in leather or simply by the contact of leather on the skin. The terms have been acceptable in the gay community for several decades but are now widely understood and used. *See also* RUBBER QUEEN (under 'RUBBER MAN').

leave a chalk mark when you're finished! Coarse catch phrase

between men, implying that one man's sexual partner has – as a result of 'promiscuity' – an overly large or overly used vagina. Insulting to women and betraying blatant double standards, but very common.

lech or **letch** A simple abbreviation of lecher, which has meant 'one with base or vile desires' since the 18th century (OED). To lech means to look at with sexual gratification in mind, while lech and even more commonly old lech (a form of mild rebuke, usually approbatory) were popularized in the early sixties and survive in current usage. While lecher may appear in newspapers, lech is invariably used in speech.

leg *See* THIRD LEG.

leg over Sexual intercourse. Following the pattern of the 'active man' imagery in 'straight' sex, leg over is still the most common of the graphic 'leg' compounds. Thus 'I know you took her out for a meal, but did you get your leg over afterwards?' Invariably a straight male term, and not one accepted by the 'liberated' female. 'Leg over' now replaces such dated terms as lifting one's leg, leg lifting and leg business, all of them synonymous.

length, a The penis. More commonly used in compound form, as in 'Did you slip her a length?' or 'Did you give her the full length?' Straight male usage

119

for the most part and probably among the more humorous of such terms. *See also* YARDAGE.

les A lesbian. Widespread abbreviation, used from the fifties on in the US and UK, but not always acceptable to lesbians who prefer to use the word in full. Most of the other variants are puns on les and mostly used by males. These include les-be-friends, lesbo, lesby, les girls, Leslie, less-than-a-mans, lezbo, lezzy, and lizzy.

letch water Sexual transudate. Connected in the popular imagination with 'lecher', but taken from the literal OED definition – a stream flowing through a muddy ditch or bog – and as such peculiarly and graphically offensive. *Contrast* with LATHER.

let go To ejaculate. A time-honoured euphemism among men, but also used, if only jokingly, by women. ('He let go inside me' as the soft porn magazines would have it.) Interestingly, 'coming' – a term acceptable to both male and female – is now much more popular than 'letting go', the definition of which is so loose that it can also be taken to mean (and does in general slang) to urinate, to vomit or to defecate.

let one's hair down To declare oneself to be actively homosexual. Originally US, now widespread and virtually synonymous with 'come out' (q.v.).

120

let's ball! An invitation to sexual intercourse. Originally US, from the rock'n'roll/groupie circuit. Thus, groupie to rock star: 'Are you in a band? That's great, let's ball!' Surprisingly, this expression has dated very quickly and is now likely only to be used in a jocular context. However it is synonymous entirely with the surviving 'let's do it!', 'let's fuck!' and 'let's screw!'

Levy and Frank Masturbation. Originally cockney rhyming slang = wank. Invariably shortened to Levy. *See also* JODRELL BANK.

lewd infusion Sexual intercourse (Partridge). Convoluted and now rarely heard.

lick, to To perform cunnilingus. Widespread US and UK usage. Obvious origin and as common as 'suck' for fellatio. Affectionate when used by a female – 'You can lick me if you want to' – but can take on tones of proud aggression when used by a male – 'I licked her box out'. 'To lick out' is the more graphic, and equally common, extension. Partridge also gives two related nouns: lick spigot = the woman who is being licked; and lick twat = the man who is doing the licking, but both are dated and not often heard.

life preserver The penis. Amusing and almost exclusively English.

light up To achieve orgasm. A

primarily female euphemism. The imagery is in keeping with the 'LAMP OF LOVE' (q.v.).

lili, or **leelee** The female genitals. Personal slang of one English woman, shared only with her daughter – and then with great embarrassment. For other instances of private slang, *see* TUDS, TICKLE TORTURE.

limpwrist A male homosexual. Straight 'macho' usage, taken from the popular mythology that gays make exaggerated, and 'feminine' gestures with their hands. Normally addressed as an insult, the word has the additional connotation that the other man isn't even strong enough to be a 'wanker'.

Lincoln Tunnel *See* CHUCKING A WORM UP THE MERSEY TUNNEL.

line-up A series of men performing sex with the same woman (in straight usage) or the same man (in gay usage) one after the other. Although quite innocent-sounding, this could be as violent (and indeed often is) as gang rape. To most people it's an easier and more polite way of saying 'gang bang'.

lingam The penis. From the Indian classics (= phallus, a Hindu expression) and briefly taken up by the hippy generation in the sixties. Now rare. *See also* YONI.

linguist A practitioner of oral sex.

The word goes back to at least the 19th century in the UK, with the specific meaning of a man who practises cunnilingus, but has enjoyed new popularity among the gay community over the last two decades; obviously meaning a fellator.

lips The labia. Often 'cunt lips'. Contemporary male usage in the UK and US. Less offensive than alternatives like 'beef curtains' (q.v.).

lips, the The wrinkled skin around the anus. Male gay usage.

liquid hairdressing Semen. Colourful (or possibly colourless?) analogy. Principally male gay, from US to the UK.

liquorice stick A black penis. Obvious imagery, camp US gay usage only.

little bit on the side *See* BIT ON THE SIDE.

little finger The penis. Coy, dated and 'feminine' usage; unlikely to be uttered by anyone born after WW2.

little friend A period. Originating in the pre-Pill fifties – by the arrival of a period a girl realized she wasn't pregnant, hence the welcoming term. Outmoded (Partridge). Also 'little visitor'.

little heeler A prostitute. A term originating in the north of England where it's still common.

From the high-heeled shoes prostitutes are supposed to wear. *See also* LOW HEEL.

little man in the boat The clitoris. Affectionate term used by male and female. The origin is Latin, from *naviculans* meaning clitoris, and *navicula* meaning boat, but such worthy roots haven't stopped widespread usage in Britain and (especially) Ireland. Occasionally 'little boy in a boat' and it's interesting to note that there has been no attempt to change the phrase to little woman/girl in a boat! For other examples of male names of female parts *see* TOP BOLLOCKS.

little sister The vagina. Limited female usage.

liver tickler The penis. *See* LUNG DISTURBER.

living in sin Alluding to heterosexual couples who share a home – and/or have sexual intercourse – and who are not married. Old fashioned, but still used in the UK, either ironically by young people, or euphemistically by the older generation.

LM *See* LEATHER BOY.

load The ejaculated semen. Invariably used as part of a sentence, invariably by men, straight or gay. Thus 'to come one's load', 'drop one's load' or 'shoot one's load' (to name but three) all simply mean to ejaculate. There are infinite variations

with the most common being 'lighten the load'. The phrases refer to any form of ejaculation, whether the result of intercourse, masturbation or fellatio. *See also* LOT and WAD.

loaded with it, he's A man considered by another man to be 'oversexed'. Occasionally simply 'overloaded'.

lob, to To have sexual intercourse. Thus to 'lob it' or to 'lob it up' is synonymous with 'knob it' or 'give it one'. Casually aggressive male usage. A popular Irish variant is 'lobbing it through an open window'.

lobcock A large penis. Normally used to describe the organ in repose, in a non-sexual masculine context (showers, changing rooms etc.)

lobster, to To have sexual intercourse with a woman. Originally forces slang, now widespread. Perhaps the image of this (delicious) creature – but with massive claws – strikes a chord of sexual fears in the male, and hence its enduring popularity? Usually used in a joking context – 'What were you doing last night? Lobstering?' The continuing thread of 'oceanic' and/or piscine analogies for anything to do with the female sexual organs is worthy of note. *See* LOBSTER POT and also OYSTER, KIPPERVILLE, FISH *et al.*

lobster pot The vagina. Mostly

male usage, but not necessarily intended in a derogatory manner.

Lolita Young woman (generally under the age of legal consent) who is considered sexually attractive to older men. The term was taken from Vladimir Nabokov's novel of the same name, which celebrated an older man's lust for a young girl, and has become popular in the US and the UK since the sixties. Hence the *News Of The World*: 'Scandalised MPs are demanding that doctors be compelled to examine the birth certificates of gymslip Lolitas before prescribing birth control drugs for the under-16s' (6 Nov 1983).

lollipop The penis. Straight and gay male term. Although the image is that of something on a stick and there to be 'licked' the word doesn't carry any notion of power, strength and aggression and usage is, more often than not, self-denigratory. The old-fashioned 'lady's lollipop' is similarly jocular.

long and thin (goes right in) ... Ironic description of the shape and size of the male organ. The full rhyme runs: 'Long and thin/Goes right in/And doesn't please the ladies/Short and thick/does the trick/And gives them all the babies.'

long eye The vagina. As obvious as it is venerable, with origins as far back as the 18th century. Mostly male usage.

lot The ejaculated semen. Virtually synonymous with 'LOAD' (q.v.) and interchangeable in all the compounds noted there. Additionally 'to have spent one's lot' has the parallel meaning of ejaculation and/or exhaustion as a result of sexual activity.

lot, the The male genitalia. A female euphemism, usually used in phrases like 'He showed me the lot', or (from women talking about a male strip show) 'What did you see? The lot!' Enduring and very common, but a description still shunned by men.

lousy fuck, he's (or she's) a One of the most common putdowns in current usage when the desire is to communicate that a sexual partner is not 'satisfactory'. Also 'lousy lay'. Equally used by men and women.

love bite A bruise left on the body (literally anywhere) after it has been bitten and sucked by a sexual partner. From the forties onwards and now across the board usage. *Compare* HICKEY.

love bubbles Breasts. Common 20th century slang with an appealing imagery. Mostly male UK usage.

love butter Semen. From the sixties onwards, from the US to the UK. More often male usage. A variant is love juice, which is

123

slightly earlier in origin, and can have the concurrent meaning of sexual transudate. *Compare* CREAM.

love handles Flesh around the upper hips that can be gripped during sexual encounters. From the fifties on. Affectionate usage, often by females describing their own bodies. 'I *haven't* put on weight, those are my love handles'. Synonymous is 'side steaks'.

love pole The penis. Dating back over a century in the UK, now rare. *See also* POLE.

low countries The vagina. Sometimes The Low Countries. Euphemistic and dating back to the 18th century (Partridge) with a possible pun on 'cunt'. Now considered flowery and more literary than literal. Largely obsolete.

low heel A prostitute. Perhaps by association with 'down at heel'. This description is Australian in origin. *Contrast* the English LITTLE HEELER.

lowlands, the The vagina. Origin as for 'LOW COUNTRIES' (q.v.) and now little heard.

lube Sexual transudate. Originally US, now more widespread. From the obvious abbreviation of lubricant. Some American sources make the distinction between lube = pre-coital secretion from the penis, and luke = pre-coital

secretion from the vagina (Rodgers).

lubra A woman. Principally Australian and principally derogatory – the word is originally Aboriginal for female, and its usage by whites carries a strong measure of racism.

lubricate, to To have sexual intercourse. Old-fashioned British usage and one comparing the – usually female – body to 'machine' (= object) that needs to be serviced. Hence generally male usage. *See also* SERVICE.

lucky bag The vagina. A euphemism sounding still modern after two centuries of usage.

luke *See* LUBE.

lumpy Pregnant. Standard, but coy; British origin and usage.

lunch The male genitalia. A British anachronism enjoying new popularity. Hence 'Put it away, you don't want everybody to see your lunch!' Straight and gay usage.

lung Breast, or breasts. A colourful Australianism, usually male approbatory – 'She's got plenty of lung' – of a woman with large breasts.

lung disturber The penis. Jocular, boastful male usage. The imagery goes beyond the colourful to the ridiculous. *See also* KIDNEY WIPER and LIVER TICKLER.

M

machine The genitals, male or female. Rarely used in conversation, but occurs in bawdy songs and lyrics as in the Irish song 'I showed her the works of my threshing machine'. In the line of slang that refers (usually) to the penis as a valuable and practical piece of 'equipment' – see also GEAR, TOOL etc. 'Machine' also has the less common meaning of condom (Partridge).

macho The qualities attributed to the traditionally 'masculine' man – such as aggression, virility, strength, toughness. Its root is from the Spanish word for virile. But increasingly, as attitudes towards gender identities change, to call a man 'macho' is an insult, especially from women, and implies that he lacks the qualities of vulnerability, sensitivity and kindness which are becoming more highly valued. Hence the quip by Zsa Zsa Gabor: 'Men who try too hard to be macho are generally not mucho.'

madam A woman who owns or runs a brothel. In the UK an old-fashioned term, because now an old-fashioned institution. But another example of how words that were originally a mark of respect or sign of a woman's rank – like 'Dame' and 'Mistress' – have systematically been devalued and overlaid with a sexual meaning. This is what feminist etymologists have called 'the systematic semantic derogation of women'.

In shortened form as 'mam', Partridge gives the 40s London meaning lesbian.

Mad Mick Penis. From cockney (and also Australian) rhyming slang with prick. 'Mick' also has the sense penis in its own right. See also DICK, JOHN THOMAS et al.

Mae Wests Breasts. From rhyming slang and also from the name of the buxom actress – which in turn became the name of the life preserver strapped to the chest.

maggot The penis. See GALLOP THE MAGGOT. A refreshingly diminutive term if used by a male.

125

Compare with ACORN and BUT-
TON MUSHROOM.

make, to To have a sexual
relationship and/or sexual intercourse with. Most commonly in
the form 'to make it' – as in the
pop song 'I want to make it with
you' (although this also passes
muster on the less explicit level of
being a success).

Some very common equivalents
are 'to make love' (which has a
classier, more respectful ring to
it), 'to make out with' (a distinctly
North American variant), and 'to
make up to', a now somewhat
old-fashioned UK form. Note that
historically each of these had a far
milder, less explicit meaning.
Indeed 'to make love' to a woman
in the novels of writers like Jane
Austen meant no more than to kiss
a hand or show a romantic
interest in her.

'On the make' and 'to make
out' also have the meaning to be
looking for sex or a sexual
relationship.

make a pass To make sexual
advances. Used by, and of, either
men or women. The phrase
suggests a degree of chancing
one's arm – as in 'The boss makes
a pass at me at the office party
every year.' Also in the classic
rhyme with its unquestioning
double standard: 'Men seldom
make passes at women in glasses.'

make scissors, to A US equivalent for 'do the bowling hold'
(q.v.).

126

make the blind see To fellate an
uncircumcised man (Rodgers).
The same blind image is implied in
the word 'mole' for penis, sometimes also known as 'blind meat'.

make the chimney smoke 'To
cause the female to experience the
orgasm' is Partridge's definition of
this rarely heard 20th century
phrase. But it is interesting for its
relationship with more common
and widespread expressions such
as 'You don't look at the
mantelpiece while stoking the
fire', and the old joke: *Q.* Do you
smoke after intercourse? *A.* I don't
know, I've never looked.

mammaries The breasts. This
pseudo-anatomical term is enjoying a new vogue amongst sections
of the middle-class young, as in:
'Do you think she should be
jogging? It might damage the
mammaries.'

man The penis. Affectionate –
but uncommon – male usage, as in
: 'Then I took out my little man
and gave her one.' Also, as a verb
'to man', sexual intercourse of a
man with a woman. The identification of men with their organs
in slang is very strong – *see* DICK
et al – and is even projected onto
women's organs so that the clitoris
becomes the 'little man in the
boat'.

Related terms are the US and
UK 'manhole' for vagina, and
'manhole cover' for tampon or

sanitary towel. Also 'man Thomas' for penis (*see* JOHN THOMAS) and 'man trap', meaning woman *and* her sexual parts.

Manchester Cities Breasts. From cockney rhyming slang with titties. Often shortened to 'Manchesters.' *See also* BRISTOLS, CAT AND KITTIES.

man in the boat The clitoris. *See* LITTLE MAN IN THE BOAT for a full etymology.

man mad Preoccupied with men and sex. Said of women, by both sexes. But the term – dating back to the 20s – is fairly genteel and forgiving, implying usually that a young woman is going through a stage. As in the 'Forty Minutes' TV documentary on finishing schools, in which one upper-class girl affectionately describes her friend as 'man mad'.

manual exercises Masturbation. 20th century slang and still common amongst men in the US and the UK. Generally male usage, and another reference to the hand – *see also* MOTHER PALM AND HER FIVE DAUGHTERS.

marbles Testicles. One in the many of the 'balls' line. UK slang from the 19th century and now widespread. *See also* PILLS.

margarine Uncomplimentary nickname given to a woman who is considered sexually 'promiscuous' – i.e. she 'spreads easily'. This form is from a Dublin schoolboy source, but an old-fashioned UK parallel which uses the same imagery is 'buttered bun' – applied to a woman who has sex with different men one after the other. In contrast, males who are considered 'promiscuous' are given the more complimentary titles of 'cocksman' or 'knob artist', to name but two.

Margery When applied to a man, the female name implies that a man is effeminate, if not homosexual. This sense is now largely obsolete in the UK, but the sense has been picked up in the US where it means 'affected' (Rodgers) among the gay male community. Other women's names such as Molly, Mary, are similarly used in slang – *see* NANCE.

market, on the Sexually available. This belongs to the same slang genre as 'available' and 'unattached', reflecting modern trends by omitting reference to marriage.

Ironically, it was not so long ago that the term meant 'available for marriage' (Partridge), and in some less 'modern' circles, it still does. *See also* MEAT MARKET, under MEAT.

mark of the beast The female sexual parts. Partridge traces this back to 1715 (when beast simply meant animal) and it is now obsolete. Yet it is of interest in relation to old, but still current terms like 'beast with two backs' –

sexual intercourse. Contrast current use of 'beast' in tabloid newspaper headlines, where a common tag for rapists and/or child molesters is 'sex beast'.

Marquis of Lorne Penis, or erection. From cockney rhyming slang with horn. Not in widespread usage. *See also* ALL FORLORN, and COLLEEN BAWN.

matinee Sex in the afternoon. Largely US slang with affectionate overtones of relaxation and entertainment as in: 'We left work early for a quick matinee'. *See also* AFTERNOON DELIGHT, MORNER, FUNCH.

maul, to To fondle sexually in a clumsy and/or unwelcome fashion. This is a common term of distaste among younger people who might use it in observation of people at a party – as in 'Did you see him mauling her while they were dancing?' As such it is very close in emphasis to 'grope' and 'paw', but slightly stronger in its aggressive, animal connotations.

meat Flesh – in its multifarious forms. Chiefly as the body, male or female, in a sexual context – i.e. 'a bit of meat' is sexual intercourse, 'fond of meat' is to be sexually keen, and anything 'meaty' whether a film, magazine or book, is 'sexy'.

In gay slang a 'meat rack' is any place that homosexuals frequent, and in the UK and US a 'meat market' is any place like a bar or disco where people congregate with the specific aim of finding a sexual partner, paid or unpaid. 'Raw meat' is the naked body.

But more specifically 'meat' refers to the sexual organs, male and female, and most commonly to the penis. As in 'meat and two veg' – the male genitals. And there are any number of variants, naming specific types of meat – *see* PORK DAGGER, and MUTTON.

Given how widespread the use of 'meat' imagery is, it is distressing to realize just how debased a view of sex and the human body it represents. Meat suggests something animal, chopped up, insensate. One of the more disgusting manifestations of the image appeared on the front of the 'pornographic' magazine *Hustler* – a picture of a woman's body being fed through a meat mincer.

Yet it is a very old image. Partridge records 'bit of meat' as dating back to the 16th century, as well as other dated forms like meat house – brothel, meat monger – wencher, the price of meat – the cost of a prostitute.

melt, to To experience sexual pleasure and/or orgasm. Although this is the kind of language one would expect to find in romantic fiction, it is generally used satirically in slang. Its imagery of heat and oozing liquid has made it a favourite for generations: Partridge records 'melted butter' for semen, 'melting pot' for vagina, and 'melting moments' for sexual intercourse. He also notes that 'melt' has the straight slang meaning 'to beat' – like many other words for sexual activity, e.g. bang, fuck.

member The penis. This is widespread UK slang – presumably from the Latin *membrum virile*. But beware: in the US it also has the slang meaning of gay, as in member of the homosexual community.

merkin The female genitals and/or pubic hair. The word comes from the name given to the pubic wig sometimes worn from the 18th century, often to disguise the shame of those who had been shaved in the treatment of venereal diseases. But it survives in the vaguer genital and pubic sense, so that a couple of young women friends living in Dublin told the authors they were known as the Merkin sisters on account of their tightly curly hair.

mess about or **muck about** An umbrella term for sexual activity from kissing to intercourse. As in: 'Sally's parents haven't let me take her out since they caught us messing about.' Hollywood has given it an American adolescent ring – conjuring up petting sessions in the back of enormous cars. But in reality the expression has been well established in the UK since Victorian times. It meant 'to take sexual liberties' in

1873, and 'to be unfaithful', from 1915. The person who does the messing about is, of course, 'a messer'.

mickey Penis. Also sometimes as 'mick'. Common in Irish slang, and rhyming with 'prick'. Affectionate male and female usage, and another instance of a male Christian name being applied to the organ – *see also* DICK, and JOHN THOMAS.

middle finger The penis. Also as 'middle leg' and 'middle stump'. Dating back to the 19th century but still common male usage in the UK. Mostly male usage, euphemistic and not as common however as 'third leg'. Additionally the 'middle finger' is also used as a description of the digit used to stimulate the clitoris prior to intercourse – again primarily male usage.

mile high club, the A fantasy club for which the only criterion of membership is that a person has been fortunate enough to have had sexual intercourse whilst flying as a passenger on a plane. First heard during the international flight boom of the early seventies and swiftly picked up by popular newspapers in the US and the UK. Still very popular (presumably people are 'joining' every day as air traffic steadily increases). Gays are also eligible, with the captain's announcement 'we are now cruising at 30,000 feet' often causing amusement on US flights. One memorable British equivalent is the 'three foot six high club' whose members join by having sex during a British Rail journey (Nick Van Hear, 1980), although this club has as yet escaped the newspapers' attention.

milk Sexual transudate, especially semen. 'To milk' is to cause ejaculation, and so a 'milker' is a vagina or a masturbator. These terms go back as far as 16th century England, but are now obsolete. *See* CREAM and ICE CREAM, however, for current equivalents.

milky way Breasts. Also sometimes as 'milk bottles'. Dating back some four centuries and now archaic in the UK. *See also* JARS, JUGS, DAIRY.

minge The female genitals. From British underworld slang of the 19th century; possibly from a Romany word. Now very common and largely UK working-class usage. During World War I it was used amongst military men as a collective noun for women. The term 'mingy', often used to signify meanness or unpleasantness, is probably from a combination of 'mangy' and 'stingy', and not – as some people suppose – from 'minge'.

mivvy Woman or girl. Long standing, mostly northern English slang which sometimes becomes a nickname for a woman.

mixed marriage A relationship – or marriage – between a heterosexual and homosexual. This is US gay slang, and demonstrates a remarkable difference in the preoccupations of different social groups: in Ireland the same term means a marriage between a Catholic and a Protestant, and in the UK it generally means marriage between people of different races.

mixed wrestling Sexual foreplay and/or intercourse. A working-class and mostly north of England term, considered innocuous enough to put into the mouth of the disco manager in ITV's Coronation Street, 18th January 1984: 'You get a bit of mixed wrestling thrown in with the job of DJ'.

moff A hermaphrodite or homosexual. Working-class UK and Australian slang (Partridge).

mole The penis. Apt blind burrowing image and one of many which see the organ as a small wriggling creature – *see also* RABBIT, MAGGOT, FERRET. The 'mole catcher' is the vagina.

molly A homosexual or effeminate man. Moll, the woman's name, originally meant a woman – as in 'gangster's moll', and 'to moll' or 'mollying' had the meaning of going about with or having sexual relations with women (Partridge). But its application to homosexuals began as far back as the 19th century, when 'to molly' also meant to bugger and a molly house was a male brothel.

And now in the US the word has come full circle to 'molly dyke', a gay term for a 'passive lesbian' (Rodgers).

monkey The female sexual parts. The monkey, as a furry, mischievous but likeable animal is a common image in sexual slang. Hence the query 'Did you find where the monkey sleeps last night?' is to be heard over Sunday morning drinks in at least one London working men's club (C. Harkins, 1981).

'Monkey tricks' has the old-fashioned UK meaning to take 'sexual liberties', while 'monkey traps' once meant female finery worn to 'catch men'. 'Monkey business' still has the widespread meaning of sexual dalliance, used by both male and female.

mono Mononucleosis, or, in the UK, glandular fever. In North America mono is also called 'the kisser's disease' as it is transmitted orally, and adolescents who fall prey to it are also subject to searching enquiries as to the source.

montezumas Breasts. Another term which is popular for its comic sound – *compare* BALOOBAS and JALOPIES.

month, wrong time of the The

menstrual period. Also 'the monthlies'. Yet another negative euphemism – *see also* CURSE.

morner Sex in the morning. US and mostly gay slang, as in the verse 'A morner is a nooner, only sooner' (Rodgers). *See also* MATINEE, AFTERNOON DELIGHT, FUNCH.

mot Girl or young woman. This is a word very commonly used in Ireland, generally to signify a girlfriend, but surprisingly it is virtually unknown in the UK or US. This is in spite of its old English and possibly French origins. Lexicographers disagree as to its root, but some argue it derives from the 16th century 'mort(e)', – woman or wife. Like other words with these simple meanings, it took on a debased sexual connotation, and a 'mot-cart' was a mattress, while a 'mot-case' was a brothel (Partridge). As such it is clearly related to the Dutch *mot-huys* for brothel.

Another theory however, is that it evolved from a shortening of *amourette*.

mother of pearl Girl. Cockney rhyming slang. Also ocean pearl. But usually as 'my old mother of pearl', or (confusingly to the uninitiated) as 'my old mother'. First recorded usage is 1870 (Partridge).

mother palm and her five daughters, a meeting with Male masturbation. One of the many

131

convoluted images to describe this still seemingly guilty act. The reference is to the hand and five fingers. *See also* FIVE FINGER KNUCKLE SHUFFLE, HAND JOB.

mottob Bottom. Back slang. Dated and rarely used. *See also* DELOW NAMMOW.

mount, to Sexual intercourse. Also 'a mount', for woman. Clearly taken from the animal kingdom, and dating back to 16th century England. Now widespread, especially in soft porn, in the UK and US. Related to slang such as 'ride'.

mouse The penis in its flaccid state according to UK 19th century and 20th century usage. Also in gay US slang during the 60s, a fellator. Another wriggly rodent image – *see also* MOLE, RABBIT.

mouth The female genitals. This is very rarely heard today, but the imagery is clear and Partridge cites the old-fashioned forms 'the mouth that cannot bite', 'thankless mouth' and 'the mouth that says no words about it'. Yet although it may be practically obsolete in the language, it is a concept used every day by advertisers with their glossy pictures of phallic lipsticks painting red mouths or a female mouth opening to whatever item of food is for sale.

mouth job Fellatio. Less common than 'blow job'. Contemporary usage, mostly US but also UK.

muff The female genitals. The popularity and strength of the term probably comes from its association with muffle, and the fur muff which keeps women's hands warm. It is most commonly heard in the form 'muff diver' – a cunnilingist.

'Muff' dates back to the 17th century and passed from underworld slang into the widespread 'slanguage' of sex (Partridge).

muncher boy Male fellator. Dated Forces slang. *Compare* GOBBLE.

mutton The flesh, and more specifically the genitals. To 'jerk one's mutton' is male masturbation, while to 'unbutton the mutton' is to take out the penis. As a woman – or 'loose woman', mutton is one of the oldest forms of slang: Partridge records a usage in Skelton from 1518. And even today it is very common to hear an older woman who likes to wear more youthful clothes described (insultingly) as 'mutton dressed as lamb'.

See also MEAT.

mutton sword The penis. Contemporary UK and US male usage combining meat and weapon imagery. *Compare* JOY PRONG; *see also* PORK DAGGER.

N

NA Not available. Used conversationally by either men or women to describe another person's state of sexual availability. A 'trendy' abbreviation, mostly British from the seventies on. More common is 'unavailable'.

nackers The testicles. Easier spelling, but not as common as the generally accepted 'knackers' (q.v.).

naff The vagina. Sometimes spelt simply naf (strictly = navel); a venerable term dating back at least to the 18th century (Partridge) and now rarely used in this context. In the forces from 1940 onwards, and in general usage since the late seventies, naff has simply meant unfashionable, useless and laughable (*The Complete Naff Guide*, 1983), but whether this is semantically linked with the old meaning of 'cunt' is debatable.

Also today as an insult. Princess Anne was reputed on one occasion to tell photographers to 'naff off'

– but if one did, did one know what one was saying?

naff omi A straight man. Common gay slang in the US since the sixties and the UK soon afterwards. Used to distinguish whether another man 'belongs', in the street, in the bar, or at a party. The opposite is bona omi (a male gay), and, commonly, just naff and bona are used in conversation. 'Stop teasing me, are you naff or bona?'

naggy (sometimes naggie). The vagina. Old colloquial usage, often extended – as so many words for vagina are – to mean a woman. As such insulting, as the image is that of something that is old and worn out and which the man 'rides'. The insult is even greater in the compound phrase 'tether the nag', i.e. have sexual intercourse, now thankfully rarely heard.

naked as nature intended, as Nude. One of the more common similes, intended to inject sexual connotations into the word naked wherever possible. As such, widely used by both male and female. Other variations include naked as a jay bird (principally US in usage), stark naked, stark bollock naked (in the UK usually just bollock naked). The more old-fashioned similes noted by Partridge such as naked as a needle or even naked as the truth have now disappeared.

nance A man exhibiting 'effeminate' characteristics. A straight man describing any other man as a nance is automatically calling him 'gay' and it is this shortened form that has survived both as a noun, and as a verb. To nance = make exaggerated 'feminine' movements, such as hand waving and hip swinging. The word was in popular usage from the thirties right through until the sixties 'gay liberation', after which it was used either jokingly or only by the uneducated male as a term of derision. In the gay community it survives to distinguish between the macho and effie (q.v.) male, and as such is a term of affection. The more straightforward Nancy Boy, from which nance derives, also survives, but the original nan-boy, dating back to the 17th century, is now rare. The alternative usage of Nancy Boy, meaning a young man kept by a lover for the purposes of buggery or fellatio ('a catamite' – OED) is also extant but more common in the US.

134

nanny house A brothel. Old fashioned, euphemistic and now very rare, as are so many words for brothel. Nanny, meaning prostitute, had all but disappeared by the turn of the last century after a 300-year lifespan.

nap A dose of venereal disease (VD). Pedantic, literally something which is caught or landed, and now considered old-fashionedly euphemistic.

napkin ring A rubber or leather ring placed round the base of the penis (or sometimes the penis and testicles). Such items are often advertised as 'penis extenders'; quite literally they trap the blood in the erect organ and while not actually increasing length and firmness can often prevent premature flaccidity. Originally camp gay slang, but since the boom in 'sex aids' in the early seventies now a common and affectionate euphemism.

nasty The vagina. Originally Australian, now with limited use in the UK also. One of the more 'modern' words for the female's sexual organ and although coined jokingly (*Bazza Pulls It Off*, Barry Humphries 1968) it is calculatedly offensive to the female – *see also* (do a) NASTY. The 'joke' extends into ribaldry with compound phrases and similes like 'as dry as a nun's nasty'. *Compare* the old usage JACK NASTY-FACE. There is limited alternative usage for nasty

= arsehole. Both are used exclusively by the straight male.

nasty, do a To have sexual intercourse with a woman. Again a 'joke' expression used by the straight male. Virtually interchangeable with 'do a naughty' (*see under* NAUGHTY).

naughty Sexually titillating. A product of the 20th century and possibly even more euphemistic than 'blue'. The compounds are endless but a few of the more common usages are the naughty, the vagina; do a naughty, have sexual intercourse; naughty knicks, sexually provocative underwear. In the 1980s in Soho the euphemism became even more widespread, and equally ridiculous. In strip clubs and peep shows 'a naughty show' was one where, for an extra charge, the stripper would display her vagina to the client in private.

naval engagement Sexual intercourse. Originally Forces slang used by the straight male, and as such a pun on navel engagement = intercourse with a woman. The term now has general, if limited, usage and is largely outweighed by the meanings listed under Navy, (q.v.).

navel *See* PROUD BELOW THE NAVEL.

navels, wriggle To have sexual intercourse. UK usage from the 19th century. A lusty, if slightly old-fashioned expression. A more modern equivalent is slippery belly (q.v.).

Navy cake The rectum. Thus to have a bit of Navy cake is to have anal intercourse (usually, but not always, with a man). Long standing Forces slang, now more general usage; UK only.

navy style Anal intercourse. Primarily US equivalent of the last entry and principally male gay slang.

N-boy A young gay, or one who, to a straight male, tends to exhibit 'gay' characteristics. Short for nancy boy.

near the knuckle Verging on the sexually explicit. Slightly old fashioned and usually only heard in conversation as 'a bit near the knuckle' = verging on the sexually offensive. Unlikely to be used seriously by anybody under 40. The popular newspaper equivalent is much more commonly 'blue' (or perhaps 'slightly blue').

Nebuchadnezzar The penis. A venerable – and by now mostly literary – description of the male organ, usually only uttered as a joke. The ponderous etymology draws on the biblical image of Nebuchadneazzar's liking for 'grass' (= either the pubic hair or the vagina). Now only surviving in a humorous sense of lofty and overly important imagery, much

necessaries

in the same way as the synonymous Jereboam and Matumbi.

necessaries The male sexual parts. Again, almost invariably male usage but with a limited currency among women as a euphemism. From the 40s in the UK. *Also* occasionally with the meaning = contraceptives: 'Have you got the necessaries with you?'

necessary, do the To have sexual intercourse. A contemporary, primarily British expression and one used almost invariably by straight males. Mildly insulting to women, as a phrase like 'I felt I ought to do the necessary' implies that a man feels almost obliged to provide a woman with a 'service'. *See* NECESSARIES.

needle The penis. Now little used, especially by males, as the image is somewhat scornful; derived from 'prick' maybe, but something that is short and thin. Most often used in a self-deprecatory sense or as part of a compound.

nest, on the In bed, with and sometimes without, the connotation that one is having sexual intercourse. In most normal conversation the former is almost invariably the meaning. Thus, in response to a question about activity or whereabouts of another person, on the nest = having sexual intercourse. In current usage nest has the dual meaning of either the innocent bed, or the vagina. More elderly expressions

such as nest in the bush, meaning vagina, have largely been superseded.

nibbets Faecal matter remaining on the anal hair. Principally US and Canadian usage but synonymous with the UK clinker and dingleberries (q.v.). In a sexual context mostly camp gay slang.

nibble, a Sexual intercourse. Almost polite in the same way as 'slap and tickle', and, unless jokingly, not favoured by the younger generation. Nibbling, denoting sex, is definitely old fashioned, although undeniably more affectionate than more current words like bonking or screwing.

nice cheek A desirable anus. Originally camp gay slang from the US, more likely to be used (properly) in the UK as 'nice cheeks'. Not entirely confined to male gays, as 'What a pair of cheeks' is the sort of expression commonly used by straight men about women.

niche The vagina. Obvious imagery and from the 18th century in the UK, but now rare, especially in speech.

nick, the The vagina. Another obvious term dating back two centuries, but largely taken over now by the gay usage below.

nick, the The buttock cleft. Common male gay slang in the US and the UK, but sometimes also

136

used by straight males and females, usually as a joke. As such, synonymous with wedgie. Also 'Happy Valley'.

nick, to To have sexual intercourse. It would be tempting to trace an etymology back to the notions of 'stealing' (from the male point of view) but this isn't the case. Now very rare.

nick-nacks (sometimes knick-knacks) The sexual parts. An entrenched euphemism used by male and female alike; but now the male is more likely to favour nacks, or knackers, while the female is likely to opt for a more direct description of her sexual organ.

nicotine stains Faecal stains on underwear. Principally US male gay slang among whom their presence or absence is regarded as of potentially sexual significance and may lead to a male being regarded in a different way. The non-sexual UK equivalent is 'skid marks'.

niffy Malodorous. Only sexual (and insulting) when applied to a partner's sexual parts. Niff = smell is virtually Standard English. In the UK usage is confined to the male (about the vagina) but the word enjoys some camp popularity in the States describing the anus.

nifty, do a To have sexual intercourse. Although the description has a history dating back

several centuries it is still considered popular, euphemistic and funny although far more likely to be used by a male than a female.

niggle, to To have sexual intercourse. Unlike 'do a nifty' this (and niggling) have not survived the passage of time and are rarely used.

night games Any act of sex by any combination of male or female (or multiples of both). A 20th century euphemism, but one so well entrenched and 'respectable' that song titles and films frequently use the description. The association of sex with night is a venerable one (despite the apparent lessons of Adam and Eve in the Garden of Eden!) and brings forth a tedious plethora of compounds. Night work (= sexual intercourse) is probably the oldest, with night starvation (= lack of same; once used innocently as an advertising slogan by Horlicks) following up. Ironically, to be on the night shift is now used as a joke to mean having sex during the day.

Nimrod The penis. From the old legend which has Nimrod as the 'mighty hunter' (Partridge) but achieving popular male currency after a missile was developed post-World War II called the Nimrod. As such a tedious continuation of the 'penis as weapon' litany.

nip, to To have sexual intercourse. Like 'niggling', not really surviving in present usage, although the partner word nippy (= penis) still has some schoolboy appeal.

nipped in the bud Circumcised. Principally US usage where the operation is much more common outside the Jewish community than it is in the UK.

nipples Once an entirely innocent word, now has very strong sexual overtones, especially in descriptive conversation and in compound phrases. The nipples are considered a sexually provocative part of the body and many a soft porn magazine has been sold on the basis of printing a picture of a 'celebrity' nipple. In recent times vast press coverage also has been devoted to such cases as the little-known Wimbledon tennis player whose nipple appeared accidentally on Centre Court, while the male obsession of such a 'glimpse' was perhaps best evidenced in 1981 when a huge Press and TV controversy raged over whether Princess Diana's nipple had 'slipped out' of her low-cut evening dress as she was leaving a car. 'Is this or is this not the Royal nipple?' the tabloids demanded, printing a grossly blown-up picture of the relevant area. Meanwhile the unfortunate Anna Ford was obliged to spend five minutes on 'News At Ten' analysing the issue. It was a shadow, the nation later decided.

nipples bigger than my wife's tits Prominent nipples. A common UK catch phrase to describe a woman with 'large' nipples. Invariably male usage, as are some of the other examples cited below. Hence 'Ice cube nipples' (first coined by 'glamour' photographers who actually use ice cubes for this purpose) are those prominent due to atmospheric rather than sexual attention. But there are 'nipples like chapel hat pegs' and 'nipples like radio dials' (*see also* RADIO DIALS).

A man passing a woman with prominent nipples may comment 'I didn't realise it was that cold!', but the more common soft porn images of nipples becoming 'engorged' or 'inflamed' indicate that the male is sometimes as anxious about the state of desire of the female as he is about his own organ.

nips Breasts and/or nipples. An obvious shortening, but in camp usage the word is meant to be dismissive and demeaning (especially if used about women). 'Ninnies' is synonymous. Both are contemporary US and UK usage.

nixies Knickers. An almost childish abbreviation, but also with a feeble pun on 'next to nothings'.

nob Either the penis, or, to nob = to have intercourse. A variant on the much more popular 'knob' for both usages.

nobble, to To have sexual intercourse. Also, a bit of nobble. Compare the last entry, although the principal usage derives from the aggressive notion of 'seizing and catching hold of' (OED). An almost jokey word, used by straight males.

nock The vagina. Origins obscure, but on the verge of being insulting and now rarely used.

nocturnal emission The 'official' description of a male wet dream and, as such, not strictly slang. Yet its very pedantry leads to common jocular conversational usage. 'What did you have last night? A nocturnal emission.' (Laughter.)

no harm in asking Outdated catch phrase that has now become clichéd. As in 'Would you like to go to bed with me? No? Well, no harm in asking.' Or perhaps the more common male interchange 'Does she go then? No harm in asking.'

nookie Sexual intercourse. Also, a bit of nookie. Standard UK euphemism (not as common in the US) dating from the 1920s and still in extremely common currency. Sometimes seen as nooky. A rarer, but still extant, usage is nookie, meaning a woman. Derivation is from the literal meaning of nook (= hole or space) but just

as likely to be used by male or female despite the originally insulting connotations.

nooky push-push Sexual intercourse, either between male and female or male and male, but since this is US camp in origin more often used to describe the latter. Among male gays a more affectionate word than many describing the same activity.

norks The breasts. Originally Forces slang from WW1, developing into a young male joke word with enormous popularity. In fact by the seventies so well accepted it began to be used by females as well. UK use only. One source (Brophy and Partridge) suggests the origin is from Norco butter adverts (a now deleted brand) which depicted a large-uddered cow. A dated variant used by the female is norgies, and equally outmoded are norgs and norkers. All are now superseded by norks.

Norma A straight male. Camp gay usage, obviously derived from normal but punning on the female name. A rarer, and less interesting, variant is norm.

Norma Snokkers Any woman regarded by a male as having large breasts. Norma = enormous, snokkers = knockers (Cooper, H. 1983). Pseudo-comic UK usage only.

north or south? Circumcised or uncircumcised. A question usually preceded by 'are you?'. US male gay usage (Rodgers).

North Pole The anus. Rhyming slang on (bum)hole. 20th century origin but now rarely heard.

notch The vagina. Dismissive male term, more common in the UK than in the US. Several centuries old but (unfortunately?) still in common slang parlance.

nothing below the waist A female refusal of any sexual activity beyond kissing and breast fondling. Coy young female usage dating back to the fifties.

not tonight A refusal to participate in sexual activity. So widespread that it has become a cliché. Usually used in compound form as in 'Not tonight, I've got a headache' (surely the best known catch phrase); usually attributed to the female by the 'frustrated' male. More old fashioned is 'Not tonight, Josephine' (supposedly derived from Napoleon's refusal of his lover) in which the roles are interestingly reversed. Extra emphasis can also be added, as in 'Will you go to bed with me?' 'Not today, not tonight, not ever.'

novelty, the The vagina. Quaint, 18th century in origin, and now all but obsolete except in euphemistic usage.

nub To have sexual intercourse. Thus also nubbing. Venerable, dating back to the 18th century, but still extant.

nubbies Breasts. Almost a joke word, used more in Australia than anywhere else. Post WW2, from the literal sense protuberance.

nuddy, in the Naked. Dated euphemism, now only finding slight favour among the older generation. Obviously a pun on nude, but a tortuous one!

nugget A girl. Australian and American from WW2 onwards, but gradually losing favour. Literally 'a piece of gold'.

nugging Sexual intercourse. Possibly related to nub (q.v.) and dating back at least as long – first usage being traced back to the 18th century. Related are nugging house, meaning brothel, and the affectionate term among males, nugging cove, a man of great sexual prowess. All are dated terms and now rarely used.

number nip The vagina. Dating back two centuries and now rarely heard. Usage has now translated into number = woman ('that nice little number standing over there on her own') by males only; another example of the almost inexhaustible woman = vagina examples.

numbers game An 'uninhibited' sex session (Rodgers). US male gay slang. In this case 'number' is either the sexual partner (and it's assumed there will be several) or the sexual preference; 'What's your number?' *Contrast* the more innocent UK straight usage of NUMBER *under* NUMBER NIP.

number three Sexual intercourse or masturbation; usually the latter. Dated young UK male usage from the turn of the century. The origin is obviously number one = urination, number two = defecation, number three = sexual relief, and as such only likely to be heard among schoolboys.

nun A prostitute. Dating back to the 17th century and now rarely heard, as is nunnery meaning brothel. While these dated euphemisms have lost ground a nun's chastity has been restored in the popular imagination. 'As dry as a nun's nasty' simply means very dry indeed (*see under* NASTY).

nunga munch Cunnilingus. An obscure Australianism from the sixties onwards. Male usage only.

nursery The vagina. A tortuous 19th century euphemism now all but obscure. Punning on a place to play and even (?) where things grow.

nurtle Sexual intercourse. Australian in origin from 1940 onwards. Rare.

nuts The testicles. Now a popular term in the UK, especially among males, although the etymology is curious. The OED records the now obsolete meaning of glans penis, from 1758. This was later resuscitated as nutmegs, meaning testicles, in the 19th century. Shortened to nuts the description enjoys a widespread usage as an affectionate equivalent to balls.

Variants and compounds verging on the borders of non-sexual slang include nut-bags and nut chokers for male underpants, both popular post WW2.

nylon milkpails A bra. From the 1940s onwards a camp US male expression, rarely used by a female.

nymph A 'young and beautiful woman' (OED). From 1584, this worthy source suggests, but a word that has taken on an entirely new (and salacious) meaning in the 20th century. A nymph, nymphet or occasionally nymphette is any young girl from the age of puberty regarded as sexually available by an older man. The word also has pornographic and sadistic overtones and sexual liaison of this nature can actually be outside the law if the woman involved is under the age of 16 (in the UK). Yet it still has widespread currency, and is even occasionally used by national newspapers. One common male description of 'paradise' dating from the '60s was 'hot and cold running nymphets'.*See also* LOLITA.

nympho Nymphomaniac. The most common conversational shortening of a word used to describe a woman whom males consider to be 'sexually overactive'. Although strictly borrowed from the medical profession the word is in widespread usage and is invariably insulting to the female when used by the male. Any woman who has had more than two lovers in a short space of time can often be heard described as 'a raving nympho'. Similarly, women unfortunate enough to have a greater sexual desire than their male partner can also be insulted by being called a nympho.

O

oats, to get one's To have sexual intercourse. Originating from terms like sowing wild oats and have one's oats, both dating back to the 18th century (Partridge), suggestions that a man was behaving in a 'wild and dissolute fashion' before settling down; i.e. sowing wild oats instead of good grain. Modern usage is more widespread and less moralistic: 'Did you get your oats last night?' means simply, did you have sex? Male and female UK usage.

obvious Pregnant. A 'high society' euphemism since the last century. Now only heard in 'polite' conversation, as in: 'Can't you see, she's obvious,' i.e. obviously pregnant.

occupy, to To have sexual intercourse. Originally having the 16th century meaning 'cohabiting', the verb became vulgarized very rapidly and was considered equivalent to tup and fuck in the 18th and 19th centuries. Time has now rendered it no more than a harmless – and rare – euphemism.

odd Having homosexual leanings. Supposedly (to the speaker) one of the most inoffensive ways of describing something he or she purports not to understand. Thus, easier than saying 'gay' or 'queer'. *Compare* DOUBLE-GAITED. A UK euphemism dating back to the turn of the century.

off *See* GET OFF WITH.

off the brush Living together out of wedlock. A 20th century UK expression, mostly heard in the north and Scotland. A common phrase for which the authors would welcome suggestions as to a derivation.

ogle To eye amorously (OED). Scarcely slang, having entered Standard English by 1600, but a good example of a word that is now used 'salaciously', both in speech and in popular newspapers. For a man to be described as 'ogling women' now means that he is a 'lecher' rather more than an interested observer. Similarly, ogler is a term of abuse, often applied by women to men, and the practice of ogling is equally frowned on, with the assumption that it is something only done by

143

'dirty old men'. In this sense only 'eyeing' and 'eyeing up' retain their innocence.

oil painting, she's no (Rarely, 'he's no oil painting'.) A woman considered unattractive by a man. A common catch phrase in the UK from the 1930s on and not always as insulting as it may first appear. The authors have heard several middle-aged men making remarks like 'I know the wife is no oil painting but I love her just the same,' in which case the usage is definitely affectionate.

old Adam The penis. Two or more centuries old and virtually obsolete, but perhaps the first of male names for the penis. *Compare* JOHN THOMAS, and PERCY *et al.*

old bag A woman, usually a wife. Dating back to the 19th century. Male UK usage only. A frequent alternative is the more insulting 'old battleaxe'. *Contrast with* CHINA, and 'ER INDOORS.

old Brown Windsor The anus. Waggish, late 19th century, from the colour of the faeces. Surprisingly never taken up as a camp or gay expression and now only used by public school boys.

old enough to butcher, old enough to bleed Catch phrase applied to a female old enough (legally) to have sexual intercourse. Crude UK male usage from a Merchant Navy source.

oldest profession, the The business of prostitution. Common for many centuries but since WW2 *the* most acceptable and fashionable euphemism for an age-old practice. Equally common is 'professional' for prostitute, both often shortened to 'pro'.

old fashioned Homosexual. A coy euphemism dating back at least a century. Teasing male UK usage only. 'I wouldn't play tennis with him, he's old fashioned.' More pedantic is the term 'a member of the old school', also meaning a homosexual. Both have relations with 'the Greek way' (= buggery).

old fella (sometimes old fellow) The penis. Affectionate male personification since the 1920s at least. Most often heard in phrases like 'I took the old fella out and gave her one'. UK and Australia usage still in popular currency. The earliest recorded etymology cites old man, meaning penis (Partridge) but this is now obsolete.

old flame A former sexual partner. From the turn of the century, and now so euphemistic it has almost become coy. Irish folk singers Foster and Allen scooped the charts in 1982 with a song called 'Old Flames', reviving several ancient clichés: 'Old flames don't hold a candle to you/ No-one lights up my life like you do'.

old hat The vagina. Endearingly dated from the 17th century and seldom used today but worthy of mention after Grose's definition 'because frequently felt'. Similarly dated is the 18th century 'old ding', a dismissive male word for vagina.

old horn An erection. A florification of horn (q.v.).

old lady A wife or girlfriend. Affectionate male usage, and the meaning wife dating back to the 19th century at least. However the expression found renewed popularity from the sixties on, especially in rock music circles. 'That's no groupie you're talking about, that's my old lady'. When *not* used in that sense it is synonymous with old Dutch and old china. *See* CHINA.

old lady five fingers Masturbation. Common from he 1920s onwards and invariably male in usage. Virtually synonymous with five finger knuckle shuffle, and Mother Palm and her five daughters.

old maid An unmarried – or unattached – woman. Although the term specifies old age, a female of almost any age may complain of being an 'old maid' if she has no relationship with a man, and the expression is also used dismissively of any single woman, as in 'Don't mind what she says, she's just a silly old maid.' The implication is that without a male partner

women become dried up, frustrated, even twisted. Contemporary UK and US slang.

Note that the only male equivalent is the infinitely more positive 'batchelor', although a single man may be called an 'old maid' as a term of abuse.

See also SPINSTER, and ON THE SHELF.

old one two, the Sexual intercourse. A heterosexual and usually male term from the 19th century onwards. Still in current usage but not as common as 'a good going over' and 'a good seeing to'; perhaps it's too euphemistic?

omi (sometimes omee) A man. Widespread UK and US usage among the gay community, who first coined it in the forties, and it's being going strong ever since. Often preceded by naff (in this context meaning straight) or bona = homosexual. *See also* BONA OMI.

omnibus A woman regarded by a male as either a prostitute or sexually 'promiscuous'. From the 19th century (when it also had the dual meaning of cunt) and still current. Literally, somethig that is ridden on, and as such insulting to women. Not as popular however as bike, or town bike.

on Menstruating. Female usage and a useful euphemism, although come on (= have one's period) shouldn't be confused with the other meaning of come on (= to

145

achieve orgasm). *See also* OTR, OTB, and ON THE RAG.

one-eyed trouser snake The penis. A male 'joke' term for the virile member, but one more likely to be used when referring to urination rather than sexual intercourse. Australian, from the fifties, now UK. The earlier equivalent, still used occasionally, is 'one-eyed milkman', which has greater sexual overtones. *See also* POLYPHEMUS.

one finger exercise The stimulation of the clitoris. 20th century male term, mostly UK. Interesting transferrence of attitude; masturbation is a 'five finger exercise', similar female arousal requires only one!

one in the box Pregnant. Venerable phrase virtually synonymous with 'bun in the oven'.

one in the bush is worth two in the hand Common UK and Australian catch phrase punning the original and commenting on the fact that sexual intercourse (here bush = vagina) is better than any amount of masturbation (= a hand job). Male usage only.

one night stand A sexual encounter that takes place only once. Imported from the US to the UK in the fifties and now a popular enough phrase regarded as so tame it can be used in tabloid newspapers. Male and female usage, straight and gay, as the emphasis is on the briefness of the affair, not what actually took place. In the US the person with whom one has a one night stand is either a 'oncer' or a 'one-timer', although in the gay community both these terms mean a merely casual encounter, not necessarily lasting a night.

one piece overcoat A condom. Sometimes just shortened to overcoat. Common UK euphemism from 1950 onwards.

one track mind, you've got Usually followed up with 'and that's a dirt track' and a common chastisement of anyone regarded as being preoccupied by sex (Partridge). Mostly UK, used with equal facility by male and female from the forties onwards, although usage now is regarded as somewhat quaint by the young.

one with the other Sexual intercourse. 19th century UK euphemism rarely heard today.

on for it Sexually available. Widespread recent UK and US usage, both by male and female. Can be harmless or provocative depending on conversational context; a male would say to another male 'She's definitely on for it', while a female might enquire of her partner 'Are you on for it tonight?'. Virtually synonymous, but more in the male domain, is 'up for it'.

ONS *See* ONE NIGHT STAND

on the blob Menstruating. *See* OTB.

on the game Engaged in prostitution. A widely used euphemism dating back to the turn of the century and recently so common that it has entered 'newspaper speak'.

on the job Engaged in sexual intercourse. Hearty male usage, mostly in the UK. 'I'm sorry I didn't answer the phone, I was on the job.' The phrase carries connotations of the male 'servicing' the female: *see* SERVICE, TOOL, and DO.

on the rag Menstruating. 20th century UK usage where rag = sanitary towel. Male and female usage, with the latter preferring this phrase to others regarded as more insulting and offensive. *See*, for instance, RED SAILS IN THE SUNSET.

on the shelf An unmarried female. Dated phrase from the last century still used today. 'You'd better hurry up and get a man otherwise you'll find yourself on the shelf.' *Compare* OLD MAID. Note that there is no male equivalent.

ooh la la From the French, a well-worn 40s retort to anything slightly 'saucy'. Used by UK newspapers in the sixties where scantily clad models were 'ooh la la girls', but now becoming dated and unfashionable.

oojah pips Breasts. Originally Forces slang, then more general male jocular usage in the UK, but now fading into obscurity.

open arse Originally prostitute, from the 17th century onwards in the UK. But increasingly having the concurrent meaning of *any* woman when used by a male. *See also* SPLIT ARSE.

open up! A male plea for a woman to submit to sexual intercourse, i.e. to 'spread her legs'. As in the song 'Open up' by Lloyd Charmers, from the LP 'Censored' (1970). 'Open up' is also used by male gays. In the US to open the gate means to submit to anal intercourse.

orchestra stalls Testicles. From cockney rhyming slang with balls. Frequently shortened to 'orchestra', or the expletive 'orchestras!' An example of how this form of slang takes the most unlikely of images for its rhymes – and thereby gives the expression humour. *See also* COBBLER'S AWLS, COFFEE STALLS.

organ, play the To masturbate. Common male slang from the 19th century onwards and still extant. Can also mean to have sexual intercourse. Widespread UK and US male usage. *See also* PERFORM.

orks A shortening of 'orchestra stalls' (q.v.) – i.e. rhyming slang with balls, perhaps also with a pun on norks (q.v.). Limited UK usage, and now dated.

Oscar A homosexual male. From the 19th century wit Oscar Wilde who made no secret, even in those times, of his homosexuality and 'campness'. Even though the word is fading from popularity it threw up a whole host of variations including to oscarise (= to bugger), to oscar (the same) and the ancient practice of Oscar Wildeing (anal intercourse). UK usage.

OTB Menstruating. Coming from the initials of 'on the blob' and used by women either to other women conversationally or to a sexual partner – 'We can't have sex tonight, I'm OTB'. One of the more humorous and affectionate descriptions of the menstrual cycle. *Contrast*, for instance, THE CURSE. UK usage from the 70s onwards.

OTR Menstruating. *See* ON THE RAG.

out An admission of homosexuality, usually in the phrase 'He/she has come out at last'. In the US and the UK the more common and accepted form is 'out of the closet'. *See* CLOSET GAY.

out for trade Going out on the streets looking for a sexual encounter. Originally used by prostitutes in the UK, now widely adopted by the US male gay community. *See also* CRUISING.

oven The vagina. A 19th century anachronism (because hot?) only surviving today in the phrase 'bun in the oven' (q.v.). *See also* INGLE NOOK.

overs and unders Overt and latent homosexuals respectively (Rodgers). US camp and gay usage.

over the shoulder boulder holder A bra. A tortuous joke phrase almost exclusively used by school children. Current UK usage.

over the time (sometimes 'over my time'). A late period, possibly caused by pregnancy. The period is known as 'the time of the month' in polite female UK usage. Now outdated, and replaced by the term 'late'.

owl taming US gay slang for 'cruising' the streets at night in search of a sexual encounter. In the UK 'owl' has the meaning prostitute (Partridge), but this is dated.

oyster Also oyster bed. The vagina. Another term which portrays the female sexual organ as fish or mollusc (and also edible). Dating back several centuries but now obsolete. *See also* PERIWINKLE, WHELK, FISH.

Oyster also has the concurrent meaning of semen, but this usage is rare.

P

package The male genitals, as observed under clothing. A common US, but rarely UK, term as in – 'That's a fine package he's got'. *Compare* TOOL, EQUIPMENT.

painters in, to have the Said of a menstruating woman, generally by men. The image is of great swathes of cloth spread to protect from drips, and comparable to 'red sails in the sunset', and 'flags flying'. Limited UK usage, imported from Australia and the US.

paint the bucket, to Sexual intercourse. US, mostly gay slang. Comparable to the British phrase 'like dangling string in a bucket'. *See* STRING IN A BUCKET.

pair Breasts. Extremely common male UK usage. Usually in commentary, such as 'Look at that pair', or 'She's got a fine pair'. Comparatively modern slang and peculiarly British.

pair off with To form a sexual relationship with a male or female. Common UK usage, as in 'Everybody's getting paired off these days'.

pancake The female genitalia. Again, the body as food – *see also* CRUMPET, BEEF CURTAINS etc. Rare and old-fashioned usage (Partridge).

pansy Male homosexual. Derisive heterosexual usage in both the UK and US, since the 20s. Hence *The Sun* ran this news item on 25 Feb. 1984: 'A man dressed as Andy Pandy for a fancy dress party claimed three gays mistook him for Andy Pansy – and tried to chat him up. But Bristol Crown Court found that (he) attacked the gays in a case of "queer-bashing".'

Also 'to pansy up' – for a man to dress himself up, and 'to pansy about' – to act in an effeminate manner. Again, the clear inference is that gay men aren't 'real men' but semi-female. *See also* FAIRY, NANCE.

panters The breasts. From their

149

proximity to the 'panter' – the heart. Old-fashioned, and virtually obsolete UK usage (Partridge), similar to 'heavers'.

papaya Vagina. Limited US usage. Comparable to 'fig' in describing the female parts as luscious fruit.

parlour Female genitals. Also 'front parlour'. UK male usage, now obsolete, but in the tradition of describing the body as real estate – 'To lie back and let out one's parlour' is an old-fashioned expression for prostitution (Partridge). Another old-fashioned term is premises.

parsley Pubic hair. Also 'parsley bed' as the female genitals, and 'take a turn in the parsley bed' for sexual intercourse (Partridge). Now virtually obsolete, but *see also* GREENS, and GARDEN.

partner Lover, male or female. Another of the awkward euphemisms applied to modern relationships since pre-marital sex has become the norm and homosexuality more socially acceptable. UK and US widespread usage, but sometimes as the more camp 'passion partner' in America.

parts The genitalia, male or female. *See* PRIVATE PARTS.

pash Infatuation. An abbreviation of 'passion' which came from the US to the UK during the early 20s. It enjoyed a heyday amongst English schoolgirls who would

have 'pashes' on each other and their teachers, but is now distinctly dated and rarely used. Far more fashionable is to have a 'crush'.

pastry A woman. A variation on the theme of a 'tasty' woman as 'jam tart', 'crumpet' etc. Limited UK male usage.

Pat and Mick Penis. Cockney rhyming slang for prick. Mad Mick is an equivalent. Now virtually obsolete. *See also* HAMPTON WICK.

paw, to A contemptuous term for unwanted or inept fondling, conjuring the image of a fawning dog. Similar in usage to 'grope' – as in 'Did you see that old drunk pawing her at the party?' A modern term, but 'paw-paw' was a nursery word for 'improper' as far back as 1720, while 'paw-paw tricks' was masturbation.

PE An abbreviation of premature ejaculation. Embarrassed UK male and female usage in modern times.

peach A sexually attractive woman. Originally American, this term came to the UK at the end of the 19th century and is now a widespread term of approval for a person, usually female but sometimes male. A trendy variant amongst young people is peacherino – i.e. especially 'peachy'. Sometimes regarded as slightly passé among the young, but equally likely to become fashionable as quickly as it may seem to disappear.

pearl necklace The drops of semen spilling out of the fellator's mouth and down his or her neck after fellatio. Originally US male gay slang from the fifties, but also limited US heterosexual usage. Rare in the UK.

pebbles The testicles. Old-fashioned and limited UK usage. But *see also* PILLS, NUTS.

pecker The penis. Widespread UK usage since the 19th century. Now also used in the US in terms like 'pecker tracks' – semen on clothing. The image probably derives from the synonymous 'beak', as something hard and protruding. The expression 'to keep one's pecker up' however, is not as risqué as it sounds. It is derived from the other slang meaning of 'peck' as appetite, and is a way of saying 'stay in good health'.

peeping Tom Man who watches through curtains or spy holes to catch a glimpse of (usually) women's nudity. A widespread UK expression. It originally meant an inquisitive person, from the legend of Lady Godiva (1785: Grose). *See also* BOGGLE.

peep show A booth where males can watch naked females dancing. Usually there are several

individual booths around a circular dance floor. Insertion of a coin in a slot gives up to two minutes 'viewing'. UK and US, especially London's Soho and New York's Times Square.

pen The penis. Dating back to the 16th century, this is both a phallic symbol and an abbreviation of penis. 'To have no more ink in the pen' is an old catch phrase for sexual exhaustion in the male. 'Pencil' was also a 19th century word for penis, while 'pencil and tassel' was the penis and scrotum (Partridge). All of these are virtually obsolete.

pendulum The penis. Rarely used, but *see* the more popular DINGLE DANGLE.

percy The penis. Most commonly heard in the famous Barry Mackenzie phrase from Australia – 'to point percy at the porcelain'; i.e. to urinate. Now enthusiastically adopted by British males.

Male names for the organ are common: *see also* DICK, JOHN THOMAS, MAN *et al.*

perform, to For a man to have sexual intercourse with a woman. UK male usage, common and contemporary. Also with the meaning fellatio, in US gay usage.

periwinkle The female genitals. Possibly from the name of the bright blue flower – but more likely a reference to the mollusc if other slang is an indication. *See* *also* BEARD-SPLITTER. Limited UK usage.

perv A sexually deviant male, such as a 'flasher', or 'peeping Tom'. Contemporary UK male and female usage, and an abbreviation of pervert – as in 'I'm sure there was a perv staring in my window last night'.

pestle, to Sexual intercourse. The penis is also 'the pestle', while 'the mortar' is the female genitalia. Old-fashioned UK usage, now virtually obsolete, but *see also* POUND THE MOUND.

peter The penis. Another in the long line of terms ascribing a Christian name to the male organ. Used by males from school days onwards, UK and US. Current but regarded as slightly twee, unlike John Thomas or Dick (q.v.). *See also* PETER METER.

peter meter Implement for measuring the penis. Mostly joking male usage, in the US and UK, focusing on the male preoccupation with length of the organ, 'Peter' is unlikely to be used on its own, but is in the tradition of male names for the penis – *see also* DICK, PERCY, JOHN THOMAS, MAN.

phyllis A euphemism for 'syphilis'. Limited UK usage, now largely obsolete.

pick up, to To make acquaintance with a person with the intent of having sex. It is generally, but not always, men who do the 'picking up'. The social setting in the UK is often a disco, pub or party, while in the US singles bars are often called pick-up parlours or pick-up joints, and women who go along into bars are assumed to be there for a 'pick-up'. Once the relationship is formed, the woman (usually) is rather contemptuously referred to as 'a pick-up'. Modern usage and still predominantly American.

piece A sexual object, mostly male UK (and some US) usage to describe women. Often as piece of flesh, piece of goods, piece of crumpet, piece of ass, nice piece. Equivalent to the equally common 'bit'. Note that both imply less than a complete person. This usage of 'piece' dates back to the 14th century.

pig A woman considered by gay men to be sexual competition. US gay usage. 'Pig suck' is a contemptuous gay term for a heterosexual male, while 'pig pile' or 'pig party' is a homosexual orgy. *See also* DOG, for a UK equivalent.

pillock The penis. This term has ancient roots, traceable back to the 14th century as 'pillicock' and 'pillcock'. Shakespeare's King Lear has the line 'pillicock sat on pillicock hill', in which 'pillicock hill' is the vagina. Although rarely used to mean penis today, pillock is still a term of mild abuse between men, and is often heard in Ireland. As in 'Don't be such a stupid pillock'. Comparable to 'bollock'.

pillow talk Lovers' intimate bedtime conversation. Affectionate and widespread UK usage. 'Pillows' also had the old-fashioned meaning of breasts, while a pillow-mate was a lover.

pills The testicles. Widespread male UK usage, considered 'vulgar' since the late 19th century. A precursor of the cockney rhyming slang 'Beechams' or 'Beecham's pills', also meaning pills, i.e. testicles. However, less popular than the ubiquitous 'balls'.

pin The penis. Limited, derisory UK usage. Still popular however is the catch phrase referring to a woman's supposed 'promiscuity' – 'She's had more pricks than a pin-cushion'.

pink oboe The penis. Comparable to 'blue veined trumpet'. Originally Forces slang, now common straight male UK usage.

pintel Also pintle. The penis. An ancient word, to be found in the bawdier verses of Robert Burns and now only used jokingly among his followers. Also pintle case – the vagina, pintle fever – syphilis, and pintle-bit or pintle-maid – a mistress or prostitute; all 19th century. Now obsolete.

pipkin Also pitcher. The female genitals. Old-fashioned UK slang, now obsolete; as is the related term 'to crack the pipkin' or 'to crack the pitcher', i.e. to take a woman's virginity.

piss flaps The labia. Contemporary male UK term and only marginally less nasty than the US equivalent 'beef curtains'.

piss hard on An erection caused by the need to urinate. UK male term and comparatively recent.

piss proud Also sometimes 'morning pride'. An early morning erection caused by the need to urinate. Dated UK male slang. *See also* EMBO.

pit A place for sex, as in 'passion pit' or 'snake pit'. Widespread US usage, but UK usage is generally non-sexual, pit having the simple meaning of a place to sleep.

pit job To ejaculate into the armpit. Also 'pit queen', one who enjoys the practice. *See* HUFFLE for a full description.

plaster of warm guts Sometimes also 'poultice of warm guts'. Sexual intercourse – as therapy. As in the 1785 dictum, 'One warm belly clapt to another (is) a receipt frequently prescribed for different disorders.'

Yet despite its age this catch phrase is making a comeback with the UK young, in preference to the standard advice, 'What you need is a woman.'

plates and dishes Wife. From

cockney rhyming slang for missus. Also sometimes slang for kisses.

play, make a To proposition, or attempt to seduce a man or a woman. Common contemporary UK usage, male and female.

play away, to Euphemistic for an illicit or extra-marital affair. From the sporting terminology of 'home' and 'away' matches. As in this recent *Sun* story about the Parkinson 'affair': 'The shock revelation that glamour-boy MP Cecil had been "playing-away" with secretary Sara Keays cannot have come as any great surprise to (his wife) Ann.'

play hard to get To feign indifference to a person's advances in order to make them try harder. Widespread UK and US usage, especially among younger people of both sexes who are still 'playing the field'.

play hospitals *See* HOSPITALS.

play the field To experiment sexually with different people. Generally approved activity for younger, unmarried people. Rather sporty modern British usage.

play the organ Fellatio. US gay slang. Both the pun and the reference to oral sex as music are characteristically camp.

play windmills For one man to watch another urinating. US gay

154

slang, from the practice of 'making windmills' – urinating in overlapping circles (Rodgers). For further male gay preoccupation with urination *see* GOLDEN SHOWER.

play with oneself Masturbation. Euphemistic and long-established British usage, often used of children, as in 'How do you stop your little boy from playing with himself?' Also some affectionate adult usage, with regard to masturbation as a pleasurable activity. *Compare* the less positive WANKING and the more graphic JERK OFF, TWANG THE WIRE.

pleasure gardens The female genitals. Old-fashioned UK usage, probably dating back a century, but still sometimes heard – as in the phrase from an old woman patient, told to the authors by a nurse, 'Are you going to wash my pleasure gardens dear?'

Parallel to the now obsolete 19th century 'pleasure boat'. The garden image is still a common one: *see also* GREENS, PARSLEY, GORILLA SALAD.

plonker The penis. Contemporary male and female UK usage, in the same line as 'donger' and 'chopper', and dating back to World War I.

plug, to To have sexual intercourse. Also 'plug tail' the penis, from the 18th century. Both of these are now out of date. Note, however, that 'plumbing' – the genitals – lives on in US slang.

pocket billiards, to play For a man to fondle his own genitals via his trouser pockets. A widespread UK term – usually in the form of a jocular accusation between men – as in 'Stop playing pocket billiards and take your hands out to pay for a drink.' In the US however, 'pocket pool' is the more popular term.

pocket the red, to To experience orgasm. An old-fashioned UK term, rarely heard today. From the snooker or billiard term, meaning to pot the ball.

poke, to To have sexual intercourse. Contemporary UK male – and sometimes female – usage, as in 'I haven't had a poke in ages', or 'Is he really poking her?'. Hardly a romantic concept, but in the same vein as the less popular 'prod'.

pole The penis. Also 'pole work' and 'poling' for sexual intercourse. Old-fashioned UK usage, but now virtually obsolete.

polone, or **palone** Woman. UK gay slang, now also US usage. Often as 'bona polone' – nice woman. There is no agreement about the origin: it could be a derivation from the Italian *pollone* – sprout, or from the Spanish *pollo* – hen. Some sources however believe it comes from the Romany, and passed into gay slang during the 30s.

For the male equivalent *see* OMI.

Polyphemus The penis. Now obsolete, but an old-fashioned term amongst the British literati, denoting 'the one-eyed one', from the one-eyed giant of Homer's *Odyssey*. Compare the contemporary 'one-eyed trouser snake'.

poof Also pouf. Male homosexual. A derisive heterosexual, usually male, UK term. Dating back to 1932, with the variants 'poove', 'poofdah', and the Australian 'poofter'. However its precursor 'puff' – tramps' slang for a homosexual – is recorded from 1870. While 'puff' is no longer heard in the UK, it is slang for 'gay' in the US.

Another recently popular equivalent among UK males is 'woofter', punning on P.G. Wodehouse's immortal Bertie Wooster (who, ironically, wasn't a homosexual) and simply rhyming with poofter. On the same note a gay man is also likely to be referred to as a Bertie Woofter, or simply 'a Bertie'.

poor man's blessing The female genitals. Old-fashioned and affectionate UK usage dating back to the 19th century, no longer in popular currency.

pork West Indian term for a white woman, in contrast to 'beef' – a black woman. One of many references to the body as meat. Also a gay US term for penis, but

155

limited usage. *See also* SALT AND PEPPER.

pork dagger The penis. Recent male UK usage, with explicit reference to the penis as a piercing weapon (*see* PRICK, and PRONG).

pound the mound Sexual intercourse. Male UK usage, only recently popular in slang. Again, the male is active and aggressive to the female's passive 'mound' and an attractive female is called 'poundable'.

pound the pork Sexual intercourse. Also, sometimes, to masturbate. An Australian male equivalent of 'pound the mound' (q.v.). Pork sometimes has the meaning, penis (as in masturbation) and sometimes, woman.

pouter The vagina. 19th century UK slang, from 'diddly pout' – rhyming slang with spout. Now obsolete.

pranny The female genitals. A contemptuous term used by UK men since the 19th century and now commonly a mild term of abuse, as in 'Don't be such a pranny!'

prat, or **pratt** Although generally used in the UK as a mild term of abuse – as in 'He's a silly prat' – this word also means cunt. It came into slang as 'buttocks' during the 18th century and persisted as 'behind' during the 19th. A 'pratting ken' was a brothel at this time. The word became explicitly 'the female genitals' in the 20th century, which usage remains.

prick The penis. Perhaps the most common UK and US term for the male organ, and in the UK equally common as a term of insult to a man – as in, 'What did you do that for, you stupid prick?'

The OED notes the use of prick for penis as far back as 1592, and it was Standard English until 1700. Since then it has been considered a vulgarism. A prime example of the notion of the penis as a piercing tool; *compare* SWORD, PRONG, DAGGER.

prick lick Fellator. US male gay usage from the 50s.

pricks, more than a pin cushion Usually prefixed by 'she's had ...' and an exclusively male term for a woman regarded as overly sexually active. *Contrast with* a bisexual phrase 'He/she's had more rides than Lester Piggot', used to convey either disapproval or approbation.

prick tease A woman who arouses desire in a man, but who won't have sex with him. A widespread contemporary term of insult in the UK, often abbreviated to PT. It is also a product of sexual double standards: a woman is supposed to be attractive to men, but is not supposed to be 'promiscuous' – inevitably some women who conform to both expectations will be called 'PTs'. Note there is no equivalent term for a man.

pride and joy Boy. Cockney rhyming slang.

private parts The genitalia, male or female. Often shortened to 'privates' especially by UK males. A 20th century euphemism, still widely heard in the UK although now less common among the younger generation.

pro Prostitute. UK and US usage since WW2. An abbreviation of professional (and also of prostitute), as a woman who makes a profession of selling her body. In the UK 'prossie' is also a popular equivalent.

promiscuous Indiscriminate in sexual relations. The word is related to the Latin *promiscuus*, meaning confused – from *pro* = for and *miscere* = to mix. The term is commonly applied in a disapproving sense to a person who is thought to have an excessive number of sexual partners. How many is judged to be 'excessive' varies with sexual mores and gender of the person: women, who are still expected to be one man's sexual property, are far more likely to be judged promiscuous than a man for the same sexual behaviour. Julia Stanley (1973) found 220 words for a sexually 'promiscuous' female and only 20 for a sexually 'promiscuous' male.

prong The penis. Recent male UK usage. Comparable to the more widespread 'prick'.

proud below the navel Having an erect penis. Limited and dated UK male usage, with venerable literary roots.

prow The breasts. The comparison is with the great jutting front of a ship, and the term is generally applied by UK men to women with large busts. Contemporary usage.

PT *See* PRICK TEASE.

pull, to To attract and/or seduce. In the UK a male's ability 'to pull the birds' is of great importance, but sometimes it is women who do the 'pulling' – as in this recent piece in the *Sun* headlined as: 'A bird pulls Robin'.

'Super bird-puller Robin Askwith finds himself irresistibly drawn to sexy Charlotte Rampling ... For a change (Robin) is on the receiving end of amorous advances.'

And anyone like Robin is said to have 'pulling power'.

pull the wire Male masturbation. Contemporary male UK usage, also, occasionally, 'twanging the wire'.

pump To have sexual intercourse. Also the female, and male, genitalia. 'The pump handle' is the penis, and 'to pump off' is (mostly male) masturbation. Originally 18th to 20th century but no longer fashionable.

pussy The female genitals, and as an extension of this usage, a

157

collective term for women. One of the most widespread terms of its kind in the UK and the US, amongst men and women.

Although definitely not polite usage, it is less offensive to some women than 'cunt', which has been so thoroughly debased, and although choice is limited women have told the authors that this is a word they find relatively acceptable to describe their own bodies.

In the form of 'puss', it dates back to the 17th century as in this quote from Cotton:

'Aenaeas, here's a Health to thee
To Pusse and good company' (Partridge).

put them back on again The derisive — and aggressive — cry sometimes heard from men in the audience at a strip show. The inference is that the woman's body is so far below their expectations that she will be doing them a favour by getting dressed again. UK usage from the 50s on.

Q

Q A homosexual male. Originally Forces slang from the twenties – 'He's Q for sure' (Partridge) and simply the initial of 'queer' (q.v. for a detailed etymology). The initial is in widespread usage in the UK and the US and has a host of spin-offs which include Q-boy (a young male gay), Q'er (a male homosexual) and the peculiarly American Q-card (a business card listing a male gay's credentials, sexual preferences and phone number, usually distributed in a gay bar).

QANTAS hostie A female sexual partner. From the days of the early sixties when Australians flocked to London on the Australian national airline, and a myth developed that any hot-blooded Aussie should be able to seduce a hostess *en route*. In England the term rapidly became popular, with humorists such as Barry Humphries (*Bazza Pulls It Off* 1968) coming up with terms like 'She features (= has sexual intercourse) like a QANTAS hostie'.

In recent years however the airline has acquired an entirely different reputation. It now flies with a large number of male stewards, and from the early seventies on QANTAS has been affectionately known to all and sundry as '*Q*ueers *A*nd *N*ancies *T*ogether *A*s *S*tewards'.

quail A woman. Originally a prostitute (Partridge), but now more generally applied. *Compare with* BIRD. The word also has the occasional dual meaning of vagina (= tail), while in the US quail has the camp meaning of 'a migratory man who chases after young chicken (= boys)' (Rodgers).

quaint, the The vagina. Now largely obsolete but a polite euphemism dating back to the 14th century (Grose) from the Middle English *queinte* and *queynte*. Now more of a 'literary' joke word than anything else.

159

qualify, to To have sexual intercourse. From the 19th century 'cultural' usage and now rare. Originating from the notion of 'qualifying as a man' by having sexual intercourse. *See also* PERFORM.

quandong A woman, especially one who is thought to be sexually available. Originally Australian, from the fruit, 'hard on the outside, soft in the middle' (an aboriginal definition). Synonymous is the Australianism 'native peach'. *See* PEACH.

quarry The vagina. Male UK usage only from the last century, and insulting. *Contrast with* other dismissive words for the female sexual organs such as hole, gap, gash, cleft.

quean *See* QUEEN.

queen A male homosexual. The word comes from the old English *cwene* (*cwena*) and originally meant woman. From the 16th century until comparatively recently it was spelt 'quean' and meant either a 'loose woman or harlot'. The OED quotes Robert Burns writing in the 18th century 'I see her yet the sousie quean'. In this century, from the fifties onwards it came to mean an effeminate man. Only since the sixties has the word been adopted by male gays who now use it to delineate every aspect of their sexuality. 'A designation of appearance, preference and character' (Rodgers). Any preference is usually spelt out then followed by queen in conversation, as in 'rim queen' and 'rubber queen'.

queer A male homosexual, but sometimes also used by straight males to describe lesbians. Dating back to the twenties in the US, it had reached the UK by the thirties where it was originally used by 'straight' people. Since the sixties however, the word has been 'reclaimed' by male gays, and is generally used in a defensive, jokey manner. 'Of course I'm queer, dear, don't you love it?'

queer bashing The beating-up of homosexuals by straight males. Although the unpleasant practice has been around for a long time it wasn't until the seventies that popular newspapers coined the phrase. Now in widespread usage in the UK and the US, although increased attention has done little to halt the activity. *See* PANSY.

quelch, to To have sexual intercourse. A UK variant of 'squelching' (q.v.).

quickie, a A short sexual encounter. UK and US usage from the forties onwards and as innocuous as 'afternoon delight' (q.v.). Male and female usage. The notion that a quickie is necessarily 'a rushed act of copulation' (Partridge *and* Rodgers) is erroneous. The word has become a euphemism for sex at an unusual time and/or unusual place. Sometimes also 'a quick one'.

quiff A man who performs fellatio for another man. US gay slang since the fifties. 'To look for a quiff is to look for someone who will oblige with a blow job' (Rodgers).

quiff, to Sexual intercourse. A venerable verb now rarely heard. But *see* the revived (and revised) meaning above.

quim The vagina. One of the oldest examples of a word for the female sexual organ. It once enjoyed a comparatively respectable status, until it was forced 'underground' in the 17th century and came to be considered obscene. Grose cites a 17th century origin from the Spanish *quemar* (= to burn), while Partridge suggests that it may derive from the Welsh *cwm* (= a cleft or a valley). Today it is in wide usage again, especially in the UK, where it is common in pornographic magazines. Mostly male usage.

Obsolete variants include queme, quim-box (still occasionally heard) and quimsby.

quim bush Female pubic hair. Again from 'quim', and also dating back three centuries. Descriptive but rarely heard, as are quim whiskers and quim wig, meaning the same thing.

quimming Sexual intercourse. From 'quim' and now very rare, with quim remaining isolated as a noun. Other obscure terms include quim-sticking and quim-wedging.

quim stake The penis. Also from the worthy 'quim', but unlike the term for the female organ the male equivalent is almost obsolete, as are the synonymous quim-sticker and quim-wedge.

quoits The buttocks. Originally Australian from the fifties (Partridge), now rare but affectionate usage by male and female alike in the US and UK. From the notion of something round and rubbery to play with?

R

rabbit To have sexual intercourse. From the 19th century and still current in the UK. The word is also featured in a myriad of variations most notably 'live rabbit' (= penis), 'rabbit pie' (= vagina) and 'have a bit of rabbit pie' and 'skin the live rabbit' (both meaning intercourse). Also heard by the authors in the contemporary joke phrase exchanged between two men: 'I hope your rabbit dies' (I hope you lose your virility).

radio dials Prominent nipples in a female. 'You could pick up Radio Luxembourg from the front of her T-shirt' (Simon Archer, 1983). From the shape and protuberance. Contemporary UK usage, and not always confined to the male. Female usage is invariably jocular and affectionate. *See also* NIPPLES BIGGER THAN MY WIFE'S TITS.

rag A sanitary towel. Since the forties, but *see* ON THE RAG.

rails, the The labia. UK only, from the sixties and still current in the south. A peculiarly graphic image, one often exploited in pornographic magazines where men talk of 'sliding it in up the rails'. Male usage only.

raise a gallop To have an erection. Originally forces slang from WW2 onwards, now general. Mostly UK usage. Often used in a dismissive, contemptuous sense, especially if used by women. 'We tried to have sex last night but he couldn't raise a gallop.' *See also* GALLOP THE MAGGOT.

rake out To have sexual intercourse. Male UK term dating back several centuries. Almost synonymous with 'stoke the boiler'; in both terms the vagina is 'the fire'.

ramrod The penis. One of the most venerable terms for the male organ, dating back to the 17th century but still in popular currency in the US and the UK. Rarer forms are rammer and ramming stick yet none of them has ever been accepted as anything but slang. 'To ram' (sometimes 'ram it home') meaning sexual intercourse, is equally common.

randy Sexually aroused. Although originating in the 18th century it's only recently that the word has become 'liberated' and is now used freely by members of both sexes about themselves or each other. A woman is equally as likely to say 'I'm feeling randy, let's have sex' as is a man, although the term up until World War II was confined to the sexual desires of the male (Hudson). He cites the example 'I bought a lot of brandy/When I was courting Sandy/With the aim to make her randy/When all I had was shandy' ('Billericay Dickie' by Ian Dury, 1977). Usage is now so obvious and innocuous that popular newspapers in the UK use the word indiscriminately. Indeed the Queen's second son, Prince Andrew, is invariably dubbed by the newspapers as 'Randy Andy'.

ranger The penis. From the last century in the UK and now not often heard.

rasp, to To have sexual intercourse. From the 19th century and becoming rarer. An unpleasant image of abrasion during coition (until 1920 rasp meant vagina) not helped by the more brutal 20th century Australian equivalent 'rasp away' (to have sex).

rat The penis. Another in the long line of 'male organ equals a live animal' associations. Limited contemporary usage. 'Rat trap', meaning vagina, dates back to the last century and is now rare. *See also* RABBIT.

rat-fucked 'Fucked to the point of exhaustion' says an American correspondent. Recent US usage – an especially enjoyable bout of intercourse (straight or male gay) would be described as a 'ratfuck'.

rattle, to To have sexual intercourse. From the last century and more humorous than violent. *See also* ROLL IN THE HAY.

raunchy Sexually provocative, exciting. From the US to the UK in the early sixties, and common ever since. Not always overtly sexual – 'You'll like her, she's a raunchy lady'. Has some parallels with randy (q.v.) but is a less personalized word, one more likely to be used by a male.

raw Naked. More commonly 'in the raw' (and sometimes 'in the raz'). A 20th century UK euphemism now so general that it is used universally. Occasionally the even more euphemistic 'in the buff' is substituted. *See also* NUDDY.

raw meat The penis *or* the vagina. Although of 20th century origin usage varies from region to region and from person to person. A case of one man's meat is another man's poison? Meaning vagina, the phrase follows the 'insulting male usage only' line, as in 'chopped liver' and 'veal cutlet'. Meaning penis the usage is again invariably male and used by gays and straights alike, although in the US gay usage is more predominant.

ready for it, she's Low catch phrase used in the UK between males, indicating that a woman is (supposedly) sexually available. As such, insulting. Can also be heard in a leering party interchange: male to female 'Are you ready for it, darling?' Almost interchangeable is 'dying for it', but with more extreme connotations of sexual availability. US and UK.

ready to spit On the point of ejaculation (of a male). Common 20th century male UK usage. Synonymous is 'foaming at the mouth', but for a more humourous alternative *see* VINEGAR STROKE.

rear entry Anal intercourse. Virtually self-explanatory and a term originating in the thirties to describe what was then known as buggery. Now widespread, especially in the UK, and not always necessarily describing intercourse between two males; a man is just a likely to give a woman 'a rear

164

entry job'. *Compare* BACK PASSAGE.

red ace The vagina. Dated UK usage from the last century, but now virtually obsolete.

red cap The penis. UK usage from the twenties. Comparable is 'red hot poker', while 'red end' also has its devotees. The former, Partridge interestingly notes, is 'feminine usage', although this is unlikely today. *See also* POCKET THE RED.

Redfern, get off at To practise the 'withdrawal method'. *See* JUMP OFF AT HAYMARKET for a full etymology.

red rag A sanitary towel. *See* ON THE RAG.

red sails in the sunset To be having one's period. Joke phrase from the fifties (and after the song of the same name) now used invariably by males. 'I wouldn't touch her, mate, she's red sails in the sunset!'

red wings The coveted badge awarded to Hells Angels who perform cunnilingus on their partners ('old ladies') while they are menstruating. The badge is more coveted than the ordinary 'wings' awarded for cunnilingus at any other time. (*The Hells Angels*, Hunter S. Thompson). US usage from the sixties, now sometimes used outside the ranks of the Angels.

relations have come, the A dated late 19th century euphemism for menstruation. Used as a female excuse (although now rare). A more tortuous alternative is 'she's gone to see her country cousins', again used as a 'feminine' excuse (Partridge).

relief massage The manual inducement of an orgasm in a male by a female, usually when the male has paid for the 'service'. The boom in massage parlours began in the seventies in the UK and the US with many premises offering massage in 'luxurious surroundings'. The male customer pays the basic fee for a shower and a massage and is then asked if he wants any 'extras'. In 1983 the going rate for massage in London's Soho was around £18-£20, while to bring the client to orgasm would cost at least another £25. Other extras, such as topless massage (when the client can touch the masseuse's breasts) and executive massage (where two girls perform the service together) cost more. In many cases 'massage' is a widely understood euphemism for sexual relief, while a 'massage parlour' can often be a euphemism for a place where sexual services can be obtained (for a fee!).

rent boy A man who provides homosexual favours for another man, either in return for lodgings or for money. Sometimes simply described as 'rent' and dating back to the thirties at least. Now widespread UK and US usage. *See also* TRADE.

retired to stud Married. Affectionate male UK slang from the early 20th century now becoming obsolete. *See also* STUD.

rhubarb The vagina. Male UK slang since the twenties. Now obsolete.

ride, to To have sexual intercourse. As in 'the ride', 'to have a ride' and 'get a ride'. Usage is mostly UK, dating back to at least the 18th century (whence virtually synonymous with 'mount') but Partridge notes 'feminine usage' in the 19th century, which has now virtually disappeared. Now mostly male usage, as in 'Why are you looking so sad, didn't you get a ride last night?' A woman is often described as a good ride (or bad ride!), a rider is a man who performs sexual intercourse, while to ride barebacked is to have sex without contraception.

rifle, to To have sexual intercourse. Male UK usage, dating back two centuries. Also sometimes riffle. The rifle is the penis, and both noun and verb carry the unpleasant image of the male shooting into the woman. Still extant, with the most common contemporary usage being when a man talks of 'rifling it into her' when boasting of his sexual exploits. *See also* SHOOT.

rig The male genitalia. From the US to the UK in the 20th century, and used by male and female, although it will be the former who talk of being 'well rigged' (meaning 'well hung'), especially among male gays. Females are more likely to say 'I like his rig'. *See also* PACKAGE, and TACKLE.

right, bit of *See* BIT.

rim, to To perform anal intercourse, from the 19th century in the UK *and* to suck the anus, from the 20th century in the US. While 'to rim' carried the original literal sense of 'to bugger' this has largely been superseded by the latter meaning and is almost exclusive to the male gay population in the US and (increasingly) in the UK. Thus rimming is 'to lick or suck the anus or to lubricate the anus with saliva; to perform anilingus, to use the medical euphemism' (Rodgers). Occasionally also 'ream out', meaning the same.

rim queen A male gay who enjoys sucking the anus. Affectionate contemporary gay usage, US and UK.

ring The vagina. From the 19th century in the UK and still popular. A more graphic variant is 'hairy ring'. In contemporary male gay usage the ring is anus however. *See also* RING SNATCHING.

ring snatching Sexual intercourse. From ring (q.v.), originally of somebody who was prone to deflowering virgins, but now more general and contemporary. Also 'ring snatcher'. Also used by male gays for someone who performs anal intercourse. US to the UK from the sixties. 'Ring queen' is an affectionate male gay term for someone who enjoys anal intercourse.

ring the bell From the 19th century in the UK this was a polite euphemism for becoming pregnant. In 20th century US however, it is a euphemism for manually stimulating the clitoris. 'Honey, you can ring my bell any time you want to.' The latter usage is now more common. *See also* DING DONG.

rise, get a To have an erection. Several centuries old but still very popular, especially in the UK. Mostly male usage – 'I could feel myself rising up as she took her clothes off.'

Ritz crackers! Male gay phrase said about another male who has an unwashed or malodorous penis. Very common in the UK from the seventies. From the brand name of the biscuits that are often eaten – or flavoured – with cheese.

rocks off, to get your To have sex. Often as part of a question 'did you get your rocks off?' From the US to the UK in the sixties and widely used by the younger generation. Some suggest the origin from rocks=diamonds=testicles, but more likely derived from the US black expression from the forties 'rock and roll'=sexual intercourse. The phrase is now used with impunity by both male and female, straight and gay, especially in the US. *See also* JOLLIES.

rod The penis. Also 'to rod', to have sexual intercourse. Since the 18th century in the UK at least, but still one of the most widespread and popular male words for their sexual organ. Conventional 'penis as weapon' imagery but sometimes made more affectionate when used as 'fishing rod'. *See also* RAMROD.

roe The semen. UK, from the late 19th century. Now rarely used. *Compare* the modern term CREAM.

roger, to To have sexual intercourse. Lusty male usage from at least 1650. One explanation for the word is that Roger was a very common name for farm bulls (Partridge). Invariably male aggressive usage – 'I gave her a good rogering'. Sometimes 'rodger'. Both variants are confined to the UK in current usage.

roll in the hay A sexual encounter that can be anything from a kiss and cuddle to sexual intercourse. Very general and innocuous UK euphemism from the turn of the century onwards, and now used by male and female alike.

rollocks The testicles. 20th century UK from the original rhyming slang Tommy Rollocks = bollocks. More often used as a mild expletive than a sexual term. Less common is the abbreviation 'rollies'.

rooster The penis. UK usage from the 19th century and now rare. From the pun on cock. In the 19th century rooster also had the concurrent meaning of vagina but this is now obsolete.

root, to To have sexual intercourse. 20th century US and UK and very common. Hence also 'root on' (= erection) and 'the old root' (= penis). Invariably male usage. Note the male is the active 'rooter'.

rose The vagina. Literary UK term dating back two centuries. Now rare, but a more pleasant image than most.

rough *See* BIT OF ROUGH under BIT.

rough trade Sadistic male gay who inflicts pain or injury on a partner after having anal intercourse or fellatio. Also, simply, a male gay who is violent. From the US to the UK since the sixties. *See also* TRADE.

rub bellies To have 'straight' sexual intercourse, and also – in the gay sense – to rub the penis against the stomach until orgasm.

167

The former is UK usage from the forties on (*compare with* SLIPPERY BELLIES), the latter has been generally accepted gay slang since the sixties (also with limited lesbian usage, *compare with* BUMPER to BUMPER). Limited usage, by both male and female.

rubber A condom. From the thirties at least and now universal, used by male and female alike.

rubber man, or **rubber woman** A rubber fetishist, somebody who gets their 'kicks' from either dressing in rubber or using rubber as an aid to sexual fulfilment. Common from the sixties onwards, US and UK. The male gay equivalent is rubber queen, meaning the same.

rub up An act of sexual intercourse. UK from the 19th century but rarely used in this way now (but *see* RUB BELLIES). It's interesting that the common UK phrase 'Has somebody been rubbing you up the wrong way?'

probably isn't as innocent as most people think.

rudies 'Joke' word describing anything to do with heterosexual sex. British and regarded as a delightful, homorous euphemism by people of all ages. Thus comedian Jim Davison on his TV show on 11 Jan 1984: 'Don't get it wrong, he thought 'e was trying to do rudies wiv her!'

rumble, to To have sexual intercourse. From the 19th century UK and now very dated indeed, as is the synonymous 'rummage'.

rump, to To have sexual intercourse. Again 19th century UK and also very dated, as are rump splitter (= penis) and rump work (= the act of intercourse).

Rupert The penis. From the forties on, and one of the latest in the tradition of male names for the male organ. *See also* JOHN THOMAS, MICKEY, DICK, PERCY *et al.*

168

S

SA Initials for sex appeal. British slang from the 30s, but rarely heard in this form today, although 'sex apeal' is a common term in the UK and US.

sack The scrotum. US usage from the 50s, now widespread.

sack, in the In bed, generally (in slang) for sexual purposes. As in the phrase – 'I'm still trying to get her into the sack'. Mostly male UK and US contemporary usage.

sack, two ferrets fighting in the *See* FERRET.

safety A condom. Old-fashioned Australian slang, from the 20s, but now obscure. Also 'a safe'.

salad *See* GORILLA SALAD.

salami The penis. Contemporary UK male slang. Also 'a bit of salami' – a woman, or indeed sexual intercourse with a woman. To 'have a bit of salami', or 'to hide the salami' is to have sexual intercourse with a woman in US and UK slang.

salt cellar The female genitals. 19th and 20th century UK slang, but virtually obsolete. 'To salt' was an 18th century term for sexual intercourse. According to one source however, 'salt' – as a female sexual partner – re-emerged during the 60s, as in this letter to *Oz*, June 1969: 'I had a game of soccer this afternoon and afterwards popped a bit into my salt' (Hudson).

sausage Penis. Affectionate and contemporary US and UK usage. Sometimes also 'live sausage', which dates back to the 19th century.

saw off a chunk, or **saw off a piece** To have sexual intercourse. Canadian slang from the 20s, but rarely heard in the UK.

scale, to To have sexual intercourse with a woman (the male is the active partner). Limited UK male usage, dating back to the 17th century. The imagery is that

169

of 'climbing up': 'I've scaled a few in my time.' *See* MOUNT.

scene A sexual relationship. Current UK usage by men and woman, as in 'Did you ever have a scene with him?' Principally homosexual usage in the 70s, but now widely used by heterosexual youth.

schnarf, to To sniff women's bicycle seats. UK contemporary male usage, but limited. *Compare* the Oxford equivalent 'snurge', and the Irish term 'gowhunk'.

screamer A homosexual who makes no secret of it. UK male slang from the 1950s, comparable to 'a roaring queer'. With the growing acceptability of homosexuality however, this word has almost faded from slang.

screw, to To have sexual intercourse. UK slang since the 19th century, and now widespread in Britain and America. Hence 'a screw' – a woman or man as a sexual object, as in 'Where do you get your screws?' – from the TV series 'Jewel in the Crown'. Often qualified in phrases to express particularly vigorous sexual activity – as in 'screw the arse off' (him or her), or 'screw the back legs off'.

Still considered a somewhat aggressive and unloving word in the UK, although more openly used in America. And note the slang title of Britain's biggest selling Sunday newspaper which features a great deal of sexual scandal – *The News of the Screws*, or *The Screws of the World*.

scrubber A term of abuse for a woman considered coarse or 'promiscuous'. Originally British Army slang from the 20s, by the 50s it had come to mean 'a girl not at all glamorous' (Partridge). In Liverpool it specifically means prostitute, and this sense underlies its use elsewhere in the UK. Christine Keeler, discussing a recent book about her life, objected to being called a 'scrubber': 'Scrubber implies someone who can't talk properly and wears horrible clothes but I always had a bit of class to me. I'm sure Jack Profumo wouldn't have gone out with a scrubber' (*New Society* 13 November 1983). *Compare* SLAG, TART.

scrubbing brush The pubic hair. 19th and 20th century British slang, but now out of fashion.

second innings Sexual intercourse for the second time in one session. Affectionate and jocular UK usage, from the language of the genteel sport of cricket. A favourite of H.E. Bates in his novels about the Larkin family. UK post war usage.

separate showers As in the jocular comment from the UK male when he feels under threat from the presence of a homosexual – 'Make sure we take separate showers!' The context is invariably sporty, and the inference is that every gay man is just waiting for the opportunity to assault him from behind. *Compare* 'DON'T DROP YOUR CAR KEYS', and 'IF YOU DROP A FIVER IN BANDON KICK IT ALL THE WAY TO CORK'.

service, to To have sexual intercourse. Also as 'a service' – as in the humorous expression among some British women, 'Well, I've had my service for this year at least!' In the UK the sense is affectionate, drawing on the language of animal breeding combined with that of mechanics. Note that it is the male who is the doer. Growing in popularity since the 70s.

In the US however, the gay community uses the word to signify a more literal sexual 'service', often paid for – as in intercourse or fellatio. The location for such 'servicing' is known as a 'service station'.

services rendered, for Generally a jocular phrase, with the innuendo that a reward or payment has been earned by sexual 'services'. Widespread UK slang – as in ironical the aside by a secretary about a lecherous boss 'I got a great Christmas bonus this year – services rendered, you know.'

shaft, to For a man to have sexual intercourse with a woman. UK slang since the 40s, as in – 'It's a long time since I had a good shafting', or 'What she needs is a good shafting'. Hence 'shaftable' – referring to a woman considered worthy of the act. Now also US slang.

Shaft also has the parallel US meaning of cheating, beating or swindling – generally 'screwing somebody up.' The 'Shaft' films of the 70s played on the double imagery with a sexy, black, violent hero called Shaft.

shag, to To have sexual intercourse. A widespread term in the UK among homosexuals and heterosexuals. Often as a term of abuse – as in 'The shagging car won't start', and marginally more acceptable socially than 'fuck'. Dating back to the 18th century, the term is probably related to the now obsolete slang meaning 'to shake about'. It enjoyed widespread popularity amongst soldiers during the First World War, and has been a part of British speech ever since.

shake, to To have sexual intercourse. UK male slang dating back to the 16th century, although rarely heard today. In 19th century London a shake was a prostitute. Possibly a precursor to the term 'shag' (q.v.).

shake hands with the wife's best friend *See* WIFE'S BEST FRIEND.

sharp and blunt Vagina. From cockney rhyming slang with cunt.

171

See also GASP AND GRUNT, GROWL AND GRUNT, GRUMBLE AND GRUNT.

shaving brush The pubic hair. Slang in the UK from the 19th century but now obsolete.

shirt lifter Homosexual man. Derisive male heterosexual usage in the UK, and comparatively modern. *Compare* BENDER.

shoot, to To ejaculate. Sometimes in reference to a 'wet dream', especially as 'to shoot the bishop'. Widespread UK and US male usage, dating back to the 19th century. Now old fashioned – but related -- are the phrases 'to shoot in the tail' – to have sexual intercourse, and 'to shoot in the brown' or 'to shoot up the straight' – to have anal intercourse. Also 'shooters hill' – the female pubic mound, and in reference to male virility 'plenty of shot in the locker'.

The penis as weapon imagery is common – *see also* PORK DAGGER, BAZOOKA.

shrimp job *See* BIG J.

sin *See* LIVING IN SIN.

sit on my face A request that is the precursor to cunnilingus. Modern US and some UK usage. Also 'Sit on my face – and I'll guess your weight'.

sixty-eight As in the gay joke: Q. 'What's a sixty-eight?' A. 'Suck me and I'll owe you one.' *See* SIXTY-NINE.

sixty-nine A position for the practice of reciprocal oral sex. Derived from the shape of the two numerals 6 and 9, as curled round each other in the number 69.

Adopted from the French *soixante neuf* in the 19th century and used in this form by upper-class British society by the turn of the century. The French form is still sometimes heard today. During the First World War it became popular Forces slang as 'swaffonder' or 'swassonder', and by the 20s it had entered UK slang for good.

Note the gay joke: Q. 'What's the square root of sixty-nine?' A. 'Eight something.' *See also* SIXTY-EIGHT.

skirt A generic term for women, among UK males. As in, 'Any skirt going at the party?' or 'That's a nice bit of skirt'. From the 19th century when it had the sense 'prostitute' and still widespread.

slag Widespread contemporary UK term of abuse for a woman, implying that she is a prostitute or 'loose' woman. Hence this comment from a Soho stripper: 'It can be very frightening standing naked on a stage with a crowd of men shouting "slag" at you.'

According to a comprehensive survey of London teenagers (*New Society*, 13 Oct 1983) 'The commonest insult, used by both sexes, is "slag". But all the insults (the survey) came across seemed to relate to a girl's reputation – although they might bear *no* relation at all to a girl's sexual behaviour. One problem for girls is that there aren't equivalent terms that they can use against boys ... that amount to an attack on their whole personality or social identity.'

A likely root for the word is the early 20th century 'slagger' – brothel keeper.

slap and tickle Euphemism for a variety of sexual activities. Affectionate and only slightly 'naughty' UK usage among men and women. Comparable to 'nookie'.

slap her and ride in on the waves Catch phrase referring to sexual activity with a chubby woman. Contemporary Irish male usage, as in – 'Don't let that worry you, just slap her and ride in on the waves'. *See also* RIDE.

sleeping with A euphemism for having sexual intercourse with. Widespread contemporary slang, among men and women, and one of the few such phrases to be acceptable in polite company. One of the oldest euphemisms for the sex act, dating back to the year 900. Like 'having relations', it omits nothing *but* the sexual aspect of a relationship. 20th century UK and US usage.

slippery belly, doing Having

sexual intercourse. Contemporary Australian, especially Sydney, slang among men and women (M. Fry, Sydney 1983). *Compare* POULTICE OF WARM GUTS.

slit The vagina. Male usage in Britain and America. A common image, dating back to the 17th century. *Compare* SPLIT ARSE, CLEFT, GASH, GAP.

slut 'Promiscuous' and/or dirty woman. Widespread as a term of abuse in the UK. Young women especially, before marriage confers sexual respectability, risk being called a 'slut' if they have more than one boyfriend. Note the lack of equivalent terms for males, reflecting the sexual double standard. The usage of 'slut' is practically interchangeable with that of 'scrubber' and 'slag'. *See also* the reverse insult TIGHT.

The broad association of 'loose' morals with sloppy personal habits makes it a general – and powerful – insult. Women who don't keep up with the housework or who appear in scruffy clothes are commonly called 'sluttish' as if a 'low standard' in these traditionally feminine areas of responsibility indicates a propensity towards 'low' sexual morals.

SM, or **S and M** Initials for sado-masochism, or sadism and masochism, in which sexual 'pleasure' is derived from inflicting and/or experiencing pain, domination etc. Sadism is from the name of Marquis de Sade (1740-1814), notorious for his enjoyment of cruelty,. The word first appeared in English in 1888. 'Masochism' is taken from the Austrian novelist Leopold von Sacher-Masoch (1836-95) who describes the practice as we now know it. The compound 'S and M' was first used in 1915 (Neaman and Silver). Current US and UK slang. A US synonym is 'Sadie-Masie' or 'Sadie-Mazzy'. *See also* B AND D.

snatch The female genitals. Widespread male UK usage, dating back to the 19th century when 'snatch-clatch' was a popular synonym. In the north of England 'snatch' also became a collective noun for women.

In the 17th century snatch had the meaning – a hasty or illicit copulation.

snekkers Any woman who is regarded as sexually available. Principally Scottish, from the seventies (Jimmy The Blade, Dingwall 1983). Thus 'She's snekkers', or 'I had snekkers last night'. Carries the parallel meaning of sexual intercourse.

snogging 'French' kissing. Also a more general term for sexual cuddling. Widespread contemporary usage by young people of both sexes in the UK, as in – 'It's enough to put you off your pint to see those two snogging in the pub'.

snorker The penis. Modern UK

usage, connected to the same slang word for a sausage – as in 'Poor old Pete, he's only got a tiny little snorker'.

snowdropping Also snowballing. The practice of exchanging semen orally through passionate kissing after fellatio. Originally slang, but adopted in the US by the heterosexual community – especially among 'groupies'. *See also* WHITE RUSSIAN (Rodgers).

snurge, to For men to indulge in the practice of sniffing women's bicycle seats. A popular Oxford term since WW2. *Compare* TO SCHNARF, and one who (in Limerick) schnarfs – a GOWHUNK.

social worker *See* DO SOCIAL WORK.

sod A homosexual. Common UK abbreviation of 'sodomist' since the beginning of the 19th century, but more often used as a general insult – as in 'What does that silly sod think he's doing', or 'Sod off and leave me alone' – addressed to men *or* women.

Originally from the Hebrew Sodom, the biblical town destroyed by God. In American gay slang, 'Sodom' is a name for any place heavily populated by gays, and a 'Sodomy factory' is a jail where men are inculcated into homosexual practices. 'Sodom' – as a place of corruption – was also a literary nickname for London during the 19th century.

sow Term of abuse for women, from its meaning of female pig. Male and female contemporary usage in the UK, with the strong suggestion that a woman is fat, dirty and over-fertile. More insulting than 'cow', and comparable to 'bitch'.

spindle The penis. UK usage from the 19th century, but now obsolete. Also 'spindle-prick' – a man deficient in energy. The image is still a common one – see PRICK.

spinster A derogatory term for an unmarried woman, generally implying that a woman is old, unwanted by men and a virgin not by choice. As such used widely in the English speaking world as an equivalent to 'old maid'. Note the absence of a male equivalent.

However, in recent years, with the change in attitude towards marriage the word has been 'reclaimed' by feminists. They have turned attention to its original, dignified meaning from Middle English of a woman who earns her living by spinning wool. As such, 'spinster' was appended to women's names to denote their occupation. Only in the 18th century did it come to mean 'old maid'.

Mary Daly in her feminist classic 'Gyn/Ecology' (1978) makes 'spinster' into an emblem of women's creative power: 'Spinsters spin and weave, mending and creating unity of consciousness' she writes. This new meaning of the word has been adopted by groups of British women, and in London at the beginning of the 80s, women's centres would sell 'spinster' badges.

split arse Woman. UK and especially Scottish male slang, dating back to the 19th century. This nasty image is nearly as full of hatred and fear as 'cat with its throat cut', and is often bandied about in pub and club conversation.

sporran The pubic hair. UK usage from the 19th century but now rarely heard.

spunk Semen. Widespread UK and US slang, with connotations of potency and pungency from its root 17th century slang meaning 'mettle, spirit, pluck' (Partridge). Note the common description of a person as 'spunky' or 'full of spunk', i.e. vital and full of life, which is applied to women as often as to men.

squelching Sexual intercourse. Contemporary UK expression, brought to prominence by the (now desceased) Sex Pistols star Johnny Rotten, who dismissed the sexual act as 'two minutes of squelching noises' (NME 1978).

stallion Male believed to have a large sexual organ – as in 'He's hung like a stallion'. UK and US male usage. Contemporary. *Compare* STUD, and HUNG LIKE A DONKEY.

stiffy An erection. Personal slang of a young English woman who said she didn't like any of the other available slang (Sandy, 1984). Individual women often have private slang words. *See also* LILI, TUDS, TICKLE TORTURE.

stonk, stonk-on, stonker An erection. Contemporary British usage among young men and women, as in 'I saw him at the swimming pool with an enormous great stonk-on.' Synonymous with 'bonk on'.

storm and strife Wife. Cockney rhyming slang. One in a multitude suggesting matrimony as a battle ground – *see also* TROUBLE AND STRIFE.

street walker *See* WALK THE STREETS.

stretcher A large penis. UK mostly male usage, as in 'Did you see the size of his stretcher?' Also sometimes as 'leather stretcher', while the vagina was 'leather lane'. Dating back to the 18th century, but now limited usage.

string in a bucket, like A comic simile for the condition of the penis in relation to the vagina. Either in derisive commentary from a woman as in 'Exciting? You must be joking, it was like dangling string in a bucket', or in rueful description of his imagined performance by a male. Note that the comment is double edged: not only is the male's limpness a source of laughter, but the female's orifice is under attack as being grossly gaping. Contemporary UK slang.

stud Man as a sexual athlete. As in the semi-derisive comment – 'Didn't you know he was a real stud' – about a man who has had many sexual partners. Usage is sometimes admiring, but depending on the tone and attitude of the speaker can also be derisive or ironic, as if to say: 'he really fancies himself, doesn't he?' The 'stud' is often admired in the gay community, hence the definition in Rodgers *Gay Lexicon* – 'the epitome of manhood'.

From the mid-18th century stud was simply an abbreviation of the American term 'stud-horse', i.e. a stallion used for breeding, but it entered slang with its current meaning during the 50s. Now widespread in the US and UK.

stuff, to To have sexual intercourse. Most commonly in the form of the abusive UK comment – 'Why don't you go stuff yourself'. Male and female usage from the mid-19th century.

stump A small penis. Contemporary Irish usage and sometimes used in the form of the nickname 'Stumpy' for a man not 'well endowed'. Mostly affectionate however.

suck, to To fellate. This dates back to the 19th century, but today is more often expressed as 'suck off'. 'A suck' was also slang for homosexual, while 'a sucker' was a lesbian in the last century, and is now US slang for gay man, although straight usage is equally widespread.

The term is more freely bandied about in the US than in Britain, and a common insult in America is 'cock-sucker!'

Among the US gay community 'sucksy' means attractive, the 'suck hole' is the mouth, and a 'suck shop' is a coffee shop frequented by gays.

Amongst the straight community a 'suck-off' is an act of fellatio performed by a woman.

sugar daddy Wealthy, older man who lavishes generosity upon a younger, usually female, object of his infatuation. Originally American and popularized in the UK by Hollywood movies from the 1930s.

Still common in British speech, generally in reference to a fantasy figure, as in 'What I need now is a sugar daddy, and I'll never do another stroke of work'.

Also gay usage in the US.

SWALK Initials for Sealed With A Loving Kiss. Often written by romantic young people on the back of love letters. Also sometimes SWAK – Sealed with A Kiss, and SWALCAKWS – Sealed With A Lick Cos A Kiss Won't Stick. This tradition dates back to 19th century Britain.

switch hitter Bisexual. US usage, from the baseball term for a left-handed batsman. *See also* AMBIDEXTROUS, AC/DC, DOUBLE-GAITED.

SYT Initials for Sweet Young Thing. Dated UK slang.

T

tackle The male genitalia. Obviously related to 'equipment' and a lusty British word for several centuries. Still contemporary male usage (often heard is 'getting the tackle out and getting down to business'). *See also* PACKAGE, and WEDDING TACKLE.

tadger The penis. Modern slang in the UK, mostly male affectionate usage. Suggestions as to its origin would be welcomed.

tail Either a woman, or the vagina. Both usages date back to the 18th century, but after a spell of obscurity, the term resurfaced in the US during the thirties and is now widespread. Contemporary terms are 'chasing tail' (synonymous with 'chasing pussy', looking for a sexual partner) and a 'nice piece of tail' (an agreeable woman). Male usage only and more common in the US than in the UK. Variants such as tail pick, tickle tail and tail pin (= penis), tail hole for vagina and tail juice

for semen haven't survived the test of time.

take in hand To masturbate. Glaringly obvious pun from 19th century UK, now rarely heard.

talent Sexually attractive and/or sexually available men or women. Male and female usage, as in 'I always go down to the Hammersmith Palais on a Saturday, the talent's magic' (thanks to Peter Barbour, 1983), or 'She complained all evening about the lack of talent at the party'.

Tale of Two Cities Breasts. From cockney rhyming slang for titties. *See also* TOWNS AND CITIES, BRISTOL CITIES and MANCHESTER CITIES. Now virtually unknown, except (from the second reference) in the shortened form 'Bristols'.

tap, to To have sexual intercourse. A rare variant on tup (q.v.).

tart A woman and/or a prostitute.

Originally affectionate from the 19th century, and a shortening of jam tart (= a sweet thing). The current usage, however, is more disparaging. Both male and female will now describe a woman they think is 'loose' as a tart. Christine Keeler commented to *New Society* (13 Nov 1983) that she didn't like being described in a book about her as 'just a pretty scrubber ... I wanted them to change it to "tart".'

Note also the common jibe 'cheap tart'. However, 'to get tarted up' simply means to put on new clothes and makeup, and the term carries no more sting than 'all dolled up'.

tasty A sexually attractive person. Usually applied by UK males to females. Consistent with the widespread usage of terms denoting the body as food, as in 'crumpet', 'meat' etc.

It had the 1762 meaning 'tasteful and elegant', and took on its current sexual connotations at the end of the 19th century.

tease *See* PRICK TEASE.

telephone sex So far a peculiarly American phenomenon, whereby a male 'customer' dials an advertised number and is talked to by a woman, always on explicitly sexual topics. Starting in New York in the early eighties the 'service' has burgeoned, with adverts for phone sex littering newspapers in major American cities. Customers pay by credit card. There are also a few numbers where free phone sex can be obtained; these usually take the form of a recorded message using explicit sexual language. So far no-one has imported phone sex to the UK.

tenuc The vagina. Back slang for cunt since the 19th century but still very popular in working-class Britain (R. Wilder, 1983).

thatch The female pubic hair (or very rarely the male pubic hair). Contemporary and in the same line as 'bush' or 'nest' in imagery. Male and female usage, mostly UK.

Thatcher's girls Prostitutes. A British phenomenon since the economic policies of Maggie Thatcher's government have caused widespread unemployment, especially in the north of England. In consequence many women on the bread line travel south to London to look for work; and in many cases the only 'work' available is in the sex industry. Defiantly, they call themselves 'Thatcher's girls'. Recent UK usage. *See also* HAVE IT AWAY DAY.

that there The vagina. A euphemism from the last century, now surviving as 'that' (sometimes 'that thing'). UK usage.

that way Homosexual. Obviously from 'that way inclined'. Rather prim usage from the thirties, but still common among some of the older generation. 'I had no idea he was that way.'

thing The penis or the vagina. A generic term for the sexual organs now only used as a 'joke'. 'He got his thing out and I started laughing.' *Compare with* THAT THERE. Mostly UK usage.

third leg The penis. Male UK usage since the twenties; often in affectionate reference to the speaker's own organ.

Thomas The penis. A shortening of John Thomas but popular in its own right. From the 19th century, UK male usage. *See also* MICK, DICK, PETER, for other examples of the penis having a male name.

thread the needle To have sexual intercourse. Graphic imagery and an originally Irish male expression from the twenties, now also used in the UK.

three in a bed scenario Troilism. A term popular in the UK since the seventies and still extant.

threepenny bits Breasts. From cockney rhyming slang with tits. Now as little in currency as the coin itself. *Compare* BRISTOLS.

throw a leg over To have sexual intercourse. Dating back two centuries in the UK and sometimes shortened to 'throw over' or 'throw'. Still contemporary male usage often as 'get the leg over', or to be in a 'leg over situation'.

thrust, to To have sexual intercourse. The word has been around since the 18th century and is still used by straight and gay males. Also 'thruster' for penis. In a similar line are the more dated 'thump' (have sexual intercourse), which is now rare, and the synonymous 'go through', still popular, especially in the UK.

tickle tail The penis. Also tickler. Slang from the 19th century at least but not much used today. *Contrast*, however, with the current 'tail'.

tickle torture Female masturbation. The hitherto private slang of one young woman, invented in childhood to name something she understood was naughty. Sometimes also called 'TT' or 'twenty twenty' (T is the twentieth letter of the alphabet) to further disguise the true and guilty meaning. An instance of how women's slang is often coined and confined among immediate family and friends. *See also* TUDS.

tickle your fancy Homosexual. From cockney rhyming slang with nancy, or nancy boy.

tickle your fancy Sexual innuendo with various levels of meaning, depending on the context. 'Does he tickle your fancy' can mean anything from 'Do you fancy him?', to 'Do you have sex?', in which 'fancy' stands for the female part. Affectionate usage from the 19th century, mostly

UK. Synonymous is 'have a tickle'.

tight Sexually cold. Perhaps the most common accusation levelled at women who refuse a man's sexual advances. Hence this comment from a schoolgirl, interviewed in a 1983 study by Sue Lees from North London Polytechnic: 'It's a vicious circle. If you don't like them, then they'll call you a tight bitch. If you go with them, they'll call you a slag afterwards.' The video made concurrently is entitled *Tight Bitch or Slag?*

tit man Male who is attracted to women – or not – according to their breast measurements. It's not uncommon to hear men in the UK expressing their preferences, or reactions to women, by saying 'I'm a tit man myself', or alternatively, 'I'm not a tit man, I'm really a bum man'. Current and pervasive male usage, with no female equivalents.

tits Female breasts. Sometimes as 'titties'. 'Tit' originally meant young girl or woman in the 17th century, and even then was regarded as vulgar. Throughout the latter half of the 20th century it has always meant breasts, and is used openly by both sexes. Women rarely feel embarrassed about referring to their 'tits' in normal conversation – 'My tits have been sore ever since I went on the pill' – while male usage can range from the derogatory to the affectionate. 'Tit' is on the verge of modern respectability and will occasionally crop up in newspapers, although until recently only as part of a quotation. There are many variants such as tit mag (a euphemism for a pornographic magazine) and tit'n'bum (newspaper pictures that are supposedly erotic, usually showing topless models). Similes are invariably used by males in commentary on women's bodies – hence 'tits like cherry stones' and 'tits like elephants' bollocks' (J. Lynton, 1983).

'Tit' is also common as a term of abuse, by women and men, as in 'Stop making a tit of yourself'.

toilet talk Conversation between men about sex. A 'joke' term in the UK and Australia from the sixties, but slowly fading from popularity. However still used by male gays in the US – 'Let's talk toilet'. Toilet is a gay euphemism for the anus.

tom A prostitute. Police slang in the UK from the thirties. *See also* EDIE.

tomato A woman. Common in the US from the twenties but becoming outdated. Originally from a 'luscious juicy fruit'. (See for example Damon Runyon's *On Broadway* or *Guys And Dolls*.)

tommy The penis. Dated UK slang now perhaps only used by schoolboys. Following in the long line of words giving a man's name for the penis, but also possibly from the 19th century rhyming slang Tommy Rollocks (= bollocks). *See also* THOMAS, DICK, PETER etc.

tongue, to To perform oral sex. No usage recorded before the 20th century but since the sixties, in the US and the UK, one of the more popular descriptions of either fellatio or cunnilingus (or indeed anilingus). Usage is straight, gay and lesbian.

tonk The penis. Curent UK male usage, generally persisting from schooldays, and less common than prick etc. *See also* BONK.

tool The penis. Centuries old but right up there along with 'prick' as one of the most common words used by men about their sexual organ, both in the US and the UK. Common too as a term of abuse for male, from both men and women – as in, 'Don't be such a tool', or 'time you stopped tooling about'. Also current are 'tool it' (= to have sexual intercourse) and 'tooling' (meaning the same). 'To grind the tool' however, is now rare. *Compare* EQUIPMENT, TACKLE.

top bollocks The breasts. Contemporary male UK usage, and especially popular in Ireland, giving male characteristics to the female body. Also sometimes as 'top buttocks' (from the forties, especially in Australia) and the simpler 'top 'uns' (also 20th century). *Compare* front bum = vagina.

topless Referring to exposed breasts. The word can be used to describe anything from a newspaper pin-up (the topless Page Three girls in *The Sun* newspaper having been a talking point since the early seventies) to an innocent sunbather ('Brighton beach goes topless!'). London's Soho abounds with topless bars (where girls serve drinks undressed from the waist up), there are always topless discos (where a woman dances for an audience with her breasts exposed) and also topless massage (*see* RELIEF MASSAGE).

toss off To masturbate. Dating as far back as the 18th century (Grose) and still in widespread usage in the UK and the US today. 'I didn't find a woman at the party so I went home and tossed myself off'. Almost invariably male, although women can say they have 'tossed a man off'. Variants like tosser and toss-pot are used as terms of abuse directed at males. *Compare* WANK.

touch it with a barge pole, I wouldn't A derogatory catch phrase used about a woman by a male (usually to another male). *See* I WOULDN'T DO IT WITH SOMEBODY ELSE'S.

town bike A 'promiscuous' woman – because 'She's been ridden by everybody'. *See* BIKE.

towns and cities Breasts. From cockney rhyming slang for titties. *See also* BRISTOLS, MANCHESTER CITIES, TALE OF TWO CITIES. Only 'Bristols' is in common UK usage today.

trade A sexual partner. A prostitute calls her clients 'trade', and in gay slang the term refers to any partner or potential partner. UK and US contemporary usage.

tram lines The female genitals. 20th century UK male slang, as in 'I'd like to give her one up the tramlines'. *Compare* the equally graphic RAILS.

tramp A woman. From the US to the UK since the twenties and still in general usage. The meaning is normally affectionate (That's why the lady is a tramp, sang Frank Sinatra) but used by male and female alike to suggest sexual 'promiscuity'.

trannie Transvestite. An affectionate abbreviation, in vogue amongst sections of the gay community. *Compare* CUNNI.

trick A prostitute's client. UK slang since the forties. Also gay usage for any sexual partner.

trolley and truck Sexual intercourse. From cockney rhyming slang with fuck. *See also* CATTLE TRUCK, and FRIAR TUCK.

trouble and strife Wife. Cockney rhyming slang. Although this term has its original usage in a small London community, the image of the wife as a battleaxe has appealed to men acros the country and this is now one of the more widely known cockney terms.

trouser snake The penis. *See* ONE EYED TROUSER SNAKE.

trumpet The penis. Often as 'blue veined trumpet'. 20th century UK male slang, invariably as a joke. *Compare* the synonymous PINK OBOE, and BLUE VEINED STEAK.

tuds Breasts. One young English woman's personal slang, shared only with her female friends.

tumble, to To have sexual intercourse. Also to become pregnant, presumably from the sense 'to fall'. British slang dating back to the 18th century and now obsolete. *See* ROLL IN THE HAY.

tummy banana The penis. Popularized by *The Adventures of Barry McKenzie* (Barry Humphries, 1968), and now highly prized by 'Bazza' fans in the UK, male and female alike.

tup, to To have sexual intercourse. Dating back to the 17th century, this term is still current among men in the UK, and it is men – according to usage – who do the 'tupping', while the question to women is 'Has he tupped you?', or 'Never been tupped?'

turd burglar A male homosexual. Although turd – once a respectable word – dates back to the 11th century, this expression, currently popular with straight UK males, is strictly modern. The related 'turd packer', which enjoyed brief popularity amongst US gays in the 40s is now dated. For similarly derisive terms *see* CHOCOLATE BANDIT, CHUTNEY FERRET.

turned on To be sexually excited. A very common contemporary expression in both US and UK, among men and women. A person can be a 'real turn-on', if there is something about them that is a 'turn-on' – i.e. their way of dressing, their humour or idiosyncrasies. Related, no doubt, to the drug terminology of the 60s when in a different sense people 'turned onto' drugs (i.e. became excited and enthusiastic about them). The reverse of course is to be 'turned off', i.e. uninterested in sex, and anything from a boring person to the odour of his or her socks can be a 'turn-off'.

TV Initials for transvestite. UK and US slang among groups of men – as in 'Right on, Soul Brother, out the door with my coloured TV' (Rodgers). Some clothing shops in the UK – where attitudes are mellowing towards men who dress in women's clothes – now advertise themselves as TV shops.

twang the wire Male masturbation. 20th century men-only usage in the UK. *See also* PULL THE WIRE.

twat The female genitals. Long-established slang dating back to the 17th century, and still popular in the UK and US. Not a loving expression however, and frequently used as a term of abuse – as in 'Leave me alone you silly twat' (addressed by and to either men or women) – but still less aggressive than 'cunt'.

two ferrets fighting in a sack, like In reference to the agitation of flabby buttocks on a perambulating person. A Dublin expression, of limited application, noted during the 70s but elsewhere unrecorded (B. Stickland, 1981).

U

udders Breasts. Not a complimentary term, likening the woman (or sometimes man) to a cow and implying that the breasts are large, droopy and wrinkled. But sometimes used by men to register astonishment at a woman's bust – as in 'Just take a look at those udders over there'. Other slang terms for breast also emphasize the milk-carrying function – *see* JUGS, JARS, DAIRY, etc.

Ugandan affairs Sexual intercourse, usually illicit. The term was coined by the satirical magazine *Private Eye* during the regime in Uganda of President Idi Amin: Amin attempted to discredit one of his own government ministers the Princess Elizabeth by accusing her publicly of having sex in a toilet while on a diplomatic mission to Europe. Since then the term has become firmly entrenched in middle-class English slang. The variants and compounds are understandably immense – 'East African affairs', 'discussing East Africa' (= sexual intercourse) and 'consultation with the Third World' are just three of the euphemisms spawned by this embarrassing non-event.

unattached Without a sexual partner. Since the 60s more and more people are involved in sexual relationships which don't fall within the traditional alternatives of 'married' and 'single', and so words that don't refer to matrimony now prevail when describing a person's standing socially and sexually. Hence the dinner party set are frequently heard to complain – 'There are so few unattached men these days'. *See also* PARTNER, GIRLFRIEND.

unbutton the mutton To display the penis. Male slang only, with reference to the male organ as meat again predominant. Originally Australian, now general.

Uncle Dick The penis. Rhyming slang with prick. *See also* DICK.

under par A small penis. While

185

the macho myth persists that a man's masculinity, virility or ability as a lover are in direct relation to the size of his organ, this remains a dismissive insult to the male. As likely to be used by a female as a male, although the term originates from a male-dominated sport.

unemployed, the The penis. Used with heavy irony, usually by a man about his own organ. Hence the old joke: Q. Do you (or does the Pope) wear underpants in the bath? A. Yes, it doesn't do to look down on the unemployed.

unload To ejaculate. From the US slang for semen – a man's 'load'. Also emphasizing the sense of 'relief'. Primarily a dismissive male term.

unparliamentary Obscene. This term entered slang a century ago as a reference to the type of language not permitted in Westminster by the Speaker of the House of Commons. These days it is confined to erudite, euphemistic usage.

unsliced Uncircumcised. Mostly US slang, with more than a hint of sadism.

up Sexual intercourse with. As in the generally male question – 'Has he been up her yet?', or the well-worn phrase 'Up her like a rat up a drainpipe'. Also in reference to anal intercourse in gay and heterosexual usage, as in

up the bum, up the back passage, up the Yang Yang (New York gay usage).
Widely used too as an obscene expletive or insult, such as 'up yours!' or 'up your arse!'
Partridge records the old-fashioned usage of 'up' as a verb – as in 'I have up'd her'.

up, get it To have an erect penis. Most commonly found in the negative form as a mortal insult to a man – 'He can't get it up'. The latter is a rare example of female derision in sexual slang.

upper deck Breasts. Mostly UK male slang. Clearly a boating pun and yet another comical euphemism for this part of the female body which seems to attract far more innocuous and nursery-style slang than the other sexual parts. Also 'upper works' and 'top deck'.

upright Sexual intercourse performed standing up – as in 'doing an upright'. Less common than the more graphic 'knee trembler'. An alternative is 'perpendicular'. Australian slang also has 'upright grand' (= sex while standing) as a pun on a type of piano (Partridge), but in US gay slang this has the meaning 'an erect penis'.

up the duff Pregnant. Widespread English and predominantly working-class slang. Perhaps related to the synonymous 'in the pudding club' via the meaning of 'duff' as food.

uptight Tense and anxious – with a strong implication that the root of the problem is sexual repression. First used in the 60s to denote what every good hippy should *not* be, the term is still in wide use today and in the US is virtually interchangeable with 'tight assed'.

urge, the Sexual desire. A euphemism more commonly used by women than men – as in 'I don't know what's wrong with me, I haven't had the urge for ages.' Less explicit than contemporary – and generally American – equivalents such as 'having the hots' and 'feeling randy'.

V

vache A male homosexual. US male gay slang, slowly spreading to the UK. From the French *vache* (= cow) – in widespread use as an insult to women – and considerably less affectionate than the omnipresent QUEEN (q.v.).

vacuum cleaner The mouth of a fellator. Principally US camp, gay slang. 'You haven't had the vacuum cleaner out for over a week.'

vag (almost invariably pronounced 'vadge') The female genitalia. Obviously a colloquial shortening of vagina, but generally applied in a non-specific way by the male. Thus 'Her vag was hairy', and so on. Women are often loath to refer to their genitals by name as so many of the available words have been appropriated by men as terms of abuse. But like cunt, which some women are attempting to 'reclaim' (*see* Introduction), vag is also increasingly used by women as an affectionate nickname. For instance the term is used in hospitals between nurses and women patients, meaning something less 'medical' than vagina while less taboo than 'cunt'. It also recently (19 March 1984) appeared in the *Guardian*'s women's page in this description of intercourse: 'Sex – dull, grunting married, five-minute vag-wash sex …'.

valley The vagina. A literary euphemism dating back several centuries but still extant. Sometimes rendered even more flowery as the 'valley of love'. Not as aggressive as 'cleft' or 'hole', with occasional (if affected) female usage.

valley of decision The small of the back, leading down to the anus. A US gay slang expression meaning that the success of a manual approach to this area will indicate whether a man will or will not consent to anal intercourse (Rodgers).

valve The vagina. Insulting male term in the UK, because 'it is opened by a cock'. Slang from the 19th century but now rare. Possibly from confusion with 'vulva'. *Compare* also with CYLINDER.

vamp A 'loose' or sexually provocative woman. A dated term from 1918 onwards and gradually becoming classy enough to be now acceptable newspaper terminology. A part of its sterilization process has been its adoption as a term in fashion, in which 'vampish' looks suggest heavily 'sexy' makeup and clothes. A vamp can also be a man however – 'to vamp it up' or to be 'vampy' or 'vampish' means to flirt, and used by gays and straights alike, US and UK.

One suggested origin for the term is 'vampire' and one of its earliest symbols was the Hollywood actress Theda Bara who pretended to be a Hungarian from vampire country.

vampire An ardent homosexual and (especially in the US) one who is likely to steal a prospective sexual partner. Male gay slang and quite widespread.

vampire run, to go on a To go out at night looking for a sexual encounter, especially if the hour is late. Mostly US male gay slang from the sixties onwards.

Van Dyke A lesbian with prominent facial hair. From the famous painter who was bewhiskered, and also a pun on 'dike' and 'dyke'. 'Humorous' but insulting US gay slang only.

vanilla Conventional sex. Principally any sex that doesn't involve S & M (sado masochism) or B & D (bondage and domination). Synonymous with bambi (q.v.). Spreading from the US to the UK in the seventies with usage now widespread.

vanilla bar A bar or club which is essentially 'straight', i.e. no sexual encounters take place there. *Contrast with* DEGENERATE BAR. Jokey US male gay usage from the seventies onwards.

vanilla queen A black male gay. Colour-conscious camp US gay usage from the sixties onwards, but mostly affectionate.

vaseline villa Any place where male gay sexual encounters take place, house, hotel or YMCA. From one of the more common lubricants used to facilitate anal intercourse. Very much a modern US gay alliteration. Two other alternatives, both synonymous, are 'KY cow house' (from the lubricant KY Jelly), and 'Crisco cottage' (from Crisco, oddly favoured as a lubricant by 'fist fuckers' – *The Fist Fucker's Manual* 1981).

Vatican roulette The rhythm

189

method of contraception. Humorous working-class UK slang from the forties onwards.

vault The anus. Male gay slang, UK and US, dating back to the sixties. 'I'd love to open his vault some time.'

VD Venereal disease. Since World War II Forces usage so commonly accepted as an abbreviation that it has become Standard English, both in the US and the UK. From the sixties 'VD clinics' have been openly advertised.

veal cutlet The vagina. A recent coining in the UK and another in the unpleasant line of sexual organs as 'meat'. *See also* BEEF CURTAINS, PORK SWORD, MEAT.

vegetable stick The penis. One of the more anachronistic male gay images for the sexual organ. US from the fifties onwards.

vegetarian A male gay who doesn't perform fellatio on his partner(s). Dismissive gay usage in the UK and the US from the seventies. Literally one who doesn't eat meat (in this case meat = penis).

vehicle A woman. Again the dismissive image is of 'one who is ridden on or in'. UK from the forties, but not as widespread as 'bike'. *See also* SERVICE.

velch The action of ejaculating into the anus of a partner and then retrieving the semen with the

mouth immediately afterwards. A term originating in America, and virtually exclusive to the male gay population. The expression has spread with the activity and is now accepted usage among UK gays. Now often part of an invitation, as in 'Are you velching tonight?' Synonymous are 'felch' and 'fletch'.

velvet The vagina. Although literary from the 19th century, an affectionate, if rarely used, word to describe the female sexual organs. Partridge also notes the interesting 'tip the velvet' meaning cunnilingus.

velvet job A particularly delicate act of fellatio, or 'a soft blow job' (Rodgers). Male gay usage and contemporary, not to be confused with the meaning of velvet (q.v.).

velvet orbs The testicles. Male gay usage from the sixties onwards, US and UK.

Venus with a penis A sexually attractive young boy or man. Contemporary gay catch phrase – 'Look, there goes a venus with a penis' – but mostly confined to the US.

vibes In a sexual slang sense, feelings of attraction between one person and another, straight or gay, male or female. A shortened form of vibrations, which has also been used universally since the late fifties. One of the earliest written forms came with the

Beach Boys' sixties hit 'Good Vibrations' – 'She's giving me good vibrations/Keeps giving me good vibrations'. Although 'vibes' became more general in the seventies, coming to mean feelings or sensations ('Everything oppressive will automatically collapse through the accumulated good vibes', *Spare Rib*, Feb 1979 – Hudson), the sexual sense is still never far away.

view master A man who takes pleasure in looking at other men, either in bars or in the street. US male gay slang, usually used in a dismissive sense. Sometimes 'view queen'. Contemporary.

village people Now dated, but originally meaning gay men from New York's Greenwich Village (a home for the avant garde from the fifties). From the large number of gays and gay meeting places in the area. In the late seventies a pop group briefly flourished called Village People, whose predilection was to dress up as macho stereotypes (from leather man to construction worker) and several of whom were gay. The term has little credence now, even in the US.

vinegar stroke, the Referring to the point of sexual excitement just before ejaculation in the male. As in this contribution from a local at the Tulse Hill Tavern, south London, in reference to masturbation, 'I was just on the vinegar stroke when the phone rang.' Contemporary UK usage.

virgin's dream The penis. Lofty and self-congratulatory description used by men. UK, from the 19th century but now very dated.

vitals The male genitals. UK slang from the forties on, but often used in a sporting sense, and by males only. 'I got the ball right in the vitals'.

vital statistics The measurement of any sexually interesting part of the body. From 1945 the Standard English form meant a woman's bust, waist and hip measurements and in this sense it is used in newspapers and elsewhere even now. But 'vital statistics' is also used by women (and by male gays) to describe a man's penis. As heard in 'He's got big hands and a big nose, I wonder what his vital statistics are?' Contemporary, and when used by women a rare example of the female sex 'getting its own back'.

VPL The initials of *v*isible *p*anty *l*ine. Since the seventies spoken so universally that it has become nearly as acceptable in polite company as BO (body odour). Sexual slang, because to many people (especially in the US) the outline of underwear beneath tight trousers is regarded as a 'turn off', or occasionally as a 'turn on', depending on predilection. US and UK, male and female usage in all contexts.

VSI The initials of *v*igorous *s*exual *i*ntercourse. Coined by ex-*Sunday Times* writer Allen Brien in the late sixties and steadily gaining popularity in the UK ever since. Often used in speech as a joke, as in 'Do you know what the best cure for a hangover is? VSI every time!'

vulture An elderly, lecherous gay (Rodgers). US camp gay slang from the sixties onwards. Literally, because 'he preys on young meat'.

W

wad The semen. Usually used as part of a phrase: i.e. to 'shoot one's wad' is to ejaculate, whether while masturbating or during sexual intercourse. Mostly US male usage, as in the UK 'wad' retains its innocent 'straight' meaning. Contemporary male slang.

walk the streets, to To work as a prostitute. *See* STREETWALKER. UK slang from the turn of the century.

walk up fuck, a Sexually available woman. Originally Australian term for a woman judged to be 'promiscuous'. The idea is that all a man has to do is walk up and ask her.

wallflower A woman, or sometimes man, who is ignored by the opposite sex during social gatherings. Originally the term had the literal meaning of a woman 'keeping her seat by the wall because of her inability to attract partners' and Partridge cites this 1820s verse:
'The maiden wallflowers of the room
Admire the freshness of his bloom.'
Today the term keeps its old-fashioned ring, but a mother might well urge her daughter to dress up for a party – 'because you don't want to be a wallflower.'

wally Although this is now a widespread UK term for 'twit' we suggest that it may have had a sexual origin. At the end of the 19th century, wolly or wally had the meaning a cucumber pickled in brine (Partridge), and as such wally could be the UK equivalent of the US word dill/dildo – also after the pickled cucumber, an obvious phallic symbol.

waltz, invitation to the Sexual intercourse. This comically polite euphemism is still used by some middle-class and middle-aged people today. As overheard from a

193

woman describing her embarrassment when a man arrived in her bedroom after she had told him she was going to have an afternoon rest – 'He must have thought it was an invitation to the waltz!'

wand The penis. Used in parody of the notion of a magic wand, a joking expression for sexual intercourse is 'waving the wand'. Also, occasionally, 'waving the magic wand'.

wandering hand In reference to a man who has a reputation for 'groping' women. It is still fairly common to hear (especially young) women comment about a man: 'Well, he's got a wandering hand problem, hasn't he?' The term is well established: WHB has had the meaning 'Wandering Hand Brigade' since the late 19th century. But young women today are learning that they don't have to pass off unwelcome 'groping' with jokes about wandering hands, and when the WHB are men in the workplace the problem has been dignified by a new name – sexual harassment. *See* WHT, DESERT DISEASE.

wank (occasionally **whank**) To masturbate. Probably the most common term for masturbation – used by males and females – in the UK, and also widespread in America. In the US however, 'jerk off' is more popular.

But it is the way it is used in general conversation that sheds an interesting light on attitudes towards the practice. If a person is wasting time, being ineffectual or self-indulgent, the common retort is 'Stop wanking about'. And any person (male or female) who is considered irritating, stupid, dull or useless is called a wanker. An object that is of no use or a machine that isn't working is 'wanky'.

Men in particular will accompany the accusation of 'Wanker!' with the appropriate hand movements, conveying dislike and contempt. This gesture now rivals the traditional 'V-sign' in popularity.

Despite the attempts of the sex educators, the idea that masturbation is a contemptible, wasteful and degrading practice is still very much alive in popular slang.

Old fashioned – and mostly of Forces origin – are wank pit = bed, wanker's colic = pain in the gut, wanker's doom = debility, and wanker's spanner = the hand (Partridge).

wank mag Pornographic magazine, principally to aid the solitary self-gratification of the 'straight' or 'gay' male.

was it OK for you? The question after intercourse which the modern man was not so long ago expected to ask in deference to the new interest in women's sexual needs. But today it has become such a cliché that any man who utters it risks being called a 'wally'. Indeed in 1983 *The Sun*'s list of ways to tell a wally included this same question.

weapon The penis. The image of the penis as weapon and penetrative sex as violence predominates in much slang and has done since Shakespearian times at least. Words like lance, spear, stick, sword, pork dagger and pistol – and even prick – are now commonplace words for penis. Another equivalent is weapon of peace – in the multilateralist line of thinking perhaps?

wear one's hair out against the head of the bed Said of a man who is going bald, this jocular catch phrase is now out of date but the sexual innuendo is based on a popular myth, still extant, that prematurely balding men are exceptionally virile.

wear the kilt, to To be the passive partner in male gay sex. The term is current US usage, but it was in use in the UK from WW2. It probably evolved in opposition to the well-known phrase about women who are dominant partners in their marriages, i.e. who 'wear the trousers'.

wedding tackle The penis. In the same tradition of workmanlike phrases about the 'equipment' that 'does the business'. Very widespread lower middle-class UK

phrase, used in a lockerroom/sports club context. Closely related to 'wedding kit' – Forces slang from WW1.

wedge, to Sexual intercourse. British West Indian in origin from wedge, wedger and wedgie – meaning penis – the verb has developed as wedging = to have sexual intercourse.

wedgie The white buttock area exposed when bikini bottoms or swimming trunks are whipped down by strong ocean rollers. Hence a triumphant cry to be heard off the surfing beaches of Cornwall and the West of Ireland – 'Look! A wedgie!'

well endowed A person with supposedly remarkably large sexual parts. The term most commonly applies to men with big genitals, and as the size of their organs is still a matter of obsession with many men, being well endowed or well hung is considered a compliment worth more than its weight in gold. Women however tend to be less interested in this mythical aspect of virility. The term is also sometimes used in reference to a woman's large breasts. *See also* WELL HUNG.

well hung Having large genitals (male). Still in very common usage; the term dates back to the early 19th century (Partridge). *See also* WELL ENDOWED.

welt The penis. Originally Armed

195

Forces slang, this word still carries unpleasant sadistic overtones, perhaps from another slang sense of 'welt' – to flog or strike a blow. Obscure and now obsolete.

wench A woman. Today the term is used semi-affectionately in the consciousness of its medieval and Shakespearian flavour. The so-called medieval banqueting halls that have sprung up in rural Britain and Ireland to entertain tourists with a taste of 'genuine' history employ 'serving wenches' to pour out the mead, look buxom etc.

The word has an interesting history. It derives from *wencel* which had the Old-English meaning unsteady, inconstant (OED). It also meant child, then female child. By the 16th century it had come to mean a girl of the rustic or working class and in late Middle-English a 'wanton woman, a mistress' (OED).

The OED cites Chaucer – 'I am a gentil womman and no wenche', and Shakespeare – 'Prythee, how many Boys and Wenches must I have'.

To wench – and wenching – as a verb – came to mean consorting with woman and/or prostitutes, and the noun wench kept the disparaging 'promiscuous' sense.

The development of its meaning is a good example of what Dale Spender has called the systematic semantic derogation of women.

wet bottom, get a Also 'do a

bottom-wetter'. To have sexual intercourse. This old-fashioned phrase speaks for itself, but 'wet' was probably the old equivalent of the modern 'hot' – denoting readiness for sex. For wet Partridge gives 'of women when secreting letch water' – from the mid-18th century.

It is still used in an intimate sexual context, and in pornographic writing.

wet dream Erotic dream that culminates in orgasm in males. Dates back to the 18th century at least. Note the late 60s phrase for joyless sexual intercourse: 'like a wet dream pushed up with a spoon.'

wet patch *See* DP (for 'damp patch').

wet T-shirt competition A form of 'beauty' contest originating in America in the late 70s, now widespread in Britain. Based on the spurious principle that the contestants are more 'decent' than topless models because dressed in wet T-shirts, in reality the cold water used to drench the girls causes their nipples to become erect and some men find this a more titillating sight than nudity.

whack it up Sexual intercourse. Widespread term in the tradition of violent, penetrative imagery.

whack off Masturbation, generally male, but sometimes trendy female usage. Hudson cites *Oz*

1973 – 'Her mother catches Janis in the bath singing the Kozmic Blues and whacking off'. 'Wrap off' is a US variant.

wham bang thank you ma'am Originally US but now widespread slang phrase for a casual sexual encounter – so quick that it was literally a case of 'wham bang' and goodbye. Used by both sexes, thus entirely interchangeable with 'wham bam thank you man' in gay usage.

whanger The penis. Probably deriving from the slang word whang – meaning to strike heavily and resoundingly, and as such another in the line of words which uses the image of penetration as a blow. *Compare* WHACK IT UP, BANG etc.

what for Used in sexual innuendo – as in the working-class expression 'I'd like to give her a bit of what for!' Synonymous with 'a seeing to'.

what number, what colour? Question to ascertain a person's sexual preference. Common in US where people may be offended by the UK assumption that heterosexuality is the norm.

wheel, grease the Sexual intercourse. Of northern English origin, now rare. Also the old Yorkshire expression 'keep cart on wheel' – to keep a sexual relationship going.

whelk The female parts. This is cockney working-class in origin and well over a century old. But the oceanic image is a common one, as in 'periwinkle', 'bearded clam', the 'French mollusc' and the popular 'lobster'.

where the monkey sleeps The female parts. Usually heard in the man-to-man question: 'Did you find where the monkey sleeps last night?' Generally working-class usage and Scottish in origin (C. Harkins, 1983).

whim The female parts. Also 'whim wham'. This is now largely obscure, but perhaps related to 'quim'. It also has the sense of a trinket, something of no consequence; hence little used.

whipped cream Semen. A rather self-congratulatory term – *see also* LOVE BUTER.

whirligigs Testicles. Obscure.

whisker splitter *See* BEARD SPLITTER.

whistle The penis. Childish usage, from the obvious phallic imagery.

white blow Semen. Old-fashioned posh English term. Perhaps related to whitewash – for sexual intercourse.

White Russian Practice in which semen is passed from the fellator's mouth to the mouth of the ejaculator. Synonymous with 'exchanging loads' and 'snowdropping'. A mostly gay male expression.

white wedding A wedding in which the bride is supposed to be a virgin. These days when some UK brides are pregnant on their wedding day and marriage is less popular than it has ever been in living memory, white weddings are rarely taken seriously and the term most often occurs in the facetious question – 'I suppose you'll have a white wedding?'

Who are you leaning on these days? Query about identity of a man's latest girlfriend. The expression has been heard in Ireland where the image of a man leaning on a woman – whether figuratively or in a bar – is not uncommon.

whoopee, making Sexual intercourse. US in origin and largely outdated since the 60s, this term derived from the original, purely innocent, slang meaning of having a good time.

whopper Large penis. Jocular and inoffensive usage – as in 'Cor, what a whopper!', which, ironically, could just as easily refer to a fish!

whore Prostitute or woman considered sexually 'promiscuous'. Etymologically the word has moved a long way from its Latin root – *carus* = dear, through the Norse *hora* and Middle-English *hore*.

Today it is probably the most common term for what the OED calls 'a prostitute ... or unchaste

or lewd woman', and in slang is used as a general – and serious – insult to women (and sometimes men) – as in 'Fuck off you silly whore!' It is interesting that despite the so-called sexual revolution, one of the most widespread ways of expressing contempt for a woman is an accusation of 'promiscuity'.

There are any number of compounds with whore, such as whore house = brothel, whoremonger = promiscuous man, whore's melt = bastard (Scottish and some Irish usage), whore's musk = perfume, whore pipe = penis, whore's bird = debauchée, but these are mostly dated.

The word can also be used lightly, in a camp or semi-affectionate sense, but the speaker will generally pronounce the word in mock Scottish or 'Oirish' as hoor or hoo-er, to show that he or she is joking.

WHT An abbreviation of 'wandering hand trouble'. As in the comment from one UK woman to another:

'I think your boyfriend's got a bad case of WHT.' Modern, mostly female usage. *See* WANDERING HAND, DESERT DISEASE.

why buy a book when you canjoin a library? Catch phrase implying there is no need to go to the expense of 'having' a wife when there are women sexually available without so much expense. A parallel expression is 'Why buy a cow just because you like milk?'

wick The penis. From Hampton Wick, rhyming slang for prick. Dip the wick is sexual intercourse, a widespread male expression. 'It gets on my wick' i.e. 'it gets on my nerves' has the same root, but the expression is so many stages removed from its origin that the literal meaning penis is generally forgotten and women *and* men use the expression.

wife In slang usage a girlfriend or lover. As in the pub closing-time expression 'The wife says its time to go home'. Also as a slightly embarrassed euphemism for a lover amongst the middle classes: an old-fashioned 19th century form for mistress was 'wife in watercolours' – i.e. no permanent bonds.

Wife also had the archaic prison slang meaning of ball and chain.

Also passive partner in homosexual sex – which speaks volumes about the notion of the wifely role! US gay slang from the '60s.

Wifey is widespread Scottish usage for woman.

wife's best friend The penis. Common male usage, comically self-congratulatory. Usually appearing in the phrase 'to shake hands with the wife's best friend' – meaning male masturbation (or, occasionally, urination). *See also*

MOTHER PALM AND HER FIVE DAUGHTERS, OLD LADY FIVE FINGERS.

willy, or **willie** The penis. Widespread, schoolboyish usage. Sometimes William also. *Compare with* DICK, and other men's names for penis.

wilnuts An Irish schoolboy version of 'bumtags'. *See also* CLINKERS, WINNET.

wimp A feeble, pathetic, 'unmanly' man. Someone who is 'wimpy' or 'wimpish' or whose actions are a 'wimp out' is considered weak and a failure.

One source suggests that the term originates from the character Wimpy in the Popeye cartoons, but from about 1920 'wimp' meant girl – Partridge suggests from 'whimper'.

wind do twirl Girl. Cockney rhyming slang. Rare.

wink, to To be uncircumcised – as in the query 'Does it wink?' Mostly US usage. Not to be confused with 'wink the brown eye' – to expose the arse in 'mooning'.

winkle The penis. Affectionate and mostly childish usage.

winnet Faecal blob found on the penis after anal intercourse. Also a Mancunian word for 'bumtag'.

wire The penis. Usually occurring in the widespread phrase 'pulling

the wire' (or 'twanging the wire')
– male masturbation.

woman Principally the word
which emancipated females used
to describe themselves and each
other, in contrast to 'girl' which is
rejected as being patronizing.
Feminists tend to avoid using 'girl'
for all but females under the age
of about 12, preferring 'young
women'. Some have changed the
spelling to delete the 'man' from
'woman', using 'wimmin' and
'wombyn' instead. These alternative forms are found in feminist
newsletters and periodicals like
Wires and *Spare Rib*.
A glance through the OED will
demonstrate why many women
are sensitive about the way the
word is used. Its old English origin
is wif+man, defined as 'an adult
female human being', and listed
among its meanings is 'With
allusion to qualities attributed to
the female sex, as mutability,
proneness to tears, or physical
weakness; also to their position of
inferiority or subjection'. It also
has the meanings 'a female
servant ... a kept mistress, a wife'.
But the women's movement has
made the general public aware of
the bias of the word: hence a
newspaper cartoon (*Guardian*,
November 1983), showing an
adult telling a child, 'Don't cry, be
strong, be a woman'.
'Woman oriented woman' is an
originally US and feminist term
for a lesbian.

womanist Of, by and/or for
women. The term is parallel to
'feminist' but lays claim to a wider
frame of reference. It is a
brand-new US word, which has
not yet made its way across the
Atlantic. The US writer Alice
Walker uses it to describe her book
of 'womanist prose' – *In Search of
our Mothers' Gardens*, which is
about black women in relation to
their mothers, families, each other
and the world at large.

woman of the night Prostitute.
Old-fashioned usage.

wong The penis. US gay usage –
an inevitable variation on the
theme of whanger/donger etc.

wooftah Male homosexual, a
variant of pooftah. Usage is
widespread among men, and
invariably disparaging.

woolies Pubic hairs. Mainly US
usage, but a universal image.
Contrast the more fanciful GOR-
ILLA SALAD.

worm The flaccid penis. Affectionate and schoolboyish usage, as
in 'He's got a little worm in his
underpants' or 'Did you see his
little tummy worm?' In the same
class as winkle and willy.

**would you eat chips out of her
knickers?** A Dublin expression
indicating distaste for a female. It
has become a throw-away phrase
among a small group of Dubliners,
male and female, and will probably share the same fate as the

equally obscure 'I'm on the floor for ye Gloria!', now only a memory for a few.

wriggle navels, to Sexual intercourse. Affectionate, chummy usage, perhaps related to the now obscure wriggling pole – penis. *Compare* the Australian SLIPPERY BELLY.

wrinkle The vagina. Semi-affectionate – if not exactly flattering – usage. Mostly US.

wrist job An act of masturbation. Also 'wristing' and 'giving it one off the wrist'. Invariably male usage, used in male company. 'If I don't pull tonight it'll have to be a wrist job.' Contemporary UK and US usage.

X

x Sex. A principally American abbreviation, as in 'Did you have x with him last night?' More likely to be used by women than men, as such a coy euphemism. *See* X-EY.

X-certificate Pertaining to sex or sexual provocation. Common currency was achieved with the introduction of censorship in the cinema, with the British Board of Film Censors first granting an X-certificate to films not to be shown to anyone under 18. Since then anything slightly 'blue' or 'sexy' has been described as 'X-certificate stuff'. But the abolition of the old certification scheme in the early eighties in the UK (with X being replaced by 18) hasn't caused the term to become obsolete. More American is 'X-rated' – meaning provocative or sexy among 'straights', and generally deviationist or sado-masochistic among male gays. Yet X-rated is also a convenient tabloid expression for anything 'sexy' or titillating. 'Curvy Carol Dean shows off a bewitching bodysuit ... in her X-rated Xmas undies she's a perfect stocking filler.' (*The Sun*, 24 Nov. 1983).

x-ey Sexy. A coy, almost 'preppy' American abbreviation.

Y The vagina. Common abbreviation, probably suggested by the shape of a woman's legs when apart. Affectionate generally male usage. *See also* YMCA.

YA Youthful (and/or) inexperienced homosexual. Abbreviation of young action, mostly US.

Y, dining at the Cunnilingus. Australian in origin, now mostly male jocular in usage. 'Eating' is a common enough term for oral sex, while the 'Y' is the vagina.

yaffle (Of a male) to perform cunnilingus. From the previously vulgar yaffle (= snaffle); to eat, gobble or snatch. Obscure. *See also* GOBBLE.

yang The penis. Possibly from the concept of yin and yang, the female and male principles in Taoist philosophy. Fanciful US gay usage.

yanking Masturbation. Male usage. A combination of the sense of 'pulling off', and the synonym 'wanking'. One of the less common terms for this activity.

yansh The 'arse'. From the original Yoruba (West African dialect). British black use only, but a word equally employed by men and women.

yardage In reference to the penis of a 'well-endowed' male – as in 'Did you see the yardage on him?' Further illustration of the male obsession with the length of the penis.

YMCA The vagina. An Australianism popularized by Barry Mackenzie (*Bazza Pulls It Off* 1968). Taken from the notion that the YMCA is where young women stay, hence it is the home of sex – to continue the allusive chain – the 'home' of sex equals the vagina. Sexist, as any notion that 'all women are cunts' invariably is.

YMCA, dining at the Cunnilingus, simply a variant on dining

at the Y (q.v.). *See also* YODEL-
LING UP THE VALLEY and DON-
NING THE BEARD for other
Australian synonyms.

yodelling up the valley Performing cunnilingus. Originally Australian and humorously graphic.
Invariably male usage in male
company; sometimes shortened or
lengthened for effect. Thus in its
shortest form, yodelling = cunnilingus, while recorded American
tortuosities include 'yodelling in
the canyon of love' and 'yodelling
in the fishy forest'.

yoni The vagina. From the Indian
classics and briefly fashionable
amongst the hippy generation of
the sixties. Now rare. *See also*
LINGAM.

**you'd fuck a hedgehog if it
didn't have spikes on!** Crude
catch phrase usually implying that
a man is at once sexually
insatiable and indiscriminating.
As such often used by men to
express envious admiration. Usage
is invariably jocular; a form of
male banter. *Contrast with* the
female usage of a phrase like
YOU'D RIDE A BIKE IF IT HAD A
KNOB ON.

Here, as in the following list of
equivalents (which are apparently
endless and as yet undocumented)
the recurring theme is that of the
male as the active pentrative
partner while the female is merely
an 'object' to be 'had' at all costs:
you'd fuck a frog if it didn't jump;

you'd fuck a hole in the ground if
it smiled at you; you'd fuck a
snake if it didn't wriggle; you'd
shag a barber's floor if it had
enough hair on it.

**you don't look at the mantel-
piecewhen you're stoking the
fire** This popular catch phrase is
used to convey the idea that it
doesn't matter what a woman
looks like while a man is having
sex with her.

The imagery is of woman as a
hot gaping hole, the male –
literally – a poker. And although
the original idea is sexist to a
degree, such is the comedy of the
phrase that it is invariably used in
fun – by men and women – and
rarely causes offence. The authors
last heard it on the lips of a young
Somerset woman talking about a
local love affair – and she had the
occupants of the pub where she
presided in stitches.

Contrast the cruder usage of
YOU'D FUCK A HEDGEHOG IF IT
DIDN'T HAVE SPIKES ON, etc.

**you'd ride a bike if it had a
knob on** (sometimes **she'd**)
Expression addressed to a woman
considered sexually insatiable and
indiscriminating. Less common
than the equivalent expression to
males – *see* YOU'D FUCK A
HEDGEHOG, etc. – and less likely
to convey grudging admiration
than disgust.

**you'll die like a mule with the
seed in your belly!** Jibing catch

phrase directed from one man to another who has produced no children. The popular notion is obviously that he has been unable even to have sexual intercourse. Dated, but often addressed from the older generation to the younger, much in the manner of 'Why don't you get on with it?' (C. Harkins, 1982.)

you look at the worldthrough the hole in your prick! Coarse catch phrase said by one man to another supposedly obsessed by sex. *See* YOU'VE GOT A ONE-TRACK MIND!

you've got a one-track mind! Rebuking catch phrase to a person who thinks or talks only about sex. Used by both male and female in polite company, now considered rather coy, especially if the phrase is extended with the addition of '... and that's a dirt one!'

yoyo A small penis. Literally a tiny and insignificant plaything. The word is invariably used as an insult – sometimes in derisive comments by women. *Compare* with BUTTON MUSHROOM, IBM. *Contrast* with YARDAGE, and WELL HUNG *et al.*

yummies Either the physical pleasure involved in sex (in which case getting your yummies is synonymous with getting your rocks off – (q.v.)) or the body's erogenous zones, i.e. genitals or nipples. Across-the-board American usage; unlike yummy (q.v.) this particular form of Yankee euphemistic approbation hasn't survived the Atlantic crossing.

yummy A sexually attractive woman or girl (Hudson). Yummy as an adjective has been around (via the US) since the early sixties, usually used by females to describe something pleasurable or exciting. However the use of yummy as a noun, to describe a potential sexual partner, was one of the spin-offs of the so-called rock revolution in the late sixties and early seventies. A yummy could be a groupie or vice versa, but just as easily a female that caught the eye. This usage is now rare, largely being superseded by the American usage of YUMMIES (q.v.).

Z

zab The penis. From the original Arabic, little heard outside of the ethnic community and (occasionally) by 'travellers' or those trying to impress.

zig-zig Sexual intercourse. Entering common currency after WW2, from the Middle Eastern and North African description of sex. First used by British Armed Forces but attaining new heights of popularity once the 'hippy trail' began in the sixties. For the younger generation it was a new word which came back with new experiences. Also the similar jig-a-jig, and fucky-fucky.

zipper sex Fellatio. The term generally implies a hurried or clandestine act in which the man does not even remove his trousers. Almost entirely confined to the gay community, especially US. Also closely related is 'zipper dinner'. Rodgers also gives the obscure 'zipper club', oddly defined as 'an after-hours establishment.'

Zogg's Sex Wax Surfboard wax. An innocuous enough trade name, but worthy of inclusion as its advertisement (as every surfer knows) reads 'The best for one's stick!' The stick, of course, is the surfboard, but sexual allusions about the power of Zogg's are common in surfing slang.

zoo number Sex with an 'animal'. In camp gay usage the term can mean simply having sex with another person possessing 'animal' characteristics (*see*, for instance, GORILLA SALAD). The straight male would use the term to describe sex with either someone he regards as a physically ugly woman or possibly one that he considers 'abnormally' sexually active. Hence a male active in this direction becomes a zoo keeper (the straight term) or a zoo queen (the obvious gay synonym). Oddly the term doesn't cover having sex with a *real* animal.

zubrick The penis. Fanciful term comparing the male 'organ' to an obscure musical instrument, although it has been suggested that the word is rhyming slang for prick.

206

THE PRIVATE PARTS

An unselective list of words in common usage for the male and female genitalia.

Male

Acorn
Accoutrements
Almond
Almond Rock Candy

Baby Maker
Bald Headed Hermit
Basket
Bazooka
Beard Splitter
Beechams Pills
Bell End
Big Foot Joe
Blue Veined Steak
Boy
Brush
Button Mushroom

Cherry Splitter
Chopper
Club
Cock
Colleen Bawn
Copper Stick
Corker
Cory
Crown Jewels

Dagger
Dangler
Dark Meat
Dead Rabbit
Derrick
Dibble
Dirk
Dingle Dangle
Do Hickies

Donkey
Dork
Down There
Dolly
Doodle
Drapes
Driving Post

End
Equipment

Family Jewels
Fancy Work
Ferret
Flowers and Frolics
Fornicator

Gear
Generating Tool
Giggle Stick
Goolies

Hampton
Hair Splitter
Hammer
Hangers
Head
Helmet
Horn

IBM
ID
Inch
Irish Root
Ice Cream Machine

JT

Jewels
Jewish Compliment
Jigger
Jock
John Thomas
Joy Prong
Joy Stick

Key
Kidney Wiper
Kit
Knackers
Knob

Lob Cock
Lot
Lung Disturber
Lunch

Machine
Mad Mick
Maggot
Man
Marbles
Marriage Gear
Marquis of Lorne
Member
Mickey
Middle Finger
Mole
Mouse
Mutton

Nebuchadnezzar
Necessaries
Needle
Nick Nacks

Nimrod
Nuts

Old Adam
One-Eyed Trouser
  Snake

Pat and Mick
Pecker
Pen
Pendulum
Percy
Pillock
Pin
Pink Oboe
Plonker
Pork Dagger
Prick
Prong

Quim Stick

Rabbit
Ramrod
Ranger
Rat
Rig
Rod
Rupert

Salami
Sausage
Sword

Tadger
Tackle
Thing

Third Leg
Thomas
Tickle Tail
Tool
Tommy
Tonk
Trouser Snake
Trumpet
Tummy Banana

Under Par
Unemployed
Uncle Dick

Wand
Weapon
Wedding Tackle
Welt

Whanger
Whirligigs
Whisker Splitter
Whistle
Whopper
Wick
Wife's Best Friend
Willy

Winkle
Wire
Worm

Yoyo

Zab
Zubrick

Female

Ace of Spades
Agreeable Ruts of
  Life
Artichoke

Beaver
Beef Curtains
Bite
Box
Button

Cat With Its Throat
  Cut
Cave
Centre of Bliss
Chink
Chopped Liver
Cleft
Clit
Commodity
Coyote
Crack
Cranny
Cunt
Cylinder

Dead End Street
Diddly Pout
Dot
Down There
Drain

End of The Senti-
  mental Journey
Eve's Custom House
Expressive Button

Fanny

Fig
Fish
Flange
Flower
Front Bum
Fud
Gap
Garden
Gash
Gee
Geography
Gim Crack
Glue Pot
Growl and Grunt
Grumble and Grunt
Gut Entrance

Happy Hunting
  Ground
Hair Pie
Hole
Horse Collar
Hortus
Housewife
Husband's Supper

Ingle Nook
Inner Sanctum
Irish Fortune
Ivory Gate

Jelly Box
Jerusalem Artichoke

Kennel
Kettle
Kitty
Knick Knack

Ladder
Lamp of Love
Lapland
Leading Article
Leak
Leather
Lili
Little Man In The
  Boat
Little Sister
Lobster Pot
Long Eye
Low Countries
Lowlands
Lucky Bag

Man In The Boat
Mark of The Beast
Merkin
Minge
Monkey
Mouth
Muff

Naff
Naggy
Nasty
Niche
Nick
Nick Nacks
Nock
Notch
Novelty
Number Nip
Nursery

Old Hat

Pancake
Papaya
Parlour
Periwinkle
Pleasure Gardens
Prat
Pussy

Quim

Rails
Red Ace
Rhubarb
Rose

Salt Cellar
Seed Plot
Sharp And Blunt
Tail
Tenuc
That There
Thing
Tramlines
Twat

Vag

Whelk
Where The Monkey
  Sleeps
Whim
Wrinkle

YMCA

The Fall
of
Constantinople

NANAMI SHIONO

Translated by Kerim Yasar

Published by Vertical, Inc., New York.

Originally published in Japanese as *Konstantinopuru no Kanraku* by Shinchosha, Tokyo, 1972.

ISBN 1-932234-17-9

Manufactured in the United States of America

First American Edition

Vertical, Inc.
257 Park Avenue South, 8th Floor
New York, NY 10010
www.vertical-inc.com

THE PRINCIPALS

CONSTANTINE XI..............Byzantine (Eastern Roman) Emperor

DIEDO...................................Venetian sea captain

GEORGIOS............................Learned monk of Constantinople

GIUSTINIANI.......................Genoese mercenary captain

HALIL...................................Grand Vizier of Ottoman Turkey

ISIDORE ....Catholic Cardinal and Papal envoy

JULIA ....Spanish consul of Constantinople

LOMELLINO ....Magistrate of the Genoese settlement

MEHMED II ....Sultan of Ottoman Turkey

MIHAJLOVIC.......................Serbian cavalry captain

MINOTTO.............................Venetian ambassador to Constantinople

NICOLO ....Venetian noble and physician

NOTARAS.............................Chief Minister of the Byzantine Empire

ORHAN.................................Turkish prince in exile

PHRANTZES ....Minister of the Byzantine Empire

TEDALDI..............................Florentine merchant

TREVISAN............................Venetian admiral

TURSUN...............................Sultan's page

UBERTINO...........................Philosophy student from northern Italy

URBAN ....Hungarian military engineer

ZAGANOS............................Turkish Pasha

Chapter One

The Two Protagonists

The City of Constantinople

It is not unusual, in the annals of history, for the fall of a city to be bound up with the destruction of a nation. Yet how many times in the long history of the human race has the fall of a city heralded the end of an entire civilization, and one that had exerted a significant influence on the surrounding world over the course of many centuries? Furthermore, how many such occurrences can be pinpointed not only to the exact year, but to the exact month, day, even *hour*? Constantinople is unusual because we know with certainty not only the day of its death, but the day of its birth as well.

This city on the Bosphorus Strait was known as Byzantium until May 11th, 330 C.E., when it took the name Constantinopolis ("The City of Constantine") in honor of its founder, the Emperor Constantine. For 1,123 years it served as the capital of the Greek-speaking Roman Empire, also known as the "Eastern Roman Empire" or the "Byzantine Empire."

In these pages we will use the anglicized name "Constantinople." This is fitting in a sense because during the millennium or so of its flourishing, the city was known by a number of names other than the "Constantinopolis" used in Greek and Latin. Every ethnic group that had any connection with the city pronounced the name in its own way. The Italians, for example, who had a very close relationship with the city during its final years, called it "Constantinopoli." The current official name of the city, "Istanbul," is the Turkish variation on "Constantinopolis," but one so altered by the passage of time that its etymology is difficult if not impossible to guess.

Similarly, "Adrianopolis" is known in modern Turkish as "Edirne." When Constantinople fell, however, Adrianopolis ("The City of Emperor Hadrian") had already been the Ottoman capital for over a hundred years, so referring to it here by its Greek or Latin name would not be quite appropriate. At the same time, though, since not even the Turks of the time had yet begun to call the city "Edirne," for the sake of consistency let us refer to it by the rendition that would be most congenial for us, Adrianople.

The rapid development of Constantinople, also called "New Rome," was quite enough to draw the attention of the neighboring peoples of the time, all the more so because the Western Roman Empire was in decline. Situated where Europe meets Asia, the city was destined from birth to become the capital of the Mediterranean world.

This "New Rome," however, was completely different from the Rome to the west in one important way. Eastern Rome was an empire born with Christianity as its defining constituent. The cloak worn in public by the emperor of the Eastern Roman Empire was not purple, but crimson. The Christian church had made purple, which had been the color of the ancient Roman emperors, the color of mourning—in other words, the color of death.

Although it is said that when Eastern Rome was founded in the fourth century it was already a more vibrant society than western Rome, in the final analysis it didn't actually become the capital of the Mediterranean world until the original Rome met its ruin in the late fifth century. Less than a century after that, in the mid-sixth century, the Eastern Roman Empire's sphere of influence reached its greatest extent. Although it didn't match the ancient Roman Empire at its zenith, the Byzantine Empire under Emperor Justinian extended from the Straits of Gibraltar in the west to Persia in the east, from the Italian Alps in the north to the upper Nile in the south. (Map 1)

By the time the Crusades began in the 11th century, however, the empire had diminished considerably. The Byzantine Empire had become the base of the Greek Orthodox Church, whose doctrinal disputes with the Catholic Church had led to schism, and so its allegiances during this period of conflict between the Christian powers of the West and the Islamic forces in the East were not completely clear. It was during this time, as well, that the Byzantines lost control of the eastern Mediterranean Sea to the maritime city-states of Genoa and Venice. (Map 2) With such a state of affairs, it was only a matter of time before the empire was lost. The final push came with the Fourth Crusade in 1204, which also saw the founding of the Latin Empire. During this period only the Nicaean Empire, which had been founded in Asia Minor by exiles fled from Constantinople, kept the bloodlines of the Eastern Roman Empire alive.

The Byzantines were able to regain Constantinople after a mere sixty years, but to their great misfortune an archrival to the east continued to grow in size and strength in the meantime: the Ottoman Turks, who were consolidating their strength in the Anatolian plain. For the next century the Byzantines suffered a string of defeats. It is the guiding principle of history that all that prospers must eventually decline, but even so, the debilitation of the Byzantine Empire was notably precipitous. (Maps 3 and 4)

As the Turks crossed the Bosphorus Strait and conquered

one European holding after another, the once-glorious Byzantine Empire was reduced to nothing more than Constantinople, its environs, and a portion of the Peloponnese peninsula. The Aegean Sea to the south was firmly in the grip of the maritime city-states of Venice and Genoa, each of which had a population of no more than 200,000.

During the Byzantine Empire's flourishing between the sixth and tenth centuries, the population of Constantinople and its outskirts was said to have been around a million. By the beginning of the fifteenth century, it had fallen to less than a hundred thousand. The population density in the city proper was lower than that of either Venice or Genoa. Furthermore, the Italians of the time had given birth to Renaissance civilization and made coolheaded, rational thinking their trademark. To them, the Byzantines—who would not separate the church, whose affairs are spiritual, from the state, whose affairs are temporal—were a collection of medieval-minded irrationalists, prone to superstition, whose only interest was in religious sermons and who completely lacked the active and cooperative spirit absolutely essential to the efficient administration of a community.

Physically surrounded by the Turks, militarily negligible, economically at the mercy of the trading nations of Western Europe, the Byzantine Empire of the fifteenth century was led, coincidentally, by a man who shared the name of the city's founder: Constantine XI. This emperor, who would be the Eastern Roman Empire's last, was a physical embodiment of the elegant, dying civilization he oversaw: a refined, 49-year-old gentleman with a tranquil disposition who revered honor above all. Twice married and twice widowed, he had no

9

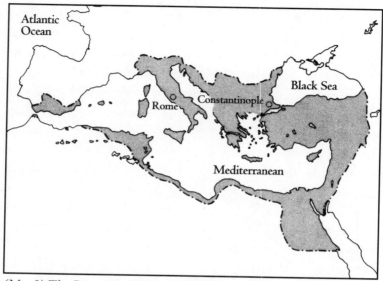

(Map1) The Byzantine Empire in Justinian's times, ca. 565 C.E.

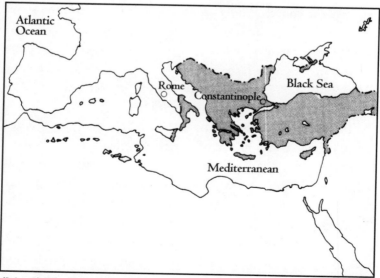

(Map2) The Byzantine Empire during the Crusades, 11th century

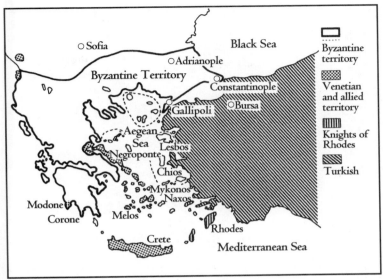

(Map3) The East Mediterranean, distribution of power in 1340

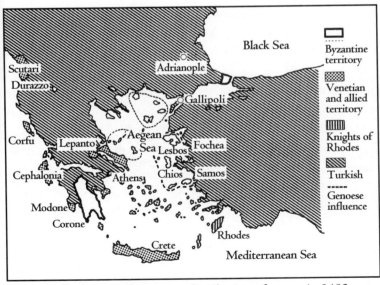

(Map4) The East Mediterranean, distribution of power in 1402

children.

It was Emperor Constantine's charge to defend the city of Constantinople, symbol of the Byzantine civilization that had imbibed the influence of the Orient as well as that of classical Greece and Rome, while still maintaining its distinct individuality. His opponent would be a young Turkish man who had just turned twenty years old.

Sultan Mehmed the Second

It is a given that, around the year 1300, nobody was paying any attention at all to the Ottoman Turks who had begun to consolidate their power at that time in the Anatolian plain in Asia Minor. Within 28 years, however, the Turks would go on to conquer the city of Bursa near the Sea of Marmara. With the very formidable Mongol Empire to the east and the weakened Byzantine Empire to the west, it was natural for this nomadic people to choose to expand westward. The Turks made Bursa their capital. Asia Minor was now completely within their control.

But this wasn't enough to satisfy them. Their march west continued, and in 1354 they captured Gallipoli. Situated on the shore of the Dardanelles, Gallipoli was not in Asia: it was very much a part of Europe, even if only at its periphery. The fall of Gallipoli gave the Turks control of the strategic stretch of land running from the Dardanelles, through the Sea of Marmara, all the way to Constantinople. This was not something that would go unchallenged, either by the Byzantine Empire from whom the city was taken, or by the Western city-states who passed through those waters in order to conduct trade with Constantinople and cities on the Black Sea. The first reports of the menace presented by the rising power of the Turks appeared in the Republic of Venice, which had the most comprehensive information network at the time, during that same year 1354.

The Byzantine Empire didn't have the forces to repel the invaders on its own, while Venice and Genoa were locked in internecine squabbles; the Ottomans proceeded steadily into the Balkans and the chance to stop them quickly slipped away.

1362 fall of Adrianople
1363 castle at Philippopolis captured

These two conquests put all of Thrace in Turkish hands. At the end of these two years they moved their capital from Bursa on the Asian side to Adrianople on the European side. There could be no clearer indication than this that they intended to continue their march westward. Neighboring Bulgaria, Macedonia, and the Byzantine Empire itself were suddenly jolted. Both Macedonia (officially under Byzantine rule) and Bulgaria became vassal states of the Ottomans, forced to pay annual tribute and to provide troops. The Byzantine Emperor not only had to pay annual tribute to the sultan, but also had to lead, or send a member of the imperial family to lead, a Greek regiment fighting alongside the Turks whenever the sultan set out on an expedition.

The Ottomans continued to win one battle after another, seemingly impervious to defeat. In 1385 they took the Bulgarian capital of Sofia. In 1387 the Macedonian capital of Thessaloniki also fell into their hands. The subjugation of the Byzantines progressed so far that when infighting among the imperial family made it impossible to decide the next successor to the throne, they would await the decision of the Ottoman sultan who, in his own time, would dispense his sanction. Thus by the end of the fourteenth century, all that remained of the Byzantine Empire was Constantinople, its environs, and the inland portion of the Peloponnesian peninsula. It was around this time that the emperor went to Western Europe begging for reinforcements to hold back the Ottomans. Anybody who knew the reality of the eastern Mediterranean of the time could see that the Byzantine Empire was clearly on the brink of collapse. To assert that the Ottoman encirclement of Constantinople was not complete would have been impossible even for an optimist.

Rushing home upon hearing that the Turks were advancing on Constantinople, Emperor Manuel learned instead that the Ottoman threat had vanished in the course of one morning. In that year, 1402, Ottoman forces led by Sultan Beyazid suffered a complete defeat in Ankara at the hands of a Mongol army led by Timur. The sultan himself was taken captive. Hunted down by the Mongol forces, the great Ottoman army had vanished without a trace. Although the Turkish soldiers were famed for their cruelty, the Mongolian forces were even more vicious: it was said that where the Mongol army had passed, one could hear neither the barking of dogs, nor the singing of birds, nor the crying of children.

Having tasted its first defeat and with its sultan in the hands of the enemy, the Ottoman court immediately splintered into factions. This infighting continued beyond the death of Timur three years later and the rapid collapse of the Mongol Empire that attended it. All of the Ottomans' vassal states, from the Byzantine Empire down, saw this as a good opportunity to regain their independence. During the twenty years that it took the Turks to recover from their defeat by the Mongols, these states shrugged off their tributary payments and refused to send troops, but they did nothing to enhance their own capacity for self-defense. Indeed, when the Turks went on the offensive once again after those twenty years, the former vassal states could do nothing to stop them. Constantinople was again surrounded, the Byzantine Empire and the other vassal states conceded to Sultan Murad's demands, and the twenty-year hiatus of tribute payments and troop offerings came to an end. It was back to 1402.

But Murad, believing perhaps that simply maintaining the lands under his control was the best policy, did not launch any large-scale acts of aggression for the next thirty years. Battles were fought, mainly of a defensive nature, but they did not occur close to Constantinople. The city at that time, despite being the nominal capital of the Byzantine Empire, was rather in the position of a free port city. The commercial city-states of the West, Genoa and Venice, as well as the trading peoples of the Orient—the Arabs, Armenians, and Jews—all used the city as the base from which to compete economically with one another. The Turks, unlike their coreligionists the Arabs, were essentially a nomadic people and unskilled in the art of commerce. Perhaps for this reason they were willing to give tacit consent to the existence of a simple free port city, the activities of which enriched their capital of Adrianople as well. It was well known that Murad's most trusted vizier, Halil Pasha, was sympathetic to the West and to the Byzantines. Venice and Genoa had publicly signed friendship and trading agreements with the Ottomans, and both sides had secured considerable profit from trade via Constantinople with cities in Asia and on the Black Sea coast. The Ottomans' policy of rule during the first half of the fifteenth century was a pragmatic recognition of compromise as a means toward mutual benefit. That compromise was allowing the Byzantine Empire, which had been reduced to only Constantinople, to continue to exist.

What the powers of the West and the Byzantine Empire didn't know, however, was that a young man with an extraordinary interest in Alexander the Great and Julius Caesar was coming of age in the plains of Asia Minor.

Mehmed the Second, the third son of Sultan Murad, was born in the Ottoman capital of Adrianople in 1432. His mother was low born, a slave who had been forced to convert from Christianity to Islam. Sultan Murad, perhaps because he felt no special favor towards Mehmed's mother, sent the boy, his mother, and his wet-nurse to the Anatolian city of Amasya when the boy was two. Amasya was then governed by Murad's eldest son, who died three years later. The governor's post was not considered to be anything particularly important, and so was handed down to five-year-old Mehmed. As the sultan's son, Mehmed was also occasionally invited to banquets given at the capital in Adrianople. After a short time, Mehmed's remaining older brother was given the Amasya governorship while he was put in charge of Manisa.

In 1443, however, his older brother was killed by an unknown assassin. Eleven-year-old Mehmed was now the only heir to the throne, which prompted his father Murad, who had never given Mehmed any particular attention up until this point, to summon him to the capital. Separated from his mother and still only a child, Mehmed had to serve as the regent while his father was away fighting in various campaigns.

Mehmed's advisor during these times was Halil Pasha. More than an advisor, he was in fact Mehmed's overseer. When he disagreed with the young ruler's words or actions, he not only protested in a loud and commanding manner, but also often forced Mehmed to retract his previous statements. Unlike most of the other ministers, who were former slaves and converts from Christianity, Halil alone was the son of a former vizier and a pure-blooded Turk. Yet his high birth was not the only reason he was able to do as he pleased: Sultan Murad had absolute confidence in Halil's political acumen and sense of balance. He instructed his son to call Halil Pasha (who was in fact officially Mehmed's servant) by the honorific term *lala*, or "tutor."

The next year, however, Sultan Murad suddenly abdicated the throne. He had just dealt a severe blow to the Christian armies at Varna and perhaps felt that Turkish territories were now secure. Not only the Turks, but the peoples of Europe as well, couldn't but be startled that Murad, still in his prime at forty years old, should retire so early. His viziers implored him to change his mind, but Murad held firm in his decision. He handed over his throne to his twelve-year-old son and quickly retired to Manisa. For some time after that, though, the espionage organs of Venice, unwilling to believe that a complete transfer of power had occurred, referred to Mehmed in Adrianople as the "Sultan of Europe" and Murat in Anatolian Manisa as the "Sultan of Asia."

In fact, Mehmed's hold on power was short-lived, as his father returned after less than two years to retake the throne as suddenly as he had abdicated it. The instigator of this *coup d'état* of sorts was none other than Halil Pasha, who is said either to have been alarmed by the fourteen-year-old Mehmed's germinating designs on Constantinople or to have been desperate over the fact that Mehmed hadn't won the confidence of the elite Janissary troops. Although Halil Pasha was the one who asked Murad to return, two other ministers, Ishak Pasha and Saruja Pasha, also concurred with the decision. Mehmet, unaware of these machinations, was sent out hunting on the day his father returned to the capital; by the time he arrived back at the palace, it was too late for him to do anything.

Murad ordered Mehmed to be confined to his quarters at the palace in Manisa. Sending him to the same city where he himself had passed his short-lived retirement was tantamount to exile. Murad once again took the helm and proclaimed that his three viziers, Halil, Ishak, and Saruja, would remain at their posts. Among the viziers, only Zaganos Pasha was demoted and sent to Asia along with Mehmed, for dereliction of duty.

Mehmed's honor was shattered by this humiliation, as might be expected, since he was already fourteen, an age when it was not unusual for a man to be treated as an adult, and since he had a naturally very proud character. No doubt he passed his days at Manisa in a very different frame of mind than he had at the palace in Adrianople. His father occasionally allowed Mehmed to join him on military campaigns, but nothing about Mehmed's performance on these occasions was considered particularly noteworthy. Given the fact that Mehmed would later display a most remarkable strategic and tactical prowess, the only possible reason for this is that his father the sultan didn't allow him near the theater of combat.

Mehmed was much better known at the time for his sexual exploits with both genders in far-away Manisa than he was for his skills as a warrior.

In the second year of his exile, Mehmed fathered a son, Beyazid. The mother was an Albanian, a former Christian slave much like Mehmed's own mother. A year later he took as his official wife a young woman from a Turkish family that was prominent enough that her older sister had been given to the sultan of Cairo. This new bride was considered to surpass her sister in beauty, yet it appears that her sixteen-year-old husband did not even bother to make love to her. They had no children. At around the same time, Mehmed's mother passed away.

In February 1451, the fifth year of his exile, Mehmed learned of his father's death. Murad, who was a heavy drinker despite Islam's injunctions against alcohol, suddenly collapsed one day and never regained consciousness. Three days later he was dead, at the age of 47. Grand Vizier Halil followed the protocol for such occasions and did not immediately announce the sultan's death, instead sending a messenger to Manisa. Mehmed received the news three days after the fact.

The young man, two months shy of his nineteenth birthday, didn't wait for the formal preparations for a new sultan's entry into the capital to be properly completed.

"Those who are with me, come!" was all he said. He mounted his beloved Arabian stallion and galloped northward. He knew full well what the viziers and Janissaries had thought of him until that point. Furthermore, he knew that he had an infant half-brother whose mother, born of an elite Turkish family, had been one of Murad's favorites. He drove his horse through the day and the night, only stopping to rest while aboard the boat crossing the Dardanelles.

On February 18, 1451, Mehmed the Second formally acceded to the throne. The leading citizens of Turkish society crowded into the Great Hall of the palace, but nobody, with the exception of the Chief Eunuch of the Harem, was allowed near the young sultan's throne. Even the Grand Vizier Halil Pasha and the viziers Ishak Pasha and Saruja Pasha, were standing quite some distance away. Everybody in the hall that day knew why, and the atmosphere in the room was very tense.

"Why are my ministers so far away?" Mehmed asked, for all to hear. Then he turned to the Chief Eunuch. "Tell Halil Pasha he should return to his seat."

At that moment the heaviness in the air lifted. With this it was decided that Halil Pasha and all of the viziers beneath him would be allowed to retain their posts. Mehmed the Second turned then to the three men who had in the meantime lined up to the right of his throne, and continued:

"Ishak Pasha, I would like you, as the head of the Anatolian Corps, to accompany my father's body to the cemetery in Bursa." Ishak Pasha stepped forward to the throne and knelt down so that his forehead touched the ground in the customary Turkish sign of respect. The former sultan's favored mistress then stepped forward to offer her felicitations on the occasion of the new sultan's accession to the throne. Mehmed the Second graciously accepted his stepmother's congratulations and then offered her to Ishak Pasha as a wife, thereby saving her from an uncertain future. While this spectacle was unfolding in the Great Hall, however, an infant was being drowned in a tub in the Harem baths. With this, Mehmed the Second established the Ottoman custom of murdering one's siblings upon taking the throne.

Halil Pasha could have just as easily been beheaded, but things were not as simple as believed by those who breathed a sigh of relief at his retention as Grand Vizier. It was well known that Ishak Pasha was Halil Pasha's sworn friend and had been sympathetic to the plot to reinstate Murad on the throne. After Ishak buried the former sultan he was relegated to Anatolia and not allowed to return to the capital. Mehmed had shrewdly cut Halil off from one of his closest friends and supporters, and replaced him with Zaganos Pasha, the vizier whom the former sultan had demoted.

Neither the Byzantine Empire nor the powers of the West thought very deeply about the meaning of this chain of events. This was because the new sultan had renewed his father's non-aggression pact with the Byzantine Empire and its less prominent neighbors without presenting any difficult obstacles. The renewal of the trade and friendship agreements with Genoa and Venice had also been completely trouble-free. The young sultan also repatriated the King of Serbia's younger sister, Mara, who had been offered to Sultan Murad's harem and was in fact one of his official wives, but who had failed to bear him any children. He not only returned her dowry money but even gave her numerous presents and an allowance for traveling expenses. Since it was well known even in the West that Mara had maintained her Christian faith throughout her stay in the harem, there were many there who took this as proof of the new sultan's moderate attitude towards Christians. The countries of Europe judged the new, nineteen-year-old sultan to be a vessel consecrated only to the continuation of his father's legacy of greatness in battle and noble-minded justice.

There were a few people, very few, who couldn't take such an optimistic view. One of them was the Byzantine Emperor Constantine XI. Regardless of the fact that the Turks and Byzantines had renewed their mutual non-aggression treaty, less than a month after Mehmed the Second's enthronement he sent an envoy to Western Europe requesting military reinforcements. Yet, any such request would immediately become tied up with the problem of reunifying the Greek Orthodox and Catholic Churches, and even the Emperor himself knew not to expect a simple resolution.

Chapter Two

The Eyewitnesses

Summer, 1452 Venice

"Why are hospitals everywhere so noisy?"

This question turned through Nicolo's mind as the sick-rooms passed by, one after the other. The answer was obvious, yet the question continued to gnaw at him. Ten years had already passed since he entered the medical faculty at the University of Padua, and the only thing that hadn't changed since the day he first followed his professor into a ward was his irritation at the noise and clamor of these places. He had to smile ironically, though, when he recalled that the noise didn't bother him at all when he had entered the hospital, not as a doctor, but as the relative of a patient.

The patients weren't the noisy ones. It was the family members, who talked loudly with no consideration for others and whose voices echoed back from the arched stone ceiling as an indistinct cacophony. The quietest were those patients who had no relations here in Venice and who had fallen ill returning from their pilgrimages. They were also the only ones staring blankly at the depictions on the walls of Christ's miracles, solitary sufferers whose eyes anxiously followed the doctors and nurses around the room.

Walking out of the especially noisy hospital, Nicolo saw the black-robed man standing near a water tank in the middle of the square whom the gatekeeper had told him about. The gatekeeper had said only that there was somebody who wanted to speak with him near the well; Nicolo assumed it must have been a relative of one of the patients. When he realized that the man was an acquaintance of his from the Admiralty, he hesitated in surprise. The man approached him. In a quiet, polite voice he said, "Admiral Trevisan would like you to make a discreet visit to the Admiralty tonight at the ringing of the vespers."

"I'll be there."

The man nodded slightly and Nicolo returned to the hospital.

In order to get from Nicolo's hospital in the San Paulo district to the Admiralty in the San Marco district, it was necessary to cross the Grand Canal. Unfortunately Nicolo, who had changed from his white hospital garment into his usual black robe, arrived at the foot of the Rialto Bridge just as it was being raised in order to allow a ship to pass. He was forced to wait for quite some time. He looked at the masts of the ship passing by, a sight to which he should have been thoroughly accustomed, with a sense of freshness and wonder; behind him the bells of the Church of San Giacomo gently began to announce the vespers. Nicolo was seized once again by the question that had filled his mind all afternoon: Why had Admiral Trevisan, who was supposed to be on the island of Corfu, secretly returned to Venice?

The Admiralty was located in the Palazzo Ducale. Nicolo knew the building well; he entered through the door facing the San Marco wharf and went directly towards the Admiralty division without need of direction. As a member of the Barbaro family, it was Nicolo's aristocratic right, and indeed duty, to serve in the Great Council of the Republic, which was precisely what he did every Sunday as long as he was present in Venice.

The entrance to the Admiralty would have been bustling with people going in and out earlier in the day, but it was the custom in Venice's official bureaus that the ringing of the ves-

pers, barring some emergency, signaled the end of the work-
day. Now the only person standing in front of the imposing
door to the Admiralty was the man who had come to visit
Nicolo that morning. Without saying a word he led Nicolo
inside and through five separate rooms until they reached a
locked door mounted with a ring-shaped iron rapper. The
man knocked three times, and without delay the door opened
from inside to reveal the imposing figure of Admiral Trevisan
on the other side. The admiral smiled at his old friend and
politely gestured him into the room, quietly shutting the door
behind them.

Like Nicolo Barbaro, Gabriele Trevisan was an aristocrat.
Nicolo led the more unconventional life of the two: he had
chosen medicine against the wishes of his older brothers, who
had gone into trade. For the aristocracy of a maritime power
such as Venice, a life at sea such as that chosen by Nicolo's
brothers or Trevisan was the more common. Trevisan's exceptional talent, even among such a competitive field, was
acknowledged by many: he was deputy commander of the
fleet stationed at Corfu, a post for which he was chosen twice
in a row. For the Venetians, who believed that naval superiority in the Adriatic was the key to their nation's security, such
a responsibility was the equivalent of entrusting him with
their own personal safety.

Indeed, Trevisan also possessed a physique that inspired
confidence in those around him. No doubt his long years at
sea had merely forged a body that was already robust to begin
with. The only physical signs he showed that he was already in
his early fifties were the gray hairs that had started to multi-
ply on his head and in his beard.

Nicolo had already taken two voyages with the admiral,

serving with Trevisan's fleet during merchant vessel escort missions. The first voyage was to Alexandria in Egypt; on the return leg they had sailed to Syria and made ports of call at Cyprus and Crete. It was common for Venetian doctors to serve aboard ship even after they had begun working at the university or a hospital, so there was nothing special about Nicolo's case. Nonetheless, duty on an escort fleet was somewhat dangerous, and in fact Nicolo had witnessed three naval battles, albeit small ones, during the journeys to and from Egypt. These and other factors had delayed their return to Venice by two full months.

The second voyage had been to Negroponte in Greece, with a return via Crete. Since this voyage had been confined to waters firmly in Venetian control, they had been able to return home on time and without incident. It was during this occasion that Nicolo came to know Trevisan well, both his deep humanity and his calm composure, unwavering in peace and war.

Trevisan dispensed with formalities and began to speak as soon as Nicolo was seated. "I think you may already have some idea of why I've called you here. It was resolved two days ago in the Senate, although it still hasn't come before the Great Council, that the Republic of Venice will send a fleet to Constantinople in response to a request for aid from the Byzantine Empire. I have been appointed commander of this fleet. I want you to join me as the fleet's doctor. I have sailed with many doctors, but I believe that *you*, despite your youth, are the one best suited for this duty."

Hearing these words from Trevisan, whom he had long revered, suddenly made thirty-something Nicolo feel much younger. Depending on the company, a man in his thirties can seem to have the presence and maturity of a man a full decade younger or older than he actually is.

"I've never been to Constantinople. It would be my pleasure to accompany you," Nicolo replied.

"We may see battle."

"Ever since I was a child I've been hearing that the fall of Constantinople was only a matter of time. Yet still it endures. Surely it can continue as it is for some time longer?"

Nicolo, not having given the matter much thought, was merely regurgitating the opinions of his colleagues in the Great Council. Despite being an aristocrat, Nicolo had chosen his own path in life and essentially didn't have much interest in politics. He attended the parliamentary sessions because it was his duty as an aristocrat and because, if he missed even a single session without a pressing reason, he would be penalized nearly two years' pay; but in the fifteen years since he had assumed his position, he had barely spoken twice, and only then because they were discussing countermeasures against the plague. Trevisan blinked at the young doctor's stated opinion and continued speaking:

"The fleet will be composed of two large galley warships. We set sail in mid-September, in ten days. The official reason that will be given to the Great Council for the dispatch of these warships will be to meet a merchant fleet sailing from the Black Sea at Constantinople and then to escort the same back to Venice.

"As the chief medical officer, however, it will be your responsibility to select and procure the necessary medical supplies: you need to know more than just the official explanation. The reason I've asked you to come here tonight is to fill in the missing pieces."

Nicolo tended to become quiet when he was tense. He nodded wordlessly and Trevisan continued:

"As you are aware, people have been saying that the Byzantine Empire is in mortal danger for a long time. If we begin counting from the date that their emperor first asked the Western powers for military assistance, a whole half-century has already passed. During those fifty years there were periods when things took a turn for the better, but at present, the empire is completely surrounded by Ottoman territory except for the sea; it is completely cut off by land. Twenty years have passed since the first time that a Venetian Ambassador had to be sent off to Constantinople with instructions as to what to do if the ruler of that city, upon arrival, were no longer the emperor but the sultan. It would be fair to say that, in terms of the Byzantine Empire, a state of emergency has become the everyday state of affairs.

"That said. What those who are entrusted with the safety of others must be most wary of is the making of false judgments simply out of habit. Even if a state of emergency has become the norm, it's always possible that at any time it could turn into a *real* emergency, and one has to be prepared with a response for such a case. We have received reports that the sultan is building a stronghold along the Bosphorus. I would like you to join this mission with the understanding that you will not merely be a ship's doctor. You will be a military doctor."

Nicolo finally felt as if the fog had lifted. Yet as he listened to Trevisan he felt a certain doubt begin to form within him and now couldn't help expressing it out loud. "In that case, Admiral, aren't two galleys rather too few?"

Any further explanation from Trevisan was motivated simply by his personal good will towards Nicolo; with avuncular patience for Nicolo's naivete, he answered, "As you yourself know our country has long had a non-aggression treaty with the Turks; in fact, it was just renewed last autumn. At the same time, our friendship treaties with the Byzantine Empire have a long, continuous history. In other words, we are on good political and economic terms with both the aggressor and the defender. The Turks, furthermore, have made no declaration of war against us. At the same time, if we were to refuse a request for aid from a fellow Christian nation, our standing in Western Europe would inevitably be compromised. We also cannot forget that Constantinople is an essential base for our trade with the Orient. Under such circumstances, even if we *had* fifty ships to send, we wouldn't be able to. Two galley warships is the norm to escort a merchant convoy in peacetime.

"As for sending reinforcements, I'm sure the government will give that matter its utmost consideration. Since there won't be time to come back to Venice to deliberate, it is my duty, in addition to commanding the fleet, to decide which reaction to events will be most favorable to Venice's interests. If that means fighting and dying, so be it."

Trevisan said these words in a very matter-of-fact way, and that was the spirit in which Nicolo took them. Yet even if Trevisan's tone had been more dramatic or animated, Nicolo would not have been fazed. Although he had little interest in politics, Nicolo Barbaro was a member of the aristocracy. He had been taught from an early age by his father and grandfather that he possessed the qualifications to belong to the front ranks of the ruling class, and this of course demanded a certain standard of behavior.

At supper that evening, when Nicolo told his oldest

brother that he was sailing to Constantinople with Trevisan's fleet, the only reply was, "I see." His brother, who sat on the Senate, clearly must have understood all of the implications of that statement. Nevertheless, he said nothing more about it, and made no effort to find out just how much Nicolo knew about the situation. His second brother on the other hand, who was involved with trade and in charge of overseeing the family fortune, had just returned from a trip to Alexandria and was full of energy and things to say.

"Take a good look around when you get to Constantinople. See how the capital of the once-glorious Eastern Roman Empire has fallen into ruin. And furthermore, when you see just how high-handed the Genoese there are, even *you*, the very model of calm, will come to hate Genoa in a day, at most. I think it was very wise of Venice to move the base of our Orient trade to Alexandria."

The conversation never turned to the wife and young child that Nicolo would be leaving behind: it was a given that their livelihood would be taken care of by Nicolo's brothers during his absence, in perpetuity if it came to that. These were the unspoken values of the Venetian nobility. Nicolo himself was most concerned about drawing up a table of the necessary medical supplies and choosing a successor for his work at the hospital.

Two days later, when he was passing the drawbridge at the Church of San Marco on his way to the Admiralty to deliver his completed supply requisition, he came upon a long line of sailors waiting to board ship. This was a common sight in Venice and normally he would have kept walking, but the thought occurred to him that this might be his own ship and so he went to the head of the line.

His hunch proved correct; he found Trevisan standing there. Seated at a desk next to him was a scribe who was writing down the names of all of the sailors into a ledger. In the Republic of Venice, neither the captains of merchant vessels nor those of military vessels chose their own men; rather, sailors applied to serve aboard the ships of captains of their own choosing. Since the captain's identity was always confirmed ahead of time, simply posting his name on a notice board should have obviated the need for him to be there during the recruiting, but his presence was nonetheless customary and expected. Perhaps this was to allow the sailors to look once into the eyes of the man to whom they were entrusting their lives, and thereby fortify their resolve to serve him to the end.

As he walked away from the long line of waiting sailors, Nicolo thought to himself that he and the sailors were in complete accord on that much: Trevisan was a captain they could trust without reservation.

Summer, 1452 Tana

In Tana, which was located at the innermost part of the Azov Sea at the northern edge of the Black Sea, the harbor became crowded with ice floes as early as late autumn. Since merchant vessels had to leave the harbor by mid-autumn, summer was an extremely busy time of preparations. Of all of the Venetians and other Italians' trading ports, Tana was the furthest to the north and to the east. It took longer to sail back home to Italy than it did to sail north up the River Don all the way to Moscow. But it was still attractive enough to

European traders that they were willing to endure its long, harsh winters: it was a noted source of slaves, fur, salted fish, and wheat.

A lone figure was walking along the pier overflowing with people and cargo; one could tell from a glance at his long black robe fluttering in the salty breeze that he was a European trader. He was Jacopo Tedaldi, a Florentine merchant. His gait was as buoyant as ever, but his head was spinning with the rumors he had just heard at the Venetian Mercantile House. Apparently the Turks were in the process of building a massive fort on the western bank of the Bosphorus. Tedaldi, who had been busy buying furs along the upper reaches of the Don, was hearing for the first time information that had been the talk of Tana since the beginning of the summer.

For the past ten years, Tedaldi had used Constantinople as the base for his trade in goods from the Black Sea coast, and thus he knew that the mere building of forts was in itself not cause for alarm. There were already two imposing Genoese-built citadels on the hilltops along the thirty-kilometer-long Bosphorus, but those were built solely for observation purposes and not to attack the ships passing below. The Turks, however, were building a fort *on the banks* of the strait—and at the *narrowest* point of the strait, no less. In fact, they already had one fortress, albeit a smaller one, on the Asian side. Tedaldi felt he had no choice but to agree with the conjecture of the Venetian merchant who had told him the news:

"They're building it to control passage of the Bosphorus. Surely they're going to attack Constantinople."

The city was blessed with a geography that was strategically advantageous to the defenders, and it was known to have the strongest ramparts in the Mediterranean. Even for someone like Tedaldi who intimately knew the grim state of affairs in the Byzantine Empire, it was hard to believe that Constantinople would fall easily. But it was a plain reality that, even if the capital were successfully defended, trade in the Black Sea would become difficult.

"I think it's about time I finish my work here and go back home."

He had left his wife and child in Florence and hadn't returned there in five years. Having made up his mind, he turned on his heels and went back the way he came. He would return to the Mercantile House and book passage for himself and his cargo.

"There are quite a few days left before the ship sets out; maybe I can use that time buying some wheat. I'll take the fur back to Europe and sell the wheat in Constantinople—that way I can make the most of things until the last possible moment."

When Tedaldi imagined what his life would be like, approaching forty-five years old and back on land for good, a wry smile floated across a characteristically Florentine face which looked like all of the excess fat had been trimmed off of it.

Summer, 1452 Serbia

Mihajlovic stepped out of the royal palace and took a deep breath. He looked up and the cloudless summer sky filled his eyes. He had reason to be excited. He had just turned twenty-two. Despite his youth, he had just been put in charge of a 1500-man cavalry regiment. "Lead this regiment of horsemen to Asia," the king had ordered.

Serbia was one of the Christian nations that had the misfortune of bordering on an Ottoman Turkey that was expanding westward with frightening vigor, having left only Constantinople standing as if it were some kind of undesirable wasteland. Despite their almost touching efforts at defending their country, the Serbs had suffered a terrible defeat at the hands of the Turks and had just barely kept their independence by offering one of the royal princesses to the sultan's harem. Yet when Sultan Murad died a year earlier Princess Mara had produced for him no heirs. The new sultan's actions had also been deeply worrying, so much so that the king couldn't sleep at night. Yet while the young sultan had cold-heartedly disposed of his deceased father's other wives and concubines, he granted Mara, and only Mara, her wish to be returned to her home country. This was something quite unexpected for a fanatical Muslim to do, and created a buzz of speculation. In Serbia, in particular, people believed that the young sultan simply could not but respect Princess Mara's virtue and cultivation.

This had reassured the king for the time being that the Turkish threat was receding, as did the fact that the sultan had sent him a request for military reinforcements. The Bey (or ruler) of the principality of Karaman was leading periodic uprisings against the sultan in the provinces of Anatolia and the sultan had wanted help in subduing him; the wording of the letter had been quite polite. It would have been out of the question for the Serbian king to refuse. Although it meant helping the Turkish heathens, the situation was redeemed for the Christian Serbs by the fact that the enemy they were being asked to fight were also Turks. The king decided to send 1,500 riders just as the sultan requested. When he assigned Mihajlovic to lead the regiment he also gave him a letter addressed to Mehmed the Second from Mara. The letter read, "Praying that the suppression of the rebellious Turkish tribes may be hastened, we offer you these 1,500 horsemen. There would be no greater happiness than to know that they were of assistance to you."

Mihajlovic was also entrusted with selecting the soldiers who would serve under him. He decided that the primary criterion for selection should be the ability to handle horses on the harsh Anatolian landscape; his candidates were therefore younger horsemen in their twenties.

Mihajlovic wasn't surprised by the fact that they were scheduled to depart during the winter. In order to reach the Turkish capital of Adrianople they would have to set out east from Serbia and cross Bulgaria. After assembling in Adrianople they would have to move east once again, crossing the Bosphorus near Constantinople and then moving on to Anatolia. In order to avoid the harsh Anatolian winter and arrive in time to fight during the summer, they would have to leave Serbia while it was still winter.

Mihajlovic spent the days and weeks before their departure training his men. Sultan Mehmed the Second had asked Serbia to send fifteen hundred of their finest troops. The sultan held the key to their homeland's security: to guarantee it they would have to fulfill his every request, to the letter.

Summer, 1452 Rome

For the past few days Cardinal Isidore had struggled to hide the deep emotion welling up within him and maintain the proper dignity of his position. Were he to give in to his natural impulses he would probably forget his rank and his fifty years of age and run through the streets of Rome shouting for joy. His firm hope and conviction of twenty years, one he had maintained even in the face of cold stares from his friends, was finally coming to pass. What was more, it had been made his own personal duty to make his dream come true. He felt no doubt that it was the only possible way to save his homeland, the Byzantine Empire. He firmly believed that a reunification of the Greek Orthodox and Catholic Churches and the assistance that it would elicit from the nations of Western Europe would effectively counter the Turkish menace.

While the path to unification would be fraught with difficulties, the cardinal's own life history, rather ironically for one whose life had been devoted to the service of God, was perhaps no less stormy.

He had been abbot of the Saint Demetrios monastery near the Sea of Marmara in Constantinople when, in 1434, the then Emperor Ioannis ordered him to attend an open council in Basel. Having just turned thirty, Isidore was the youngest member of the Greek Orthodox delegation and threw himself into the work; it was his first opportunity to meet high-ranking clergy from other countries, and the experience left its mark. For his part, he left an indelible impression on those assembled as a theologian of great ability; the reputation he established at the meeting led to his appointment as the Patriarch of Kiev as soon as he had returned to Constantinople. This was the highest ecclesiastical position in all of Russia, and because of this Isidore became an indispensable member of the Orthodox delegations to the subsequent councils in Ferrara and Florence.

These visits to Italy, however, had brought about a fundamental change in his thinking. In Venice, in Ferrara, in the "City of Flowers," Florence, Isidore was able to sense, feel, and have his eyes pried open by the new intellectual movement that would later come to be called the Renaissance. There was no trace of this in Byzantine civilization, where religion regulated every last aspect of life and therefore tended to stifle the unhindered expression of human vitality. Italians respected Byzantine civilization and vied with one another to emulate certain of its aspects, but only those they found agreeable—all else they ignored. Those scholars who had forsaken Greece in favor of Italy had done so because, in Italy, they were surrounded by people who took a genuine interest in their work; life there was far more energizing than in Constantinople.

Isidore, until then skeptical, had begun to believe that a synthesis of Byzantium and Western Europe was possible. He had even reached the conclusion that there was no choice but to reunite the Western and Eastern churches and that this would occur under the banner of Roman Catholicism; the Byzantines had once looked down upon the western Europeans as barbarians but now it was they, and not the Greeks, who were overflowing with newfound energy. Only one other leader of the Greek Orthodox Church, a peerless theologian named Bessarion, shared Isidore's beliefs. Five years after moving to Rome, he and Isidore were baptized as

Catholics and made cardinal.

Isidore and Bessarion had never believed, however, that it was a realistic possibility for the Greek Orthodox Church to incorporate itself with the Catholic Church. Despite that, they continued arguing for such a unification in the belief that it was the only hope for their doomed homeland. In their eyes, those Greeks who opposed unification and treated them like traitors were obstinate fools, anachronistic dreamers clinging to past glories.

While Bessarion remained in Italy living the life of the scholar, Isidore bore the weight of his compatriots' hatred for both of them. The next ten years were exceptionally busy; he was sent to Russia to preach unification to the Orthodox followers there, and failing to convince, spent time in jail.

He eventually managed to escape and return to Rome, after which he traveled back and forth to Constantinople countless times. Even these trips home couldn't shake his conviction that the two churches should be united, as there were many Byzantine statesmen and intellectuals who shared his view; the opposition came mainly from the monks and the general public. He believed, however, that their antipathy would fade once concrete aid came from the West.

And now Isidore was about to depart for Constantinople with ships and soldiers provided by the Pope. He could already hear the magisterial joint Mass of the Catholic and Orthodox Churches in the Hagia Sophia. He could hear, too, the war cries of a united Christian army routing the Turkish infidels.

Summer, 1452 Constantinople

If one turned north halfway along the boulevard leading from the Gate of Charisius to the Hagia Sophia and followed the gentle slope down towards the Golden Horn, one eventually came to the monastery of the Holy Church of the Almighty Messiah. One of the rooms of the monastery belonged to Georgios, who had lived there for over two years.

Georgios hadn't always been a monk. After studying ancient Greek philosophy and theology he began teaching privately; the depth of his learning soon became known to the court and he was employed as the emperor's secretary. He attended the Councils in Italy along with Isidore and Bessarion. But unlike Isidore, who was a few years his senior, when Georgios returned home from Italy he began to work against a unification of the two churches.

He had not been oblivious to the stirrings of a vital new era in Italy. And he was not opposed to a unification of the two churches per se. What he opposed, and what Isidore and Bessarion supported, was a reunification on terms set by the Catholic Church. In Italy he had had the acute impression that Byzantine civilization and Western European civilization were fundamentally different. It would be impossible to carry out the unification under the aegis of Catholicism without doing away with what might be called the spirit of Greek Orthodoxy. The end result of a forced unification would be repeated divisions within the Greek Orthodox Church and its eventual disappearance. Georgios could see that, once they were severed from the Greek Orthodoxy that connected them, he and his coreligionists would devolve into mere Greeks, Slavs, Armenians.

Of course he knew that the Turkish sultan was building a new fort on the banks of the Bosphorus. He shared the concern of the Emperor's aides that this was a harbinger of Constantinople's downfall. Yet, from his standpoint, even if Constantinople fell and the Byzantine Empire along with it, that would simply be the fate appointed by God. It would be the Byzantines' divine punishment. To forsake your religion in order to defend your nation was blasphemy. What kind of true believer would sacrifice his eternal salvation to protect his ephemeral existence?

Georgios believed that the powerful faith of those Greek Orthodox Christians living in countries already under Turkish rule was proof of his thinking. Even if they threw away their long-standing traditions and managed to sew together a unified church, those Orthodox believers in every country who opposed such a step would turn away from the Church; it would be better to be defeated by the Turks while continuing to maintain their faith than to lose the Orthodox Church altogether. This was the conclusion that Georgios, who avowed a love for the Byzantine Empire as great as any man's, had reached.

For him, the outward collapse of the nation was nothing more than a relative concern. There were many Greeks who shared his thinking, and his monastery had become the focal point of resistance against unification.

Summer, 1452 Constantinople

A young Italian was among those who regularly visited

Georgios's cell. He was a student named Ubertino who had just turned twenty-one. He had been born in a northern Italian protectorate of the Republic of Venice called Brescia, and after studying Greek philosophy had longed to deepen his knowledge of the subject in the center of the Greek world; he had arrived in Constantinople two years earlier in the spring, and had been Georgios's pupil for over a year.

Although it was customary for Western Europeans studying Greek philosophy and language in Constantinople to live on a stretch of land along the Golden Horn known as "the Latin Quarter," Ubertino alone chose to live among the Greeks. The only time he went to the Latin Quarter was to claim money sent to him by his family at the bank in the Venetian mercantile center, or to pick up letters from the post office of the Venetian embassy.

In truth Ubertino, as a Catholic, couldn't help feeling some discomfort sitting through Georgios's heated religious discussions with other monks and visitors. At some point though, after he had grown accustomed to all aspects of Byzantine life both good and bad, he began to feel that he could no longer so easily divide things into the acceptable and the unacceptable—those that residents of the Latin Quarter very rationally rejected and gave no further thought to. Although the lessons in philosophy grew further and further between, the young Italian student continued to visit his tutor with enthusiasm unabated. He didn't take part in the discussions, instead sitting unobtrusively outside of the ring that surrounded Georgios. While the fanatical Greek monks may have *ignored* him, they at least didn't *denounce* him.

Ubertino of course knew about the fortress that had been completed on the shore of the Bosphorus, which was all that people in the Latin Quarter could talk about. Among the Venetians, who made up the majority of those living in the Latin Quarter, the number of people who took the threat seriously enough to evacuate their wives and children was growing by the day—but in Constantinople in the summer there were few ships available for that purpose. All of the merchant vessels were taking advantage of the fair-weather summer months to maximize their profit; even to evacuate to the Venetian protectorates of Negroponte or Crete meant waiting until the ships returned from the Black Sea in autumn.

The Greeks living in the neighborhood where Ubertino lived showed a different reaction than those they called the "Latins." They believed that the Turks had built the fortress, called "Rumeli Hisari" (Turkish for "Roman Castle," i.e., the castle on the European side) in order to rein in the trading activities of the "Latins" as they passed through the Bosphorus on their way to the Black Sea coast. Many Greeks resented the fact that the Western European merchants were using their city for heedless self-enrichment, and felt a secret satisfaction at the thought that the Black Sea trade would run into trouble; there were very few who understood that their own well-being was also at stake. Furthermore, the Turks had tried to conquer Constantinople twice in the past, and both times had had to break off the siege. Few Byzantines seriously entertained the possibility that the capital would fall. And if the worst *did* come to pass, they felt, there was nothing to do but resign oneself to the will of God. In true Byzantine fashion, the Greek residents of Constantinople combined within themselves optimistic predictions along with a fatalistic worldview.

One afternoon, after yet another meeting where instead of

discussing philosophy or religion Ubertino merely listened to the others' impassioned speeches, he was surprised to be stopped on his way out by Georgios, who asked to speak to him privately.

"Have you thought about returning to Italy? My reputation is not very good over there so I won't be able to write you any letters of introduction, but it shouldn't be difficult for a young man of your abilities to find a good tutor or employment. At this point the study of Greek philosophy would probably be more profitably carried out in Venice or Florence or Rome than here. Italy has more teachers and more books."

Ubertino merely thanked his teacher for his concern and left the monastery. Of course what Georgios had said was correct. Unlike the merchants who had interests to supervise in the city, Ubertino had really no reason to remain in Constantinople. Yet it was difficult for him to set his heart on returning home. He himself did not know why. It was just that making a definitive decision too soon felt somehow unnatural. Perhaps he had taken on that Byzantine habit, routinely denounced by the Latins, of missing the forest for the trees. He hadn't smiled in a long time, but the thought brought a bright smile to his faintly boyish face.

Summer, 1452 Galata

From the top of Galata Tower one could enjoy a commanding view of the entire city of Constantinople on the other side of the Golden Horn. One could see the ports where the groups of merchant ships were docked, and beyond them a castle wall with towers at strategic positions. There were openings here and there, gates through which workers busily ported cargo back and forth in the midday sun; they looked like small toy soldiers at that distance, but were still large enough to count. On the other side of the castle wall could be seen the Latin Quarter with its warehouses, mercantile centers, and shops. The port was always bustling with people, cargo, and ships.

Hagia Sophia occupied the highest point in the city, from which its copular rose to an even more imposing height. Looking toward the west, one could exhaust oneself simply from counting the bell towers of the many churches for which Constantinople was famous. In the far distance could be made out the tall, square imperial palace, as well as the castle wall that extended to the shores of the bay of the Golden Horn. Standing here in this place, taking in the expanse of the largest city in the Mediterranean, Lomellino felt an extreme tightness in his chest. Indeed, he felt it every single time he had to stand there.

"Why do I of all people have to be in this mess at this point in my life?"

He sighed again heavily, indifferent to the fact that those around could hear him.

Angelo Lomellino was the *Podesta*, or magistrate, of the Genoese settlement in Galata, also known as Pera. Facing Constantinople from across the Golden Horn, his district was an important stronghold of Genoese trade. With this,"the Genoese Tower," at its center and including a castle wall that extended down to the Golden Horn and the Bosphorus, the district had been the exclusive preserve of the Genoese for two hundred years. The island of Chios in the Aegean, Galata, and the Black Sea port of Caffa were the three main centers of Genoese trade, and it was because of these holdings that the Genoese merchants had been thoroughly able to overwhelm their long-time rivals, the Venetians. Everything in Pera, from the docks to the rows of warehouses, was for the exclusive use of the Genoese. This was in stark contrast to the Venetians; though they may have been the main tenants of the Latin Quarter across in Constantinople proper, they had to share the space with merchants from Florence and Ancona, as well as those from Provence and Catalonia. Galata Tower, which provided a commanding view of the workplaces of their rivals, was symbolic of the position of the Genoese within the Byzantine Empire.

The building of this tower and the two fortresses in the hills along the Bosphorus had been eminently sensible measures. Genoa had invested all of its resources in the Black Sea trade. The Venetians had long held control of trade with the Orient and the south, Alexandria in Egypt and all of Syria. Constantinople (and the trading ports of the Black Sea to which it was the gateway) was only one of the many bases of the Venetians' diversified business dealings.

If for that reason alone, the post of Magistrate of Galata was truly an important one for the Genoese economy. For the honest yet sluggish Lomellino, it was too heavy a burden. He himself understood this better than anybody, and wouldn't have taken the position if not for the fact that he was promised that his tenure would be short. Indeed, a new magistrate was appointed a mere three months after Lomellino took the post. He awaited the arrival of his replacement with eager anticipation. All he prayed for was that his time in office would pass as uneventfully as possible.

This was not to say that he was negligent in carrying out out his duties. He immediately sent word back to Genoa when the Turks started building their fortress in the spring, and it was he who advised that this development would very likely have serious consequences for the Genoese economy. Later, alarmed at the speed with which the fortress was progressing, he kept asking how Pera would cope with the attack that these developments portended. It was only now, months later, that Genoa had replied that they were sending two ships and five hundred soldiers.

The safety of the residents caused Lomellino considerable worry. Unlike the merchants in the Latin Quarter who were there for the short term and had left their families back home, the Genoese were long-term inhabitants and most of them had their wives and children with them; there were even quite a few "Genoese citizens" who had been born and raised in Galata. Such people had their whole lives invested here. The current situation was not something that could be solved just by issuing an evacuation order.

Lomellino was responsible for solving the most difficult problem imaginable in an already difficult situation: how to do everything possible, in light of the fact that Genoa's orient trade was wholly dependent on the retention of Galata, to maintain friendly relations with the Turks without provoking the ire of the Byzantine Empire and Genoa's Western European neighbors. There is nothing as difficult as maintaining neutrality when your existence is not absolutely necessary for either side, but that was the task the Genoese government had given him. In his mid-sixties, Lomellino had already crisscrossed the Mediterranean as a merchant, but was now at an age when most men return to their native land and quietly enjoy their retirement. He had lost his wife and had no children. He had been ready to hand over the businesses he had built in Pera to his nephew, and return to Genoa to quietly pass the remainder of his days with his brother's family. Yet just as he was about to leave, this tremendous responsibility had fallen upon his shoulders; he had good reason to keep sighing.

"Maybe I should send another couple of goodwill ambassadors to both the Emperor and the Sultan, just to be safe," Lomellino mumbled to himself as he carefully descended the spiral staircase of the Galata Tower.

Summer, 1452 Constantinople

Phrantzes could not suppress the warmth that filled his heart whenever he appeared before the Emperor. Phrantzes had been twenty-seven when he began working as a secretary for Constantine in the days when the latter was the ruler of Morea. Constantine was three years younger than he, and although he Phrantzes had been promoted to Minister of Finance when Constantine had inherited the throne from his childless older brother Ioannis four years earlier, the fond veneration he felt for his ruler hadn't changed at all since the days when he was a mere secretary. The Emperor, too, could sense this devoted loyalty that had spanned twenty-four years, and it was still his habit, whenever anything called for secrecy, to rely on Phrantzes.

"There is nobody more noble in body and mind than my Emperor."

Phrantzes said this with pride almost as if he were speaking of himself. Indeed, Constantine XI, although thin, was tall and well proportioned, with a narrow, deeply-chiseled face, a beard, and warm eyes. His appearance combined regal bearing with human warmth. When he rode his white horse with his crimson cloak fluttering in the wind, not only Phrantzes, but all who saw him, were fascinated by this figure as imposing as the caesars of old. His personality, too, was a perfect model of integrity, probity, and truthfulness. He patiently listened to the opinions even of those with whom he disagreed. Even Georgios, who led the movement against reunification with Catholicism, could only venerate the Emperor as a man. Constantine was also, needless to say, beloved of the people.

Yet Phrantzes had to admit that he felt no little pity at just how unfortunate Constantine's family life had been. Constantine's first wife, whom he had married when he was twenty, died a mere two years later. They had no children. Thirteen years later he remarried, this time the daughter of the lord of the island of Lesbos, but she too died young and left him no children. He remained single thereafter until assuming the throne, at which point he could remain single no longer if he were to continue the royal lineage. Two years earlier, the search for an empress had begun, under the direction of Phrantzes.

Among the candidates were the daughters of the Doge of Venice and the Emperor of Trebizond, but the most appropriate choice of all was thought to be Princess Mara of Serbia. The first reason was that she was still young enough to bear children. The second reason was that she had not converted to Islam while in the previous sultan's harem, and was a fellow follower of the Greek Orthodox Church. But the most important reason of all was the fact that she was respected by the new sultan, Mehmed the Second. The relationship with the Turks was an issue of paramount importance to the Byzantine Empire, and this qualification alone was considered a more than sufficient "dowry." Another member of the Byzantine imperial family had already set a precedent by marring the widow of a sultan, so that presented no obstacle.

As ideal as this arrangement seemed, however, it was ruled out by Mara's refusal. The Christian princess who had entered the harem in order to save her country had sworn to God that if she ever made it out of the harem alive she would never marry again. Hearing this, there was nothing the Emperor could do. In the end, the bride they settled upon was the princess of the small nation of Georgia in the Caucasus Mountains. The previous autumn Phrantzes had traveled to Georgia to finalize the arrangements, but the princess had to sail the Black Sea to reach Constantinople. Although she would try to arrive as quickly as possible, it was impossible to set a firm date for the ceremony.

The Emperor for his part wasn't permitted the ease of mind to be counting the days he had to wait until the wedding. He had barely been able to enjoy a moment's rest since February of the previous year.

The chain of events that had occurred during that month never left the Emperor's mind: the sudden death of Sultan Murad, who had allowed the Byzantine Empire to remain in its current state, followed by the ascendancy of the young Sultan Mehmed the Second, whose real intentions were difficult to ascertain. This development filled him with unease, which was only somewhat alleviated by the fact that the reliable Halil Pasha and his three ministers had retained their posts and the non-aggression treaty had been readily renewed. After all, the Ottoman Empire was an autocracy. The Byzantine Empire was surrounded by the Turks on three sides. And now those Turks were being led by a twenty-year-old whom the seasoned Emperor found more or less inscrutable. He sent even more envoys to the West to request military aid.

That had been the spring of 1451. The delegation, headed by a member of the imperial family, immediately left Constantinople; in April they arrived at the home of the Este family in Ferrara, and went from there to Venice. In August they arrived in Rome, where they met with Pope Nicolo V. From there it was on to Naples, where they planned to request aid from the King of Aragon. In terms of who had the most invested in Constantinople, the best candidate for aid would have been the Republic of Genoa, but as a polity Genoa was too weak to take much action. In any event, the aim was to appeal to the nations of the Christian West to help counter the Muslim Ottomans. The first duty of the delegation was to inform the Pope that the Emperor was willing to allow the reunification of the eastern and western churches under the banner of the Roman Catholic Church.

That autumn, Pope Nicolo V sent a letter to the Emperor promising military assistance given the terms of reunification offered. Venice agreed to offer financial assistance and promptly ordered the Venetian bank in Constantinople to transfer a payment, but refused to send a military force on the grounds that Milan and Florence were engaged in a civil war; Venice certainly couldn't send its own army by itself; the only hope was for civil war to be brought under control and a grand coalition of Western nations to come to

Constantinople's aid together. The King of Naples demanded the Emperor's throne as a condition for sending military aid, a condition that Constantine needless to say could not accept. The highest secular authority in the Catholic world, the German emperor of the Holy Roman Empire, was engaged in a war with fellow Catholics of the Kingdom of Hungary and couldn't be bothered with what was transpiring in the Orient. The King of France was equally indifferent. Spain had its hands full fighting the Muslims within its own borders.

The coming of a new year, 1452, didn't herald any great changes in the situation in Europe. The anti-unification faction learned of the Emperor's stance and showed signs of stiffening resistance; that was all. A single day didn't pass that mobs of monks did not gather in front of the heart of Constantinople, Hagia Sophia, shouting their disapproval as they marched in procession, followed by hordes of gloomy commoners. At the center of it all was the black-robed figure of Georgios.

Resistance began to show itself in the Emperor's inner circle as well. His chief minister and relative Lucas Notaras even went so far as to say, "We would rather be buried under a sea of Turkish turbans than have to look at the Pope's triple crown!" The only person among those in the inner circle who felt the Emperor's agony as if it were his own was Phrantzes. Even if the Emperor didn't say anything, he could tell that Constantine's one and only hope was that armies from the West would appear and somehow soften the resistance among his own people to reunification.

Yet by February of that year there was still no sign of an army coming to the rescue; news that Mehmed the Second had ordered five thousand workmen to be assembled took

Constantinople by surprise. At first many predicted that the sultan was just going to have a new palace erected in Adrianpole. They could only fall silent when they saw that the workmen were gathering hundreds of miles away from Adrianople, on the far side of the Bosphorus. Then, on March 26th, the sultan himself arrived, accompanied by thirty ships. The sultan's fleet emerged from Gallipoli, sailed north through the Sea of Marmara, and then entered the Bosphorus in front of Constantinople. The Byzantines, who had no navy, could do nothing but watch helplessly. A military force exceeding 30,000 men had marched east from Adrianople and then met up on the European shore of the Bosphorus with the force that had arrived by sea. They immediately got to work building the fortress.

Responsibility for the building was divided among the three major ministers, Halil Pasha, Zaganos Pasha, and Karadja Pasha. A spirit of competition sped up the construction considerably. In a surprisingly short period of time the fortress took shape in front of the watchful eyes of Mehmed the Second, who gave it the name *Rumeli Hisari*, or "Castle of Rome"—that is to say, the castle on the European shore. The fortress on the other, Asian bank, was named *Anadolu Hisari*, or "Castle of Anatolia."

The Emperor of course immediately lodged a formal diplomatic protest. The *Rumeli Hisari* was quite blatantly being built on Byzantine territory. While construction of the *Anadolu Hisari*, which had been built by Mehmed's grandfather, began only after receiving approval from the reigning Emperor of the time, Mehmed began building the *Rumeli Hisari* with no prior consultation.

Another cause for protest was the fact that a Greek

Orthodox monastery at the building site had been unceremoniously torn down and its stones appropriated for the fortress. In response Mehmed argued that the fortress was being built to secure safe passage through the strait; the Byzantines had just as much to gain as the Turks from an end to the piracy then rampant along the Bosphorus. When the Emperor's young envoys dared to complain that surrounding villages were being plundered in order to feed the workmen and soldiers, however, the two twenty-year-olds were immediately beheaded without a further word.

The Emperor had the six hundred Turkish residents of Constantinople arrested and imprisoned, but there was nothing else he could do. The Byzantine Empire not only had no navy, it also had no army worthy of the name. In the end Constantine released the Turkish prisoners, and sent the sultan a gift of wine along with a request that no further harm be done to the local villagers.

Mehmed took note of this request, but to his way of thinking the only villagers who should be spared were those who put up no resistance; if they did resist, they were in transgression of his agreement with the Emperor. Indeed, those towns which, giving up any hope of the capital rising to their defense, put up their own resistance, were completely massacred. Any Byzantine cavalry group that ventured outside of the city walls was invariably decimated, with only a handful of riders returning home alive.

The fortress was completed at the end of August. Shaped like an inverted triangle, the *Rumeli Hisari* was built on an ascending foundation that hugged the rising landscape of the shore. It was 250 meters long, 50 meters high, and was surrounded by a wall three meters high. It had three high towers

70 meters tall and nine smaller towers that gave a clear view of every conceivable tactical point. A battalion of soldiers was stationed inside, while the high towers on the waterfront were outfitted with large-scale cannons. Even with this information in hand, which had been provided by Venetian spies who had infiltrated the enemy camp, the Byzantine Empire couldn't count on the help of the Europeans.

A fresh terror soon assailed the Emperor. Once the *Rumeli Hisari* was completed, Mehmed would have been expected to return to Adrianople over land, but instead he remained with his entire army right outside the castle walls of Constantinople. While the residents held their breath behind the locked gates of the city's triple-layered castle walls, the Turkish army stayed its ground, tents still erected. The Emperor had trouble bringing himself to imagine exactly what this meant. From the city wall next to the Imperial Palace, he could readily see the clusters of Turkish tents in the far distance. Among those of various colors was one that was especially conspicuous: a large, red tent that no doubt belonged to the Sultan. Three days later, when the Turks finally struck their tents and their men and horses receded into the west, the Byzantine people were able to breathe again at last.

Autumn, 1452 Adrianople

Anybody who even glanced at twelve-year-old Tursun couldn't help but be astonished at the young Turk's beauty. His extremely smooth, white skin, cool to the touch, was like porcelain; beneath his thin, crescent-shaped eyebrows, his black almond-shaped eyes exuded a quiet, passive sexuality. He had a slender, lithe body and moved with reserve and unruffled grace.

Tursun had been employed as Mehmed's page for the past two years. There were many pages working in the Sultan's palace, but pure-blooded Turks were rare. It had been custom since the reign of Mehmed's father Murad to bring, by force, teenage boys from Christian lands under the Empire's rule to the capital every few years; from this group, those of both superior intellect and appearance were converted to Islam and made pages in the court, where they received an education that prepared them for careers in the imperial bureaucracy. The remaining boys were also made to convert, but groomed instead for service in the Sultan's elite Janissary corps, which was famed for its bravery in battle. The Turkish name for the Janissaries, *Yenicheri*, means "New Troops." Because of this practice, unique to the Turks, almost all of Mehmed's pages were actually Christian slaves who had been forced to convert to Islam. The reason that Tursun, a pure Turk, was chosen was that he had been a servant to Mehmed even before he became Sultan.

When Tursun began his service, Mehmed was serving as Governor of Asia Minor, but in title only; although he was the designated heir, he wasn't allowed to remain longer than a few days in the capital, and his posting was little more than a glorified form of exile. Although Mehmed could look forward to a complete transformation of his circumstances once his father died, Murad was still in his prime in his mid-forties. In those days Mehmed passed his days in drunken revelry and sexual indulgence with both genders. He was indeed a difficult lord under whom to serve, a wounded beast of sorts, and yet Tursun's service was exemplary. That Mehmed went against precedent by bringing this page along with him when he ascended the throne was due not only to Tursun's matchless beauty but also to the fact that Tursun, who literally grew up by Mehmed's side, understood him better than any of his other pages.

When the Sultan felt thirsty, Tursun was already there behind him, kneeling down and holding up a cup. One could tell from the coolness of the water inside that it had just been poured. When the Sultan felt cold, he turned around to find Tursun waiting with his cloak in hand. When Mehmed once flew into a rage and threw his wine cup against the wall, Tursun didn't grow pale or begin groveling the way the other pages did: he understood that the Sultan was angry because he had seen the triple walls of Constantinople reflected in the wine of his tilted cup. While the other pages jostled with one another to win the Sultan's affection but only managed, each and all, to meet with his antipathy, Tursun alone was high above the fray.

This is not to say that Tursun was indifferent to the pleasure that came along with the pain that seemed to pierce his spine when his lord bestowed his affections upon him. He simply understood that when Mehmed was preoccupied with something, he forgot all else: wine, sex, hunting. If his master didn't call for him, that merely meant that his master had lost himself in his thoughts and that it would not be appropriate for Tursun to disturb him with his own expressions of desire. The beautiful twelve-year-old boy seemed to know, if only subconsciously, that to play the coquette in this manner would actually fan the flames of his master's desire.

Although he felt that nobody could guess the wishes of the lord better than he could, Tursun knew that this was only true when it came to the trivial matters of daily life. This feeling only grew stronger by the day after Mehmed became Sultan. This is not to say that Mehmed's appearance and manner had changed at all. Although he certainly didn't give any impression of weakness, Mehmed still had the slender, narrow body of a man in his early twenties, still had the pale, long face, still had the black almond-shaped eyes that seemed to swallow whomever they beheld, still had the hooked, slightly prominent nose and the light red lips that he had when Tursun first became his page. Yet now there was something more of a distance between Mehmed and his retainers, as well as a new gravity to his bearing that was rare in one so young; the impression he gave had indeed changed.

Tursun had heard many voices critical of the young new Sultan. Mehmed's father Murad had been frank and open; he had enjoyed mixing among the common soldiers, and his relationships with his ministers were bonded with trust. He had the genuine devotion of his subordinates, whereas they saw Mehmed as haughty. Where Murad had lived with simple austerity, his son loved ostentatious clothing and demanded gorgeous pageantry in everything. In contrast to his father the rough-hewn warrior, Mehmed's words were polite and courteous to the point where one could hardly believe that here was a ruler with absolute power in his hands. From Tursun's perspective as his servant, however, this was nothing more than a sign of Mehmed's cool detachment. Indeed soon this young ruler, who would allow no one to glean the workings of his mind, began issuing orders that took his ministers wholly by surprise.

The first of these was his decision to recall the army sent to put down the unrest in Asia Minor, even though the rebel forces had by no means been completely subdued. It was no simple matter to suppress the forces of Kuraman Bey in the mountainous terrain of Anatolia, and Mehmed decided that it was enough for the time being simply to limit their sphere of influence and to leave it at that.

Then, in the spring of the following year, he ordered a large number of workmen to be recruited. He told his ministers that he wanted to build another fortress at some point along the shore opposite the *Anadolu Hisari* in order to ensure safe passage across the Bosphorus. Ottoman territory straddled both Europe and Asia, and crossing the Bosphorus was the only way to travel from the western to the eastern regions of the empire. For the past few years, however, Spanish pirates had been a conspicuous presence in the waters of the Bosphorus and had been creating headaches for the Venetian and Genoese merchant vessels that also plied those waters. Mehmed's stated objective thus seemed reasonable to everybody—everybody, that is, except Halil Pasha, who suspected that it was actually preparation for an eventual attack on Constantinople.

The building of the *Rumeli Hisari*, based on sketches of European fortresses and on Mehmed's own ideas, proceeded extraordinarily quickly for a project of its type. Instead of relying on one building supervisor, it was Mehmed's idea to assign each of the three major towers and their surrounding embattlements to a separate supervisor. Knowing that the Sultan was perpetually looking over their shoulders, the three supervisors vied with one another to do the best job in the shortest time; the effectiveness of this method was proven by the fact that the fortress was completed far sooner than anybody had anticipated. Mehmed the Second was able to return to his capital Adrianople on a fine, clear day at the beginning of autumn.

A Hungarian by the name of Urban appeared in Adrianople in late October. He visited the palace, claiming to be able to build a cannon that could break through the castle walls of Constantinople. At first the courtiers laughed at him and waved him away. Yet, at the same time, there was their inscrutable Sultan to worry about: one of the palace officials, fearing that he would be beheaded if the Sultan learned of such a missed opportunity, decided it wouldn't hurt at least to announce Urban's presence. Mehmed ordered the man to be brought to him immediately.

Urban, whose lower face was buried under a thick, curly, reddish-brown beard, was led to the Sultan's chamber by Tursun. He had a bundle of scrolls under his arm, which he unrolled on the ground for the Sultan one by one after taking his seat on the Turkish rug as instructed. Tursun couldn't make sense of the wild tangle of lines drawn on the pages, and at any rate didn't have much interest in a cannon that was claimed to be able to break through the wall of Constantinople, reputed to be the strongest wall in all the Mediterranean, a wall so strong that even Allah might not be able to strike it down. In fact, it made much more sense to Tursun that this Hungarian, before coming to Adrianople, had gone to the palace at Constantinople to offer his services and been rebuffed.

Yet Mehmet seemed different when Tursun glanced at him sitting on his low, Turkish-style chair. The young Sultan was listening without saying a word, his gaze transfixed on the drafts rolled open on the floor in front of him. From that day on, he would be Urban's patron. Mehmed promised him three times the fee that Urban had requested of the Byzantine Emperor. From that moment, there was one person and one person only who was allowed an audience with the Sultan unannounced: not the Grand Vizier Halil Pasha, not even his own son Beyazid, but rather this Christian with long hair and a scruffy beard.

The Sultan's appearance soon changed. Even during the daytime he seemed as though possessed, so much so that even Tursun was a bit hesitant to approach him. There had been times before when Mehmed had been lost in thought, but never for such long stretches. At night Tursun could hear him in the next room, tossing and turning in bed, unable to sleep. The young Sultan no longer drank and had seemed to lose all interest in sex. Until then there had been times when Tursun could sense the heat of the Sultan's lusty stare when he bowed to excuse himself as he left the room, but now it seemed as if his beautiful page no longer even existed. Although Mehmed was normally exceedingly conscious of his grooming and dress, these days he often forgot even to trim his beard. His once beautiful, almond-shaped eyes glared instead beneath sunken eyelids. The pages and slaves shrank back. Only Tursun, maintaining his usual reserved manner, remained by the side of Mehmed the Second. He now understood. His young lord had finally found a way to realize his long-standing dream.

Now the Sultan began to go out onto the street disguised as a common solider. Accompanied by Tursun, also dressed as a soldier, and a black slave famed for his physical strength, he would sneak out into the streets of Adrianople in the dead of night and head to his soldiers' garrison. If any of the soldiers he encountered recognized him and attempted to make the appropriate salutation, the soldier was immediately cut down by the slave.

One evening after midnight, Tursun heard the Sultan calling from his bedroom, ordering that the Grand Vizier be summoned immediately. Halil Pasha soon appeared with the black slave sent to bring him; the fact that he had been summoned at such an odd hour made him suspect that the inevitable day of reckoning had finally arrived. He walked into the Sultan's chamber carrying a silver tray heaped with gold coins, many of which fell to the floor as he crossed the threshold. Tursun rushed to pick them up.

Mehmed, dressed in his nightgown, was sitting on his bed. The aged Grand Vizier knelt before him, touching his forehead to the ground. He pushed the tray of gold coins forward as if in offering.

"What is the meaning of this, teacher?"

When Mehmed had briefly assumed the throne at the age of twelve, his father Murad had instructed him to think of Halil Pasha as his teacher and to listen to his advice. From that time on, and even now that he had become the undisputed ruler of the empire, Mehmed addressed Halil Pasha with the honorific title *lala*, or "teacher."

The aged Grand Vizier replied, "My Lord, when a ranking retainer is summoned by his ruler in the dead of the night, it is the custom that he cannot arrive empty-handed. I am merely following this tradition—but, in all honesty, what I bring now belongs to you, and not to me."

"I have no need for such things. There is something you can give me far more precious than this. There is one thing, and one thing only, that I want from you.

"That city. I want that city."

Standing to the side, Tursun could see the Grand Vizier's face grow pallid and stiff. Mehmed's face, on the other hand, was as placid as the waters of a still lake. Mehmed the Second didn't utter the word "Constantinople," but he didn't have to; in fact, the choice of words made it clear to Halil Pasha that the Sultan's determination was something quite out of the ordinary.

Grand Vizier Halil Pasha knew that the policy of co-existence and mutual prosperity that he had believed in for so long was collapsing around him. Drained of strength, his head bowed down, he had no choice but to promise to do everything in his power to satisfy the Sultan's desire. As he escorted the old man out of the room, Tursun was surprised to realize the grand old vizier no longer looked like much of a vizier at all.

Chapter Three

To Constantinople, One and All

After stopping in Parenzo to stock up on water and fresh foodstuffs, the two battle galleys under Trevisan's command proceeded, with no further ports of call, to the island of Corfu, which defended the passage to the Adriatic Sea. The voyage proceeded without a hitch, not only because the weather and winds were favorable, but also because the ship was a "fast galley." Even Nicolo, who knew very little about ships, could understand why they were called that: narrow and low off the sea's surface, they could cut easily through the wind and water. When he proudly mentioned this insight at the dinner table to the veteran Trevisan, as if it were some new discovery, the Admiral laughed and proceeded to explain another reason for their speed.

"Our fleet is made up of only two ships, and they are both of the same type. When we are accompanying merchant fleets, many times there will be sailing vessels added to a number of large merchant galleys. Since it's very rare to have steady tail winds in the Mediterranean, even with a narrow light warship such as this one we constantly have to hoist and lower various sails so as not to outpace the other ships. In this case, since we're not burdened with such a responsibility, we can let the ships go as fast as they're able."

Indeed, after stopping in Corfu they proceeded further south to the port of Modone on the southern edge of the Peloponnese peninsula. The rowers had nothing to do because the winds were so strong, and they killed time by gambling on deck. Their days of luxury ended, however, after the ships left Modone and entered the Aegean Sea. They were headed to the northeast and facing stiff headwinds from the Black Sea. At least they were within Venetian waters as far as the Greek port of Negroponte. The busiest were the rowers and the helmsmen; the crossbowmen on the other hand had no reason to be on their guard just yet.

The crew was planning to spend five days docked at Negroponte. Trevisan would be busy during this period discussing military matters with the Venetian commander in charge of the Aegean, Jacopo Loredan. Nicolo spent the time looking around the bay where the Greek ships of antiquity that attacked Troy were said to have assembled.

As they set out from Negroponte, the crew of the two galley ships felt a new tension. Even the oarsmen donned breastplate armor, and the crossbowmen held their positions with the understanding that battle could commence at any moment. From this point until Constantinople they would pass close by heavily armed Genoese islands, after which they would enter the Dardanelle Straits, which were under Ottoman control. Nonetheless, they made the voyage without a single engagement, entering the Dardanelles with the ancient battlefield of Troy passing by to their right, and even sailing past the one and only Turkish port of Gallipoli without any trouble. Continuing north they would pass through the Sea of Marmara to Constantinople. The reason the voyage took an entire month, despite the favorable conditions, was that they'd spent days for military reasons at the naval bases at Corfu and Negroponte.

Not a single person grew ill during the voyage, which made Nicolo's life aboard ship rather dull, but after they left Negroponte he was able to enjoy looking at the islands appearing one after the other, and the days seemed to pass quickly; this was his first time in this part of the Mediterranean. They arrived in Constantinople at the beginning of October.

Nicolo had no special interest in history, but when he first saw this city, the largest in the Mediterranean, bathing in the full light of the autumn sun, he couldn't restrain his excitement. Connecting innumerable towers, the high city wall stretched from the shore to the left to the Sea of Marmara on the right. The wall was so intimidating that it seemed literally to push one back. Even the oarsmen, who must have been exhausted from having rowed all through the previous night, found renewed vigor as they approached their destination. The flag of the Republic of Venice was fluttering atop their mast; slightly below it was a smaller standard indicating that the commander of the fleet was aboard.

The two ships continued north following the path of the city wall. Constantinople's wall was so long that Nicolo began to wonder whether they would ever reach their destination. They passed two ports along the way but the Venetian ships continued northward. According to the boatswain, the ports along the Sea of Marmara were too small to accommodate large Venetian and Genoese ships.

Nicolo knew that when they turned left, with the towering dome of the Hagia Sophia to their left, they were entering the mouth of the famous Golden Horn. To the right of that was the mouth of the Bosphorus. Soon after entering the Golden Horn, Trevisan's ship entered port. The sentries along the wall must have seen the Commander's flag and passed word to the port guards. The Venetian Ambassador to Constantinople, Minotto, was waiting to greet them.

*

Even though he had made this journey more times than he

could count, whenever Tedaldi entered the Bosphorus after having traveled from Tana in Crimea, with stops along the way at the Black Sea ports of Trebizond and Sinop, he had the feeling of having come home and would feel his body relax. But this time things were different. At all of the European trading posts along the Black Sea—at the Venetian merchant base in Tana, at the exclusively Genoese-controlled Caffa, and even in the independent city-state of Trebizond, the one and only topic on everybody's lips was the fortress the Turks had built along the Bosphorus.

Both the *Rumeli Hisari* on the European side and the previously existing *Anadolu Hisari* on the Asian side were equipped with large cannons; passing ships were ordered to stop and forced to pay exorbitantly expensive "toll fees." Ships that disobeyed the order to stop received volleys of cannon fire from both sides of the strait. Even the Byzantine Empire, which technically had sovereignty over the Bosphorus, had never charged a toll in order to pass through. The Genoese and Venetian merchants fumed that even if they *were* to pay such a thing, these matters were supposed to be regulated by the trade agreements between Genoa, Venice, and the Ottoman Empire and could only be considered as a new condition to be negotiated when the agreement was renewed. To make such demands unilaterally while the previous agreement was still in effect was completely unreasonable. This was one thing that the Genoese and Venetians, who were normally fierce rivals, could agree upon.

Merchants from other, less economically prominent, states such as Florence, Ancona, Provence, and Catalonia were all in agreement that the Turkish action was both illegal and barbaric. They agreed among themselves that they would refuse any order to stop and refuse to pay the toll.

But having spent many long years traversing the Bosphorus to travel back and forth between Constantinople and the trading cities on the Black Sea, they knew full well that this strait, even though only 30 kilometers long, required a surprising degree of skill to sail through. North winds blew in from the Black Sea, south winds blew in from the Sea of Marmara, and the moment one entered the strait, hemmed as it was on both sides by rising hills, those winds grew a measure stronger. Furthermore, the strait did not extend in a straight line from the Black Sea to the Sea of Marmara: it snaked and twisted along like a winding river. Since the water level was higher in the Black Sea, the current usually flowed south from the Black Sea to the Marmara, regardless of which direction the wind was blowing. Under such circumstances, one had to avoid increasing one's speed at blind corners where the wind could suddenly change direction—one had to choose those points along the strait where the wind and current provided no danger or hindrance.

This level of seamanship was not a tall order for preeminent mariners such as the Genoese and the Venetians. They felt just as much at ease when entering the Bosphorus as they did when throwing anchor at dock in Constantinople. But things were a little different now. At the strait's narrowest point, where it was a mere 600 meters across, they had to evade cannon fire coming from both sides of the shore. The thought of laying one's life on the line in order to do trade with heathens was not terribly pleasant.

One of the Genoese merchants, laughing, said, "Hoist a yellow flag. They surely won't stop us then."

All present broke into laughter, Tedaldi included, but the

good cheer soon ended. A yellow flag was internationally understood to mean that somebody with the plague was on board. It might have worked for *one* ship to try that trick, but obviously they couldn't all sail down the Bosphorus with yellow flags flying. The conclusion that the European merchants reached was to no longer travel in fleets, as they had customarily done, but rather to keep a suitable distance from one another to avoid the cannon fire and to sail through the strait at full speed.

The Venetian merchant galley that Tedaldi was aboard finally entered the Bosphorus. The feeling of unease that gripped the entire three-mast galley extended to him as well as he stood in the shadow of the ship's bridge. To show their mettle, the sailors hoisted the flag of the Republic of Venice, a scarlet background with the lion of San Marco embroidered in gold thread. The fact that the three staysails were filled with the north wind but were not jigging from side to side was a testament to the skill of the helmsman. The oarsmen adjusted their rowing to suit the strong wind as well, by taking slow, wide strokes. They were clearly tense with concentration. Although the sound of the boatswain's flute, meant to keep them in rhythm, was lost in the wind, the two-hundred-plus oarsmen managed to keep perfectly in sync.

After passing through a third of the strait they could see the Genoese castle high in the hilltops. They passed a steep bend along the Asian side, and after traveling roughly the same distance yet again, they saw a cylindrical tower rising high into the sky. Atop the tower was the red flag with white crescent moon of the Turks. This was no doubt the *Rumeli Hisari*.

Drawing closer, they could see the fortress walls extend

down to shore. Finally, at the edge of the wall they saw another large tower rising from the point where the wall ended. They heard one of the cannons fire a blank shot: that was the order to pull up along shore and stop. Of course the Venetian ship didn't alter its direction one bit. As they turned another corner, the entirety of the *Rumeli Hisari* came overwhelmingly into view.

It was a western-style inverted triangle fortress, with walls extending in either direction from the center tower on the waterfront meeting up with two large towers. It was larger than they had imagined, looming oppressively above the shore. Yet they couldn't escape by sailing close to the Asian side of the strait—for there was the *Anadolu Hisari*, smaller but no less dangerous.

A couple of minutes passed. Then a cannonball fired from the central tower threw up a pillar of water. The Venetian vessel didn't have a cannon to fire back, and even if it did, it would have been hard to aim toward land from a moving vessel. The crossbowmen who were an essential part of any merchant vessel's crew also didn't make a move: even though they could see the Turkish soldiers firing the cannon from the base of the main tower, they were out of range. All they could try to do at this point was escape. Captain Coco shouted angrily: all hands on board had to work together for one goal and one goal only: to proceed south as swiftly as possible. When they turned another corner, they felt as if they could finally breathe again. The fortress was still in view behind them, but they were out of the cannon's range. But their partner vessel somewhat behind them had been tilted almost horizontally by the force of a cannonball that had nearly scored a hit. Their hearts quaked with fear for their comrades. Thanks to the extraordinary skill of the helmsman, however, the ship was soon able to right itself. And then, like a mirage in the unusually misty autumn morning, the city of Constantinople appeared on the horizon. The Venetian sea hands felt a sense of relief like never before. The oarsmen, too, slumped over their oars once the danger had passed.

But Tedaldi felt a palpably physical discomfort well up in him, something like a sudden seizure. He kept staring at the Turkish flag, now a red dot in the distance, until it disappeared completely.

✱

Cardinal Isidore's voyage from Europe to Constantinople, unlike that of Nicolo and Trevisan, took much longer than a mere month. Although he left the papal port of Civitavecchia on May 20th he didn't arrive until five months later, on the 26th of October. Unlike the galleys for which the wind conditions made little difference, he traveled to Constantinople on a sailing vessel that couldn't even budge if there was no wind; furthermore, it had been his job to recruit soldiers along the way.

Pope Nicolo V gave Isidore a war chest and ordered him to charter a Genoese vessel and hire the soldiers. Although it was more advantageous to charter the boat itself in Europe rather than elsewhere, it was decided that it would be more convenient to employ soldiers from a locale closer to Constantinople. So Isidore set out for the Orient in a ship carrying only sailors. First he had to stop in Naples to try to convince the Neapolitan king also to send a contingent. He didn't succeed in this effort.

After leaving Naples, he proceeded to the Sicilian city of Messina. After passing the strait there, he and his crew began their voyage eastward; they enjoyed favorable winds all the way to the Aegean island of Chios, which was controlled by Genoa. It was still midsummer then. Charged as he was with the heavy responsibility of uniting the eastern and western churches, Isidore was in a hurry to get to Constantinople and make that ambition a reality. Yet his wishes were frustrated by the unexpectedly long time it took to recruit soldiers on Chios. The three main bases of Genoa's orient trade were Caffa on the Black Sea, Galata in Constantinople, and the island of Chios in the Aegean, and if for that reason alone the news reaching the island was certainly up to date: they knew that they would be going to a place where war could likely erupt. It was a waste of time trying to convince the native Greeks of the island to go help their fellow Greeks. In the end Isidore had no choice but to hire Genoese who had lived on the island for generations and who understood that the fate of Chios was closely connected to that of Constantinople. They were soldiers of high quality, but their fees were correspondingly high. Even if he threw in all of his own personal fortune, the most that Isidore could afford with the money given him by the Pope was two hundred men. They all boarded the vessel, and then set off from Chios, along with a merchant galley bound for Caffa. By this time the sunlight had already taken on a paler autumnal cast.

Those many travels back and forth between East and West had all been for this day, Isidore thought. He could barely suppress his happiness at the belief that a successful resolution was near at hand. As if to reflect his bright frame of mind, the skies of Constantinople were clear. At the dock, the high-ranking palace ministers sent by the Emperor were waiting in their long, sumptuous robes. The Cardinal mounted a steed that had been brought for his use; the ministers followed him to the gate of the city wall, also on horseback. The two hundred soldiers Isidore had brought followed, dressed in full armor. They walked in a single line up a gentle slope towards Hagia Sophia. When they passed through the Latin Quarter the people on the streets clapped and cheered, but once they entered the Greek neighborhoods they were met only with silence. Even then, clad in steel from head to foot, they seemed much more intimidating than a force of a mere 200 men, and the Greeks were duly impressed.

At the main square in front of Hagia Sophia, two stretched-silk chairs were prepared on a scarlet carpet that had been unrolled. One was a high chair, the other was only slightly lower. Isidore was greeted by the waiting Emperor. Emperor Constantine XI took the higher chair while the papal envoy took the lower. After the Emperor spoke some brief words of greeting, the Cardinal, speaking in the Pope's name, made a prayer for peace and then said that the Roman Catholic Church, in order to save the Byzantine Empire during a time of peril, had agreed to unify the eastern and western churches and to send military assistance. It was also announced that a formal ceremony to commemorate the unification of the two churches would be held on December 12th in the rotunda of the Hagia Sophia.

While the Venetian ambassador, the Genoese magistrate, the Catalonian consul and the representatives of the other European communities all knelt down simultaneously to demonstrate their allegiance, the high Byzantine ministers, arrayed in their magnificent formal gowns, merely bowed their heads lightly. The Greek onlookers packed in behind them remained stonily silent. Ubertino looked on, sitting not with the Latins, but mixed in among the Greeks.

*

In order to travel from Hagia Sophia to Georgios's monastery, one had to be prepared to travel halfway across the vast city of Constantinople. Ubertino, though, had been so deep in thought that he didn't even notice the distance. When he arrived, the normally quiet monastery seemed to be seething with feverish agitation. Groups of monks were engaged in loud debate, not only in Georgios's cell, but also in the cloisters around the cypress-lined central garden. Georgios's noble figure was also among them. Ubertino guessed that they would pour out into the streets as they had a year earlier to protest the unification loudly. The common people would rally behind them. In the Byzantine Empire, the influence wielded by monks was far, far greater than that of monks in Western Europe.

Despite their fervor, when the lunchtime bell rang they went to the dining hall as usual. Ubertino, wanting to say hello to his teacher, approached Georgios, who was a head taller than everybody else and easy to spot. Georgios noticed him and called out, "Are you still in Constantinople?" The young disciple replied that he had been to Hagia Sophia and back that morning. He asked his teacher to explain something that he had been thinking about since the ceremony at Hagia Sophia, as if trying to confirm it one more time in his own mind. Why were the Greeks so opposed to unification? Georgios, unruffled by the fact that Ubertino had rudely stopped him from going to lunch, answered in a quiet tone. Nobody else was around.

"Byzantine civilization is the sum of all of the elements it absorbed from the ancient Greek and Roman civilizations and from the Orient, and yet something more. It is its own complete entity, not merely a composite of elements from diverse civilizations. In a sense it is a mistake to call it the 'Eastern Roman Empire.' In 330, when Constantine moved the capital of the Roman world from Rome to Constantinople, he created a completely unique *spiritual* empire which had its own way of responding to difficult problems and its own repercussions, its own architecture, its own law, its own literature. It's not without reason that Western Europeans, influenced by ancient Greece and nursed at the bosom of old Rome, find the Byzantine Empire and those of us who live here unfathomable and dislike us, even if they're not aware of it. We Byzantine Greeks are not purely Europeans, you see.

"In the thousand years that have passed since the fateful founding of the Byzantine Empire, Greece has been part of a giant octopus that straddles Asia, Europe, and Africa. When the Western Roman Empire collapsed and Europe entered its dark age, the people of Constantinople fashioned a new civilization that fit our way of thinking; the blossoms of our 'exoticism' began to bloom. Our preeminence in the Mediterranean world was demonstrated not so much in practical affairs, but most conspicuously in the spiritual realms of religion and art. Of course our political characteristics are an inseparable part of this: we believe firmly that our church and our state, our religion and our politics, must remain as one. This is the fundamental rule and guiding principle of the

Greek Orthodox Church.

"In Western Europe you have reached the point of wishing to separate the church and state as much as possible, perhaps because before that so much confusion and bewilderment had been caused, for so long, by the mixing of the two. The flourishing of your Italian city-states is the fruit of that decision. But for us Byzantines it is impossible to accept such a separation, despite the fact that it has been possible in Europe and has yielded many benefits. For the Byzantines, it is unthinkable to imagine a government where the seamless unity of religion and politics isn't the primary assumption and consideration."

The young disciple looked up at his teacher's face, listening intently so as not to miss a single word. The teacher continued:

"You surely realize that the social unit that makes up the foundation of this great and truly noble civilization is the congregation of coreligionists. The composition of this group is decided neither by geographic divisions nor by ethnic differences—after all, the people of the Byzantine Empire are tied to practically all the different ethnic groups. Whether one belongs to the Byzantine Empire or not depends on one thing only, one supreme criterion: a shared belief as Christians.

"A unification of the eastern and western churches under the umbrella of the Catholic Church, with the standardization of the mass and so many other factors, would not be an easy task. It would mean taking two totally different civilizations and forcibly melding them into one. It would be an unacceptable and ultimately futile act of violence."

Georgios looked kindly at his young disciple. His last

words were, "Return home. You are a Westerner."

✳

Starting the next day, the streets were filled for over a week with monks and commoners loudly protesting the unification. As usual, at the center of the protest was the figure of Georgios clad entirely in black. His name was on a list of religious leaders who were invited to the Mass at Hagia Sophia on December 12th commemorating the unification of the Catholic and Orthodox churches, but he didn't attend. What's more, he and seven other representatives of the Greek Orthodox Church refused to sign the document attesting to the unification. After the unification mass took place, even the average Greek refused to set foot in Hagia Sophia, despite the fact that it was the most important church in Orthodox Christendom.

✳

In December, as the north wind from the Black Sea grew a measure harsher, the "Latins" in Constantinople not only wore thick woven underwear under their usual black gowns, but also always tightened their gowns with wide belts that kept the cold out. Ubertino hadn't set foot in the Venetian merchant house in quite some time; the sight of the merchants there scurrying back and forth in their thick clothing reminded him that winter had indeed come.

This was the busiest time of year for the Latin Quarter. One merchant ship after another arrived from the Black Sea, congesting the docks and piers; at the same time, one ship after another took advantage of the tailwinds to sail south into the Aegean and then on to Western Europe. But December of that year, 1452, was indeed different from usual. A certain incident had given considerable shock to the Venetians and indeed all of the Western Europeans in Constantinople.

On November 26th, a Venetian vessel packed with wheat was sailing south down the Bosphorus from the Black Sea when it was sunk by a volley of cannon fire from the *Rumeli Hisari.* A consort ship a little distance away was able to escape, although a cannonball struck the stern bridge, killing the captain, a man by the name of Erizzo. The captain and thirty crew of the other, sunken vessel were able to swim to shore, but both those who made it to the Asian side and those who crawled ashore on the European side were immediately apprehended. When the Venetian ambassador Minotto received word of the accident from the crew of the consort ship, he immediately sent an envoy to the Sultan to protest the capture and ask for the men's return per the stipulations of various treaties between the two nations. To no avail. The Sultan replied curtly that the matter was not open to discussion; on December 8th, on the Sultan's order, the captain was killed by impalement while the thirty crew members were sawed in half.

The Venetian settlement in Constantinople, which had enjoyed a favorable relationship with the Turks since the time of Murad's reign, realized beyond a doubt that those days were over. Some of them raged and demanded nothing short of a declaration of war. If this was how the Turks treated citizens of a nation with whom they had formal treaties, the merchants of other countries such as Florence, Ancona, France, and Spain had good reason to worry. Many merchants had decided to close up shop and return home, which was why the merchant house was so crowded.

A few minutes earlier Tedaldi had just deposited the money made from selling his wheat. Since he had also requested that the money be transferred to his account in the bank's main branch in Venice, his money was returning home one step ahead of him. A few days earlier he had completed the paperwork to have his furs sent back to Venice; the Venetians were trustworthy in matters such as that, and by leaving it to them he saved himself a good deal of trouble. All that was left was for him to book his passage back home. Although it was difficult at this time of year to find a place on any ship bound for Venice, there were still a number of ships with open berths going to Crete, which for the time being was good enough. Yet for some reason he had a difficult time making this final decision to leave.

In Tana he had always enjoyed imagining what his life would be like after returning home, but now that this was about to become a reality, he was torn for reasons that he himself didn't completely understand. The images floating through his head were not those of the city of Florence sitting on the banks of the Arno River like a beautiful woman, but rather of Constantinople: Constantinople as it looked from the sea after his boat had veered back and forth trying to dodge the cannonballs flying at them like demons from the terrifying *Rumeli Hisari*.

Another of those who was having trouble making up his mind whether to stay or leave was Ubertino. He had also just gone to the bank, in his case to pick up money sent by his father. If he were to return home as Georgios had suggested, this money would suffice to buy passage back to Venice. He would also be able to return with the manuscripts he had bought here. All he had to do was walk over to another part of the merchant center and book his berth, that would be the end of that. Yet, like Tedaldi, he hesitated. The difference was that, in his case, the thing that kept drawing him back was the Byzantine civilization that he had grown to love. Or rather, what he had grown to love was the city in which that civilization had crystallized: Constantinople.

One person who had neither time nor reason for mixed feelings was Nicolo Barbaro: whenever a ship coming in from the Black Sea got hit with Turkish cannon fire, there was bound to be a crew member who needed treatment, even if only for minor injuries.

As he was about to leave the clinic on the first floor of the merchant center he ran into Trevisan, who was on his way in. The two hadn't seen each other in almost two months. Trevisan had been very busy since arriving in Constatinople: he had had numerous meetings with the Venetian ambassador and Emperor Constantine, he had sailed to the Black Sea and back to escort Venetian merchant ships returning to Constantinople, and he had led missions to reconnoiter the *Rumeli Hisari* from sea. He had been so busy he had hardly had time even to catch his breath. Seeing that Nicolo also looked to be quite busy he cast him an approving nod, and then accompanied him down the hall.

"I just came from a meeting with the leaders of the settlement," Trevisan began. "The Venetian community is united as one. They will answer the Emperor's call and work together to defend the city."

This automatically meant that Nicolo would be remaining in the city as well. He could tell from Trevisan's manner that his approval of the Venetian community's decision was not the product of a temporary enthusiasm. The duty given him by the Republic was to defend merchant vessels, with the authority to change his mission in time of crisis if he saw fit. He had already fulfilled his formal duty: if that had been the extent of it he could have left Constantinople for Negroponte, escorting out the last Venetian merchant ship of the year. By doing so, not only he but the five hundred crew members of the two galleys under his direct command would have been put out of harm's way.

At the same time, he was the only Venetian admiral currently present in Constantinople. His departure would mean folding up the flag and retreating in fear in the face of the Ottoman Empire's flagrant flaunting of trade treaties and massacre of Venetian citizens. Trevizano had originally been against the idea of staying, but this was a consideration he could not ignore. And so, at his third meeting with the leaders of the Venetian settlement, Trevizano had arrived at his decision. From the next day, all Venetian vessels, be they military or merchant, would be placed under the command of Admiral Trevisan.

The news that the Venetian force would remain on in Constantinople instantly made the rounds of the merchant center. Tedaldi was at a barbershop inside the building when he learned of the decision, which instantly became the only thing in the barbershop that anybody could talk about. The Florentine merchant was the only one who didn't join in the discussion; he left the shop as soon as his trim was finished. He walked briskly out of the merchant center without giving the ticket agency a further glance. He returned to his rented house in the Latin Quarter and ordered his Russian slave to unpack the belongings that the man had just finished packing.

Ubertino also heard the news while at the merchant center. Since ships sailing south were still free to leave as long as they had Admiral Trevisan's approval, he could have left whenever he wanted. Despite that, he didn't book a ticket. He had decided to join those who would stay behind. He thought of his teacher, but for some reason hesitated to go tell him of his decision right away. I'll wait until the time is right, he thought.

*

Phrantzes led Ambassador Minotto and Admiral Trevisan, who had come to give word of the Venetian community's decision, to the Emperor. When he had finished listening to Minotto's report, the Emperor conveyed heartfelt thanks in his characteristically soft-spoken manner. Shortly thereafter, word came from the Magistrate of Galata, Lomellino, that a Genoese ship filled with five hundred soldiers would soon arrive in Constantinople. Genoa and Venice were both Italian maritime city-states, but their competition for the Orient trade had made them rivals for three hundred years. This rivalry divided the society of Western Europeans in Constantinople; relations between the two were bad, and there were no public channels of communication between them. Another goal of the Venetian ambassador's visit was to sound out the possibility of establishing such lines of communication.

"Is the Genoese community still maintaining its policy of neutrality?" he asked.

The Emperor nodded with a pained expression on his face. Then, as if to defend the Genoese, he said, "Magistrate Lomellino has told me he will do everything possible. He is an honest man and I believe I can trust him in this."

Both Minotto and Trevisan knew full well that, although the Venetian settlement had made its stance clear and the Genoese settlement—to its potential discredit—had not, the official policies of the two home governments were more or less the same: neither wanted to get involved. Despite that, the Ambassador promised the Emperor that the messenger he would dispatch to inform the Venetian government of the settlement's position would also request, yet again, that Venice send military aid. The Emperor thanked him, and asked him to instruct the messenger to relay his gratitude for the fourteen shiploads of foodstuffs that Venice had sent. Phrantzes could tell that the Emperor's heart was on the verge of breaking at the endless stream of bad news that assaulted him, and could only feel pity seeing the Emperor's effusive gratitude for such a trifling form of assistance.

Not a single one of the messengers that the Emperor had ceaselessly sent abroad to request military aid had returned with good news. Genoa and Venice were willing to send money and food, but because of the wars then raging among the Italians, they were unwilling to be the only ones sending battleships and soldiers. In Rome, the Pope seemed to think that agreeing to a unification of the two churches and sending two hundred soldiers was enough to clear his conscience. The King of Naples never made his intentions clear. Their most reliable and trustworthy ally in Eastern Europe, the Hungarian Regent Hunyadi, had signed a three-year truce with Mehmed in 1451 and seemed to have no intention of doing anything to endanger that by helping Constantinople. The Emperor's two younger brothers, who governed the Peloponnese peninsula, had already been beaten down by a force sent earlier by Mehmed, and could do nothing to help. The Emperor realized that Mehmed had already cleared away any potential obstacles to an attack.

The Turks could appear over the horizon at any moment; all the Emperor could do was try to secure enough food to keep the city alive in case of a siege, and strengthen the city walls. The walls facing the Sea of Marmara and the Golden Horn were not a concern, even though they had only one layer, as an attack from sea was unlikely. But those facing land, even with three layers already in place, had to be fortified. The Byzantines knew that the Ottomans were essentially a land-based power that had invested in a large army. Anybody could predict that their attack would come from land. The Emperor entrusted Phrantzes with the responsibility for building the fortifications, who was pleasantly surprised at just how obediently the Greeks recruited for this task did their jobs. The fact that the Emperor himself visited the construction sites from time to time surely had something to do with this. Although the common people had opposed the unification of the two churches, there wasn't a single one of them who disliked the Emperor as a person.

*

On the last day of 1452, Nicolo took advantage of a lull in his work at the clinic to see the city wall. There was nobody who lived in the Mediterranean who didn't know about the triple walls of Constantinople. He wanted to be able to take a good look at it, at least once. He had to sail to the interior of the Golden Horn to reach the point where the landward part of the wall began. He disembarked and began to walk south.

This part of the wall, meant to protect the Imperial Palace, rose upwards from the shore. From here until the point where it finished curving around the palace it had only one layer—it was five meters thick, however, and its apparent strength was awe-inspiring. A second and third layer began where the palace portion of the wall ended. A little further south was the Gate of Charisius, the busiest in the city. This was the gate that opened out onto the road to Adrianople; if one followed it into Constantinople one could go more or less in a straight line to the main coliseum of the city. It was the central thoroughfare.

Nicolo entered the gate and began following the wall along the inside. In front of him was the innermost layer of the wall, 17 meters high and 5 meters thick. It was marked at a 40-meter interval with square watchtowers that looked to be 20 meters high and 10 meters across. "Breaking through this is practically impossible," Nicolo said to himself admiringly.

There was a 5-meter corridor between this inner wall and the outer, which was 3 meters thick and 10 meters high from the other side. This wall also had, at the same intervals, smaller towers that still looked about 15 meters tall and 6 meters wide each. The towers of the two walls were staggered evenly.

Beyond this outer wall, which would have sufficed alone for another city, was yet another corridor 10 meters wide, at the end of which rose a third wall, lower but lined on top by a wooden fence. Moreover, there was a moat, twenty meters across, in front of this stockade. The moat was meant to be filled with seawater but had been left empty for many years. The outer grounds finally began here, which meant that a full sixty meters separated them from the inner wall. (Figure 5) This distance shrank only at the heavily studded gates along the triple walls.

Constantinople was a hilly city with many peaks and troughs, and so the wall naturally followed the gradations of the landscape. The elevation was highest from the Imperial Palace to the Gate of Charisius, then started to descend and reached its lowest point at the Military Gate of Saint Romanus. It then returned to its original height near the Gate of Rhegium. To the south were Pegae Gate, and the Golden Gate which (as even Nicolo knew) got its name from the fact that it was the one the Emperor passed through whenever he made a triumphal return to the city. Although there were other gates used by common people and by the military, these five, in addition to the Gate of Caligaria that faced the Imperial Palace, were strategically the most important.

This landward wall, extending from the Golden Horn to the Sea of Marmara, was over six-and-a-half kilometers long. From the outside it seemed to rise as if to block out the sun, and was no doubt the strongest in the Mediterranean. Yet Nicolo suspected that the population of the city was much too small to defend the wall's entire length: six and a half kilometers facing land, five kilometers facing the Golden Horn, almost nine kilometers facing the Sea of Marmara, for a grand total of nearly twenty-one kilometers. According to Ambassador Minotto's estimates, Constantinople's present population was no more than 35,000. With a population that size it would have made more sense for the residents of the city to retreat within the older city wall dating from the era

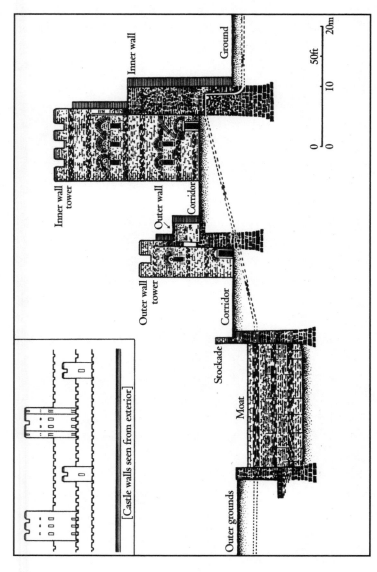

(Figure5) Constantinople, slice section of triple walls

of the first Emperor Constantine, which was half the size of the current wall. That said, the older wall was so badly damaged as to be unusable. And so, with a diminished population that reflected the decline in the Byzantine Empire's strength, the people would have to fight from the wall of Theodosius that had been built at the height of the empire's fortunes. Even Nicolo, who knew very little about the art of warfare, harbored the fear that they would not be able to put this "impregnable" wall to its full use.

✻

Tursun felt that his young lord's behavior had undergone a complete change again. It all seemed to begin with his secret conversation in the night with Halil Pasha. Before then he had seemed constantly possessed by something, but after that meeting he became quiet, almost tranquil. He no longer stole out of the palace in the dead of night, he no longer threw cups of wine offered to him against the wall. Although he still didn't enter the harem, he did resume periodic hunting expeditions. He also asked his twelve-year-old page to spend the night with him more often than he had before. One thing, the twenty-year-old Sultan's style of lovemaking, hadn't changed: it was still that of a hawk playing with the quarry in his talons.

Some short while ago, a specially constructed low desk had been placed in the Sultan's bedchamber. Day and night the desk was covered with sketches and plans. The largest of these was a map of Constantinople. The map illustrated not only the streets of the city, but also the city wall, the numerous gates of that wall, the Golden Horn, the Genoese quarter on the other side of the Horn, all up to the mouth of the Bosphorus. Whenever he had a free moment Mehmed would return to his chamber and spend long hours standing still, looking at the maps and sketches. There was a time when Tursun, still burning with desire, noticed that Mehmed was no longer lying next to him but was instead standing up, staring at his maps. Tursun wanted to reach out, to do everything in his repertoire to give his lord pleasure, but he stifled the impulse when he recalled just how cold Mehmed could be to him when he did something against Mehmed's wishes.

That Halil Pasha had acquiesced to his wishes wasn't the only thing that restored Mehmed's calm and composure. And it wasn't just that the Hungarian engineer Urban's cannon was steadily making progress. It was also because the spies that he had dispatched to Western Europe a full year earlier were finally returning, one after the other, with good news. He was able to conclude from their reports that the powers of the West would not come to the Byzantine Empire's aid. The only Christian nation that was capable of sending over an army by land, Hungary, had already sealed off that option by concluding a treaty with the Ottomans. The Emperor's brothers had their hands full keeping Turkish forces at bay; coming to the capital's rescue would be nothing more than a dream. Finally, the reluctance of the Venetians and the Genoese to act would render the Turks' only military liability, a lack of sea power, irrelevant. If the other naval powers of the West also didn't step in, Constantinople's complete isolation would be guaranteed. The young ruler, only twenty years old, hadn't made the foolish mistake of thinking that he could start such a great undertaking with force alone.

In January of the new year, 1453, Sultan Mehmed the

Second issued a mobilization order to all Ottoman territories. The countries under Ottoman control had already received demands in the past for reinforcements to quell the uprisings in Asia Minor. The mobilization order of January 1453 differed from these, however, in that the purpose of the mobilization wasn't specified. The further precaution was taken of not mentioning that this was to be a Holy War: to have done so would have made clear that Constantinople was the target.

Shortly thereafter, the first test of the new cannon took place. "The Great Cannon," as Urban's weapon was called, was a monster the likes of which nobody had ever seen before. The barrel was over eight meters long, and the stone cannonballs weighed over 600 kilograms each. It took thirty oxen in two rows just to pull the platform on which it rested. On the day of the test a notice was posted in Adrianople warning the residents not to be frightened by the sudden blast. It was then brought to the front of the Sultan's palace by a detachment of one hundred soldiers.

Urban's grandiose claims had all been true. The sound the cannon made when the first shot was fired could be heard for twenty kilometers in all directions. The cannonball flew a kilometer and a half, making a frightful sound as it cut through the air, and blasted out a crater two meters deep at the spot where it landed. The Sultan was immensely satisfied and immediately ordered more cannons of its type to be built. In order for the cannons to be transported without being damaged, he also ordered the road from Adrianople to Constantinople to be overhauled. The road had been built during the age of the Roman Empire and been neglected for hundreds of years; although the army could use it without much chance of harm, it was likely that such heavy cannons would be damaged along the way. The fact that even the roads around the capital city were in a similar state of disrepair was probably the best indicator of just how far the Byzantine Empire had fallen.

*

Although he didn't hear the resounding roar of the Great Cannon, Emperor Constantine knew that it was aimed squarely at his own breast. A short while earlier he had learned of the Sultan's unwavering determination from a secret messenger sent by the Grand Vizier Halil Pasha. The Emperor sent a secret messenger back to the Sultan offering to pay a substantial annual tribute payment if the attack was called off. Mehmed the Second refused anything less than unconditional surrender. If the Greeks surrendered and the Emperor left the city, the Sultan would spare the lives of the Byzantine people. Constantine had no intention of extending his life if that was the price that had to be paid for it. The negotiations broke down. He sent another messenger to offer a larger annual tribute, but the Sultan's answer was the same.

A few days later news arrived that somewhat lightened the cares weighing down on the Emperor's steadily graying head. Two Genoese ships with five hundred soldiers on board had arrived. They were lead by one Commander Giovanni Longo Giustiniani, a mercenary leader based on the island of Chios; his soldiers were seasoned battle veterans from the same island. Their fees were not being paid by the Genoese, but rather by the Emperor. Constantine was still greatly pleased with the arrangement, however, because Giustiniani had accepted the Emperor's promise of the island of Lemnos as payment. This skilled warrior was made the supreme commander of Constantinople's ground forces; it had already been decided that Trevisan would direct the naval forces. War councils were being held almost daily with top Byzantine ministers such as Notaras and Phrantzes; with the papal envoy and newly appointed Patriarch of Constantinople, Cardinal Isidore; with Commander Giustiniani, Ambassador Minotto and Admiral Trevisan.

The council's discussions were not exactly marked by high spirits. The session of February 17th illustrated quite well the atmosphere that pervaded these meetings.

On that day Trevisan reported that on the previous night a Venetian vessel and six Cretan ships had fled the city under cover of darkness. When it had been decided the previous December that the Venetians of the settlement would remain in Constantinople, it was ordered that any ship flying the Venetian flag would need Admiral Trevisan and the Emperor's permission to leave harbor. Such actions were thus more than just cowardice in the face of the enemy: they were a violation of the Venetians' promises to the Byzantine Empire.

Yet Phrantzes couldn't help but suspect from the calm and detached manner in which Trevisan relayed this news that he had knowingly allowed these ships to flee. Since Crete was a colony of Venice, the Cretan ships were also under Trevisan's command. What was more, a total of seven ships had fled together, with the Venetian vessel holding more than five hundred people. Unlike the Genoese, who had put down roots in Constantinople from one generation to the other, there were few residents of the predominantly Venetian "Latin Quarter" who had their families with them. And judging by the number of residents left in the Latin Quarter, a majority of the four thousand people who had fled the city were in fact Byzantine Greeks. Surrounded by Turkish territories on all sides, Constantinople was completely isolated and the only means of escape was the sea. Rats always flee from a sinking ship, and this was no exception.

The defection of intellectuals, mainly priests, who had received very favorable offers to work and settle in Italy had already been taking place for fifty years. More recently, it had become difficult to find anybody of any power in Byzantine society who hadn't evacuated at least one member of his family to Venice or Rome along with the family fortune. Even Notaras, chief minister and a member of the imperial family, had already sent his daughter to Venice with his immediate family's assets. Probably the only two people in the court who hadn't taken such precautions were Emperor Constantine himself and Phrantzes, who revered the Emperor and was prepared to follow him into death.

A further proof of the lack of common spirit was the fact that the residents of the Byzantine Empire were hardly rising up as one to defend the city. It was unrealistic even to imagine that the participants in the daily meetings were all of one mind. Even among the Greeks, there was the westward-oriented Isidore on the one hand and Notaras, who had refused even to sign the pact unifying the two churches, on the other; the two barely exchanged words. Although Phrantzes was by no means one of those who embraced Westernization, he did not much care for Notaras either. The Venetians, for their part, generally looked down upon the Greeks. Rationalists in all things, they could barely stand the sight of these Byzantines who continued to fritter away their days in theological debates at a time when their very existence was at stake. Ambassador Minotto, as if to set an example for the other Venetians, had not sent his own family back to Venice.

The Greeks disliked the Venetians in turn. Although the Venetians constantly claimed to be doing everything possible to defend this nation that was not their own, the Greeks felt in the bottom of their hearts that all the Venetians were really concerned with was protecting their business interests. The only thing that united the Greeks and Venetians was their mutual hatred of the Genoese, who maintained neutrality while hiding in their enclave in Pera. Although the Genoese magistrate Lomellino of course wasn't present at these meetings, he didn't neglect to pass on word through the mercenary Giustiniani (also a Genoese) that they were still doing everything possible to help despite their official stance. The magistrate kept repeating to the Venetians, who fiercely censured that policy of neutrality, that the Genoese in Galata had their families to worry about, were in fact far more at home in Galata than in Genoa, and therefore couldn't jeopardize everything dear to them by making any rash decisions.

Both the Greeks and the Westerners realized that there was only one thing keeping a group so devoid of solidarity from falling apart altogether: the fair and evenhanded personality of the Emperor. That, and the fact that Giustiniani and Trevisan, both of whom had been tempered in the fire of war, were warriors first and Genoese or Venetian second.

In the same calm and composed voice as before, Trevisan went on to inform the council of the current state of their naval forces. He gave as much detail as possible: not only the number of captains who had confirmed that they would stay on, but the number of oarsmen as well. According to his report, their force was composed of the following:

Five large Genoese sailing ships
Five Venetian ships, military and large merchant galleys
Three Cretan galleys
A vessel each from Ancona, Catalonia, and Provence

Adding the ten ships that flew the Byzantine flag made for a grand total of twenty-six. In reality, based on size and maneuverability, the main power of the fleet would be the five large ships each from Genoa and Venice.

Moving on, Trevisan revealed that Venetian spies had reported that the Turks were in the midst of constructing two hundred ships at their port in Gallipoli. Although Italian sailors were far and away the best in the world and the Turks had no seafaring tradition to speak of, they had drafted Greek sailors from their colonial territories to man these boats; although it was often said that it would take five Greek sailors to match one Genoese or Venetian sailor, the threat had to be taken seriously: after all, the enemy would have ten times as many ships. They were waiting for a proper fleet being assembled in Venice to arrive as soon as possible.

Giustiniani for his part also hadn't wasted any time in taking control of the ground forces. For the past several days he had been reporting on the state of the Western European defenders. Excluding the neutral Genoese in Galata, they had a total of two thousand men, which included volunteers from the Latin Quarter as well his own group of mercenaries. Since the able-bodied Greek men of the city were subjects of the Byzantine Empire, he had left it to the Greek side to determine their size and strength.

The Emperor had delegated this task to his most trusted

advisor, Phrantzes. "I want you to do this job, both because you are skilled at this kind of accounting, and because it would be wise to keep the final results a secret. I know I can rely on you to keep quiet. You needn't worry about your normal duties at court while carrying out this project. I just want you to stay in your quarters, finding out exactly how many men, arms, spears, shields, and bows and arrows we have available to use in this battle."

Phrantzes, along with his most trusted subordinates, worked day and night and was able to complete this difficult work in a very short time and in complete secrecy. He took the completed table of numbers to the palace and presented it to the Emperor. The Emperor looked over the numbers and then looked back up at Phrantzes, his eyes filled with anguish. He said nothing for a long time. Constantinople, the glorious capital of the Eastern Roman Empire, had only 4,773 adult men with the physical ability and weapons necessary to fight. Greek Orthodox monks, who could not be expected to fight alongside Catholics, were not included in this number.

Added to the two thousand Westerners, their entire force didn't even amount to 7,000 men.

"Don't let anybody know these numbers," the Emperor said to Phrantzes in a dark voice. "Only you and I can know."

This precaution was for naught, however, as the leaders of the Venetian settlement had already guessed that the numbers were about that low. For that reason, Ambassador Minotto, Admiral Trevisan, and Alvise Diedo, a Black Sea trade merchant captain who was appointed Trevisan's vice-commander, didn't press the Emperor on the issue. When the Emperor asked them to take care of the fortification of the stretch of the city wall closest to the Imperial Palace, they even consented heartily.

Trevisan and Diedo led the construction work. The construction crew was undermanned and, at the beginning, the Venetian sailors who had been assigned to the task grumbled on about how the Greeks were shirking their duty to assist in their own defense. When the Emperor came to visit the site to offer friendly words of thanks to the men, however, the grumbling stopped. There were many among them who disliked the Greeks; but there was nobody who would say a bad word about the Emperor.

*

Although they had come all the way from Serbia, Mihajlovic and the 1,500 riders under his command were not allowed within the city walls of Adrianople, and were kept waiting in their tents for over a month. Mihajlovic had requested an audience with the Sultan upon arrival, but was merely told that he had to wait until he was summoned. In addition to the 1,500 riders, there was also a foot solider and groom for each rider, making for a total of 4,500 men. It had not been a simple task leading so many men all the way from Eastern Europe during the inclement months of autumn and winter. It was also very taxing to keep so many men out of trouble during the long period of waiting after their arrival.

To make matters worse, Mihajlovic had been hearing some frightening rumors. Soldiers from other Ottoman vassal states were also encamped outside of the city walls, and word had spread among them that the purpose of their expedition would *not* be to put down rebels in Anatolia but rather to attack Constantinople. The soldiers of these vassal states,

Serbia included, were all Greek Orthodox Christians. They had come there under the specific understanding, based on assurances from Mehmed the Second, that they would be fighting to put down the rebel leader Karaman Bey in Asia Minor. Yet now all they were hearing from the rank and file Turkish soldiers was that this was going to be a Holy War upon the infidel.

Mihajlovic's interview with the Sultan came ten days after he first heard these rumors. The young commander and his two vice-commanders, both older than he, passed through the city gate and entered the Sultan's palace. Even though they came from a country that was by no means wealthy, in their eyes Mehmed the Second's palace seemed so plain that they could hardly believe it was the residence of the ruler of a vast empire. Even worse than the plainness were the regal touches haphazardly placed here and there. Everything had the slip-shod air of a temporary residence. Only the sheer quiet of the place was impressive. The many people entering and leaving the palace seemed to be afraid to make even the slightest noise.

Mihajlovic and his two deputies were led to a sitting room of sorts that was constructed to look exactly like the inside of a tent. They noticed a young man sitting upon a low, broad chair in the center of the room. They were able to guess from the reverent attitude of the frighteningly beautiful page who had led them in that this young man was none other than Sultan Mehmed the Second.

Although Serbia was in fact a vassal state of the Ottomans, as a matter of form they were classified as an "ally" and the young riders were thus only required to genu-flect to the Sultan in European fashion rather than prostrate themselves before him in the Turkish style. They presented the Sultan with a gift from the King of Serbia, as well as a letter from the king's sister, Mara. After politely thanking them for the gift, the Sultan began to read the letter from his former mother-in-law. After he finished he briefly asked some questions about how Mara was faring. Mihajlovic thought to himself that if the king could hear the warmth with which the Sultan was asking these questions, he would no doubt rest assured that the future of Serbia was safe. This feeling was quickly chilled, however, by the indifferent nonchalance of what the Sultan had to say next:

"You will be joining my army in a siege of Constantinople."

The Serbian riders closed their eyes, deep in thought. They could say nothing.

Finally: "We came here thinking that we would be fighting Karaman Bey."

Mehmed the Second was unfazed. With the same nonchalance he replied, "There has been a change in order, that's all. Karaman Bey comes next."

Mihajlovic looked into the Sultan's face; Mehmed must have been two or three years his junior, and yet he looked to Mihajlovic's eyes like an incarnation of the devil himself. If Mihajlovic refused, not only he but all of the men outside the city walls under his command would be killed. With a group of 4,500 men, escape was also out of the question. More importantly, he knew that an attempted escape would put the future of Serbia itself in doubt. He had to do what he was told. Already pallid with despair, he was then ordered by Mehmed to move in ahead of the main army and attack the villages on the outskirts of Constantinople. Mihajlovic knew that this wouldn't serve much of a military purpose but was intended rather to test the loyalty of the Serbian riders.

The painful task of informing his men awaited the young Serbian cavalryman back at the encampment. When they were told, however, the Serbian soldiers didn't even have it in them to shout out in protest; the only thing that broke the heavy silence were the groans of heartache that spilled out from their tightly shut mouths.

*

On the 26th of March, 1453, the entire Ottoman army assembled outside the Adrianople city walls and set out in strict formation towards Constantinople. At their head was the young Sultan, wearing a white mantle and white turban as he sat atop his lustrous, black, purebred Arabian stallion.

The lead force was the Anatolian Corps, led by the governor-general of Asia Minor, Ishak Pasha. The regular troops alone numbered over 50,000; they all wore the same red turbans and carried the same equipment. Behind them followed numerous units of irregular soldiers carrying a diverse mix of equipment and arms. Some of these men had been forcibly drafted, deceived into fighting as the Serbians had; others were merely those whose eyes were dark with visions of plunder. Many of them were in fact Greek Orthodox Christians. These irregular troops also numbered in the range of fifty thousand.

Third in line was the European Corps, led by Karadja Pasha. They had already cut their teeth by torching one town after another on the outskirts of Constantinople. One could tell from the energy in their step that their spirits were high.

The idea to sandwich the untrustworthy irregular troops between the regular Anatolian Corps and European Corps had of course been Mehmed's.

Bringing up the rear were the Sultan's elite Janissaries. Although they had previously been at odds with Mehmed, a doubling of their salaries had changed their attitude considerably. Perhaps in order to please the Sultan, they displayed an absolute uniformity in everything from their equipment to the rigid formation of their ranks—in fact they were all even approximately the same height. They wore white felt caps and green jackets, and white Turkish-style pantaloons, with scimitars hanging from their belts. These last and the bows they held in their left hands were their main weapons.

The Janissaries, who numbered 15,000, were made up of former Christian slaves. They had been taken from their families at a young age, converted to Islam, and never allowed to marry, and their regimented military life had successfully fashioned them into the best of the best of the predominantly Muslim army.

In the middle of the Janissaries, who were in a perfect line down to the tips of the bows in their left hands, was the Sultan on his horse. The wind rustled through his cloak, revealing a green silk jacket underneath. Like the Janissaries who had been trained since youth to serve him, he was wrapped in the holy colors of Islam, white and green. Needless to say, the spirits of the Janissaries were high; their voices rose together in songs of war. Soon the melody spread throughout the whole of the army, like a wind blowing across an empty plain.

A trumpeter played a plaintive oriental melody that was oddly mixed together with a valiant marching rhythm beat out on large kettledrums; the soldiers' hearts swelled with excitement as their voices rose to blend together with this ensemble.

From a distance the marching spear-carriers looked like a forest grove moving across the landscape. The archers looked like swaying fields of wheat, though obscured from time to time by the dust being kicked up from the road. Mehmed did not rush his men along. It was less than 300 kilometers from Adrianople to Constantinople; there was no need for haste. What was important was for each soldier's anticipation to build slowly along the way, for their individual wills and swords to congeal into one, unified force.

They repeated the same marching song over and over again, but nobody minded. Here and there red Turkish flags with white crescents fluttered defiantly above the swirling dust. Tursun, who was riding a horse behind his young lord, looked on in disbelief as the troops' fighting spirit soared even in the midst of absolute discipline. The motley crew had somehow been transformed into a single superb fighting force. And this miracle had been carried out by the person he loved more than anybody else in the world. The boy gazed upon the scene before him with immense pride.

Tursun turned around to look one more time at the city of Adrianople disappearing in the horizon. But the twenty-one-year-old Sultan whom he followed kept his sights set firmly ahead. The Ottoman capital of Adrianople was nothing more to him now than a woman he had used, and then disposed of.

Chapter Four

The Siege Begins

April mornings in Constantinople were often hazy. If the previous day had been clear and warm, the mist could last until the sun had risen high in the sky. This reminded Nicolo of the early mornings he went to work at the University of Padua in Venice. As his boat worked its way up the Prenta river it would pass through milky white patches of fog as thick as the clouds in the sky. On the morning of April 2, 1453 as well, the haze was so thick that one couldn't even see the opposite shore of the Golden Horn.

That morning, Nicolo and Trevisan were standing together on the wharf of the Constantinople side of the Golden Horn, watching two small boats that had just left dock rowing slowly towards the far shore. Each of the boats, oars moving in sync, was pulling a log connected to chains woven from iron rods twice as thick as a large man's arms. One end of the huge chain was already latched to one of the towers on the Constantinople side, and firmly secured with a leather web. The other end of the chain that the two boats were carrying across would be latched onto a tower in Galata, thereby blocking passage through the Golden Horn. The plan had been Trevisan's and had been approved by the Emperor; anything to slow down the enemy, who would have a fleet ten times as large as theirs, would be useful even if it didn't stop them completely. While making it difficult for the enemy to enter the Golden Horn, it would also make it difficult for them to escape: nonetheless, nobody among the Greeks or the Latins objected.

The heavy chain disappeared from view as its massive weight pulled it under the surface. All they could see were a row of wooden rafts being pulled along behind the boats. Even after the chain had been completely secured at both ends, the rafts would continue to serve the purpose of preventing the chains from sinking to the bottom. Since the purpose of the chain was to prevent ships from passing, it would be useless if it weren't taut across the surface. This work, which demanded more skill than one would imagine, was being overseen by the Genoese Bartolomeo Soligo.

In time the two boats returned. Although the row of wooden rafts was swaying in the current, it was still floating on the surface. As the day warmed the stubborn Constantinople fog began to clear quickly. Nicolo said goodbye to Trevisan, who was awaiting Soligo's final report, and headed to the Venetian merchant center. There he heard the news that the Ottoman advance guard was getting closer by the day.

Magistrate Lomellino was deep in gloom as he returned to his official residence after having gone to see the work being done on the boom. One end was attached to a tower on the easternmost part of Pera's city wall. When the Emperor had implored him for at least that much help, there was no way he could refuse. This was not because he was weak-willed: after all, Constantinople had shown that it could withstand a Turkish seige the last time it happened, thirty years earlier. Even though the Genoese community intended to maintain a stance of neutrality as instructed by the home government, as the man responsible for Galata's future he had to hedge his bets by keeping in mind that Constantinople could withstand an attack this time as well.

At the same time, it would be impossible to hide from the Sultan the fact that one end of the chain was linked to a tower in Galata. There were more than a few in the settlement who felt that they were too blatantly taking sides with the Byzantines, and were unhappy about the boom. Nonetheless, Lomellino didn't envy Ambassador Minotto and Admiral Trevisan, who were leading a Venetian community that was firmly united in its support of the Byzantine Empire. Even if he were jealous, there would be nothing he could do about it anyway. He decided that when the Sultan's tent had been erected he would send an envoy bearing greetings.

When Trevisan finished his work with the placement of the boom, he rushed to the Imperial Palace in the northwest corner of the city for another war council meeting. Although this meeting was no different from countless others they had held since the end of the previous year, there was an unspoken assumption among the participants that this day's meeting would be the last before the fighting actually began. The division of defensive responsibilities that had previously been determined was quickly confirmed without any objections.

Constantinople was shaped like a triangular peninsula with rounded edges. One of the bases of that triangle, the side facing the Sea of Marmara, was directly buffeted by strong winds and fierce currents coming from the Bosphorus. For that reason, in the more than 1100-year history of the Byzantine Empire, no enemy had ever attacked from that direction. Thus they believed that a single-layered wall and a limited number of defenders would suffice to protect this sector. This responsibility was given to Cardinal Isidore and two hundred soldiers under his command. Half of these soldiers were ready to act as a reserve army to defend the landward wall if necessary. Spanish consul Pere Julia and his Catalonian regiment would be positioned south of Isidore's troops, and to their south was the Ottoman prince-in-exile Orhan (who had lived almost his whole life in Constantinople) and his Turkish subordinates.

A portion of the wall facing the Golden Horn, like the wall facing the Marmara, consisted of only one layer, and this section was incomparably better protected from the Bosphorus currents and the north winds. The only time that Constantinople had been conquered—during the Fourth Crusade of 1204—it was because an attack on precisely this wall had managed to succeed. Any strategy to take Constantinople would hinge on the successful conquest of the Golden Horn. The defensive boom was meant precisely to prevent that from happening. The defense of the Golden Horn itself had been entrusted to the Venetians, so it only made sense for them to take charge of defending that portion of the wall as well. The part of the wall where most of the docks were clustered was their responsibility.

Worried that handing over the defense of such a crucial part of the wall to the Latins would be met with resistance among the Greeks, the Emperor tried to smooth things out by assigning defense of that part of the wall from the docks to the Imperial Palace to the second highest-ranking man in the Byzantine Empire after himself, the Megadux (Grand Duke) Notaras and the court nobles under his command. The Supreme Commander of the Christian fleet within the Golden Horn would be Admiral Gabriele Trevisan.

However, it was clear to one and all that the part of the wall that would bear the brunt of the attack would be that facing land. When they had attacked thirty years earlier, the Ottomans had done so by land. The majority of the defensive army would have to be placed along that part of the wall.

The single-layer stretch of the wall encircling the Imperial Palace would be defended by an army of Venetians under Ambassador Minotto. Although he was a citizen of Florence, Tedaldi, who had close ties to the Venetian merchants, was also a part of this detail. Giustiniani's group of five hundred Genoese mercenaries would defend the portion of the wall south of the palace. The Mesoteichion section, where the wall dipped into the Lycus Valley, the emperor himself (whose original plan was to guard the palace) would defend with Greek elites. Further south, where the elevation began to rise again, groups of Greeks, Venetians, and Genoese would each defend a major gate. The student Ubertino joined a Venetian force, led by a man named Gritti, that was defending Pegae Gate.

It had been the Emperor's idea to mix the different nationalities up in this fashion; he felt that this would not only lessen the animosities among the various groups, but also allow him to make the most of each group's respective capabilities. The fact that the commander-in-chief was the Emperor, the commander of naval forces the Venetian Trevisan, and the commander of the army the Genoese Giustiniani reflected this intention. This composite army so far seemed to exhibit such cohesion and unity, regardless of who was leading them, and seemed to be so overflowing with the will to fight, that the Emperor's care and foresight in this regard was probably not even necessary.

Tedaldi, who was with the Venetian detail defending the palatial wall, had just climbed to the top of one of the towers along that part of the wall together with two knights. It was their job to hoist the flags of the Byzantine Empire and the Republic of Venice from the top of this tower, which was the farthest to the northwest of any of them. The knights, one Greek and one Venetian, both experienced at this kind of work, were quickly able to hoist up the Byzantine flag, a sky-blue background with a silver-colored double-headed eagle, and the Venetian flag, red with the lion of San Marco in gold.

The two great flags could be seen fluttering together in the wind from any point in the city: from the center of Constantinople, from the defensive positions along the city wall, from the ships sailing the Golden Horn, and from the Genoese settlement in Galata. Needless to say, the Turkish army that would no doubt assemble near the landward part of the wall would see the paired flags as well, perhaps to their displeasure. Flying the flags together had been the emperor's idea, and Ambassador Minotto had readily agreed. With this, the Venetian settlement of Constantinople would give public notice to the Sultan that they were fighting on the Byzantine side.

Ubertino, assigned to a section of the wall near the Pagae Gate, hadn't been able to sleep at all the night before. This was not because he had been assigned sentry duty. Quite the opposite: he had been told to rest and so found a nook at the base of a tower along the inner wall against which to rest himself. No matter how hard he tried, however, he just could not fall asleep. This would be the twenty-year-old's first battle. When the sun began to rise that morning, April 4th, he could stand it no longer, got up, and quietly left. He climbed to the top of one of the towers along the inner wall. He was now more than twenty-five meters above ground level. Below him was the outer wall stretching out as far as the eye could see, and on the other side of it the wooden protective stockade.

Along the towers of the outer wall he could see the sentries who had stayed up all night.

It happened then. The far horizon, still hazy in the morning mist, began to sway back and forth. No, actually, the horizon itself seemed to be swelling forward. As the mist cleared away the moving line grew clearer, more distinct. Like a wave extending all the way across the horizon it slowly drew closer. Never in his life had Ubertino seen such a massive army. A throng of people who hadn't been there before were now crowded behind him. Like him, they held their breath and merely watched the wave crawling closer and closer. This, beyond a shadow of a doubt, was the main Ottoman army that had reportedly left Adrianople ten days earlier.

Thirteen was not too young an age at which to serve as a page. Yet this was Tursun's first opportunity to take part in a real battle in the service of his young lord. The wall of Constantinople, the strongest, most impregnable rampart in the whole of the Mediterranean stretched out before his eyes, filling the young boy with nothing short of awe.

"Should a wall as great as this really be destroyed?" he thought to himself, only to have his reverie broken by the seldom heard sound of his lord's voice screaming in rage.

"What is Zaganos Pasha doing?"

Without waiting for his lord to say another word, the boy jumped on his horse and rode off to summon Zaganos.

Like Tursun, this was Mihajlovic's first time to see the wall of Constantinople, and like him he looked on it with awe; yet his feeling of utter gloom was quite the opposite of the young page's elation. His pride and that of the Serbian riders under him had been shattered by the order that had just arrived from the Sultan:

"We don't need you as riders any longer. Form yourselves up as an infantry unit."

Mehmed had even ordered them to kill their horses. The meat would not be used to feed Turkish soldiers, who only ate lamb, but instead would be wrapped in sheepskin and submerged at the landward end of the Golden Horn for later use by Christian soldiers serving in the Ottoman army. The 1,500 riders who constituted the cream of the Serbian army along with their 3,000 attendants were thus turned into an infantry regiment of 4,500 who would be held in the rear for the time, but no doubt deployed to the front line when necessary.

Tursun did not have to round the Golden Horn to get to Zaganos Pasha's encampment on a hillside behind Galata. When he had kicked his horse twice, he spotted Zaganos Pasha rushing toward him, scattering soldiers away who were assuming their positions. Zaganos, who believed himself to be the only top minister trusted by Sultan Mehmed, threw the page a glance and did not even stop. The vizier began galloping towards the Sultan's encampment and Tursun could only turn his own horse around and follow.

Mehmed the Second was seated on his throne with his ministers lined up to his right. They were in the center of the sultan's exceptionally large red tent, which was embroidered with dazzling gold thread. Present were the Grand Vizier Halil Pasha, the commander of the Anatolian Corps Ishak Pasha, and the commander of the European Corps Karadja Pasha. Zaganos Pasha took his seat after arriving late and prostrating himself before the Sultan. To Mehmed's left were his generals, admirals, and senior *imams*. In other words, the leading personages of the Ottoman Empire were all assembled in one place. The twenty-one-year-old ruler seemed to have no intention of asking the senior ministers who had served under his father for any opinions or advice. He merely issued a series of terse orders to each of the men and with that the strategy meeting was ended.

The Anatolian Corps under Ishak Pasha would set up camp along the landward portion of Constantinople's wall from the southern tip to the Lycus Valley. The sultan's encampment, as well as that of the Turkish riders under Halil Pasha and the Janissaries, would be established north of the Lycus Valley in the area focused on the Military Gate of Saint Romanus. The European Corps under Karadja Pasha would camp further north, from the Gate of Charisius to the part of the wall surrounding the Imperial Palace. The Sultan ordered furthermore that the irregular troops would set up their formations behind those of the two main armies. Zaganos Pasha's division, made up of soldiers drawn from various different groups, were setting up formation in the hills of Galata from the north of the Golden Horn to the Bosphorus—in other words, they would encircle Galata.

These orders were merely the final confirmation of instructions that had previously been handed down, and the ministers merely bowed their heads in acknowledgment. They could only stare at Mehmed in utter disbelief, however, when he uttered the following words:

"Tomorrow morning, the entire army will advance to a line 1.6 kilometers from the wall."

That same day the entire army had just finished setting up camp along a line four kilometers away from the wall. Now he was telling them to break down camp and set it up again the next day 1.6 kilometers away from the wall. Yet none of the senior ministers, including the most senior of them all, Halil Pasha, dared question the young ruler's orders. The next day, after having finally completed the troublesome task of re-erecting all of their tents 1.6 kilometers away from the wall, they received a second order from the sultan:

"Tomorrow morning, the entire army will advance to a point 400 meters away from the wall."

The reason for all this wasn't clear even to the Grand Vizier himself, but Tursun, who never left his lord's side even for a moment, understood.

During the first day of the encampment, when only the Sultan's tent was standing and the others hadn't been completed yet, a group of Genoese representatives led by the Magistrate Lomellino had come to pay a visit. While the Sultan granted them an audience, his attention was focused on one of the men in particular for some reason, whom he asked to remain even when the others had left. This man, perhaps because he had been put off guard by the sultan's unexpected politeness, or perhaps driven to extremes by his worry over the fate of the Genoese settlement, freely and honestly answered all of the Sultan's questions. Mehmed learned in the course of this questioning that, although the Byzantine army also possessed a number of cannons, more often than not, when the fuse was lit, not only would the stone cannonball not fire, but the cannon itself would explode and destroy the portion of the wall on which it was housed. This report concurred with a similar assessment made by the Italian scholar of antiquity Ciriaco d'Ancona, who was very familiar with the situation in Constantinople and whom the Sultan had received recently as an honored guest.

Since the fact that the enemy's cannons presented no

threat was the only reason for drawing the encampments closer, it would of course have been easier on the troops simply to move them to the 400 meter line the first time around instead of making them move twice. Even Tursun couldn't imagine why the Sultan had done so. It was clear, however, that the atmosphere pervading the imperial court was completely different from that of the previous Sultan. Tursun knew that his lord was more feared than loved by his ministers and retainers. The truly mysterious thing was that everybody, from the ministers to the lowliest foot soldiers, all moved as if they were no more than the limbs of Mehmed's own body; an army of over 150,000 men set up camp three times in quick succession without trouble or complaint.

As they approached the 400 meter line, they felt an almost physical sense of oppression from the sheer size of the city wall. On the morning of April 7th, Tursun was accompanying the Sultan as he inspected the full army after they had completed their final encampment. Tursun noticed a group of generals staring down at them from the top of the outer wall near the Military Gate of Saint Romanus. In the center was a man astride a white horse, his crimson mantle flapping in the wind: the Emperor, no doubt. It seemed that Mehmed had noticed them as well. He boldly turned his black horse towards the wall and his young page had no choice but to follow.

Mehmed the Second may have had a youthful audacity, but he also wasn't a man to forget to take precautions: he did not ride close enough to the wall to be within the enemy's range. After staring at the men atop the wall for a time, he turned back around. Tursun, who had to turn his horse around again to follow him back, heard the Sultan mutter to himself, "It seems an imperial ruler can go nowhere without a white steed."

The heavy silence that reigned over the citizens and defenders of Constantinople continued unabated for a long time after the enemy's arrival. The bells of the churches were silent at Mass time. Even the people on the streets seemed to be walking as quietly as possible. All that could be heard were the sounds of the enemy's army advancing forward outside of the city walls, a mass of indistinct sounds like that of the wind.

Nicolo looked down with bated breath from a gap in Charisius Gate at the Turkish soldiers spreading like floodwater across the plain below. Like everybody else, including the Western military leadership, he could not figure out why the Turks had moved forward twice in such quick succession.

Although he had seen Turkish soldiers before, he couldn't help but be surprised at how meager the equipment of their commanders was: not a single one of them was dressed in armor, and surely it couldn't have been better for the common soldiers.

In contrast, the defenders' armor was of such high quality that it could have been put on display as representative of Western armor technology at its finest. Shining so brightly it could have been silver, the steel armor worn by the soldiers arrayed along the top of the wall created a magnificent spectacle; it was clear at a glance that this was Milanese armor of the highest quality, although the ones wearing it were not so much the Venetians and the Genoese, but rather the Byzantines. The armor had been imported to Constantinople from Milan, which was famous for producing the finest armor in the West by Venetian and Genoese merchants.

As might be expected from a highly educated doctor, however, Nicolo did not allow the magnificence of the defender's equipment to give him false comfort. The poorly equipped Turkish soldiers below, seemingly as tiny as ants, enjoyed an overwhelming numerical superiority. He tried to estimate their numbers by counting the number of soldiers in the nearest encampment and then extrapolating from there. Guessing that the troops on the Galatian side that he could not see amounted to a quarter of the army, he could safely estimate that the entire Ottoman force was around 160,000.

Although Ambassador Minotto and Admiral Trevisan agreed with Nicolo's estimate, others held different opinions. The Florentine merchant Tedaldi believed them to number 200,000 and the emperor's confidant Phrantzes insisted on roughly the same number. In general the estimates made by the Greeks were high: Cardinal Isidore thought there were 300,000, and there were even those who believed the Turks had 400,000 soldiers. Nicolo thought to himself with some sarcasm that this was yet another example of the Byzantines' flights of fancy, and so didn't press his opinion on them.

Once the Ottomans had completed their encampments, the leaders of the defense were able to come up with a strategy. Anybody could guess from the location of the Sultan's tent that the main thrust of the attack would be directed at the lowest point of the Lycus Valley—in other words, the Military Gate of Saint Romanus. Giustiniani and the five hundred mercenaries under his command moved south from their previously assigned location to join forces with the elite Greek troops under the Emperor in order to help defend this most problematic sector. The gap left by the Genoese mercenaries' departure was filled by a Venetian regiment. Tedaldi thought, however, that this would cause the number of defenders, already small to begin with, to be scattered even more thinly.

The next day, April 8th, a gentle rain was falling. Although they believed it unlikely that the attack would commence in the rain, the defensive forces were on guard at their respective positions. The surprise that befell them that day didn't take the form of arrows and bullets, however—it took the form of the great cannon being dragged into position by a massive team of men and oxen. Even from a great distance, Nicolo could tell that the work of positioning the cannon, with the men helping the oxen along, was exceedingly difficult. First they had to build a foundation of large stones, then cover that with a platform of thick planks, and then somehow slide the cannon atop those planks. The cannon was so heavy, however, that even in such a light rain it kept sliding and tumbling back. When this happened a scream rang out and those men who weren't working hard enough were violently pulled out of the way and another attempt was made. It struck Nicolo that the oxen were treated better than the men, and the cannon was treated better than the oxen.

The defenders didn't just idly stand by while this work continued for the next three days. As soon as they thought of countermeasures against the cannon, they immediately went to work. They fortified the protective fence that rose ten meters away from the outer wall. In front of this third wall they lined up bags filled with leather and wool to soften the impact of incoming cannonballs. On top of the fence they lined up barrels filled with dirt, which made it somewhat taller. Not only the male soldiers but also the women of the city took part in this labor.

They couldn't simply worry about defending themselves on the landward side, however. Reports were coming in that the Turkish fleet was making its way north up the Sea of Marmara. The Christian naval forces immediately went on full alert.

On April 9th, a fleet of ten ships—five large Genoese sailing vessels, three Cretan ships, one Anconian ship, and one Byzantine ship—took up their positions inside the boom. An additional reserve fleet made up of two Venetian naval galleys, three large Venetian merchant galleys, five Byzantine galleys, and six other ships was waiting in harbor. Six smaller boats, which could serve no defensive capacity by themselves, were also waiting at dock. The galleys were held in reserve because they had greater maneuverability than the sailboats.

There was another excellent reason to use the large Genoese sailing vessels as the first line of defense. Two of them were in the 1500-ton class, with one ship each in the 700-ton, 400-ton, and 300-ton classes. This reflected the fact that Genoa was a deep-water harbor that could accommodate such large boats. More importantly, these ships rose to an imposing height above water level, which made them appear from shore almost like a wall stretched across the entrance to the Golden Horn. Even a complete novice could see that they were more appropriate as a first line of defense than the 200-ton class Venetian men-'o-war. But this arrangement also symbolized the different temperaments of the two city-states: while the motto of the Venetian art of commerce was accuracy, cooperation, and continuity, the Genoese were individualists who preferred one-shot gambits.

On the 11th of April, the citizens of Constantinople seemed to shift their attention away from the cannons and towards the approaching Turkish fleet. They could only gasp in surprise as they watched the fleet pass. Led by the Ottoman Admiral Baltaoglu, it was so large that it took over half a day for all of the ships to pass by. By Nicolo's count, they had twenty galleys, seventy to eighty large vessels, twenty to twenty-five transport ships, and some smaller boats for a total of 145 vessels. Tedaldi's guess was a smaller number, but in this case, as in others, the guesses hazarded by the Greeks were markedly larger than those of the Westerners. Phrantzes guessed that they had 400 ships, and although that was a minority opinion, most guesses were still in the range of 300 ships or more.

"You can't trust what a Greek says, when you're fighting a war." This had become Trevisan's stock phrase, one he uttered whenever a strategy meeting ended.

The newly-arrived Turkish fleet dropped anchor near the mouth of the Bosphorus, at a point the Greeks called the "Double Columns" which was protected from the strong currents and north winds. They would use that part of the sea as a forward base from which to begin immediate attempts at breaking through the boom, an inevitability for which the defenders would have to be prepared.

As anxieties about the threat from the sea began to peak, the landward defenders were finishing their final preparations; the atmosphere was pervaded by the quiet that precedes battle. The Turks had their large cannons in place: two aimed at the Golden Gate, three at the Pegae Gate, four aimed squarely at the Military Gate of Saint Romanus, and three aimed at the Gate of Caligaria in front of the Imperial Palace, for a total of twelve cannons. The pale moonlight made the dew-covered barrels of the cannon seem almost to levitate off the ground. The nightly north winds the last few days had been unseasonably cold. Ubertino was on sentry duty, pacing back and forth along his portion of the wall, trying to keep himself warm, but it seemed as if the black barrels of the three cannons were following him as he walked back and forth. The enemy camp had turned ominously silent.

*

On the morning of April 12th, as if to herald the warmth radiating from the rising sun, the Turkish cannons began firing, one after the other. The massive stone cannonballs screamed across the sky. All the defenders could do was to try to evade the stones raining down upon them. The enemy seemed to lack the ability to hit specific targets with precision, but that didn't matter: their only target was the long, high city wall. Anywhere would do. When the cannonballs struck the defensive railings or outer walls, they heaved up an enveloping cloud of dust. When the dust cleared, it revealed the pitiful sight of crushed railings and gutted walls: the bags filled with leather and wool had done absolutely nothing to protect them.

This was not to say that everything was going well for the artillerymen. Perhaps because the mountings were not adequately secured, the cannons swayed violently from side to side whenever they were fired. A few of them even slipped off of their mountings. The Great Cannon was all the more difficult to handle—even when treated with the greatest care, it could only manage seven shots in one day. Nonetheless, those seven shots alone inflicted more damage than all of the other cannons put together. Nobody in the Byzantine Court had known about this cannon built by the Hungarian whom they had once laughed out of their city. And none of them imagined that these cringe-inducing explosions would continue unabated for the next seven weeks, perhaps because none of them had the time to indulge in worry: from this day onward, they would spend their nights trying to repair the damage done by the cannons during the day.

On the naval front, however, it was the Christian forces who had the upper hand. On the same day that the cannon barrage began, the Turkish navy set out from its base hoping to break through the defensive chain and enter the Golden Horn. The defensive fleet under the command of Admiral Trevisan, arrayed along the boom, braced themselves for the assault. The archers aboard the Ottoman boats released a torrent of arrows. A Turkish cannon set up just outside the east end of Galata began to fire. Closing in on the Christian ships, the Turkish vessels hurled burning logs at the enemy's boats, while sailors tried to latch hooked nets to pull them closer and forcibly board them.

All of these efforts ended in failure. The cannons were too far away, and their volleys merely landed with a splash in the sea or else struck, and sank, their own vessels. The fires started by the burning logs were quickly put out by deckhands, who were well accustomed to such emergencies, and the arrows hardly had any effect whatsoever. The large Western ships were a great deal taller than the Turkish boats, and arrows fired from the Christians' towering masts had a decisively higher kill ratio than those fired willy-nilly by the Ottoman forces. When it came to naval combat, the Venetian and Genoese forces were so far ahead of their Turkish enemies in both experience and skill that the Ottoman fleet was effectively neutralized as a threat. Indeed, when Trevisan's fleet had the boom unlatched so that they could move out of the Horn to launch a counterattack, the Turks quickly turned back to base for fear that they would be encircled and completely obliterated.

This outcome grievously injured Mehmed's pride, but he also realized that no matter how harshly he berated Admiral Baltaoglu it wouldn't improve his sailors' competence. The young Sultan instead ordered the cannon positioned outside Galata to be modified. It was Urban's duty to recalculate the cannon's trajectory, and after a few days he had adjusted the cannon to meet specifications. It was placed in the same position as before, and this time, on the second volley it struck one of the merchant ships cruising outside the boom. From that point on the Christian fleet would no longer be free to leave and re-enter the Golden Horn at will.

Whatever the happenings at sea, it was clear to all concerned that the assault on Constantinople was a battle that would be decided on land. On April 18th, fifteen days after first surrounding the city on April 4th, Mehmed the Second ordered the first full-frontal assault. The preparations had been completed.

The week-long barrage of cannon fire, despite the late-night repair work carried out by the defenders, had left many parts of the wall bare, and the protective stockades had only been patched up with barrels filled with dirt. The damage along the Mesoteichion section of the wall was especially severe. Mehmed, who didn't like to leave any of his soldiers idle, ordered those not involved in the artillery work to fill in the twenty-meter-wide moat that surrounded the wall; after days of continuous labor with cannon volleys flying overhead, they had completely filled in the dry moat at a number of points.

The full-scale assault began two hours after sunset. The main thrust of the attack, as predicted, was centered on Mesoteichion. A flame rose up toward the dim sky from near the Sultan's red tent, which shone lit up by torches. That was the signal. The sound of drums drifted on the wind across the plain, while trumpet bursts loudly pierced the air. The collective battle cry of a hundred thousand Ottoman troops seemed enough to make the very ground quake beneath them. The alarm bells in the city broke out in a frenzy of hollow peals.

Despite all of this Giustiniani kept his composure; his troops, although outnumbered, had been placed according to his precise instructions in the most strategically advantageous locations, and were free to move at will.

The defenders had their good fortune bolstered by a serious mistake on the Sultan's part: he sent in too many soldiers to attack at one time, which greatly hindered their mobility. While the Turkish soldiers jostled with one another for space, the defenders, whose equipment was adequate and whose morale was high, were able steadily and consistently to pick them off. After four hours of fighting, the Turks had to call a retreat. Their dead, including those who had been trampled by their comrades, numbered over two hundred. The defenders had suffered a few light casualties that were readily treated by the chief medic, Nicolo. They had no fatalities.

The Christian soldiers who were resting along the city wall were dead tired, but their faces were aglow. They had brilliantly repulsed a full-out assault which they had considered

the beginning of the end. This, combined with their successes at sea, gave rise to the hope that perhaps they would be able
to defend the city to the end.

In just a few hours, the church bells would toll serenly to
announce the first Mass of the morning. A day later, an event
would occur that would bolster their confidence even further.

Chapter Five

Victory at Sea

It was now two weeks since the beginning of the siege, and for most of that time a strong north wind had been blowing through Constantinople and its environs. Because of this, three Genoese ships sent and paid for by the Pope that were carrying replacement arms and ammunition were left stuck at port at the island of Chios in the Aegean Sea. All three were large sailing vessels, and thus it was impossible for them to move north against a headwind. Once the first Turkish general assault had ended, however, that north wind turned into a south wind, and the long-awaited ships were able to head north toward the Dardanelle Straits at high speed. As they were about to enter the Dardanelles, they encountered a Greek boat, also headed north. This ship, even larger than those of the Genoese, had been sent to Sicily by the Emperor ahead of the siege to procure foodstuffs and bring them back to the city. It was thus the largest, best-equipped, and most expertly manned vessel in the essentially non-existent Byzantine navy. The four ships formed a group and entered the Dardanelles together.

Perhaps because they had devoted their entire fleet to the blockade of Constantinople, there were no Turkish ships whatsoever along the straits. The convoy, blessed with favorable winds, passed through the Dardanelles quickly and without harassment. They were even able to pass Gallipoli, the Ottomans' only port, unobstructed—perhaps because they were intimidated by the convoy of four large ships, no boats left the harbor to intercept them.

They arrived within view of Constantinople on the morning of April 12th after a smooth passage through the Sea of Marmara. Lookouts, both atop the city wall and within the Ottoman encampment, noticed that a convoy flying Genoese

and Byzantine colors was approaching. The four ships carefully adjusted their sails to make full use of the favorable winds
as they continued north.

Tursun, who had just finished getting dressed, wasn't surprised when the Turkish soldier barged into his tent. He just
did what the soldier told him and went to the adjoining tent
to rouse his lord. Mehmed appeared to be awake although he
was still in his bed; Tursun told him that a soldier had arrived
with urgent news.

Mehmed didn't say anything after the soldier made his
brief report, merely turned around to find Tursun waiting
with the wardrobe for the day.

Less than ten minutes later he emerged from his tent. He
quickly dispatched several messengers with instructions for
the artillerymen on the day's targets, and then straddled his
beloved horse. Tursun alone followed his every step.

He only took care while crossing the makeshift bridge
that spanned the inner part of the Golden Horn, but then
whipped the horse along until he reached Zaganos Pasha's
camp, where he stopped to order as many brave soldiers as
possible to accompany him as quickly as possible to the
"Double Columns." They proceeded towards the Turkish fleet,
once again whipping the horses to run at full gallop. The
Sultan's pure white cloak flapped parallel to the black horse's
back as they flew through the hills of Galata, and the only
time it touched the Sultan's back again was when he had finally reached the dock.

In a deep but cutting voice, Mehmed told Admiral
Baltaoglu, "Christian ships are approaching. If possible, I
want all four ships captured. If not, I want them all sunk. No
matter what happens, I don't want a single one to pass

through."

The Turks had no naval tradition, and had quickly thrown a fleet together on the Sultan's orders. Admiral Baltaoglu, who had more or less trained himself from the ground up, remembered a few things he had learned from Greek sailors during the building of the fleet. For one, sailboats, easily diverted by the wind, were inappropriate for naval combat. He immediately marshalled all of the ships that had some means of propulsion other than sails, leaving the sailboats behind. Crack troops under Zaganos Pasha's command also boarded their large transport ships. A number of cannons were placed on board as well, but since this would be battle at close quarters it was more likely that the decisive factor would be the number of combatants they had at their disposal. It took less than three hours for these preparations to be completed. Mehmed, as well as Halil Pasha and other ministers who had arrived some time later, proceeded to the shore along the eastern wall of the Genoese settlement. From this vantage point they could see off the departing attack force and also witness the ensuing battle.

The city's defenders watched the four ships move north, their hearts pounding with fear. The first report by the lookouts had immediately spread across the city, and those defenders who were not needed to man the landward wall rushed to the Marmara wall and to the tops of the churches' bell towers to get a look. The Emperor himself stood at the top of the tower that supported one end of the boom. He was surrounded not only by his perennial attendant Phrantzes but also by Chief Minister Notaras and Cardinal Isidore. Trevisan was watching from the lookout of one of the tall Genoese ships that had dropped anchor inside the boom. Next to him a sailor with signal flags was ready to transmit his orders to allied ships, in case they needed to launch a supporting counter-attack. Nicolo was on stand-by aboard a Venetian galley anchored near the boom. Nothing could surpass a galley warship when it came to sea battle. The galley's speed would also help if Nicolo needed to tend to wounded on the Genoese and Byzantine ships which, unlike Venetian ships, did not necessarily have a doctor aboard since their laws did not mandate it.

As the sun passed through its apex in the sky, the Ottoman fleet slowly moved south like a swarm of centipedes to try to block the northbound convoy. Baltoglu quickly ordered the sails dropped. The convoy ignored this and continued forward. The current of the Bosphorus, moving north to south, was fanned into rippling waves by the wind, which was blowing south to north, making it difficult for the Turkish ships to navigate. The Christian sailors peered sideways at the Turkish ship, but continued sailing northward: the Turks tried to edge closer as the Christian boats tried to slip past. When they came within striking range of each other, sailors on the lookout of one of the Genoese boats started throwing rocks down upon the cowering Turkish sailors, while their archers let loose volley after deadly volley of arrows. The chase continued northward for nearly an hour. As the four sailboats approached the edge of the promontory at which they would turn left to enter the Golden Horn, the wind suddenly abated. The sails of the four large boats drooped down from their masts. Although the current from the Bosphorus was moving south, part of that current was deflected by the promontory and was actually moving *north*, and the four ships got caught up in that current. This phenomenon was particularly marked after a strong south wind.

The onlookers in Constantinople felt as if their hearts had stopped. The four Christian vessels were drifting north, directly towards the shore on which the Sultan was observing the proceedings, and could do nothing to change that. Furthermore, the Turkish fleet had also navigated its way into the northward current and was catching up with them.

Nonetheless, those who felt the situation was hopeless were not fully aware of the true state of things; those, such as Trevisan, who knew these waters well saw things differently. The sailors on the four Christian vessels were just waiting for the right moment to drop anchor, which they did as soon as the ocean floor came within twenty meters. The sound of the four iron anchor chains being unwound into the water echoed across the Golden Horn. Without wasting a moment or making a single false move, the combat-hardened sailors moved into battle positions to face the enemy's attack.

In a matter of moments the Turkish fleet came within striking distance. They didn't drop anchor since they had the freedom of movement afforded by their oarsmen. The anchored Christian boats kept tightly together. The Turkish fleet separated into four parts to attack each boat individually. One of the Genoese ships was attacked by five galleys, while another was assailed by thirty smaller boats. The third Genoese ship was surrounded by forty transport filled with soldiers. The large Greek ship, which had dropped anchor in the midst of the Genoese vessels as if to be shielded by them, was attacked too by a combination of more than twenty large and small boats. Mehmed looked on as the sea battle between Christian and Muslim commenced.

The Turkish troops attacked in a mad fury. They tried to ram the Christian boats with their own boats' sharpened prows, they tried latching onto the Christian ships with their rope-and-hooks, and they fired off innumerable flaming arrows. Some rowers even tried to board the Christian ships along the oars. But the courage and extraordinary skill of the Genoese sailors made up for their numerical inferiority. Even when the Turks were able to get their hooks latched onto the Genoese boats, her sailors were quickly able to cut them loose; perfectly trained to deal with such things, they put out the fires before they got out of control. The fact that the Turks had their oars out, combined with poor maneuvering skills, often resulted in oars from different boats getting entangled—and when that happened, the bunched-together boats became a perfect target for the Genoese. From their higher position the Genoese archers could take aim at the immobilized ships and fire at will. The dull whoosh of their arrows flying through the air meshed with the screams of the Turkish soldiers.

Although their navigational and combat skills were not as honed as those of the Genoese, the Greek sailors also got off to a good start in the fighting. They used barrels filled with combustibles, popularly known as "Greek fire," to devastating effect. If one of these exploded aboard a ship the entire vessel would immediately turn into a raging inferno.

The Ottomans, however, enjoyed a numerical advantage. No matter how many Turkish troops the Christians killed, more kept coming. No matter how many Turkish ships they burned and sank, there were still others in their wake. The young Sultan didn't bother to rest his legs sitting on the stool Tursun had provided. He rode his horse into the shallows of the Bosphorus, as if he were somehow taking part in the battle himself. The horses' flanks, wet from the seawater, took on a black sheen; the Sultan's soaked white cloak clung to the horse's side, but he was oblivious to this; he kept the horse pacing back and forth in the water while he shouted himself hoarse at his distant warriors, sometimes reviling, sometimes encouraging, with an almost insane fervor.

Even if Admiral Baltoglu couldn't hear his lord's enraged voice, he could no doubt see him riding his horse back and forth like a man crazed. He decided that he would ignore the three perfectly defended Genoese ships and instead focus on the Greek boat, which was clearly having a harder time of it. He immediately sent signals to his scattered ships to gather together. The Genoese, however, were able to guess at this change in strategy right away from their movements.

The measure of a crew's skill at naval combat could be judged by how quickly they could raise anchor, and in this regard even the Venetians had to admit that the Genoese were the best in the Mediterranean, as they soon amply demonstrated.

While the Turkish ships were still trying to get into formation, the Genoese boats raised anchor with a speed that was astounding for boats of such size and immediately closed ranks around the Greek ship. The people on shore thought for a moment that a fortress with four towers had suddenly emerged from the sea. To the Turkish fleet it must have seemed as if a giant iron wall had suddenly interposed itself between them and the Greek ship. The Genoese boats stuck tenaciously to this self-appointed role of defensive wall for the remainder of the engagement with the Turkish fleet, which went on until sunset.

At the precise moment the sun fell below the horizon, however, the calm sea suddenly turned rough: the wind had started blowing. The Christians were in luck: it was a north wind.

The drooping sails suddenly filled with life. The four Christian ships took advantage of this opportunity to brush the Turkish ships aside and proceed toward the Golden Horn in tight formation. The boom was lowered from the Constantinople side. With trumpets blaring, Trevisan's task force of three galleys crossed the now-open threshold into the Bosphorus. The trumpet calls were meant to fool the enemy into thinking that the entire fleet inside the Golden Horn was launching an attack.

The nightfall gave this daring plan a chance of success. Although he could still hear the Sultan screaming, Baltoglu ordered his ships to retreat. The Sultan's anger was a less frightening prospect than naval combat in the dark of night. On Trevisan's orders, the four ships, which had managed to escape from a fierce battle that had dragged out for the better part of the day, furled their sails and allowed themselves to be pulled into the safe port of the Golden Horn by Trevisan's galleys. They were greeted by the ecstatic cheers of the defenders packed along the wall.

The people of Constantinople hadn't been this wildly happy in years. The Emperor himself boarded the newly arrived ships and personally praised and thanked each of the crew members. Overflowing with high spirits, the Greeks of Constantinople began boasting to one another about how the Christian forces hadn't suffered a single fatality while the Ottomans had already lost over ten thousand men. Nicolo, who had personally tended to the casualties, had to smile sarcastically at these fantastic rumors. The Turks had probably lost about a hundred men, with maybe another four hundred wounded. The Byzantine side had lost twenty-three men, and roughly half the sailors had been wounded in some way or another. As far as he was concerned, the fierce battle at sea meant simply that he wouldn't even have time to sleep as he tended to all of the wounded. The activity outside continued late into the night as the fresh weapons, ammunition, and food were unloaded.

Mehmed, pale as a sheet, didn't say a word. He wasn't so much angry as he was tormented by humiliation. The fact that the Ottomans had no merchant fleet tradition and no naval history didn't count as an excuse in his eyes. In battle, all that mattered were the results. The humiliation was especially severe because somehow a convoy of *only four ships*, large as they may have been, had bested his fleet of over a *hundred* ships. And those hundred or so were not just small boats: at least forty of them were quite large, even if small compared to the Christian ships. Clearly this defeat was rooted in an absurd mismatch of skills.

His smooth, young skin had always had something of a faint ruddiness to it, but that night it stayed pale even as he ate nothing and gulped down liquor. His eyes remained focused on a single point. When Halil Pasha suggested that he return to his tent at the main encampment, he ignored him. When it was suggested that he at least get some rest at Zaganos Pasha's camp nearby, he said nothing. He remained in the hastily erected tent all night, drinking silently and allowing nobody to approach him except for Tursun.

The young ruler had only one thing on his mind. He certainly wasn't thinking about Admiral Baltoglu, whose execution he had ordered, only to have his mind changed by the desperate pleas of Baltoglu's subordinates; though he spared Baltoglu's life, he had his entire fortune ordered confiscated and handed out among the Janissaries. And he certainly was not thinking about the letter that had arrived from a high-ranking *imam* who was always eager to offer advice during times like these. The Sultan read it once and then discarded it. The letter said that the responsibility for the defeat rested with the Sultan himself. Many of the Ottoman soldiers were not true Muslims, just men who were fighting out of blind greed, and the Sultan had to motivate them with promises of war spoils. The letter went on to say not to worry, that the prophecy of Constantinople's fall would come true, but for this to happen the Sultan would have to deepen his faith, to believe the teachings and prophecies of Islam with heartfelt conviction.

No, the twenty-one-year-old, burning with ambition, knew that he had better things to do than listen to the words of clergymen. He was obsessed with one question and one question only: was there some way not only to improve his navy, but actually to transform it into a dominating force?

Chapter Six

The Loss of
the Golden Horn

In the early morning of April 21st, the irregular troops, who, with the exception of the general assaults, had until then just been sent out to fill up trenches, received an order to assemble at Galata. Mihajlovic had a bad feeling about this, but tried not to think about it too deeply. News about the sea battle had reached the Serbian soldiers, who had been filling trenches the whole day. Of course they couldn't say so openly, but it was the first uplifting news they had heard in a long time.

As usual they weren't told why they were supposed to assemble in Galata, but they assumed it must have been to repair the ships damaged in the battle. Mihajlovic had his troops fall into formation, checked that all were present, and then they headed towards Galata around the tip of the Golden Horn.

When Mihajlovic and his men arrived at the Bosphorus, he was struck by the odd fact that the Sultan and all of his top ministers were there, far away from the main encampment where they should have been. He didn't have time to indulge his speculations, however, as the commanders of all of the irregular units were called up one after the other to receive their assignments for the day and quickly get to work. Mihajlovic's Serbian forces were assigned to a section of the hills rising from the Bosphorus.

Their first task was to repair and fortify the road that ran alongside and slightly apart from the Genoese settlement's wall. The road had been there already for a long time and had been used for the Ottoman soldiers' comings and goings, but for some reason it now needed further, special leveling, more so than was necessary in order to be used only by people and horses. That finished, they used timber brought by another group of soldiers to begin constructing a pair of rails. It occurred to Mihajlovic, as he oversaw the work, that these rails could be used to transport the Great Cannon.

Just as they were finishing the rails, the Sultan appeared with his ministers in tow to carry out an inspection; they watched as a platform with metal wheels was pushed along the wooden rails, and also checked to be sure that the ground under the rails was firm. The last time Mihajlovic had seen the Sultan at such close range was at their meeting in Adrianople. He wondered if Mehmed would recognize him, but the Sultan didn't even glance at the Serbian commander standing next to the rails: all he cared about was the proper completion of the work. After the inspection report was delivered, he followed the road further uphill to the next work station without looking back.

The next day, the 22nd, the irregulars were called up even before daybreak and ordered to assemble at the same place as the day before. A completely different task awaited them at the Bosphorus, however. Mihajlovic looked around trying to figure out what they were going to be ordered to do. And then he saw. It appeared that the Turkish Sultan, his junior by a few years, wasn't using the rails to transport the Great Cannon: he was using them to transport his fleet overland into the Golden Horn. The young Serbian knight was more than just surprised; he was nearly trembling with fear.

Mehmed had no shortage of men or material, and he never hesitated to exploit them to the hilt. The wooden rails were completely covered with animal lard. The wheeled platforms were linked together, and resting atop them was a ship that had been pulled out of the sea. The sails were at full mast—a favorable wind blowing from the water up the hill was actually helping push the boat along. Most of the work, however, was being done by two rows of oxen that were managing to pull this unimaginably heavy boat. Large numbers of men were pushing the boats from behind as they inched their way up the hill. The highest point of the Galata Hills was sixty meters above sea level; once the boat reached the peak, oarsmen would get on board and then the boats would slide down an identical set of rails into the Golden Horn.

Once the first of the lighter ships had made it to the top of the hill, the cannon positioned along the east wall of the Genoese settlement fired off one round after another; this would distract the ships inside the Golden Horn towards the boom. At the same time, the Turkish marching band began wildly banging their drums and blowing their trumpets so that the Genoese inside the settlement walls wouldn't hear the ships sliding into the water.

When the first boat was successfully pulled to the top of the hill, loud cheers and clapping erupted not only from the Turkish soldiers, but from the Greek Orthodox soldiers from East Europe as well. The prevailing mood was not one of warfare but rather of pleasant sport, skillfully executed. Seventy more ships, one after the other, followed the first.

It was a little before noon. A sentry atop the wall facing the Golden Horn suddenly let out a heart-stopping shout. When his comrades came running to see what was the matter, he couldn't even find the words to explain it: he could only scream and point his finger in front of him. The lookouts on the ships in the Golden Horn noticed it at around the same time. They could only gape, speechless, at what they saw: one ship after another sliding into the Golden Horn, all flying the red and white star and crescent. They looked like nothing more than toy boats sliding down a chute. When they hit the water, however, the oars immediately began moving. The ships, once afloat, even maneuvered to form a protective fence in the water for the ones that were following suit. It seemed to take no time at all for every one of the ships to make it into the water. For the dumbfounded onlookers, at least, the entire process seemed to pass in an instant. Some of them wondered whether this was not some kind of waking dream or hallucination; however, the fleet that was heading west toward the tip of the Golden Horn before their eyes was very much a reality.

Within moments, the same people who had felt such a wonderful sense of solidarity from the sea victory of two days before were blaming one another for the misfortune that had materialized. The Genoese said, "The Sultan must have heard from some Venetian in his camp about how, fifteen years ago in northern Italy, the Venetians carried their fleet overland from the Po River to Lake Garda. No doubt that's where he got the idea!"

The Venetians didn't remain silent in the face of such charges. "Unlike you, at least, we're quite clear about our position towards the Sultan. Do you really think the Sultan would allow a declared enemy to approach him? Yet it is a *fact*, is it not, that the Sultan has secret agents among the Genoese in Galata? If the Sultan indeed knew of a strategy that we resorted to in 1438, he must have heard it from one of the Italians in the Turkish camp, either that classicist or the attending physician Iacopo da Gaeta. Maybe some Genoese went to him looking all loyal and passed on the information.

"Furthermore, how is it humanly possible that this construction work was going on right outside of your walls and not a single person noticed it? We can only conclude that you knew about this all along and yet didn't inform us!"

The Greeks merely looked on, trying to suppress their laughter. These "Latins" who had boasted that only their great naval power could defend the Golden Horn had had their confidence shaken. This gave the Greeks a certain satisfaction, despite everything.

Admiral Trevisan paid no attention to the rancor aboard his ship. He had realized the enormity of the situation even before all of the Turkish boats had entered the water. He immediately sent a messenger to Ambassador Minotto, who agreed with Trevisan's estimation and sent another messenger to the Emperor requesting an immediate emergency meeting of the war council. The imperial court, however, had become accustomed to a more leisurely pace of doing things and ordered the meeting to be held the next morning.

Trevisan, who was responsible for the overall naval defense of the city, decided not to wait until the next morning but rather to assume the authority of supreme commander and do what needed to be done. For the time being that meant sending a fast galley to keep an eye on the movements of the Turkish ships that had dropped anchor deep in the Golden Horn. He also ordered the Christian fleet lined up along the boom to prepare themselves not only for an attack from the front, as they had up until this time, but to be ready as well for a possible attack from the rear. They could no longer feel secure just because they were in the Golden Horn.

The scout ship reported that the Turks now had artillery set up not only outside the east wall of the Genoese settlement, but also on the shore of the Golden Horn where the Turkish fleet was now anchored. If the defenders came anywhere near the Turkish fleet, the cannons would immediately fire in their direction. The Genoese in Galata could hardly be at ease knowing that they were now hemmed in by Turkish cannons from the east and west. Boats anchored at the settlement's docks would now have to be under guard around the clock.

That night a meeting to consider countermeasures, attended only by Venetians, went late into the night.

The war council convened the next morning, April 23rd, at the Church of Saint Mary's. The Greeks were represented by the Emperor, Phrantzes, and the main Byzantine ministers from Megadux Notaras on down. On the Venetian side were Minotto, Trevisan, Captains Diedo, Coco, and four other ship captains. With the exception of Minotto, they were all men of the sea and coolly saw the latest development as a problem to be dealt with, nothing more. Also present was Cardinal Isidore in his capacity as the Pope's representative. The only Genoese who had been invited was Giustiniani, head of the ground forces.

The members of the council put forward a number of proposals. One of the Greeks suggested that they join forces with the Genoese: a joint assault on the Turks would surely prevail, he offered. Most of those present felt it highly unlikely, however, that the Genoese would forsake their neutrality in the course of one day and join their alliance. The situation called for swift measures, and so such a strategy was deemed inappropriate.

The second proposal was to send an army to Galata to

destroy the cannons the Turks had positioned there, and then set fire to the Ottoman ships in the Golden Horn. This was dismissed by most of the assembled as unrealistic. Zaganos Pasha's army was encamped in the hills above Galata. Simply to launch a credible attack on such a force would require far more men than the city's defenders could spare.

The third proposal came from Captain Coco, a man who was said to know every single sea lane in the Black Sea. He insisted that their only option was to attack at night with a small number of ships drawn from the cream of their fleet: draw close to the Turkish boats and torch them. He even volunteered to lead this attack, which he acknowledged amounted to a suicide mission. There were no objections from the Byzantine side. Trevisan put forth that a mission calling for such secrecy and speed could indeed be carried out by Venetians and Venetians only, and all gave their assent. They agreed not to inform the Genoese about the attack, and set the time for the night of the following day, the 24th.

In the end, though, word somehow leaked out to the Genoese. The morning of the 24th, they pressed into the Venetian merchant center and made their case to Trevisan: they felt it was unjust to be made into pariahs in this fashion and asked to be allowed to take part. After their naval victory against the Turks, their self-confidence had soared to new heights. The Emperor had often said that if the two great seafaring states, the Venetians and the Genoese, were to join forces they would make a supremely formidable fighting force: he urged Trevisan to grant their request. Trevisan didn't have the authority to go against the Emperor's wishes. He decided to allow the Genoese to contribute a boat to the attack force.

That afternoon, however, the Genoese sailors complained

that they wouldn't be able to prepare an appropriate vessel by sundown. They insisted that the attack be postponed for four days, until the 28th. The Venetian side had no choice but to accept this. Coco was outraged, and insisted that at a time like this, when even a moment could mean the difference between life and death, that the Venetians should go it alone as originally planned. This too, was impossible, however, as the Genoese were not the type of people who would quietly allow the Venetians to set off without them.

And yet, the more people who knew about the secret plan, and the longer they postponed carrying it out, the greater the chance that their cover would be blown. And when word of the plan reached a Genoese living in the settlement who worked for the Sultan, that was precisely what happened.

At a little past midnight on April 28th, a group of ships secretly set out into the Golden Horn from a dock on the Constantinople side. A light breeze was blowing, and the moon was obscured by clouds. Leading the attack force, according to plan, were two large ships, one Venetian and one Genoese. Both ships had bales of cotton and wool on both sides to protect them from enemy cannon fire. Behind them were two Venetian battle galleys. Trevisan was aboard the galley to the right side. These four ships actually served to hide the three smaller galleys that accompanied them, sliding across the water with oars in perfect rhythm. Captain Coco was aboard one of these three ships, which would play the main role in the attack. The three light galleys (*fuste*) were accompanied by even smaller boats that were packed with pine resin, sulfur, oil, and other combustibles. Their only navigational guides in the dark were the white sheets stretched across the stern of each ship. The two large vessels in front proceeded slowly and quietly. The forty oarsmen of the two galleys immediately following them rowed in unison with such perfect control that hardly a wave was formed on the water's surface.

Immediately after leaving port, they saw something like a flash of light from one of the towers inside Galata; they suspected it might be a signal to the Turkish forces, but the boats of the Turkish fleet inside the Golden Horn didn't react at all to this possible signal, so the Italians decided to continue forward. Their plan was to sneak up on the enemy ships, toss their combustibles on board, ignite them, cut the enemy ships' anchors, and then escape. If a battle broke out, the four large ships would fulfill their function.

When they came almost within reach of their target, the light galley under Coco's command, propelled by 72 oarsmen, began to overtake the four ships in the lead, as though Coco was becoming impatient about the larger ships' rate of progress. Once it had come to the head of the formation, it continued with unabated speed right towards the enemy.

Cannon fire suddenly erupted from the facing shore. Deafening blasts followed one another in quick succession. The third shot struck a direct hit on Coco's ship, which was immediately engulfed in flames and quickly sank. The other two *fuste* were in no position now to set the enemy fleet on fire, and instead retreated into the protective shadow of the two large ships at the vanguard.

These were far from invulnerable. The two of them got hit multiple times, and although the fires they started struck fear into the hearts of the sailors who scrambled to put them out, in the end the ships were saved from being sunk by the protective bales along their sides. The galleys, on the other hand, hadn't taken such precautions since they were too low to the water. The Turks' barrage focused on Trevisan's galley, almost as if they knew that none other than the Western fleet's commander was aboard. Two of their shots finally scored direct hits, which sent the mast flying and tilted the boat violently to its left side. Water started to enter the hull. Trevisan ordered the crew to board the lifeboats. Within moments the crew, including Trevisan, was rescued by their companion vessels. Dawn began to break as a battle began between the Western ships and the Turkish fleet that had arrived to finish the rout. The battle lasted for over an hour, but ended in a stalemate with both sides returning to their respective ports.

Forty members of Coco's crew were able to swim to shore, where they were seized by Ottoman troops. Mehmed ordered that they be taken to a spot where they could be butchered in clear view from the Constantinople city wall. In retaliation, the Christian forces took 260 Turkish prisoners who had been captured inside the city, lined them up along the wall, and beheaded every last one.

The night raid had been a grave failure. The Venetians had lost one of their galleys and one of their speedboats, in addition to almost ninety of their finest sailors. Coco was among those presumed dead at sea.

What darkened their mood more than anything, however, was the prospect that the Ottoman fleet would continue to occupy the Golden Horn. The only time that Constantinople had fallen, 250 years earlier, it had been at the hands of the army of the Fourth Crusade, which had taken control of the Golden Horn and successfully breached the wall from sea. It was fair to say that controlling the Golden Horn was the key to conquering the city.

This was not to say that complete control of the Golden Horn had already been ceded to the Turks. They would have a difficult time defeating the superior sailors of Genoa and Venice, regardless of their greater numbers. But a poisonous tension had arisen between the Venetians, some of whom insisted that the raid had been betrayed by the Genoese and many of whom quietly suspected as much, and the Genoese, who countered that the true cause of the failure was Coco's reckless desire for fame.

The last day of April saw Mehmed do something that would banish the idle hopes of those who had been trying to tell themselves that the Turkish ships, though they had made it into the bay, would accomplish nothing more. Mehmed had the fleet inside the Golden Horn construct a floating pontoon that connected Constantinople and Pera. It was constructed out of over fifty pairs of empty barrels tied together. Above them were beams supporting thick, sturdy planks. The bridge was five hundred meters long, enough to span the narrow interior portion of the bay, and wide enough to fit five soldiers across. Platforms holding cannons were jutting out from the bridge at regular intervals.

Even to a non-expert such as Nicolo, the purpose of this floating bridge was clear. Not only would it speed up communication between the main encampment, on the one hand, and Zaganos Pasha's army and the fleet at the Double Columns on the other, but, more importantly, it made it possible to fire upon the stretch of the city wall facing the Golden Horn, which only had one layer. Since the defenders had felt secure in their control of the Golden Horn until this point, they had only placed lookouts and nothing more along this wall. That would certainly have to change. Yet they were already short of men; the ground commanders racked their brains trying to figure out where those additional defenders would come from. The only silver lining was that the Turks had not yet figured out how to fire their cannons from the bridge with any lethal degree of accuracy, which somewhat lessened the urgency of the situation.

That said, the Venetians and Genoese, sea-faring people both, knew only too well that to have anything less than perfect control of the coastal waters was to be in a very compromised position. This eased some of the tension between them. The number of small boats carrying relief supplies from Pera to Constantinople under cover of night, and the number of Galata residents who volunteered to fight alongside the defenders, increased substantially. When Venetian ships docked at Galata's ports to escape enemy cannon attack, the unpleasant awkwardness that had greeted them before was gone. The Venetians for their part stopped denouncing the Genoese. Though good fortune often brings people together, it must be said that misfortune can do the same.

Chapter Seven

The Last Push

May had arrived. Ubertino, who was guarding the stretch of the wall near Pegae Gate, suddenly felt an urge to go visit his teacher Georgios. This is not to say that the bombardment they had endured for twenty continuous days had somehow stopped. Beginning with Urban's giant cannon, the shots had rung out without pause, an average of a hundred per day. Since they were not engaging the Turks in close combat, the defensive troops' main task was to repair the daily damage done to the outer wall and the protective stockade. This had been going on for twenty days already, and so the defenders had gotten a feel for the rhythm of the attacks. When they felt it was about time for the bombardment to begin for the day, they evacuated to the safety of the inner wall. They had thus all managed to escape death, although a few had been injured by flying debris. Instead of calling the cannons "cannons," they called them "bears." The giant cannon was the "Papa Bear" and the smaller cannons to both sides of it were the "Cubs." They said things like, "The Papa Bear seems to have given up the ghost—they've replaced it with a new one," and "They've increased the number of Cubs to four today."

Of course they knew about the disastrous battle in the Golden Horn and they had seen their own ranks dwindle right before their eyes, but human beings cannot live in a state of continuous tension. As soon as he heard it was May, the young man from northern Italy thought of the larks that chirped high above the wheat fields in his hometown. He asked for a brief break from his duties, and his commander and comrades all agreed without making a fuss.

In order to get to Georgios's monastery from Pegae Gate in the southwest corner of the city, Ubertino would first have to travel east along an avenue until it met another that came down from the Gate of Charisius in the northwest, and from there proceed north towards the Golden Horn for quite some distance. But Ubertino, who knew the city very well, decided instead to take a bypath extending to the northeast that was a shortcut, a narrow road that had modest vegetable gardens between the houses. He didn't hear the singing of any larks, but the grapevines already had small green bunches growing here and there. Though this was a shortcut, he still had quite a ways to travel. He was reminded again of just how large this Byzantine capital was.

When he finally arrived at the monastery, he was surprised at how quiet it was. The monks were all there of course, but the loud fervor that had dominated the place before the siege was now completely gone. The monks were quietly walking back and forth in the cloisters and plowing their vegetable gardens; Ubertino was reminded of the monasteries in Italy.

Georgios was understandably surprised to see Ubertino open the door to his cell. Yet he didn't ask Ubertino why he was still in Constantinople; he just pushed his reading stand to one side and motioned for Ubertino to sit down. He looked closely at the young man, whom he hadn't seen in some time: with a somewhat inscrutable expression he considered Ubertino's face, which seemed to have aged five years in a flash. Georgios for his part didn't look any different to Ubertino, who was relieved that the Greek monks had stopped their ranting and raving.

"Where are you?"

Ubertino replied that he was defending the Pegae Gate. The monk replied slowly, in a deep voice:

"You realize of course that the noose is tightening. Food

shortages have begun. Supplies from Pera are now our last hope, but not all of the Galatians approve of such aid."

Ubertino, as a part of the Venetian forces, had heard such reports. He silently nodded.

"The Sultan's envoy visited this morning. He secretly docked at the port on the Marmara, so most people don't know about it. The envoy, Ismail Bey, is a Greek convert to Islam. The Sultan's terms of surrender call for the payment of 100,000 gold pieces and for the Emperor to step down. The Emperor refused."

This, Ubertino did not know. The Emperor occasionally came to the wall to express his appreciation to the defenders. The Emperor was about the same age as Ubertino's father. The young student thought of the Emperor's regal bearing, his kind words. He could hardly begrudge him his decision.

Master and disciple didn't talk of the fighting any more after that. They realized that they would both continue to hold the opinions they had held up until that point. So they spoke of philosophy instead. Ubertino was practically transported back in time to the days when he had first arrived in Constantinople, and he relished the feeling. The evening bell was ringing by the time he left the monastery. Ubertino made his usual cursory goodbyes; Georgios just smiled warmly and said nothing.

Phrantzes had once again been entrusted by the Emperor with a most difficult task: dealing with the food shortages that were prompting louder and louder complaints from the people. It was no easy challenge to feed more than 35,000 citizens plus 3,000 foreign soldiers for a total of nearly 40,000 mouths. After the arrival of the four ships on April 20th, all aid from the outside world had come to an end. The food that had been brought by the Genoese in Pera hadn't exactly come cheaply, either. As the Ottomans tightened their control of the area surrounding the settlement, the Galatians themselves had begun to experience difficulty receiving their own shipments from the outside. The number of sheep and cows that were kept in Constantinople was negligible. The vegetable gardens hardly yielded enough food in this season to make a difference.

Phrantzes went to the Emperor and told him that the funds of the state wouldn't suffice; they had no choice but to appeal for contributions from churches, monasteries, and wealthy individuals, and then use that money to try to buy as much wheat as possible, which they would then distribute sparingly to each family. The Emperor approved and Phrantzes immediately went to work. The amount they were able to collect was far below what they had expected; the Emperor once again fell into a dark mood, and at this point he was no longer able to bear hearing his people's cries for help.

The barrage continued in the meanwhile. Although the "Papa Bear" occasionally fell silent due to some malfunction or explosion, the "Baby Bears" were easy to maintain and kept roaring without missing a day. Yet since the enemy soldiers were not attacking directly, nobody was killed, and as the days passed the booming sounds of cannons created a peculiar counterpoint with the church bells tolling the hours; the people of the city had grown accustomed to this state of affairs and had almost forgotten their terror at the fact that they were under attack. The siege had now lasted a month.

On the morning of May 3rd Ambassador Minotto and

Admiral Trevisan were summoned by the Emperor, who met them with only Phrantzes at his side. Constantine XI, 49 years old, occasionally stroked his progressively graying, yet still perfectly trimmed beard as he spoke to them in a grave but warm voice.

Minotto had sent an envoy to Venice on January 26th conveying the Emperor's request for military aid. He had said that it would take two months at most for the envoy to reach Venice, but when the siege had begun in early April no reply had yet arrived. There had been reports, however, that Venice had begun assembling a fleet. The Emperor said that surely the fleet must be approaching Constantinople by now; would it be possible to send a messenger to inform the fleet of the urgency of the situation and ask them to make haste? Minotto and Trevisan readily consented to this request.

Around midnight that day a ship manned with 12 volunteers, all Venetians, snuck out of the lowered boom. It was a small boat with two masts that could also be rowed. To prepare for the possibility of being seen by the enemy, the boat was flying the Turkish flag and the crew were wearing leather outfits in the Turkish style; they capped off their disguises with turbans. They were able to sneak out without the Turks noticing and just at the opportune moment caught a strong north wind that quickly swept them southward and made them disappear from sight.

The defenders, however, confined as they were in Constantinople, didn't know what had transpired in Venice.

Minotto's messenger had arrived in Venice on February 18th, less than a month after departing Constantinople. The Senate met on the 19th. Foreign affairs were debated in the Senate and its decisions were final. They decided to send a fleet of fifteen galleys, the commander and vice-commander of which would be selected later. On the 25th, they sent word to the Pope, the Holy Roman Emperor, the King of Naples, and the King of Hungary to the effect that they had decided to send aid in response to the Byzantine Emperor's request. Needless to say they didn't neglect to urge these leaders to join them in standing up against the Ottomans.

In the shipyards of Venice preparation of the fleet bound for Constantinople took place in an atmosphere close to that of wartime. An emergency expenditure of 3000 ducats paid for the work.

On April 13th, the selection of Alvise Longo as commander of the fleet was approved. Four days later, on the 17th, he was supposed to lead the fleet out of Venice. They would first sail south down the Adriatic Sea to Modone at the southern edge of the Peloponnese, where they would restock their supplies, and then proceed straight to the island of Tenedos at the mouth of the Dardanelles. They were to wait at Tenedos until May 20th for the arrival of Admiral Jacopo Loredan's fleet from Negroponte. The two fleets, as well as a third that would arrive from Crete, would come under Loredan's unified command. The combined fleet would then proceed to Constantinople.

In the event that Loredan didn't arrive by the 20th, Longo's instructions from the Senate were to sail to Constantinople alone and ascertain the enemy's strength. After arriving at the Byzantine capital he was to report to Ambassador Minotto and Admiral Trevisan and join in the defense of the city as a part of the Emperor's navy. Under no circumstances, however, was he to sail to Constantinople before May 20th.

If everything had gone according to plan, there is a good

chance that the combined Venetian fleet, with more than 30 men 'o war galleys, among other ships, would have arrived at the capital before it fell, destroyed the Turkish fleet outside of the boom, and then worked together with the Western ships inside the boom to rout the Turkish fleet in the Golden Horn. Control of the seas would have reverted to the Christian forces, the attack from sea would have collapsed, and Constantinople would have been freed from its isolation. Thus the Emperor's hopes on May 3rd that the approaching Venetian fleet could possibly be his city's salvation were well founded.

As it happened, however, the departure of Longo's fleet of fifteen ships scheduled for April 17th was put off for two days. In Negroponte, Loredan didn't receive the order to arrive in Tenedos by the deadline of May 20th until May 7th. Not only that, but he wasn't allowed to sail directly for Tenedos—his orders from the Senate were to sail to Corfu on the other side of the Peloponnese, pick up Corfu's governor, sail back to Negroponte, where he would await the arrival of the attack group from Crete, and only then sail to Tenedos. The ever-cautious Republic of Venice sent a supplementary order the next day saying that Loredan should be accompanied by the special envoy Bartolomeo Marcello, who was to represent the Republic to the Emperor—but Marcello hadn't left Venice yet and Loredan couldn't depart until he had arrived. To arrive at Tenedos by the 20th was thus a complete impossibility. As if this weren't enough, Longo's fleet arrived at Tenedos three days behind schedule. The fact that he had been late to arrive made Longo hesitate to take the ordered action—he decided instead to wait some days for Loredan's fleet to arrive.

Since the Turks had completely sealed Constantinople off by both land and sea, there was no way for the people inside the city to know what was happening outside, and no way for those outside of the city to understand just how urgent the crisis facing the Byzantine capital was.

In Constantinople the people had become visibly agitated. The enemy's cannon barrages were relentless. The cannon in Galata kept the Christian ships anchored along the boom in a state of perpetual alarm, and the cannons along the floating bridge spanning the Golden Horn daily increased the damage to the single-layered seaward wall. But the landward wall that took the brunt of the attacks was damaged beyond compare. Tedaldi, who was defending the wall along the Imperial Palace, witnessed a cannonball lop off the entire top half of one the towers when it struck a direct hit. Along the landward wall, the worst damage was around Mesoteichion and the single-layered wall adjacent to the Imperial Palace. Constantinople, the embodiment of the brilliant history of the Byzantine Empire, was being wiped away from three directions by the artillery of Anatolian mountainfolk.

In the midst of all of this, the animosity between the Venetians and the Genoese once again exploded out of control. The Venetians, already angry at the Galatians' neutrality, were also still incensed by the debacle of the nighttime raid. They couldn't shake off the suspicion that allies such as the Genoese would sooner or later desert them and flee. The Venetians therefore proposed that all Genoese merchant ships detach their anchors and sails and put them in the possession of the Emperor, as the Venetians had done. The Genoese took offense at this and replied, "What kind of stupidity is this?

To escape would be to give up Galata, would it not? It took us two hundred years to make this city what it is: our wealth is here, our sons are here, and under no circumstances will we throw them to the wolves. This settlement is where we were born and raised. We will fight to the last drop of our blood before we give it up."

They may have been rivals, but both Venice and Genoa were mercantile states, and they could understand one another at least on this much. The Venetians held their tongues. But a flourish of rhetoric wasn't enough to make them forget or forgive the fact that the Genoese were in continuous contact with the Sultan. To which the Genoese replied that the Emperor was well aware of what their representatives were doing and that these representatives could be of use to him as well.

Indeed, the Byzantine side had not given up attempts to negotiate with the Turks. The Genoese magistrate Lomellino, knowing that Pera's fate depended on some kind of settlement, did absolutely everything within his power to bring one about. Yet Mehmed's terms were unwavering: the Byzantines must pay reparations and the Emperor must step down. If these conditions were met he would guarantee that the lives and personal property of Constantinople's citizens would be spared. Many of the top Byzantine ministers were inclined to accept these terms. There were even a few who publicly urged the Emperor to do so. The Genoese ground commander Giustiniani was even more blunt:

"Your Majesty, it is pointless to wait for some army to come and save this unfortunate city. The enemy looks very close to launching a frontal assault. If Your Majesty would consider retiring to the Peloponnese for the time being, I can assure you that if you were to assemble an army to retake the capital, I, my galley, and my men would be at your disposal."

Tears were flowing down the Emperor's cheeks. "I thank you for your counsel, from the bottom of my heart. Day and night, you and other Westerners like you grind your spirits in the defense of this city that is not even your home. But how on earth am I supposed to abandon my people? No, my friends, I cannot. I would choose rather to die, together with my people, together with my city."

The Emperor still had his hopes set on the arrival of a Venetian fleet. He and Admiral Loredan had been acquaintances for some time, and he believed that Loredan's character and competence were a more powerful ally than ten galleys.

Giustiniani's prediction had been correct. Four hours after sunset on May 7th, the Ottomans launched their second frontal assault.

The Sultan didn't repeat the mistakes of the first attack. He unleashed over 30,000 troops on a two-kilometer-long stretch of the Mesoteichion section of the wall, the section most damaged by the many days of continuous bombardment. They were opposed by a thousand-man force made up of Giustiniani's mercenaries and the Emperor's finest troops. Even if one added Cardinal Isidore's reserve army, the defenders numbered less than two thousand. As before, the Turkish troops were carrying hooked webbing and long ladders with which to scale the wall, in addition to spears and bows. They swarmed across the parts of the moat that had already been filled in with dirt.

There was no cannon fire to be heard, just the ringing of the alarm bells. The attackers were urged on by a wild jumble of drums, trumpets, and flutes. Mihajlovic was among the first wave of attackers, who clung to the outer stockades with their lives. This vanguard was made up primarily of irregulars, Christians just like the defenders. The Sultan's elite Janissaries were lined up along the edge of the moat, swords drawn, to force any of the soldiers who had lost their nerve back into the fray—those who refused to return to the fighting were cut down without a moment's hesitation. Mihajlovic could sense that his own soldiers were more afraid of the Janissaries than they were of the enemy they were fighting.

The defenders fought with savage intensity, but, in that, the attackers were not to be outdone: they had nowhere to go but forward. Those who were struck with arrows or other fire were promptly trampled underfoot. The attackers scaling the stockades were impaled with spears, while those who tried to climb up using crevices and cracks in the wall were killed too quickly by the precise jabs of the elite defenders to have time even to scream.

Yet no matter how many the brave defenders killed, there were still more behind them, and there was no way to stop fatigue from setting in. The defenders didn't have enough men to spare to fight in shifts. They couldn't bring in replacements from other parts of the wall. They didn't know when Pegae Gate to the south or the area around the Imperial Palace to the north would also come under attack. Even if the Turkish troops in those areas hadn't attacked yet, they were lined up along the wall, ready to strike as soon as the attack beacon was lit. The Turkish fleets both outside the boom and inside the Golden Horn were not attacking, but their ships were in constant motion, which made it impossible for the Christian ships to make a move.

The fighting raged for three hours. The Ottoman side suffered heavy casualties but still hadn't been able to penetrate the outer wall. Mehmed lit the blue beacon ordering the attackers to fall back. The dead were left where they lay.

The defenders only had a moment to pause. Those who had been unfortunate enough to be killed or injured were taken into the center of the city, but the remaining defenders would have to banish any thought of rest: they had to work until sunrise replacing the stockades that had been pulled down and reinforcing the damaged parts of the outer wall with sandbags.

Over the next four days, until the 11th, the Turkish bombardment grew even more intense. The fire was concentrated on the Military Gate of Saint Romanus near the center of the Mesoteichion wall and on the section of the wall encircling the Imperial Palace and facing the Golden Horn. That part of the wall was already in a precarious condition thanks to the prior bombardment of that section from the floating bridge.

At Saint Mary's Church the war council discussed ways to reinforce their ground forces. Having no choice but to try to produce something from nothing, Trevisan decided to commit his sailors to the ground effort. The sailors were not happy to be abandoning their ships, but once they heard that Trevisan would be doing the same they shelved their complaints. It was also a given that nobody would object to the fact that Trevisan was handing command of the fleet over to his second-in-command, Alvise Diedo.

Diedo had no experience in naval warfare, but he had sailed the Black Sea routes so long as a merchant captain that he knew the waters of this area by heart. This, and the fact that he was cool-headed and popular with the sailors, was the reason that Trevisan recommended him. The ship's doctor Nicolo now reported directly to Diedo. The Venetian admiral, clad in armor, his left arm in a sling, disembarked from his ship and headed for the Imperial Palace wall where he would join the defenders. Nicolo was still worried about Trevisan's left arm, which had been broken by a falling mast during the disastrous night raid. Nicolo thought, I'll have to visit him at least once a day during a lull at the clinic to tend to his arm.

As it turned out, the reinforcement of the defensive forces had almost come a hair's breadth too late. That midnight the third Ottoman assault began, this time concentrating on the wall around the Imperial Palace. Fifty thousand Turkish troops swarmed in for the attack. Furthermore, these were well-rested soldiers fresh to the battle; they had been selected from the Anatolian Corps, the European Corps, and the regiment under Zaganos Pasha. Although born in different regions, they were all ethnic Turks. The soldiers from Anatolia were bold to the point of ferocity.

Facing them were under two thousand "Latin" troops, mainly Venetians, under the command of Minotto and Trevisan. There was only one layer to the wall, in height and thickness roughly equivalent to the inner wall of the triple-layered sections. Four days of continuous bombardment had badly damaged this stretch; one of the gates had even been completely destroyed and quickly replaced by a stockade, although this would not so easily be removed by the attacking forces. Though it was a simple matter to approach the wall, there were very few who dared approach the defenders atop the wall who were braced to fight back. As might be expected, the initial hand-to-hand combat started in the area around the collapsed, stockaded gate. The faces of the defenders took on a demonic cast as they carried away their fallen comrades and killed the advancing enemy.

It was a fight to the death for the Turkish soldiers as well. There was no turning back for them, no retreat—the Janissaries were waiting behind them with their swords drawn, as before. Mehmed applied the philosophy that instilling fear in your own men, even your fellow Turks, was militarily sounder than bringing fear to the enemy.

This third assault was also unable to break through the Christian defenses. After four hours of fighting, the Turkish soldiers receded like the tide. Yet the damage was severe. Twice as many defenders had died this time as the last. Looking at the Mesoteichion wall and the wall around the Imperial Palace, it was clear even to the untrained eye that these were the places where Mehmed had focused the concentrated force of his attacks. There was nothing decisive the defenders could do in response. Quite the contrary, two days later, in the morning, a sentry posted to Caligaria Gate near the Imperial Palace saw something that made every hair on his body stand on end.

The defenders had actually already considered the possibility that Mehmed would have his men dig a tunnel underneath the wall and place explosives there. Trevisan and Giustiniani in particular had mentioned that concern to the war council soon after the siege had begun. But the Byzantine side had insisted that, although the Sultan had a great many men at his disposal, he didn't have any who had the engineering skill necessary for such a task. Voted down, the two Westerners didn't push the subject further.

It goes without saying, however, that in the process of revolutionizing the Ottoman army Mehmed the Second most certainly considered using explosives to destroy the wall. This approach didn't work terribly well at the beginning. Although the Turkish soldiers had experience in stonework from having built the *Rumeli Hisari*, they had neither the skills nor the experience to dig long, subterranean tunnels. Invariably the tunnels wound up proceeding in directions completely different from those intended and were thus useless. The Sultan ordered his generals to find soldiers with mining experience. In short order Zaganos Pasha reported that there were a number of Serbian men in his regiment who had experience in silver mines. From the next day on, the tunneling work was handed over to these specialists.

Mehmed ordered them to dig a tunnel to a point directly under the Gate of Charisius. In order not to be noticed by the defenders, the miners began digging the tunnel quite a distance away from the wall, but soon after they began they hit a dense deposit of rocks and reported that it was impossible to dig further. The Sultan ordered them to dig instead towards the Gate of the Caligaria, where the wall only had one layer.

Once again the miners began from a point far away enough not to be noticed. But one of the sentries grew suspicious when he noticed some Turkish soldiers assiduously removing dirt from an opening in the ground. The leaders of the defense grew pale when they heard this news: they had no effective counter-strategy in place. They decided to feign ignorance of what was happening for the time being while they sought out men among them who had also tunneling experience.

To their good fortune they soon found an experienced

mining engineer, a German by the name of Johannes Grant, who was a part of Giustiniani's unit and who had been fighting as a common soldier until that time. Restored to his former profession, he quickly set about planning a countermine. Chief Minister Notaras put a group of Greek soldiers under Grant's command to carry out the work.

Grant's appointed task was not only to stop the enemy's tunnel in its tracks, but also, if possible, to discourage the Turks from continuing to pursue such a strategy. He began by carefully examining the ground's surface. Since it was too dangerous to exit the castle walls, he had to do this by eye from atop the wall. If any point on the surface looked suspicious, he would immediately try to guess what route towards the wall a possible tunnel from that point would take, then order his men to begin digging a tunnel from inside the wall to intercept that route.

On May 16th, barely a day after he was discovered, Grant's abilities were irrefutably confirmed. His Greek soldiers ably dug their way right into the middle of the Ottoman tunnel, where they set fire to the wooden props holding the tunnel up. A number of the enemy miners were killed in the ensuing collapse. They had not yet been able to place their explosives under the city wall.

The Sultan, characteristically, was not in the least deterred. The Greek soldiers remained under Grant's command, while the soldiers atop the wall were ordered immediately to report any unusual movements on the enemy's part. Five days later, on the 21st, a second success further encouraged the defenders. This time the Greek diggers, intercepting a Turkish mine, used especially fumy combustibles to smoke out the Ottoman miners. Of course, the Greek soldiers also made sure to refill the tunnel they had dug out from inside the castle wall.

Their labors were made easier by the knowledge that they had succeeded. Grant and his subordinates came to believe that they could even see in the black of night. Every day for the next four days they successfully destroyed a Turkish tunnel. It appears that the Sultan gave up this strategy after six such consecutive failures since Grant, whose eyes were as keen as ever, was then relieved of his mining duties.

Yet the twenty-one-year-old Sultan had by no means stopped considering every single possibility; his mind seemed almost like a mechanical contraption that worked around the clock. On the 18th, less than two days after Grant's men first demolished one of the Turkish tunnels, the Christian defenders along the landward wall were shocked by the sight of a new monstrosity rising before their eyes.

Ubertino saw it in front of the wall, halfway between the Golden Horn and Pegae Gate. It had clearly been constructed somewhere in the rear and then pushed in the middle of the night to the edge of the moat. It was a tower, constructed of wood, taller even than the towers along the city wall. Although the interior of the tower was hidden by a covering of cow and sheep leather, there was obviously a staircase inside leading to the top. Arrows came shooting down from the top of the tower upon the soldiers defending the protective stockades.

The defenders tried to set the wooden turret on fire by shooting flaming arrows at it, without much success. Throughout the day Turkish soldiers filled in passageways across the moat while protected by arrows from their mobile tower. The moat was twenty meters across, anywhere from a meter to a meter and a half deep, and five kilometers long. Filling it in completely would have been a nearly impossible task even for the sea of men that Mehmed had at his disposal, so the fastest, most effective way for him to get his soldiers and tower closer to the wall was to fill it in up to ground level only at selected points along its length. Although this work had begun quite a bit earlier, the protection offered by the turret allowed the work to proceed much more quickly.

More turrets were added. The Sultan's plan was clear, and there was no way the defenders could allow him to see it to completion. During the night a group of them snuck out of the wall and dug holes in the passageway, filling them with powder. Since the explosives were placed close to the far edge of the moat, the booming explosions not only destroyed the passageways but collapsed and ignited the wooden tower as well.

Similar explosions followed one after the other near the Mesoteichion wall and the Gate of Caligaria near the Imperial Palace. The Turkish troops, taken by surprise, could be seen fleeing in the light of the flames, a sight which greatly lifted the defenders' spirits. The next morning the only turret that had escaped the explosions was pulled back behind the front line, to the enthusiastic cheers of the defenders.

With the exception of this and Grant's countermine successes, however, there wasn't a single bright spot for the defenders. Given the repeated battles at land and sea and the uninterrupted bombardment, the number of fatalities they had suffered was surprisingly low, but the number of injured was increasing at a faster pace with each passing day. There was no hiding from anybody that their ammunition reserves had almost reached bottom and that food was scarce. Even the women of the city were saying among themselves that the arrival of outside help was the city's last hope.

It was May 23rd, in the afternoon. A sentry on the Sea of Marmara wall saw a small ship sailing north toward the city. The Turkish fleet outside the boom also saw the approaching craft and immediately sent out a number of interdiction craft. The small boat skillfully evaded them and continued north. Since no wind was blowing it depended entirely on its oarsmen. The rowers of the pursuing Turkish ships did their best, but were no match for the superior helmsmanship and rowing of the fleeing boat. By the time that the sailors aboard the anchored Turkish fleet realized that this small boat was nothing to be trifled with and sent out another wave of interceptors, it was too late. The boat slipped in through a well-timed and very brief lowering of the boom. The news that the boat that had been sent out in search of the Venetian fleet had returned quickly spread from the dock to every corner of the city. Everybody, down to every last soldier defending the wall, was filled with the hope that they would soon hear a second report that this boat had sped ahead of the approaching fleet to inform them of its impending arrival.

Minotto and Trevisan, who hadn't even had time to change out of his filthy battle garb, quickly accompanied the captain of the scout vessel to deliver his report to the Emperor. When that report was finally delivered, not only the Emperor, but all of the members of the assembled war council were left ashen.

After the small Venetian *fusta* had safely escaped, it had proceeded south through the Sea of Marmara and then the

Dardanelles, searching for the Venetian fleet. After having traversed the Dardanelles it searched each of the surrounding isles. Yet the fleet was nowhere to be seen, and the inhabitants of the islands hadn't heard even the faintest rumors concerning its arrival. When they had been searching for around two weeks, the captain of the ship realized that any further efforts would be futile and assembled the other eleven members of the crew. He told them his opinion and then said that he would leave it up to them what to do next.

One of the sailors spoke: "Brothers, when we left Constantinople the city was daily blanketed in the fear that the enemy could launch a full assault at any moment. Perhaps we didn't say so, but I'm sure all of us felt that the Byzantine capital would certainly be destroyed by that inhuman Sultan. And this, after all, would be the result of the Greeks' own incompetence.

"Thus, having fulfilled our duty, I believe we must return to our homeland. The city has probably already fallen into the Turks' hands by now."

Another sailor asked for permission to speak. "Brothers, the Emperor asked us to seek out the fleet. We did as we were asked, though unfortunately the results of that search were not favorable. But that does not mean that our duty ends here. We are still obligated to report the results to the Emperor. I believe we must return to Constantinople. It doesn't matter whether the Turks have taken the city or it is still in Christian hands—we must return. We don't know if what awaits us there is life or death, but we do know that our duty is to turn north."

The other ten sailors, which included the captain, agreed. The one sailor who had been opposed didn't object once the matter had been decided. The small Venetian *fusta* returned to Constantinople. What the twelve sailors didn't know, however, was that Longo's fleet would arrive in Tenedos six days later.

The Emperor thanked each of the twelve men in turn, tears streaming down his cheeks. A deep gloom enveloped the chamber as all of the men present let the realization settle that no further help from the outside could be expected.

All the while, the enemy's bombardment continued with undiminished ferocity. The area around the Military Gate of Saint Romanus in particular was taking such an extensive battering that, despite the desperate attempts of the defenders to repair it, the outer wall would soon be breached. Although they did everything possible to try to repair the craters left by the "Baby Bears," the 500 kilogram projectiles of the "Papa Bear" erased any trace of their labors. Only the inner wall retained its grandeur. But the defenders didn't have the men necessary to fall back and adequately defend the inner wall. They were also too exhausted, both mentally and physically, to stage such a last-ditch defense. The tolling of the evening bell that day sounded to the people of the city like a dirge.

The fiftieth day of the siege was coming to end.

Chapter Eight

On the Verge of Collapse

The people of the city felt that there was nothing left for them now expect to pray to God. But it is easy for those who cling to one aspect of the supernatural to be seduced by all the rest of it. There were a number of old folk legends that, although nobody went so far as to mention them in public, were whispered from ear to ear.

People recalled the prophecy that the Byzantine Empire would be destroyed during the reign of a namesake of the first Emperor, Constantine. There were also those who believed that since the great Emperor's statue was pointing east with one hand, this meant that the Empire's eventual conquerors would come from the east. According to another old folk belief, Constantinople would never fall as along as the moon was waxing. Yet the 24th had been the night of the full moon, and the moon had begun to wane. This in itself was enough to terrify the populace, but that terror was compounded by the lunar eclipse that had left the city in complete darkness for three hours during the night of the full moon. For the deeply superstitious Greeks, it was difficult to imagine a more inauspicious omen: the moon was the symbol of the Byzantine Empire. The unwavering idea that God had forsaken them weighed heavily on their hearts.

The following day, the citizens walked in a procession through the city center carrying aloft an icon of Saint Mary. Every person in the city, with the exception of the defenders who had to keep to their posts, took part. When the procession reached the city center, however, the icon fell off its pedestal. The procession was stopped in the confusion, while the priests tried to lift the icon up off the ground. Although the icon was merely a wooden painting, it seemed as heavy as lead and it took the combined effort of several men finally to put it back in its place. This dragged the peoples' mood even further into darkness.

Yet there were even more bad omens in the offing. When the procession began to continue its march, a thunderstorm suddenly broke out. Torrents of rain mixed with hail descended upon them, turning the streets into rivers in a flash. The procession could move no further, and all of the assembled fled back to their respective homes. The sound of the rain seemed to continue forever, while the enemy's cannons lay silent.

The next day, the city was shrouded in a thick fog from the morning on, something completely unheard of for late May. The people whispered among themselves that this highly unusual fog must have arisen to conceal the Lord Christ and the Virgin Mother as they left the city.

The nobles of the empire once again urged the Emperor to step down in accordance with the enemy's demands. The Sultan sent another messenger telling the Emperor to choose surrender. The Emperor replied only that he would share the fate of his city and his people.

The Ottoman encampment had experienced its own disturbance that same day. Although the siege had been going on for over fifty days, Constantinople was still holding out. Despite the continuous bombardment, not a single Ottoman soldier had been able to get past the outer wall. Word had arrived that a Venetian fleet was heading for the city and could appear any day now. Nobody who had seen the weak performance of the Ottoman navy up to that point could harbor any optimistic delusions about how a sea battle with a well-armed Venetian fleet would end. Furthermore, there were rumors that the Hungarians were sending an army to aid the city. If the renowned Hunyadi breached his treaty with the Turks and brought an army across the Danube while a Venetian fleet sped towards the city, the 160,000-strong Ottoman army would be unable to continue their siege. This was the situation as the Turks saw it when they opened their own war council on the 26th.

Halil Pasha had no intention of letting the opportunity pass. He spoke forcefully:

"We must lift the siege and end the attack. There is no shame in retreating from Constantinople—the former Sultan once had to do the same. The leader of a great nation should not be rash. The countries of Western Europe cannot ignore the Byzantine Empire's pleas for help indefinitely. The Venetians have already dispatched a fleet. Sooner or later the Genoese are also going to realize that they're a Christian country too, after all. The Ottoman Empire must have the courage to choose an honorable retreat when the time is right."

The words of the old Vizier, who had more experience of statecraft than any of the other men present, seemed to have had an effect on the assembled nobles. They looked at the face of their lord, as if realizing for the first time that the Sultan was actually a young man, barely twenty-one years old. Although Mehmed kept his composure, Tursun, sitting behind him, could see that his hands were clenched in rage.

The boy page wasn't the only one who had sensed the young Sultan's anger. Zaganos Pasha rose from his seat and began an angry rebuttal of Halil's argument. "The feudal lords of Europe are fighting among themselves—anybody can see that they don't have the luxury to send a combined force to come to the Byzantines' aid. Even if the Venetian fleet arrives, they certainly won't be able to drive our army away. We have a valiant army 160,000 men strong. Have you all forgotten that Alexander the Great conquered half the world with far fewer men? Withdrawing after having reached this point is out of the question. We have one option, and one option only: to continue the attack."

The young generals, one after the other, stood up to voice their assent to Zaganos Pasha's powerful speech. All present were electrified. When Mehmed announced that the next full-frontal assault would take place in three days' time, nobody objected.

Sultan Mehmed the Second, his composure completely restored, gave each of the generals his orders. Their fleet would attack the Christian fleet from both within and without the Golden Horn. Zaganos Pasha's regiment would attack the wall facing the Golden Horn, while the remainder of the Turkish army, under the direct command of the Sultan himself, would launch an all-out attack on the entire landward wall.

The people inside the city learned of this decision almost immediately. An unknown informant fired a number of arrows with letters to that effect over the city walls.

That night the Ottoman encampment was so brightly lit up that the defenders atop the wall could make out the features of each of the soldiers grouped around their tents. Not only were their torches all lit, but they had ignited flowing streams of black oil to create a wall of fire, the light from which made the Sultan's red and gold tent stand out from the rest of the surroundings. In light almost as bright as that of the noonday sun, Turkish soldiers prostrated themselves in prayer to Allah while drums and flutes played, creating an almost demonic spectacle to the eyes of the defenders. The commotion lasted until midnight, when the camp fell silent.

The next day, the 27th, the Great Cannon, apparently exempt from the fasting, was fired off all day long. The Turkish soldiers who were neither operating nor supporting the artillery were calmly at work in the rear preparing the scaling ladders and hooked webbing. One could see the white-cloaked Sultan, atop his black stallion and surrounded by his generals, whipping like a gust of wind through the regiments, inspecting them.

On the Christian side, the front-line defenders kept their morale high despite the fact that the enemy's mass assault was drawing closer. Even Giustiniani, who had been wounded by flying debris from a cannon strike, quickly returned to his post after receiving treatment aboard his ship. Along the Mesoteichion wall, which had received the worst damage, one could see either the Emperor or Giustiniani at all times.

The Turks passed that evening in the same fury of light and sound that had marked the night before. And, just as it had the night before, the commotion gave way to quiet slumber by midnight. As for the Western troops, even when their work repairing the wall or the stockades was finished they could not leave their posts—the only rest they were allowed was a few hours of sleep huddled in a corner of one of the towers.

On the 28th, after confirming that each and all of the regiments had fallen into their previously assigned formations, the Sultan ordered a day of rest. Even the Great Cannon lay silent that day. Only the Sultan, with his ministers in train, was ever on the move, going from one unit to another exhorting them to prepare for the decisive battle. But unlike his father, who enjoyed meeting directly with his troops and raising the war cries himself to rouse his men, Mehmed preferred to leave the shouting to one of his generals. That general turned to the assembled troops and began to holler.

"His Majesty the Sultan has most graciously decreed that you will be granted three days of pillage after the city has fallen. There is no God but Allah, and Mohammed is his prophet: tomorrow's battle will be a holy war, one that will bring Mohammed's prophecy to fruition. Tomorrow we will capture a great many Christians, and sell them into slavery for two ducats apiece. All of the gold in the city will be ours. You will soon be rich men. We will weave collars for our dogs out of the Greeks' beards.

"There is no God but Allah, and we neither live nor die but out of love for Allah!"

The soldiers shouted and raised their spears and swords into the air. They believed Constantinople to be the wealthiest city in the Mediterranean, and the Sultan's decree that the riches of the city would be spread among them cast a powerful spell. Soon that wealth would actually be theirs. Their heads now clear from three days of fasting, that night they no doubt went to bed early and fell into a peaceful sleep.

At that same moment, Ambassador Minotto was addressing his Venetian countrymen, all of whom had assembled in the Venetian merchant center. Minotto, who had decided to set an example by not evacuating his wife and son from the city, spoke a few words.

"Our actions, whether they end in death or are blessed

with life, are a fulfillment of our duty as Christians. I believe that our sacrifice for our country will not be in vain. I believe our country will understand why we decided as we did, and respect our decision. When the battle begins, it would be utterly futile to abandon your post; rather choose death."

All of the Venetians were then treated to wine from their homeland. Nicolo, who was tending at that moment to the wound on Trevisan's left arm, took some small comfort in the fact that it seemed to be healing.

The bells of Constantinople's churches rang continuously throughout the day. These were not the nervous clanging of alarm bells, nor were they the long, stately pealing of funeral bells. The bells were tolling as for Mass, except, continuously: the only time in the West that bells were rung in this fashion was when a Pope had died. However, that evening, on May 28th, the people of Constantinople proceeded silently to the Church of Hagia Sophia amidst that ceaseless tolling.

In the more than five months since December 12th of the previous year, when the Mass marking the unification of the two churches took place there, the people who had opposed the unification had refused to set foot in Hagia Sophia, the city's leading church. But now they were here: perhaps they sensed that this would be their final Mass. Without anybody telling them to, the people of the city, down to the lowliest commoners, began filling the church's vast rotunda and wide halls. The Emperor was of course present, surrounded by all of the city's nobles. All of the dignitaries from the "Latin Quarter," from Ambassador Minotto down, were sitting together in a row. The rites were carried out by the Patriarch and Papal Envoy Cardinal Isidore, with the participation of the very monks who had so fiercely opposed unification. Only

Georgios was absent.

The problem of unifying the Greek Orthodox Church and the Catholic Church had consumed half a century, and had involved everything from high-level theological debates to overcoming the mutual hatred felt by the respective believers. It had left deep scars in the European psyche. Yet in that moment the unification had become a reality. When Isidore gave the brothers his benediction, the people in the hall, overflowing with religious feeling, embraced the people kneeling beside them, regardless of whether they were Greek Orthodox or Roman Catholic. When the Mass ended, they all returned to their respective homes or defensive positions.

Young Ubertino started towards Pegae Gate, tears welling in his eyes. Even the hard-headed merchant Tedaldi felt something welling up in his chest as he returned to his post on the wall along the Imperial Palace. The only Italian who hadn't been able to attend the Mass at Hagia Sophia was Nicolo, who had been busy moving the clinic from the merchant center to one of the ships.

The Emperor had invited the members of the war council for a final meeting. As Phrantzes listened on, he thanked them for their hard work and their bravery in battle. He said he was particularly grateful for the exhaustive efforts of the two Italian groups, the Venetians and the Genoese. He knew that he would be able to place his full trust in them when the final battle began, as it no doubt soon would. He then addressed his Greek subjects:

"A person must be ready to die willingly for his faith or his country, for his family or his sovereign. You must now be ready to die for all of these things. I, for my part, am ready to share your fate."

The Emperor then went from man to man, asking each of them to forgive him if he had ever done anything to give offense. The Emperor may have looked haggard, but nothing could conceal his inborn nobility; an unending stream of tears ran down his face. The assembled men, also weeping, pledged to sacrifice their lives for the Emperor. As they had done at Hagia Sophia, the men now embraced one another, showing their mutual, heartfelt trust. The Westerners then returned to their respective posts. A number of the Byzantine nobles left to join a procession carrying an icon through the city.

Phrantzes joined the Emperor as he inspected the defenses of the landward wall. Once that was done, they rode their horses to the northernmost tower by the Imperial Palace, and climbed to the top.

Two flags were flying above their heads in the evening breeze: the gold double-headed eagle on blue of the Byzantine Empire, and the gold lion of San Marco on red of the Republic of Venice. The torches next to the tents of the Ottoman army outside the city walls created a sea of light that extended all the way to the hills behind Galata. Lights could also be seen flickering aboard the Turkish ships that had begun moving in the waters outside the boom.

Constantine XI, forty-nine years old, looked at the flickering lights for a long time, saying nothing. Phrantzes, who had served at his side for over twenty years, stood behind him, also silent. The Emperor finally turned and placed a hand on the shoulder of his loyal retainer. "Please check on the reserve forces in the city and report back," he said. Phrantzes didn't want to part from his sovereign's side for even a moment during these final hours, but he couldn't bring himself to demonstrate his true feelings. He merely bowed his head and climbed down the tower's stairs. As he did so, he resolved to complete the task as quickly as possible and hurry back to the Emperor, who would be defending the Military Gate of Saint Romanus.

As it happened, he never saw the Emperor again.

Chapter Nine

Constantinople's Last Day

It was an hour past midnight. Three flares traced long, red arcs across the sky's darkness. That was the signal. A full-scale assault, with all 160,000 Turkish troops taking part, had begun.

War cries broke out across the advancing front line. The better part of the attack was focused on the Mesoteichion wall around the Saint Romanus Military Gate, as expected. The bells of the city churches began wildly ringing the alarm.

The attack started with the irregulars in the vanguard. 50,000 troops swarmed in towards the wall. They had a mismatched assortment of equipment and weapons, carrying little more than hooked ladders in addition to their spears and swords. They fought for their lives to climb the scaffolding and scale the wall, but they were met by an equally fierce defense that picked them off one by one. The cannon barrage continued even now, killing Western and Turkish soldiers alike. The sounds of kettledrums and trumpets filled the silence between cannon shots. The cries of women within the city wailing in prayer for God's mercy pierced the air, as if to try to drown out the Ottoman attackers' cacophony.

The men along the wall didn't have time for prayer. Most of the 50,000 irregulars may have been second-rate warriors, but they knew that the fearsome Janissaries were waiting behind them, swords drawn: retreat was not an option. Despite this, the first wave of Turkish attackers suffered severe casualties and, two hours into the attack, appeared to be pulling back.

Mehmed was fully aware of the irregular troops' shortcomings and had planned his strategy accordingly. They may have been disorganized and poor fighters, but they had served the purpose of tiring the defenders. As soon as the first wave was pulled back, the Sultan ordered the second wave to commence without giving the defenders even a moment to catch their breath.

A regiment of over fifty thousand well-trained regular troops, dressed in identical red turbans and white uniforms, marched forward in orderly ranks. Half of them pretended to be attacking the entire length of the landward wall, which kept the defenders pinned down, while the remaining half concentrated on Mesoteichion.

Even though this second wave of soldiers was made up of his fellow Turks and Muslims, Mehmed continued the cannon bombardment. When a section of scaffolding near the Saint Romanus Military Gate was blown to pieces by a direct hit, a troop of Turkish soldiers who were attempting to climb over the fence at that exact spot were blown sky high. Nothing was visible in the thick dust and smoke. A group of two hundred Turkish soldiers managed to penetrate a breach in the outer wall in the confusion. Most of them were killed by defenders, who were quick to rush to the scene, and the rest were driven back and thrown into the moat. It was the same thing over and over: when the dust kicked up by a cannonball cleared up a bit, the defenders would resume killing and repulsing new incoming troops. Yet even before they had the chance to resolve this match, the third wave quietly drew closer.

In the pale light of the clouded-over moon, the Sultan's trusted Janissaries were approaching the wall. Wearing identical white caps and white uniforms with green belts, they crossed the moat in perfect formation. Unlike the first two regiments, the Janissaries were careful not to rush forward recklessly. When one of their number was shot down by enemy fire, they merely pushed him to the side indeed as if this had been part of the plan, and continued marching without breaking ranks. Even the tips of the scimitars they held in their right hands formed a perfect, unbroken line.

Mehmed was not content to stay in the rear watching the battle. He was at the outward edge of the moat screaming at his soldiers, exhorting and scolding them in turn. Tursun was aghast. The position where the Sultan was standing was well within range of the city wall. Although Tursun normally attended upon Mehmed kneeling on one knee, he had more important things to worry about now: he stood up to his full height and spread his arms to protect his lord. The thought never entered his mind that he was putting himself at risk.

The Janissaries responded to their Sultan's encouragement and fought with renewed daring. These 15,000 elite troops had been committed, all of them, to the Mesoteichion wall, which was less than two kilometers long. Each division took its turn advancing toward the wall, and as they repeated these waves of attack in strict order, the number of soldiers who were able to make it to the wall increased steadily.

The defenders, who had to fight new waves of fresh enemy soldiers without any rotation of their own, held up well. In particular, the soldiers along the Mesoteichion wall had, at the suggestion of the ground commander Giustiniani, locked all of the portals leading from the outer wall to the inner wall and given the keys to the Emperor. In other words, they were determined to defend at the outer wall or die. They had ceased to be Greeks or Genoese or Venetians: they were fighting as one. Giustiniani was also fighting with impressive valor, rather surprisingly for one who was quite young and a mercenary no less. Even the Emperor had his sword drawn and was fighting the Turks at the wall.

This fierce close-quarter fighting continued for over an hour. Even the Janissaries, the highly esteemed backbone of the Ottoman army, were unable in that time to score a decisive victory. Attackers and defenders swarmed together into whirling clumps of men and then broke apart again. The first light of dawn began to fill out the sky, lightly at first but steadily growing brighter. The battle had been raging for five hours.

Just as the sun was rising, an arrow fired at point blank range hit Giustiniani right above his left collarbone. As he was reeling from the shock, a second arrow struck his right thigh. Blood began pouring out of the cracks in the young commander's silver-colored armor. Screaming from the intense pain, Giustiniani asked one of his subordinates, who had come running to his aid, to take him back to his ship. This soldier knew that the doors leading from the outer wall to the inner wall and from there to the city proper were all locked. He rushed to the Emperor to ask for the keys.

The Emperor rushed through a passageway between the outer wall and the scaffolding to come to Giustiniani's side. He knelt down next to Giustiniani, took his hand, and asked him to reconsider his decision to leave. Yet it seems that the commander, who had just shown such valor, had suddenly been startled by the sight of his own blood back into an awareness of his youth and everything still left to live for. He paid no attention to the Emperor's entreaties and repeated his desire to leave the front. The Emperor reluctantly handed the keys over to Giustiniani's aides, who carried their commander away to safety.

This incident didn't go unnoticed by the five hundred

Genoese soldiers under Giustiniani's direct command. They were, in the final analysis, mercenaries, professionals. They could fight as bravely as anybody when the battle ran in their favor, but they were also the first to flee at the signs of approaching defeat. When they saw their commander being taken away, the battle was effectively over as far as they were concerned. *En masse* they made a break for the door through which Giustiniani had just been carried. The Greek soldiers, the Emperor first and foremost, attempted to stop them. The Sultan, who was at the edge of the moat, noticed that some unexpected disturbance had arisen within the city walls. In a voice louder than any he had ever wrung out he bellowed: "The city is ours to take!"

The Janissaries were completely transformed. Now they rushed as one toward the city wall to attack, and no longer were they driven back. Those who made it over the scaffolding clambered up the outer wall without a moment's rest. The defenders were finally being pushed back. Hoping to escape they jammed into the corridor between the outer and inner walls. The Turkish soldiers, who now occupied the outer wall, picked them off with their arrows, one after another.

The defenders along the Imperial Palace were by no means spared either. There were now too many Turkish soldiers pushing their way through breaches in the wall to repel. When one of the gates was demolished and the Turks started streaming in, all hope was lost. There were some Venetians who kept fighting regardless, but once they saw that the Imperial and Venetian flags flying from the tower had been taken down and replaced by the white crescent moon and star on red, they too had to concede defeat. Trevisan shouted out the order for his men to retreat to the Golden Horn.

The Emperor, too, saw the Turkish flag flying atop the tower. He mounted his white steed, and began to ride to the Military Gate of Saint Romanus. He intended to encourage his men there not to give up the fight, but the Greek soldiers had seen the red flag as well. And they were routing. Pandemonium ensued as they all scrambled in search of some means of escape. The Turkish soldiers, who had already sealed all of the outer wall's exits, slaughtered them like wolves let loose in a flock of sheep.

The Emperor realized that the end had come. He had a mere three riders in his train: a Greek knight, a Spanish noble, and one born in Dalmatia. The four of them dismounted their horses. They intended to continue fighting on foot, but the chaos around them made even that impossible. The Greek knight, who also happened to be the Emperor's cousin, shouted out that he would rather die than be captured and then cut his way into the fray.

The Emperor flung away his crimson cloak. He tore away his Imperial regalia. Somebody is reported to have heard him say, "Isn't there a single Christian here who will kindly plunge a sword into my heart?"

The final Emperor of the Eastern Roman Empire drew his sword and rushed into an approaching wave of Turkish soldiers, where he disappeared, never to be seen again. The two remaining knights followed him.

Beacons announcing that the wall had been breached lit up all across the Ottoman encampment. They didn't glow as brightly in the morning sunshine as they would have at night, but the Turkish troops' eyes were sharpened by anticipation. The entire army cheered with joy and rushed towards the city walls. The soldiers who had continued defending Pegae Gate up until this point, unaware of what had happened, couldn't have mistaken that cheer for anything other than what it was; they too began to flee for their lives. The only means of escape were the allied vessels docked along the Golden Horn, but Pegae Gate was about as far from the Horn as it was possible to get. They rushed about, eyes blinded by fear. Turkish soldiers who had made it over the wall arrived at that moment and opened the gate from the inside; a flood of Turkish soldiers rushed through it. The Golden Gate, through which the Emperors always passed when returning from a triumphant campaign during the empire's brighter days, was left standing practically unharmed. A swarm of Turkish troops entered unhindered through that gate as well.

Although the Marmara wall hadn't come into play at all during the weeks of the siege, it did see action on that morning of May 29th. When the signal came that the wall had been breached, the Turkish fleet wasted no time in sailing south and dropping anchor at two small docks facing the Sea of Marmara. The residents near the docks, perhaps realizing that resistance was futile, quickly opened the gate for the disembarking Turkish sailors and prostrated themselves. Within minutes a swarm of Turkish soldiers had surrounded the Ottoman pretender Prince Orhan and his men. Knowing the fate that awaited them if they were captured and brought before the Sultan, Orhan and his men boldly engaged a contingent many times their own size. The Prince then mounted his horse and impaled himself on a sword that one of his men had thrust out for him.

The Spanish consul Pere Julia and his Catalonian soldiers also put up tenacious resistance, fighting until the last man had either been killed or captured. For Cardinal Isidore, who was defending the stretch of the wall just north of Julia's, things were not so simple. Since it was felt from the beginning of the siege that the enemy wouldn't focus on this section of the wall, he had sent most of his men to help defend the landward stretch and had almost no men left to defend and fight alongside him. Furthermore, Isidore was not only the Patriarch of Constantinople but also the Papal Envoy. He would no doubt be the second most wanted man in the city after the Emperor. If he were captured and his identity became known, it would be as if the Pope himself, God's earthly agent and representative of all Catholic believers, had been taken prisoner by a Muslim lord. As these unpleasant thoughts were running through his mind, Isidore noticed a beggar stumbling by.

News of the rout didn't become known to everybody in the vast city right away. The first to know were those who saw defenders fleeing from the Turkish soldiers bearing down upon them. Knowing that all was lost, a few people ran in the direction of the Golden Horn, but the Greeks for the most part escaped to Hagia Sophia at the eastern edge of the city. Legend had it that if the city ever fell, the archangel Michael would descend to the top of the Hagia Sophia's dome and sweep the invaders away to the eastern shore of the Bosphorus. The rotunda of the gigantic Hagia Sophia was soon filled with refugees. They closed and locked the church's bronze doors, and knelt down to pray.

When the Christian fleet anchored in the Golden Horn saw the Turkish flag unfurled atop the Imperial Palace's tower and heard the numerous signals, they knew that the walls had been breached. Bracing for an attack from the enemy ships both within the Golden Horn and outside the boom, the ships sailed into a defensive formation. But sailors in the Ottoman fleet had other things on their mind than attacking the Christian fleet: namely, they were worried that the Turkish ground forces would get all of the spoils by sacking the city before they would have a chance at them. This was why the Ottoman ships outside the boom had rushed to the docks along the Marmara without paying the Christian fleet any attention at all. The Turkish ships inside of the Golden Horn rushed towards the gate near the Imperial Palace, where Zaganos Pasha's troops had already started pouring into the city, and joined the pillage.

For the Christian fleet this was like a gift of good fortune from the heavens above. Diedo, who had taken over as naval commander in Trevisan's absence, ordered his ships to dock along the city wall, bows pointed outward to facilitate a quick escape, and pick up as many refugees as possible. Once that was well underway, he and another captain and Nicolo boarded a small boat and began rowing across to Galata.

Magistrate Lomellino was waiting for them on the other side. Diedo spoke first: "I'd like to ask what the Galatians' intentions are now. Do you all intend to stay and fight, or do you intend to escape? If you are willing to fight, we promise to fight by your side."

Lomellino seemed at a loss. Right before the final assault one of the Sultan's emissaries had come to reconfirm Galata's neutrality. But who could say if that was a guarantee of anything?

"Could you give us a little time?" Lomellino finally said, making no effort to hide his consternation. "I would like to send a messenger to the Sultan to see if he would be willing to extend his peace terms not only to the Genoese but to the Venetians as well."

Diedo felt that such a thing was an absolute impossibility this late in the game, but all he could do was look at Lomellino with barely suppressed disdain and remain silent.

When the three turned around to board their boat and return to the Constantinople side, they discovered that all the gates to the settlement had been locked shut behind them. Yet, not all of the Genoese in Pera who saw what was happening across the Golden Horn could remain so callous. After some of these Genoese opened one of the gates for them, the three stepped out onto the dock to see that there were many Genoese and their families who didn't trust the Sultan's word and were boarding ships to escape.

The flood of escapees was reaching its peak back on the Constantinople side when they arrived there. The dock was overflowing with refugees, so much so that some people actually fell into the water. Even then the Venetian sailors never lost their nerve as they continued pulling people one by one aboard ship.

The sun approached its zenith. The number of people jamming onto the dock began to decrease. Although he should have been tending to the wounded, Nicolo was standing at the ship's stern, looking around. Trevisan was nowhere to be found. Ambassador Minotto and the other Venetian notables were not among the refugees, nor could they be seen on any of the other ships.

Diedo decided that it was too dangerous to stay in port any longer, and ordered his galley's anchor raised. He sent a signal to the other ships to do the same and follow his ship's lead out of the Golden Horn.

Yet there were still people left on the dock. Seeing that the rescuers were leaving, they began jumping into the water and swimming for the ships, which were leaving dock much slower than usual, as if reluctant to do so. Those who managed to make it to the ships were lifted to safety. Nicolo's ship rescued one poor fellow who had jumped into the water, unable to swim yet thrashing about for dear life until the rope to survival, and escape, was lowered to him. It was the Florentine merchant Tedaldi. Among the refugees huddled like corpses aboard the ships, the figure of the young student from Brescia was nowhere to be seen. And Admiral Trevisan, whose very presence was enough to put those around him at ease, never did make it to the dock.

Diedo's lead galley approached the boom, still stretched taut across the Golden Horn. Two soldiers got in a rowboat and rowed to the Constantinople side, where they cut the leather strap latching the boom to the tower. The boom slowly drifted away.

The galleys slipped through the opening. Seven Genoese boats fleeing Galata followed in their wake, which were in turn followed by a Venetian naval galley under Captain Morosini and a Venetian merchant galley. The movements of this last ship were rather hesitant: over a hundred and fifty of its crew, who had been fighting as part of the defense, hadn't returned. That ship was followed by Trevisan's galley, which, while not as understaffed as the ship ahead of it, was missing its captain. Then came two more Genoese vessels, and finally four Cretan ships filled with many Greek refugees.

Still in the Golden Horn were at least ten Byzantine ships, a few Genoese ships, and perhaps twenty other vessels including Venetian freighters. Diedo decided he would wait at the mouth of the Bosphorus for an hour in case any of these ships made it out with more escapees. In the end, none did.

Diedo also couldn't neglect his main duty, which was to be prepared for an Ottoman attack. A strong wind was blowing from the north-northwest, but it could change direction at any moment. He had to give the order to flee before this wind let up or changed direction—there might not be a second chance. When he conveyed his thoughts to the captain of one of the Genose vessels, the captain replied, "We have large sails; as long as the wind is favorable we can move very fast. We can wait for the time being, say, until sunset."

Diedo knew that the seven large Genoese galleys were well fortified and that he thus had no reason to worry. He ordered all but these Genoese boats to set off.

It was a little past 2 p.m. The four Venetian ships and the four Cretan galleys caught the strong north wind and began sailing south down the Sea of Marmara. Ahead of them was Negroponte, which, now that Constantinople had been lost, was the front line facing the Ottomans. As the boats sailed away, all on board stared back blankly at the city of Constantinople. Even the battle-tested sailors aboard the Venetian naval galleys couldn't tear their eyes away from the city slowly receding on the horizon, "The City of Romans at one with Christ."

There was no military discipline among the 160,000 Ottoman soldiers who had swarmed into the city, only the sheer intoxication of pillage. Each man was allowed to keep whatever he could carry over the next three days. The Greeks quickly caught on to the fact that their lives would be spared as long as they didn't resist.

In fact, those killed numbered less than 4,000. Within the context of the conquest of a city of 40,000, that number was not considered particularly high at the time. Most of those who were killed died right after the Ottomans breached the wall: refusing to believe that the defending combatants could have numbered less than 8,000, the Turkish soldiers were goaded mainly by fear to kill everybody they encountered. This was also the reason why most of the defenders along the wall were also killed. The blood of the dead flowed through the streets near the wall like water after a heavy rain.

It was said among the Greeks that even a Turk who has killed his own parents would rather sell you into slavery and make some money; as long as you didn't resist they would spare your life and just take you prisoner. Thus most of the citizens who couldn't escape were taken captive. The people hiding in Hagia Sophia also didn't resist and simply let themselves be tethered together by the Turkish soldiers wielding curved swords. The Ottoman soldiers made no special allowances for the many monasteries and nunneries in the city. Although there were a few nuns who chose death by throwing themselves into wells instead of falling into the hands of the heathens, most of the ecclesiastics were admirably loyal to their oaths and quietly submitted themselves as their superiors had told them to. Those who were killed despite the fact that they didn't resist included the elderly, who were considered worthless as slaves, and infants.

The captives, regardless of status or gender, were lined up in two rows. They were forced to march back to the Ottoman camp tied together with bits of rope and common silk scarves. Screams could be heard when a beautiful woman or youth was dragged out of the line to be raped by a Turkish soldier. Other than that, the captives walked along as meekly as a flock of sheep, their eyes empty of all hope.

It goes without saying that the Imperial Palace and churches were thoroughly looted, but then so were people's homes. The Turkish soldiers fought with one another for the richest spoils, and anything they didn't want was destroyed or burned on the spot. Many icons were split in two and burned. Crucifixes were discarded once their jeweled ornaments were hammered off and taken away.

Mehmed spent the morning meeting with Galatian emissaries and with Byzantine nobles who had been captured and brought before him. His main interest was the Emperor's whereabouts.

The Byzantine nobles said that all they had heard was that the Emperor had disappeared in the fighting. Two Turkish soldiers appeared, saying that the Emperor had been beheaded, and placed the severed head in front of the nobles for confirmation. The nobles all agreed, without exception, that it was in fact the Emperor. Mehmed ordered the head displayed on a column near the great hall of Hagia Sophia. The two soldiers added that the corpse was wearing stockings embroidered with eagles: this was proof enough for Mehmed that the Emperor was in fact dead.

After the audience concluded, the young victor retired to his private partition to prepare himself for his triumphant entrance into the city. He tied the green belt to his white robe, and put on his white damask cloak and white turban with a glittering green emerald in the center. The scimitar hanging from his belt was made from a gold so bright it was almost painful to behold.

Once his dress was completed, he ordered Tursun to bring his white horse to the front of the tent. Tursun doubted his ears for moment; he had thought that the Sultan would enter the city on the black horse that had served him during the fifty-six days of the siege. But he soon understood his lord's wishes. He bowed politely, and left to tell the head groom to prepare a white steed.

At two p.m., the twenty-one-year-old Sultan, followed by his ministers, his generals, his *imams*, and guarded by his elite Janissaries, entered Constantinople through the Gate of Charisius. As if wishing to savor his new possession as deeply as possible, he reined his horse to a slow trot as the procession moved along the main thoroughfare. He didn't so much as glance at the soldiers busy in their pillaging, or at the citizens silent in their captivity.

When he arrived at the entrance to the Hagia Sophia, Mehmed the Second dismounted his horse. He bowed down, took a handful of dirt, and slowly let it fall upon his white turban. Tursun and the rest assembled all understood that, with this gesture, the usually haughty lord was humbling himself before Allah.

The Sultan stood up and walked into the Hagia Sophia. The Greeks who had been hiding there had almost all been taken away; all that remained were a handful of old monks huddled in a corner. The Sultan noticed a Turkish soldier trying to pry free a marble stone from the floor, and for the first time since entering the city he became angry. The soldiers had only been given permission to enslave the people and take their possessions; it had been declared that the city, and all of the buildings in it, belonged to the Sultan and him alone. The soldier was driven out of the building. The Sultan then turned to the huddled monks, anger now gone from his voice, and told them simply to return to their monasteries.

The Sultan walked further into the rotunda, and stared, almost admiringly, at the deluge of colors afforded by the mosaics along the walls. But in due course he turned to his ministers and told them that the church must immediately be converted into a mosque. The first step would be to scrub the mosaics clean.

One of the *imams* mounted the pulpit, and began to chant: *There is no God but Allah* . . . Mehmed ascended to the altar, pressed his forehead to the ground, and gave his prayers of thanks to the God who had bestowed him with victory.

After the prayers were finished, the Sultan and his retinue visited the dilapidated Old Imperial Palace nearby. They then proceeded to the ancient Coliseum, also long neglected. After that they followed another wide boulevard to the Pegae Gate, from whence they exited and returned to their encampment. In all that time, no shots were fired, and nobody among the conquered dared to block the Sultan's way. The city of Constantinople had completely submitted to Mehmed the Second.

The Byzantine Empire had been wiped from the face of the earth. The Turkish Empire appeared in its place.

Chapter Ten

Epilogue

When the city fell, Phrantzes, along with the Greek soldiers around him, was surrounded and captured by the advancing Ottoman army. He had been on his way back to the Emperor after having checked on the reserve forces as ordered. His unassuming personality, his unimposing physique, and the fact that he wasn't wearing garments suitable to his station all led the Turkish soldiers to mistake him for a commoner. There was no way for them to guess that he was not only the Minister of Finance, but also one of the Emperor's closest confidants.

He was thrown in with the soldiers, who were made to form two columns like the other captives. They were taken to the Ottoman encampment outside of the city. There they were split into groups, and Phrantzes spent the next month penned together with other Greeks like domesticated animals outside of the tent of the Turkish soldiers who had become their new masters.

On June 22nd, Mehmed entrusted the administration of his recently conquered city to a minister and returned to Adrianople. Phrantzes was thrown in with a long train of captives who were sent along with Mehmed as part of his caravan. The number of prisoners sent with him was so large that when the Sultan's white horse at the head of the train had disappeared over the horizon, the people at the end of the caravan were still within the city walls.

During this period, Phrantzes's foremost concern was the location of the Emperor's remains. Word that the Emperor had heroically died in battle quickly spread among the prisoners and was doubted by no one, but not a single person could say with certainty where his body was. Somehow Phrantzes could not bring himself to believe that the head in Mehmed's possession actually belonged to the Emperor, yet, chained as he was to the other prisoners, there was no way for him to go and see the head for himself. Phrantzes, however, could take comfort in the fact that the emperor whom he had served with such devotion, who had secretly hoped to die, could meet his end in a heroic manner befitting the last emperor of the Byzantine Empire.

The whereabouts of his wife and children, his second concern, were also difficult to ascertain. Yet since all of the captives had similar worries, an information-sharing network quickly fell into place and news was there to be had if one paid sufficient attention. Phrantzes soon learned that his wife had become the property of some Turk. After he arrived in Adrianople, he found out that both his son and daughter were among the young slaves whom the Sultan had handpicked to serve in his palace.

Phrantzes become a slave of the Sultan's head groom. His first order of business was to find some way to buy his freedom back. Greeks in the still Greek-controlled Peloponnese as well as those in Turkish-controlled lands spared no effort to aid their enslaved brethren in Constantinople. After eighteenth months of servitude, Phrantzes was finally able to buy back his freedom with money borrowed from one of those free Greeks. Next he sought to free his wife and, with the help of a number of people familiar with Phrantzes's long years of devoted service, was able to do so.

But the fate of his children, as he later learned, was a truly pitiful one. His daughter died soon after being placed in the Sultan's harem. His son, only eighteen years old, was put to death after resisting the Sultan's advances.

There was no longer any reason or need for Phrantzes and

his wife to remain in the Ottoman-ruled land; they went to the Peloponnese to seek the protection of the Emperor's younger brother Thomas Paleologos. Phrantzes served there in Thomas's court until 1460, when Mehmed conquered that region as well and he and Thomas were forced to flee to the Venetian-owned island of Corfu. He continued to serve as a member of Thomas's court-in-exile, traveling to all of the Italian principalities, but mainly Rome and Venice, as Thomas's ambassador. In 1468, perhaps prompted by the death of his wife, he entered a monastery and spent the remaining years until his death in 1477 writing his *Chronicle*. This document, given Phrantzes's privileged position, became the most important historical document of the last days of the Byzantine Empire.

*

Chief Minister Notaras, whom Phrantzes secretly resented as the source of so many of his beloved Emperor's difficulties, suffered a different sort of drama.

When he was captured along with the rest of the ministers, his identity was obvious to all. Rumor had it that Notaras had come before the Sultan offering money and treasure; whether this was true or not, it is a fact that the Sultan showed leniency at first toward him and the other ministers; he even visited Notaras's ailing wife. Thus the high Byzantine nobles began to nurse some hopes for a brighter future. But somebody seems to have whispered in the Sultan's ear that Notaras had a young son of truly exceptional beauty, and it was only a matter of time before the Sultan sent a messenger asking for the son to be brought to him.

Epilogue

At this point, Notaras, a member of the imperial family, suddenly seemed to remember that he had noble Byzantine blood in his veins. He flatly refused the conqueror's order. The Sultan's response was swift: they were all beheaded. Notaras appealed to the soldiers who were to carry out the punishment to kill his young son first so that the boy would not have to witness his own father's death. After the boy and his cousin of the same age were killed, Notaras presented his own neck. Mehmed saw this turn of events as an opportunity to liquidate all of the remaining Byzantine ministers and did so. In actuality, Mehmed had intended from the very beginning to do away with the entire Byzantine ruling class: it had just been a matter of when.

Notaras's wife, who had become the highest ranking lady of the Empire after the Empress-Mother's death, fell ill and died as she was being sent to Adrianople. The only remaining survivor in Notaras's family was his daughter, who had been sent before the siege to Venice with most of the family's wealth.

*

Cardinal Isidore, so deeply hated by the anti-unificationists that he and Notaras could barely exchange words at the war council meetings, was also captured by the Ottoman soldiers. A bandage covering a wound to his head partially hid his face, and he had exchanged his resplendent armor for a beggar's rags; thus the Ottoman soldiers who captured him had no idea that he was the second-most wanted man in Constantinople, the envoy of the Pope. Hearsay had it that the hapless beggar with whom Isidore had exchanged clothes was immediately beheaded upon capture.

Isidore's luck continued to hold out. The Turkish soldiers who owned him and his fellow captives were in a hurry to get some money, so they took him and their other slaves to the Genoese settlement in Pera for a quick sale. He was thus spared the ordeal of the forced march to Adrianople. The Genoese man who bought this group of slaves and immediately set them free apparently had no idea that the Isidore was among them. Isidore spent the next eight days in Galata in hiding, moving from house to house, but things became even more dangerous for him when the Sultan demanded that Pera surrender and it too came under Turkish control.

Disguised as a low-class Greek, the cardinal boarded a Turkish boat bound for Asia Minor. After a very arduous journey from Asia Minor, he finally arrived at the Genoese colony of Fochea. Some of the residents there recognized him, to his great distress: although the region was nominally under Genoese control, it was surrounded by Ottoman territory. He decided he would have to flee yet again. He hired a small boat, and succeeded in reaching the Genoese-controlled island of Chios. Knowing that he could still be recognized at any time, he sought refuge aboard a Venetian ship that was about to set sail for Crete. Only upon reaching Crete was he able, for the first time, to feel at ease. Crete was far from the Ottoman lands and it was a colony of Venice, the only country that had made its anti-Ottoman position crystal clear.

He spent approximately six months on Crete. Here he wrote two letters to the Pope, one to his good friend Bessarion, one to the Doge of Venice, and one addressed to all Catholic believers. In these letters he described the circumstances surrounding Constantinople's conquest in great detail.

Epilogue

He is believed to have returned to Rome by way of Venice at the end of November of that year. He worked tirelessly to bring about an anti-Turkish crusade but died in 1463, ten years after the fall of Constantinople, without ever seeing that wish become a reality.

*

Unlike Notaras, who resisted unification with the Catholic Church only passively, Georgios had fought it tooth and nail. He too was taken captive when the city fell. All of the Ottoman troops knew that the churches and monasteries possessed great wealth, and Georgios's own monastery certainly didn't escape thorough pillaging. His monks followed his orders not to resist, and quietly handed themselves over to their captors.

Along the way to Adrianople, Georgios tried to encourage and give comfort to his wretched fellow prisoners. Despite his threadbare clothing, his noble manner and majestic physique commanded respect. Perhaps for this reason the Turkish soldiers granted his request to be unbound so that he could minister last rites to those who could carry on no longer.

Because the soldiers didn't know exactly what position Georgios occupied, it took a long time for Mehmed to find him, despite the fact that he had actively tried all possible means to do so. When Mehmed finally found him, serving as a slave in the home of a wealthy Turk, he summoned him immediately.

Mehmed's campaign for Constantinople had not merely been some rash, youthful bid to accomplish something his father had failed to do. His ambition was to expand his

empire to encompass the Byzantine Empire in all of its former glory—in other words, to occupy the entire eastern
Mediterranean. This would not be possible unless the crossroads of that region, namely Constantinople, were his, and
that, more than anything, was why he had so desperately wanted "that city."

Mehmed had decided to make Constantinople, not
Adrianople, the capital of the empire he was to build. The
administration of such a large metropolis could not be left
only to Turks who had no experience of such things—he
needed Greeks as well, Greeks well versed in the ways of the
eastern Mediterranean.

Yet, for the Sultan to be able to give them this kind of
authority, he had to be sure that the Greeks would understand
themselves to be his subjects. As long as they were willing to
submit to Turkish rule, they would be rewarded with the
recognition of their Greek Orthodox faith and the guarantee
of their safety and freedom. Mehmed was certain that the one
person who could help him make this mutual understanding a
reality was Georgios.

When Georgios appeared before him, the Sultan asked
him—indeed, it was less an order than a plea—to become the
Patriarch of Constantinople. This, in effect, meant that
Georgios would become the spiritual leader of all Greeks.
Given the circumstances, Georgios was understandably reluctant, but in the end he decided to accept this very difficult
duty. He and Mehmed the Second reached an agreement that
Constantinople's Greeks would enjoy the same rights as
Greeks in territories previously taken by the Turks: as long as
they accepted Turkish sovereignty and periodically allowed
young boys to be drafted into the Janissaries, they would be

granted religious autonomy and their freedom and personal safety would be guaranteed.

Georgios served as the Patriarch from January 1454 to the spring of 1456. During this time one church after another was converted into a mosque and even the patriarch's own church was moved several times. In the midst of all this, he worked tirelessly for the benefit of those Greeks who had been forcibly relocated to Constantinople, and he wrote many appeals and letters of counsel to those who continued to hold their Orthodox beliefs even while living under Turkish rule. Mehmed, who greatly respected the depth of Georgios's learning, visited him often. An explanation of Christianity's fundamental principles that Georgios had prepared for the Sultan was soon translated into Turkish.

After resigning as Patriarch, Georgios entered a monastery at Mount Athos, where he lived from the summer of 1456 to 1457. But unable to refuse Mehmed's persistent requests, he served as Patriarch a second time from 1460 to 1464. In 1465 he was finally able to return to the monastic life he had been longing for. He died in 1472 a simple monk. By that time Constantinople's many church steeples had been replaced with minarets.

He also left a historical document, "A Letter to Believers about the Siege of Constantinople."

It is probably safe to say that the next four hundred years (until the Greeks gained their independence from Turkish rule in the nineteenth century) were proof enough that Georgios's insistence on purity and unity of belief, even if it meant the destruction of their country, was far more effective in maintaining the resilience of Greek Orthodox believers than

Isidore's policy of religious compromise for the purpose of saving the country. For those of us who oppose fanaticism, it is rather depressing that it should not be reason, but fanaticism which excludes it, that effectively maintains strong faith, but it is alas true that such examples are legion.

The Greek Orthodox believers differed from other fanatical Christians such as the early believers who gladly martyred themselves in the jaws of lions, or the Japanese Christians who died rather than become apostates, in that they were willing to compromise in those things which were *not* essential to their belief while refusing to compromise at all in those things that *were*. It was this particular mix that allowed them successfully to maintain their faith through four centuries of occupation. Georgios, for his part, seemed to understand from the beginning that, although they were Muslims, the Turkish people were tolerant of other religious beliefs.

✳

Georgios's pupil Ubertino, who revered his teacher but who still, in the end, behaved like a Westerner, was also one of those taken prisoner. He had been defending Pegae Gate; he knew that he would be saved if he could make it to the Venetian boats in the Golden Horn and proceeded in that direction, but was surrounded and captured by a Turkish contingent on the way. The soldiers who captured him also desired quick cash, and so he was sold to a Florentine merchant in Galata. The merchant agreed to let him go on the understanding that Ubertino's parents would reimburse the man upon Ubertino's return to Italy.

Now a free man again, Ubertino boarded a ship bound for

Italy which, unfortunately, was attacked by pirates en route. He was taken prisoner once again, and would either be sold or spend the rest of his days as a galley slave. He was saved, however, when the pirates' ship was attacked by the Knights of Saint John and he was taken by the Knights to their base on the island of Rhodes. After spending a short time on Rhodes, he returned to Venice by way of Crete, made a very brief stop in his hometown of Brescia, and then proceeded to Rome where he had been summoned to serve as Cardinal Capranica's secretary.

He seems to have spent about three years in Rome. During this time he composed a lengthy epic with the title of "Constantinopolis." As a scholar of antiquity, he felt compelled to leave a record of his powerful impressions of the empire, and the civilization, that he had seen destroyed before his eyes. After his service in Rome, he returned to his home town and lived a quiet life as a teacher of Greek philosophy, translator, and poet. He is believed to have died in 1470.

*

Although he had no interest in ancient civilizations whatsoever, and no special interest in the question of religious unification, Tedaldi shared with the other "eyewitnesses" a desire to tell others of his experience of Constantinople's historically momentous fall.

The Florentine merchant, who was paradoxically saved by the fact that he had forgotten that he couldn't swim, boarded a boat leaving the Venetian naval base at Negroponte six days after the city's collapse. While the Venetians consulted with one another over their next course of action, Tedaldi passed his days telling his tale to a Frenchman who happened to be staying in Negroponte.

This Frenchman quickly translated Tedaldi's story into French and sent it to the Archbishop of Avignon. This document quickly spread around France, where the Crusading spirit was strong, and became a rallying point for the pro-Crusade faction across Europe, earning the endorsement even of Pope Nicolo V. Tedaldi became better known in France than in his native Italy. Fifteen years later, in 1468, Tedaldi's chronicle, which had been concise but rather crude in literary terms, was reworked into a proper history and came to be considered the pre-eminent historical work in France concerning the fall of Constantinople.

Although we know that he arrived in Venice on June 4th and departed for Florence on July 5th of 1453, no historical records remain of what became of him afterwards. In all likelihood he spent the rest of his days in the city of his birth, perhaps chuckling to himself every now and then at the fact that he was now a celebrity in France.

*

The Venetian and Cretan convoy that had left Constantinople at full speed couldn't feel completely safe from possible Ottoman pursuers until they had docked at Negroponte on the morning of the sixth day after their departure. Although the nearest base had been Tenedos, it was not very well protected, and Diedo had chosen instead to make for the safe port at Negroponte. He wasn't aware that Admiral Longo's fifteen-ship fleet was docked in Tenedos.

Although Negroponte was probably equal in importance

to the other Venetian bases at Corfu, Modone, and Crete in terms of maintaining Venice's naval superiority in the eastern Mediterranean, it had the distinction of being the first line of defense against the Ottomans. But the fleet there was resting quietly in the harbor as though it had only to be given an order to come to Constantinople's rescue.

The news, of course, was that Constantinople had fallen. Admiral Loredan, supreme commander of the Negroponte fleet, heard the story in detail from Diedo and the other escaped survivors. He immediately dispatched a swift messenger ship to Venice to relay the news.

After several days, the escapees from the siege continued their journeys back to their respective homes, leaving only the most severely wounded in Negroponte. The Cretan ships continued south to Crete, while the two Venetian vessels capable of withstanding the voyage began their three-week journey back to Venice. Diedo was once again in command, and Nicolo was sailing aboard his ship. Tedaldi was aboard the second vessel.

The two Venetian ships spent a day at the port of Modone at the southern tip of the Peloponnese peninsula, where they encountered a ship carrying pilgrims from Brandenburg to Palestine. These people would bring to the Holy Land the painful news that the last stronghold of Christendom in a sea of Muslims, the Byzantine Empire, had fallen.

Loredan's messenger boat arrived in Venice on June 29th. Western Europe thus didn't learn the momentous news of Constantinople's fall until a full month after the fact. The Venetian government immediately dispatched swift couriers to the Vatican, the King of Naples, Genoa, Florence, the King of France, the Holy Roman Emperor in Germany, the King of Hungary, and others to inform them of this outcome. For Genoa and Venice, which stood to lose their Black Sea trade, and for the Pope, who had just recently decided to send Constantinople more financial assistance, the news came like a bolt out of the blue. Nobody had believed that such a strongly fortified city could collapse so quickly.

Diedo, Nicolo, Tedaldi, and the other eyewitnesses arrived in Venice five days after Loredan's messenger boat. Diedo was immediately summoned before the ruling council to deliver a detailed report. Soon after that he had to deliver the same report to the Senate and answer questions from the floor. At this stage all they knew in terms of the human costs were the number of those killed in battle. No doubt Diedo had already prepared his report during the three-week journey from Negroponte to Venice: such reports were invariably expected of commanding officers involved in significant events, even merchant captains. Only when the Venetian government had received Diedo's report was it in a position to take concrete measures in response.

Venice decided, characteristically, to combine a hard and a soft strategy. The hard strategy was to send a messenger to Negroponte ordering Admiral Loredan to place the entire fleet under his command on emergency alert. They also ordered him, along with Longo's fleet of fifteen ships, to patrol the Aegean Sea. Venice would thus show its determination to fight to the bitter end to maintain control of the Aegean in the event that the Ottoman fleet sailed south to claim it. The ports at Corfu, Modone, and Crete were also placed on alert. Although the Venetian shipyards were in the midst of constructing seventeen new galley warships, the Senate felt this to be insufficient and ordered an additional fifty to be built. 52,500 ducats were set aside for this expenditure.

That said, a commercial nation such as Venice survived on the basis of trade. They couldn't afford to be too unyielding. The special envoy Marcello, whom they had sent to travel with Admiral Loredan to negotiate with the Byzantines, was now ordered to try to do the same with the Ottomans. He was ordered to proceed to Adrianople in all haste, where he was authorized to give the Sultan a goodwill gift of 1,200 ducats. He was also instructed to tell the Sultan that those Venetians who had participated in the defense of Constantinople had done so as individuals; Venice, as a state, had no intention of violating its treaties with the Ottoman Empire, and its government deeply regretted the actions of those individuals.

Marcello was told that Venice's most pressing need at the moment was to restore trade relations with the Ottoman Empire to their previous, favorable conditions. If that meant keeping silent about the enormous losses Venice suffered because of the siege—the numerous dead, of course, as well as the loss of the warehouses, the merchant center, the cargo of their merchant vessels captured in the Golden Horn, altogether worth an estimated 400,000 ducats—then so be it.

Thus the Venetian government effectively swept the sacrifices of its citizens under the rug for the greater good of the nation—but at the same time, they recompensed those citizens for their sacrifices in a way that made it clear to them that they hadn't been forgotten.

Five days after deciding to send the Sultan the goodwill gift, the Senate told Ambassador Minotto's son that he could board the *Alimonda*, then setting sail for Constantinople, to search for his father. If Ambassador Minotto were one of those taken captive, the Senate promised to pay for his liberation. This suggests that, until July 17th, the Venetian government did not know that he had died.

The next day, the Senate ordered payments to the children of Captain Coco, who had died in the night raid upon the Turkish fleet. These included a pension for each of his sons and a dowry for his daughter.

The record of the Senate meeting for August 28th shows that Ambassador Minotto's daughter was awarded a dowry of 1,000 ducats, to be reduced to a stipend of 300 ducats in the event that she didn't marry and entered a nunnery instead. Minotto's wife and son, whom he had sent away on a Venetian ship right before the city fell, were each awarded yearly pensions of 25 ducats.

Finally, two months after the city fell, the Venetian government learned that Minotto had been beheaded along with one of his sons and seven of the leading citizens of the Venetian settlement. Mehmed had not forgiven the Venetian settlement for flying its flag and defying him.

The families of the seven other victims did not receive lifetime pensions, however. Although Minotto was a member of the nobility, he was not from a wealthy family, whereas the other seven were. The *nobile* who guided Venetian society were given a great many rights, but they also had responsibilities: the first of these was to fight for Venice with no thought of the sacrifices involved.

Given this ethos of responsibility, it goes without saying that the Senate did not forget the families of the common sailors who died in Constantinople but were neither wealthy nor noble. If one reads the Senate records from the time that word of the defeat reached Venice to the end of that year, one sees that they are littered with notices of pensions being paid to the families of those who were confirmed dead, and ransom payments to release those who had been taken prisoner. The Senate record for December 10th contains the first mention of Admiral Gabriele Trevisan since the city's collapse: the record for that day shows that the Senate ruled to give Trevisan's family 350 ducats to help them pay for his ransom and freedom.

There is no record of exactly when Trevisan returned to Venice, but in the naval records of the following autumn, his name is listed among those admirals on the front lines against the Ottomans. The given name Gabriele was very common in the Trevisan family, however, so it is possible that the entry referred to somebody else.

*

There are no records of what happened to Nicolo after he returned to Venice. In all likelihood, he resumed the practice of medicine. All Venetian vessels on long voyages, including merchant vessels, were required to have a physician on board, and the name Nicolo Barbaro appears quite a few times in the registers of high-ranking officers aboard these ships. The name Nicolo Barbaro was also quite common, however, so it isn't unthinkable that these records indicated somebody else, especially since the registers do not specify in what capacity that person served aboard ship. Nicolo did, however, write a *Journal of the Siege of Constantinople.*

This work records everything from the circumstances

leading up to the siege to most of the major events that occurred during the siege itself, as well as Nicolo's own personal observations. It is believed that he assembled the book from his daily notes as well as from factual information that only became available once he had returned to Venice.

The *Journal* was the first document that allowed posterity to know precisely what happened during the siege from day to day. Although other eyewitness reports did describe most of the major events, they did not specify what day exactly these events occurred, making it impossible for those who weren't there, even contemporaries of the event, to piece together the exact chronology.

Another thing that makes Nicolo's *Journal* indispensable for historians, and far superior to other eyewitness reports, is its sheer accuracy. If one wants to know, for example, the Turks' troop strength, one will find the most reliable figures in the journals of this Venetian doctor who wasn't even part of the force defending the landward wall.

Yet this chronicle, the most accurate and cool-headed account of the siege to be produced, was virtually neglected; it received far less attention than Cardinal Isidore's letters, which terrified the Vatican, or Ubertino's extended epic, which was touted among Roman intellectuals, or Tedaldi's narrative, which became a tool in France for fanning the spirit of would-be crusaders. Until it was recognized as an important historical document and placed in Venice's Marciana Library in 1837, it lay more or less untouched in the Barbaro family archives. When Gibbon capped off his *Decline and Fall of the Roman Empire* in 1783 with an account of Constantinople's fall, he didn't even know of the existence of Barbaro's *Journal* and had to make do with Greek sources.

Epilogue

Diedo's report to the Venetian Senate no longer exists. However, it stands to reason that Nicolo must have played a significant role in its composition; the two went to Galata together after Constantinople had fallen, and spent three weeks together on the way to Negroponte, during which time no doubt Diedo was beginning to draft his report. It is reasonable to assume, at the least, that the objectivity and accuracy of Nicolo's observations were well known to Venice's leadership. Although there are maybe two or three facts that Nicolo misremembers, and perhaps a few flashes here and there of anti-Genoese sentiment, his *Journal of the Siege of Constantinople* remains the single most reliable account of the last days of the Byzantine Empire. Given the unremitting ambiguity of the Genoese's actions during the siege, Nicolo's indignation is well within the tolerable limits for a record of this sort—indeed, it rather adds to the liveliness of the work.

*

Giustiniani had fought bravely at the front; despite his youth, and the fact that he was a mercenary fighting for gain, he had been the only Genoese to win the honest respect of both the Venetians and the Greeks, who, in general, harbored very mixed feelings about the Genoese. Whatever respect he had earned from them, however, was erased by his cowardice in the battle's last hours.

He received treatment to his wounds after being taken back to his own ship. His vessel escaped the Golden Horn along with the others and, like them, remained outside the boom until nightfall for any remaining stragglers. During that time he couldn't have failed to notice the strange atmosphere that descended upon the city when the wall was breached, or the other Western ships, still trapped inside the Golden Horn, that were attacked and plundered by the Turkish fleet.

Although his mercenaries continued to revere him despite what he had done, the sailors aboard the ship, also Genoese, couldn't hide their perplexity at his shameful conduct. This appears to have wounded the once-proud commander even more than the Turkish arrows. Three days after setting out from Constantinople, Giustiniani died aboard ship.

✽

For another Genoese, Magistrate Lomellino of Galata, the days after the fall were made hellish by a combination of anxiety and powerlessness.

On May 29th, as soon as word arrived that the Ottoman troops had breached the city wall, Lomellino sent a messenger to the Sultan to plead for recognition of Galata's neutrality. Mehmed agreed to meet with the messenger, but said nothing. Two days later, the Sultan summoned a representative from Galata and ordered the settlement to surrender. For the sake of appearances the representative sealed a peace treaty with Zaganos Pasha stipulating that the settlement would be governed by a council of elders chosen by the citizens. But since any and all actions were subject to Turkish approval, this was tantamount to surrender. The following day Lomellino went himself to sign the treaty. The day after that, a Turkish regiment arrived to tear down the settlement's walls while the people of the settlement simply looked on in silence. For two hundred years the Genoese had enjoyed a privileged place among the Western traders in Constantinople; in an afternoon the wall that symbolized their glory was demolished without a trace, save for one tower at the highest point in the settlement.

Although Venice was said to have lost 400,000 ducats because of the city's fall, the Genoese settlement lost at least 500,000 ducats; if one includes the loss of real estate, the number begins to exceed a million ducats. The Venetians had moved the bulk of their eastern Mediterranean trade to Alexandria to avoid sparking off a trade war with Genoa; Genoa on the other hand had everything invested in its Black Sea and Constantinople trade. When the Byzantine Empire collapsed, it dealt a fatal blow to Genoa's economy.

Genoa's troubles didn't end there: Mehmed conquered Caffa in 1475 and the Ottoman empire took control of the island of Chios in 1566, effectively shutting Genoese traders out of the eastern Mediterranean. After a fashion, then, it was the young Turkish autocrat's extraordinary lust for conquest that drove the excellent seafarers of Genoa to turn their attention first to the western Mediterranean and then to the Atlantic Ocean.

Magistrate Lomellino, who was an honest if indecisive man, experienced his own personal misfortunes as well. The nephew to whom he wished to leave his business was taken prisoner by the Ottomans and converted to Islam. Indeed, to continue doing business in the city such a conversion was a practical necessity, and quite a few Genoese merchants went through with it. The steadfast Christians who didn't convert, many of whom were Lomellino's friends and the very soul of the Genoese settlement, were enslaved, and Lomellino lost quite a few night's sleep trying to figure out ways to raise the money to liberate them as soon as possible. This of course made it even more difficult to face his own nephew, who through his apostasy had proven himself a sore disappointment and unworthy heir. Lomellino, who was far past sixty, now had absolutely nothing keeping him in Galata.

When word arrived that his replacement, who had been supposed to arrive even before the siege began, had made it as far as Chios, Lomellino left Galata. After briefing his successor in Chios in late September, he boarded a ship returning home to Genoa. There are no accurate records of what became of him afterwards. However, a very long letter that he wrote while at Chios to his younger brother still survives. In it, he describes the siege as it was witnessed by the Galatians, the difficult position that the Genoese settlers had been thrown into, and the unstinting manner in which the settlers had done everything reasonably possible to aid Constantinople. However, he also reached the conclusion that, in the end, he, the other Galatians, and the countries of Western Europe had all underestimated Mehmed the Second. And now they were paying the price for it.

＊

It took only two years to show that the sacrifice made by the Greek Orthodox Serbian soldiers who fought alongside the Turks had been made in vain. As thanks for the 1,500 horsemen that Serbia sent in response to his request, the Sultan conquered Serbia in 1455. Mihajlovic, who had been serving in the southern city of Novo Brodo, was taken prisoner by the advancing Ottoman forces and, along with his two younger brothers, was sent to serve in a Turkish regiment in Asia Minor. Seeing no other way to survive, he converted to

Islam and joined the Janissaries. Still only twenty-five years old, he was no doubt seen as militarily useful. He remained in the Janissaries for eight years. During this period the Ottoman army, carried along by the momentum of its victory against Constantinople, carried out Mehmed's expansionist policies with hardly any credible resistance. Mihajlovic spent these days fighting as part of the Ottoman army's advancing front line.

In 1463, while fighting in Bosnia, he and his regiment found themselves surrounded by the superior forces of the Hungarian King Matthias Corvinus, who was the only highly regarded Christian ground commander in all the fighting against the Turks. Seeing this as the perfect opportunity to regain his freedom, Mihajlovic immediately surrendered himself to the Hungarian army. That year he also converted back to Christianity.

He continued his life as a soldier but, unable to return to his subjugated homeland, he joined the Hungarian army at their urging. He took part in various battles alongside the Hungarians, in Hungary, Bosnia, Moravia, and Poland. He appears to have written his *Memoirs* while living in Poland, in the period from 1490 to 1498, by which time the once youthful Serbian cavalryman was already over sixty years old. As a nod to his peculiar life history, the work is also known as the *Memoirs of a Janissary.*

*

It often happens that some turning point, some momentous event, completely changes the way in which a person is perceived. Mehmed the Second, who had been written off as immature and wildly ambitious, as one who would be lucky even to maintain the territory secured by his father, became the hero of a generation. Giacomo de Languschi, who served as Marcello's deputy during the eight-month-long negotiations to repair Venice's relations with the young victor, recorded the following impressions:

"Sultan Mehmed, twenty-two years old, has a well-proportioned physique and is somewhat taller than average. Raised as a warrior, his manner is coercive rather than cordial. He rarely smiles. He is judicious and free from any blinding prejudice. Once he decides upon a course of action, he follows it through, and does so with great boldness.

"He aspires to the glory of Alexander the Great; every day he has Ciriaco d'Ancona and another Italian read to him from Roman history. He enjoys the histories of Herodotus, Livius, Curtius, etc., the lives of the popes, critical biographies of the emperors, and tales of the kings of France and the Lombard kings. He speaks Turkish, Arabic, Greek, and Slavic, and is quite knowledgeable about Italian geography. He possesses a color map of Europe which indicates all the national boundaries as well as the region where Aeneas lived, where the Pope resides, and where the emperors have their palaces.

"He has an extraordinary desire to rule and shows the greatest possible interest in geography and the military arts. In his negotiations with us he is very skilled at asking leading questions.

"A very formidable character, one whom we Christians must now be prepared to face."

This "formidable" young man was not only extremely gifted, but also had a standing army of over 100,000 men ready to do his bidding at all times. There wasn't a single polity in Europe at the time that could assemble an army of that size.

The power of his great cannon also didn't fail to catch the attention of Europe's ruling lords. Of course Europe had cannons of its own; one hundred and fifty years earlier, Venice had begun attaching them to its warships. But Mehmed was the first to recognize, and exploit, such a cannon's full military potential. There could be no more effective demonstration of that potential than blasting through the three layers of Constantinople's wall, which was the strongest of the time. In reality of course, the cannons did not accomplish this—the defenders were simply too few to defend anything other than the stockades and the outer wall. The inner wall, the strongest of the three, was left more or less unscathed. At the time, however, there were very few people informed enough to know that. The popular image was one of cannons demolishing all three of Constantinople's walls, and that image seeped into every corner of Europe. The following year, the Venetian Senate took the lead by announcing plans for large-scale production of massive cannons, and soon the other countries of Europe, not wishing to fall behind, announced similar intentions, all of which pushed the technology forward. Needless to say, techniques of wall construction also underwent a revolution around the same time.

City walls throughout Europe, be it in the west or the east, as well as those found in the Middle East, can roughly be separated into two categories: those built before the widespread use of large-sized cannons and those built after. The difference is noticeable at a glance. Those built before are high and relatively thin, while those built after are much thicker and not as high: they seem rooted in the ground, with the lower half of the wall built at a slight slant into the

ground. The slant was thought to lessen, even if only somewhat, the impact of projectiles fired directly at the wall. The
first such walls were fashioned by the two parties that were
the first to throw themselves into the Turks' line of fire—the
Knights of Saint John on Rhodes, and the Republic of
Venice.

The new weapons also completely undercut the importance of the heavily armored knights who had been the professional warriors of the medieval period. Practically anybody,
once taught the basics, could fire a cannon. Skills for which
one had to have some innate ability and that required years of
practice to perfect, such as riding a horse or properly thrust-
ing a spear in order to pierce armor—such skills were no
longer necessary. Knights, once the glory of medieval battle-
fields, now had to step aside in favor of groups of amateurs,
artillerymen and foot soldiers thrown into massive formations
effective solely because of their sheer size.

A difference in weaponry was not the only thing dividing
the medieval and early modern periods. Though Halil Pasha
and Mehmed had been at odds over whether to take
Constantinople or leave it be, history bore out the validity of
Mehmed's choice for the Ottoman Empire's future.

Taking the capital of the Byzantine Empire gave the Turks
a claim to all of the lands once ruled by that empire. It gave
the conquerors a sense of justification. In strategic terms,
Constantinople was both a crossroads and a pivot point—by
controlling it the Turks were able to consolidate their territories in Asia and the Balkans, and thus make their empire a
continuous whole.

Three days after the city's fall, Halil Pasha, who had been
the former Sultan's right hand and a son of one of the most

famous Turkish families, was put in prison. Forced to join the procession of Greek captives to Adrianople, he spent another twenty days in prison there until he was executed by beheading. His crime: "secretly aiding the Byzantines."

Mehmed didn't waste any time making use of this new city to project his power on both land and sea. Constantinople's churches were steadily converted into mosques; construction began on the Topkapi palace; not only Turks, but Greeks and Jews were forced to move to the city to repopulate it; and preparations began for the official transfer of the capital of the Ottoman Empire from Adrianople to Constantinople. Meanwhile, the military wasn't given even a moment's rest to savor their victory.

Two years after Constantinople's conquest, the Turks took Serbia. The following year, 1456, they conquered Bosnia. Poland and Hungary became the front line against the Turkish advance.

In 1460 the Peloponnese peninsula, which had just barely held out under the leadership of the Emperor's younger brothers, also fell to the Turks. One of the brothers, Thomas Paleologos, fled to Rome, to the Pope.

Trebizond, which also bore traces of Byzantine imperial rule, fell in 1461. The Turks now ruled the entire southern coast of the Black Sea.

In 1463 the Ottoman Empire, which had been exclusively a land power, extended out into the sea. Their goal was the island of Lesbos in the Aegean. A massive army sailed in from the coast of Asia Minor, and Lesbos, a Genoese holding for over two hundred years, fell immediately into Ottoman hands.

In 1470 the Turks, moving further south down the

Aegean, tried to attack the Venetian naval base in Negroponte. This attack instigated a war between Venice and the Ottoman Empire that lasted more than ten years.

In 1473 the Ottoman army reached toward Persia and enjoyed a triumphant victory over the Persian army. The Venetians, who had hoped that the Turks would be weakened by having to fight on two fronts simultaneously, were stymied.

In 1475, the Turks sent a large army across the Black Sea to conquer Caffa. With this victory, the entire Black Sea was firmly under Ottoman rule, and Genoese traders received a final blow from which they would never recover. The Turks, on the other hand, now had inroads into the Crimea.

In 1479, Mehmed sent his troops to the southwest and eventually succeeded in subduing the Albanians, who were highly skilled at mountain guerilla warfare. All of the Balkans, with the exception of a base held by the Venetians on the coast of Greece, was now under Turkish control.

The Ottoman Empire attacked Italy for the first time in 1480, landing at the southern city of Otranto. The Pope, imagining Saint Peter's Square overrun with Muslims, must have surely passed some sleepless nights during this period. The Sultan's sudden death the following year and the subsequent withdrawal of the Ottoman forces prevented his nightmares from becoming a reality.

Mehmed the Second died on May 3, 1481, immediately after leading an expeditionary army across the Bosphorus into Asia. He was forty-nine years old. It is said that he was planning to attack Syria, Mecca, and Egypt. Europe celebrated the death of this "enemy of Christendom" by lighting torches and setting off fireworks. The churches were thronged with believers offering their thanks up to God.

Epilogue

"Mehmed the Conqueror" as he came to be called did not necessarily see all of his military adventures meet with success. The siege of Belgrade was a failure and the island of Rhodes also held out against the Turks. Despite that, during the reigns of his grandson Selim and Selim's successor Suleiman the Great, not only did Belgrade and Rhodes fall, but so did Syria and Egypt, all pieces falling into place in the master plan that Mehmed had originally drawn. Just as importantly, the Ottoman Empire didn't collapse immediately after "the Conqueror's" death. Mehmed the Second, who lived approximately twenty years longer than Alexander the Great, didn't merely conquer new territories: he had the time to bring them firmly under his control and establish the social institutions that would truly absorb them into the empire. The Ottoman Empire would reach its apex in the mid-sixteenth century under the reign of Suleiman, and it would continue to exist until the beginning of the twentieth century. His enterprise would probably never have been possible had Constantinople never been conquered.

Tursun served as Mehmed's page until 1460, when he was appointed as a secretary in the Ottoman cabinet, or *divan*, serving first as the finance minister for the Ottoman Empire's Asian territories, then performing the same function for the empire's European territories, after which he seems to have entered a quiet retirement. The exact date of his death is uncertain, but it appears to have been around 1499. Mehmed had died eighteen years earlier and the Ottoman Empire was still in the reign of Mehmed's son, Beyazid.

Now adorned with the honorific title *Bey*, the former palace page left behind a work of history, most likely begun during the years of his retirement, entitled *A History of Sultan Mehmed the Conqueror*, which was completed in 1487. It is one of the oldest historical works that the Turks possess.

* * *

For Europeans, especially for those Western Europeans who felt themselves to be the descendants of ancient Rome, the fall of Constantinople was a shock beyond words. Of course the Italian maritime states and the Vatican were aware of how weak the Byzantine Empire had become in its last days, as were Hungary and the other nations of Eastern Europe. Even people in countries less intimately tied to the Byzantine Empire knew that it had been undergoing a slow decline for centuries. The testimony of returning Crusaders that the Byzantine Empire was wholly on the defensive in the face of the Muslim onslaught had had centuries to seep through to the far corners of Europe. Furthermore, the sight of Greek scholars forsaking their homeland to live in the West and Byzantine Emperors appealing to Western rulers for military aid was one to which Europeans had already been well accustomed.

And yet, for the Byzantine Empire to be completely wiped off the face of the earth took them by surprise, and filled them with inexplicable gloom.

Even after the fall of the Roman Empire, there had been no shortage of rulers in Europe who had appropriated the title "Emperor" for themselves. Yet these men were either Franks, who had been known to the Romans as "Gauls," or they hailed from the even more "barbaric" hinterlands the Romans had called "Germania." Even if they called themselves the "Holy Roman Emperor" or wore the black embroidered double-headed eagle, they did not possess the same kind of power possessed by the Roman emperors of antiquity. Western Europeans knew this. They knew it, and never hesitated to take any opportunity to resist these so-called emperors. For these people, the true heir and continuation of the empire established by the Romans was the Byzantine Empire, even if it did happen to be ruled by Greeks. Furthermore, the Byzantine Emperor shared with them the Christian faith that the Roman emperors obviously had not. Thus, as far as Europeans were concerned, only the emperors of the Eastern Roman Empire were fully worthy of the title of emperor in every way.

And now, all of that was gone. After one of the imperial princesses of the Paleologos family married the Grand Duke of Moscow, Russia came to call itself the "Third Rome." If the Orthodox Church had moved its Patriarchy to Moscow, this would have made more sense. Western Europeans, who had denied such recognition to French and German emperors, were not inclined to accept such a claim from a Russian simply because he had married a Byzantine princess and decided to wear a white, double-headed eagle as his symbol. With the collapse of the Byzantine Empire, Europeans felt for the first time that they had been cut off from the womb of their civilization, ancient Rome.

This sense of bereavement may explain why they were so much more receptive to emotional accounts and poems of Constantinople's fall than to the accurate, objective reportage of somebody like Nicolo Barbaro. Rather than concern themselves with the sweeping revolution the event had brought about, they no doubt chose to lament what they had lost. The white, double-headed eagle had been cleaved in half by the crescent sword.

The last emperor of the Roman Empire, riding his white steed, his crimson cloak flowing in the wind, was now somewhere on the other side of the horizon.

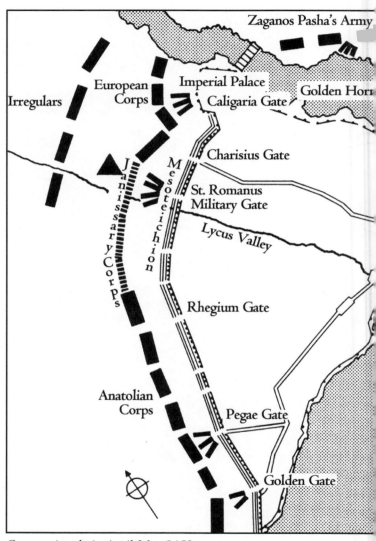

Constantinople in April-May 1453

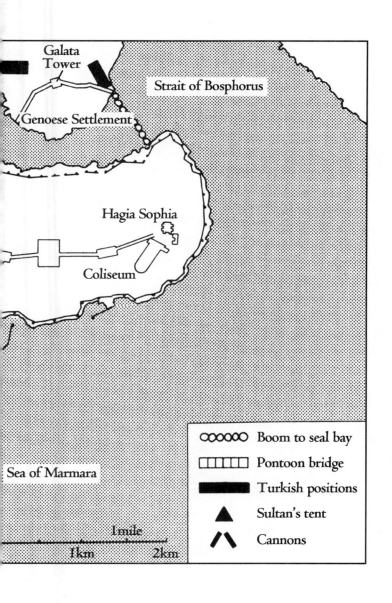

Galata
Tower

Strait of Bosphorus

Genoese Settlement

Hagia Sophia

Coliseum

Sea of Marmara

OOOOOO Boom to seal bay

Pontoon bridge

Turkish positions

Sultan's tent

Cannons

1 mile

1km   2km

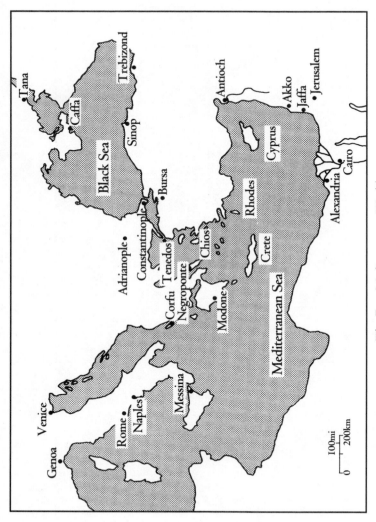

The East Mediterranean World